American Holiday Cookbook

American Holiday Cookbook

A Celebration of History, Tradition and Food

Polly Parke

Polly Parke

VANTAGE PRESS
New York

The recipes contained herein have been selected and written down by the author. They have not been tested by the publisher.

This book is dedicated to my husband, Tom, for his unwavering support and encouragement, to my children and grandchildren, and all my friends who have come to dinner, never sure of what was awaiting them as I tested recipe after recipe. Thank you.

Contents

Foreword   ix

Introduction   1
   How to Set Up a Kitchen   1
   How to Prepare/What Do I Do to Bake or Make?   10
Martin Luther King Day   26
Chinese New Year   48
Valentine's Day   77
Saint Patrick's Day   93
Easter   114
Summer Celebrations of Respect, Patriotism, Loyalty   153
   Memorial Day   153
   Fourth of July   155
   Labor Day   157
      Barbecue   159
      Clam Bake   179
      Picnic   195
Columbus Day   208
Halloween   234
Thanksgiving   263
December Month-Long Festivals of Light   303
   Diwali   304
   Hanukkah   330
   Christmas   351
New Year's Eve   419

Recipe Index   444

Foreword

America's holidays reflect our shared heritage, our diversity and the richness contained in elements adapted from other places and cultures. Our holidays are a celebration of our unity in diversity and should be shared with our friends and family.

This cookbook, first conceived for my children and grandchildren, is my attempt to help them understand their rich diversity, explain the background and history of the holidays and enjoy our shared meals and their preparation. But as I labored over this book, I began to understand that all Americans, whether from families who have been here for generations or those newly arrived trying to share in the American experience, can benefit from the same things as my family.

Being an American has been one of God's greatest gifts to me. I cherish the freedom and opportunity that has been available to me because I live in the United States. As countries around the world continue to display their intolerance towards other religions, tribes, and peoples, I count myself fortunate to have had the American experience. All of us, but for the native American Indians, at one time or another, have come to these accommodating shores for our very survival, to exhibit our own individuality, and have a new opportunity to make a fair living. In the process, we have adopted a tolerance for other ways of life and cultures. The 'melting pot' of America has done what no other people have yet been able to accomplish. It hasn't always been easy but we can look at each other and hopefully understand the pride each has in his own heritage, share it and pass it on for the next generation to celebrate.

This book has been written with the novice cook in mind, however the more experienced cook, unfamiliar with some of our heritage cooking, can benefit as well. I have tried to keep recipes as uncomplicated as possible, and have used detailed cooking instructions in case the cook doesn't know too much about the kitchen.

I hope that joyous celebrations continue in all homes, as they have in mine.

Polly Parke
January 21, 2002
Zihuatanejo, Mexico

American Holiday Cookbook

Introduction

The Introduction is broken into two sections. The first is overall information on setting up a kitchen, basic items and supplies, setting tables and making shopping lists; the second section contains information on "how to" prepare certain basic items like pie crusts, "what is" definitions, and "what do I do?" substitutes, if caught short. The terms are all listed alphabetically.

How to Set Up a Kitchen

Basic Kitchen Equipment

Following is a list of equipment basic for stress-free food preparation and cooking. More sophisticated tools can be added over the years and your budget.

Baking pans: Two 9½ inch metal pie plates; two 8 inch cake pans with removable bottoms if possible; two 9 inch cake pans with removable bottom; tart pan; loaf pan; spring form pan; tube pan for angel food cake; bundt pan; three–four heavyweight cookie sheets; circular 'pizza' pan; sponge cake (jelly roll) pan with ½ inch lip, 11½ × 17; two muffin pans
Baster, with bulb
Biscuit cutter
Electric blender
Bottle Opener
Broiling tray
Can Opener, sturdy with padded handles preferable; light-weight openers don't cut metal well
Casserole dishes, several depths and sizes
Cheese cloth
Coffee pot

Colander, metal preferred

Cookie cutters, various holiday shapes

Cooking utensils metal/stainless steel, usually 5 to a 'package' including spatula, ladle, slotted spoon, stirring spoon, cooking fork

Cooling racks for baked goods; large circles or rectangles are advisable; teflon coated is preferable

Cutting Board, at least 14 × 20; small 6 × 12 useful as well; wood

Dutch oven, large enough to roast a chicken: enameled cast iron with lid

Electric mixer, stand-alone preferable; hand-held also useful; have both if budget permits

Food Processor with metal, plastic blades and a few slicing disks, at least 4-cup. A mini prep holding only about a cup is also useful

Garlic press, heavy metal

Grater with several size holes (4–6 sides)

Juicer, electric or manual

Kettle

Knives are expensive and you should only have to buy them once. Buying a good knife is essential and you should be careful as to how they are made. The best blade is a carbon steel blade, as it holds its sharp edge, however, they rust, pit and corrode if not cared for properly. A stainless blade will remain shiny but doesn't hold a sharp edge well. Therefore, the best knife to find is one with a blade made of high-carbon stainless steel. The knife handle can be made of various types of substances, but it should always have at least three rivets holding the blade to the shaft; the shaft should extend into the handle itself. Never place knives in a dishwasher as the heat will destroy the handles and contact with other implements will dull the blade.

- Chef's knife: heavy, slice, chop, mince, dice; 8–12 inches long
- Paring knife: pare, slice, mince, trim, dice and devein, pointed tip; 3–4 inches long
- Utility knife: narrow bladed chef's knife, slice and bone; buy long blade, 10–12 inches

- Serrated knife: slice cake, bread, tomatoes, fish, paté, delicate items
- Carving knife: carve and slice roasts, dense patés, large fruits and vegetables
- Chinese cleaver: hacks through bones, slices thinly, all-purpose wonderful tool
- Metal steel rod for sharpening knives on a daily basis at a 20-degree angle away from you, full length of blade, 4–5 times each side

Mandoline, optional, for slicing

Mixing bowls: stainless steel, have at least 2 large bowls, 2 medium and 1–2 small bowls; a small variety of glass/Pyrex bowls also useful

Measuring cups: glass for liquids, 1,2,4 cup with a lip and stainless steel for dry ingredients, 1 cup, ½, ⅓, ¼ minimum

Measuring spoons set, stainless steel ¼ teaspoon size to 1 tablespoon size

Mortar and pestle

Pasta pot with inside basket/strainer

Pastry bags, plastic disposable type or cloth

Pastry cutter

Pastry tubes

Plastic spatula for no-stick cookware

Pepper grinder

Pot holders, 4 minimum

Potato/vegetable peeler

Racks for cooling baked goods, 4

Reamer for juicing, usually wood and hand-held

Roasting pan with rack

Rolling pin, cotton knit cover for special recipes

Rubber spatula, at least 2, some new materials also take the heat well

Salad spinner

Saucepans with lids, small, medium, large up to 6–8 quarts; double boiler

Scale for measuring ingredients

Scissors, heavy duty steel

Sifter

Sieve, fine mesh, small and large

Skillets; small, non-stick; medium and large with lid; cast iron good
Soup/stock pot with lid
Steamer to fit inside saucepan
Steamer, bamboo (Chinese)
Stripper for citrus strips
Storage containers: airtight in many sizes
Tea towels, cotton and terry, minimum 6
Tester, cake
Thermometers (3): instant read, candy/frying, roasting
Timer
Toaster
Tongs, metal
Toothpicks
Twine
Whisks, small and large, several
Wok, with stove ring if it doesn't have a flat bottom
Wooden Spoons: one regular type spoon, one with flat edge across bottom for sautéeing and scraping
Wraps: plastic wrap and aluminum foil
Zester

Basic Pantry

Have on hand for basic cooking.

Baking powder
Baking soda
Butter, salted, unsalted
Chocolate: unsweetened, semi-sweet; not 'candy'
Cocoa powder
Cooking spray, non-stick
Cornstarch
Corn syrup, dark and light
Eggs, large
Flour: all-purpose bleached for baking, cake flour
Gelatin, plain
Herbs, dried: basil, bay, thyme, rosemary, oregano, store away from heat and light
Milk, whole for baking, not non-fat

Molasses, unsulphured
Olive oil
Pepper, ground black, cracked if you don't have a pepper mill; white
Salt, iodized and Kosher
Shortening, vegetable (Crisco)
Sugar: granulated, light brown, dark brown and confectioners
Seeds: caraway, sesame, poppy
Spices: cayenne, chile powder, cinnamon, nutmeg, ground and whole cloves, powdered ginger, cardamom, sweet paprika, dried mustard; store away from heat and light
Tabasco Sauce
Vanilla extract
Vegetable oil, canola, peanut, not corn
Worcestershire sauce

Basic Bar

Today, fewer people are drinking hard liquor and seem to prefer wine and beer from micro-breweries. Of course, soda is always a staple. Most of the beverages in this book do not include mixed drinks, but where there is, the recipe and quantities are noted.

If you want to "stock" a traditional bar, you should have the following:

1 liter of vodka
1 liter of Scotch whiskey
1 liter rum
1 liter gin
1 liter bourbon, tends to be regional
1 liter blended whisky, rye or Canadian
1 bottle dry vermouth
1 fifth medium dry sherry
1 fifth orange flavored liqueur, Grand Marnier
1 fifth Cognac or brandy
1 fifth Anisette or Sambucca
1 fifth Fra Angelico
1 six-pack beer

6 bottles light and full-bodied red wine (3 each)
6 bottles dry white wine, to be served chilled

Bar glasses
Measuring jiggers
Ice bucket with tongs
Water pitcher
Cocktail shaker
Long-handled spoon
Strainer
Paring knife
Corkscrew
Blender, juicer, ice crusher
Ice
Cocktail napkins

Ginger ale
Club soda
Tonic water
Sparkling mineral water
Sodas, including diet for non drinkers

Orange juice
Tomato juice
Cranberry juice
Superfine sugar, Worcestershire sauce, Tabasco sauce, salt, olives, lemons and limes can be found in the kitchen
If having a party, calculate 2–4 drinks per person
One bottle of wine (750 ml) will yield about 5 five-ounce glasses.
One liter of liquor yields about 22 shots (1½ ounces each).

Before You Cook

Read through recipe carefully for ingredients and time it
   takes to complete. Make sure you have the ingredients.
Make up a shopping list if you don't have them all
Take out all the equipment and ingredients you will need
   to prepare the recipe
Preheat oven, if required
Measure carefully, especially if baking, think chemistry

Mix carefully according to the ingredients
Watch heat while cooking

Make Up a Shopping List

Decide first on a budget for your meal and then select the recipes you want to serve. Check your pantry and refrigerator for the ingredients. If you are missing some, put them on a list. Methodically go through each recipe. It may take time, but will save you later aggravation. Also check if you have the correctly sized pots, baking containers, roasting pan to fit your recipe.

If your dish involves fish, you want to buy it as close to the dinner as possible, preferably the same day, unless like steamer clams, which have to sit overnight. Also watch the recipes for items that need to be prepared one to two days in advance. Shop accordingly.

Check your bar supplies, if serving alcohol. Add any wine, beer, sodas etc. to list.

Decide on centerpiece, napkins, any special decorations well in advance to allow time to have the pleasure of putting them together, stress-free. Or wash and iron any needed. Add any missing decorative items to your shopping list.

Set the Table/Buffet

First determine your centerpiece, the colors and candles you might use. Check your tablecloths, place mats and napkins to coordinate. The size of your table and the number of guests will determine if you will have a "sit-down" dinner or serve a buffet.

If you prefer a sit-down dinner and need more space, try setting up a card table and chairs and coordinate the settings with the main table, or set up a folding rectangular table (not a bad investment with a growing family). Circular tabletops are also available to increase the size of a card table from four to six or eight. For a sit down dinner, place the dinner plate in the center of the space where the diner will sit, then place the flatware and napkin. When eating multiple courses, guests will use their silverware from the outside in towards the plate, so the setup must reflect this. On the right side of the plate, furthest way from the plate is the soupspoon, if there is a soup course, then the teaspoon and knife with the blade turned towards the plate. On the left side, furthest away is the napkin (or above or on the dinner plate), the salad fork (if there is a salad), the dinner fork and the dessert fork placed closest to the plate. If you wish, a bread and butter plate can be placed above the forks on the left with a butter knife on the dish. Salad plates are also placed on the left or on the platter if it is a separate course. Glassware is placed above the knife and spoons on the right, with a water goblet closest to the plate then a red wine glass and finally a white wine glass. Or, if serving multiple wines, change the glasses with the course with which they are being served.

If serving a buffet style dinner, make sure there are places people can sit to eat. If space is no problem, you may consider setting up a couple of card tables and chairs. Make sure that any coffee tables are cleared of clutter so plates can be placed on them. In the dining area, determine the traffic flow so people starting around a table won't get in the way of those whose plates are full. I find it best to put napkins and knife and fork at the end of the food selections so people don't have to carry them while they are serving themselves. You can fan each item or roll a fork and knife in a napkin. Dessert flatware will be placed out with dessert; you might need additional napkins. Put the dinner plates close to the start of the food. Start this with the meat or fish platters and keep any sauces for the meat or fish above those platters. Then proceed to the potato or pasta, vegetables, and salad. Don't forget to place salt and pepper near the food, butter and rolls towards the end, next to the flatware and napkins. If you have an additional surface in the dining area, you may want to put out the desserts so people can antici-pate the next course and you can 'show' them off! Dessert plates, cups, saucers, dessert forks and teaspoons will need to be pro-vided with the dessert and beverage service. Have a bar setup away from the food table so guests can help themselves to sodas or wine. Uncork a couple of bottles of red and white wine before you call the guests to dinner. Keep the white wine chilled in an ice bucket. Most red wines taste better if they have had 20-30 minutes to "breathe," especially more expensive wines; allow accordingly.

Substitutions

No matter how careful you've been with your planning, emergencies can occur and you might be missing an ingredient. Following are a few ways to get around the need.

Ingredient		Quantity		Equivalent
Baking powder	1	teaspoon	$1/4$	teaspoon baking soda with $1/2$ teaspoon cream of tartar
Buttermilk	1	cup	1	cup plain yogurt or 1 tablespoon vinegar or lemon juice plus milk to equal 1 cup
Chocolate Unsweetened	1	ounce/square	3	tablespoons unsweetened cocoa plus 1 tablespoon butter
Cornstarch	1	tablespoon	2	tablespoons all-purpose flour
Cream, heavy	1	cup	$1/3$	cup butter plus whole milk to equal 1 cup
Herbs, fresh	1	tablespoon	1	teaspoon dried
Ginger	1	tablespoon fresh	1	teaspoon powdered ginger plus $1/4$ teaspoon white pepper plus $1/2$ teaspoon lemon juice
Milk, whole	1	cup	$1/2$	cup evaporated milk, plus $1/2$ cup water
Mustard, dry	1	teaspoon	1	tablespoon prepared
Sour cream	1	cup	3	tablespoons butter plus buttermilk or yogurt to equal 1 cup
Star Anise	$1/4$	teaspoon	$1/4$	teaspoon fennel seed
Sugar, granulated	1	cup	$13/4$	cups confectioners' sugar (not for baking)
Tomato sauce	1	cup	1	can (3 ounce) tomato paste plus $1/2$ cup water
Yogurt	1	cup	1	cup buttermilk

Weights and Measures

Weights/Measures	Equivalent
Dash	less than $1/8$ teaspoon
$1^1/2$ teaspoons	$1/2$ tablespoon
3 teaspoons	1 tablespoon
2 tablespoons	$1/8$ cup (1 fluid ounce)
4 tablespoons	$1/4$ cup (2 fluid ounces)
$3/8$ cup	$1/4$ cup plus 2 tablespoons
$5/8$ cup	$1/2$ cup plus 2 tablespoons
$1/3$ cup	5 tablespoons, plus 1 teaspoon
1 tablespoon	$1/2$ fluid ounce
1 cup	$1/2$ pint (8 fluid ounces)
2 cups	1 pint (16 fluid ounces)
4 cups	1 quart (32 fluid ounces)
2 pints	1 quart
4 quarts (liquid)	1 gallon
Apples, 8 medium (3 pounds)	3 cups peeled, cored and sliced
Cheese (4 ounces)	1 cup grated
Eggs (3 large)	$2/3$ cup
1 garlic clove (medium)	$1/2$ teaspoon minced
1 lemon	3 tablespoons juice; 1-$1^1/2$ teaspoons grated peel; depends on size
Mushrooms (4 ounces)	$1^1/2$ cups sliced
1 onion (medium)	1 cup chopped
1 orange	$3/4$-1 cup juice; 2-3 teaspoons grated peel; depending on size

How to Prepare

What Do I Do to Bake or Make?

Baking in General: Remove eggs and butter from refrigerator and bring to room temperature an hour before you start baking. Preheat the oven to the specified degree. Read through the recipe.

A Word on Margarine: If you want to economize by using margarine (do not use corn oil based) the margarine must have a minimum of 60 percent vegetable oil. Below that amount, you get a lot of water in the margarine and the baked goods will not bake satisfactorily. Avoid whipped margarine, diet, liquid or soft when baking. Butter and shortening give the best results and have the best flavor.

Bake a Cake: Select your recipe and check the timing and make sure you have all the ingredients and type of pan required. Preheat the oven to the temperature on the recipe and grease or flour the baking pan(s). Baking pans can be greased with butter, vegetable shortening or non-stick cooking spray, then are usually floured, unless the recipe states otherwise. To assure a cake easily falls out of the cake pan, grease the pan, then trace the bottom of the pan onto a piece of parchment paper. Cut out the shape and insert it into the bottom of the pan and grease and flour the paper as well. Follow the recipe, measuring very carefully. Unless noted otherwise, place oven racks in the middle of the oven. Don't let the baking pans touch each other. The hot air must circulate. Don't open the oven door once baking has started, as the oven temperature will change and a rush of cooler air may cause the cake to "fall". A few minutes before it is finished, crack open the oven door to check on the cake. If it seems done, test the cake center with a wooden toothpick or a cake testing rod or bamboo skewer. If the tester comes out clean, the cake is done. The cake will also start to pull away from the sides of the pan. If it tests wet, continue to bake. Upon completion, remove the cake from the oven and invert onto cooling racks. Carefully remove pan, and then gently peel off the parchment while the cake is hot. If it sticks, take a thin blade knife and gently cut around the circumference of the pan, then try to release it. If a piece pulls up with the cake bottom, gently lay the piece of cake back onto the larger piece of cake and gently press. The icing will hold it together. Cool the cake completely. If you are not going to ice it that day, wrap it in plastic wrap when completely cool.

Why Doesn't the Cake Look Right?
It Fell
Oven not hot enough (double check oven temperatures with an independent thermometer); it might have been under mixed, not baked enough, had too much leavening (yeast, baking powder), sugar, or liquid or the oven door was opened during baking.

It Rose Too Much in the Center

Oven was too hot at the start or there was too much flour or not enough liquid.

It Stuck to the Pan

Pan was inadequately greased and floured or it cooled in the pan too long.

Cake Cracked and Fell Apart

Removed from the pan too soon or there was too much shortening, sugar or leavening (yeast, baking powder).

Cake Is Sticky

Insufficient baking, or oven not hot enough or too much sugar.

Texture Is Heavy

Over mixing when the flour and liquid were added, oven temperature may have been too low, too much shortening, sugar or liquid in batter.

Texture Is Coarse

Inadequate mixing or creaming, oven temperature was too low or too much leavening (yeast or baking powder).

Texture Is Dry

Over baked, or over beaten egg whites, too much flour or leavening (yeast, baking powder), not enough shortening or sugar.

Bake a Pie: Select your recipe, check the timing and place out all your equipment and ingredients. Make one of the pastry crusts below, roll out dough and put into the pie pan. Crimp the borders. Bake until a golden brown. Cool on a rack.

Technique

Pastry can be made in a food processor or in a mixing bowl. If selecting a food processor, fit it with the plastic blade, measure out dry ingredients (not the water) into the bowl and pulse until flour, salt and shortening are combined, oatmeal size crumbs form. Add ice cold water slowly and process until it pulls away from the sides of the bowl. You may not need more than 3 tablespoons. Do not over process or the crust will be tough. Roll out.

Otherwise, measure dry ingredients including shortening, into a medium to large size mixing bowl and cut together with a pastry cutter or two knives. You want oatmeal size pieces. Take a bit between your fingers and test consistency for shortening (butter). If it seems dry, add a bit more shortening. Weather will also affect the consistency of the crust. Wet weather can make it heavy as it picks up moisture. Add 3 tablespoons of the ice cold water and mix with a fork until it can be formed into a ball. If the dough is too crumbly, add the other teaspoon of water. Roll dough.

To get the dough off of the floured counter, pry up the edge furthest away from you with a plastic counter scraper or spatula. Place the rolling pin in front of the piece you have raised, the pin is lying on the dough. Carefully and loosely roll the dough onto the rolling pin and lift onto the pie plate. Place over one edge of the pie plate and unroll the dough across it. Gently press it into the curves of the pie plate, leaving an overhang. If you are making a two-crust pie, you will want to press the top and bottom halves together, trim with a paring knife, leaving ½ of dough to turn under to create the edge of the crust. Crimp the crust edge decoratively by using your index finger on the inside of the pastry rim and with your other index finger and thumb on the outside, pinch the crust. If there is left over dough, you can braid strips together and place on the top edge, adhering it with egg wash or milk, or cut small leaf shapes, stars, hearts with small cookie cutters, hors d'oeuvre cutters or free hand.

To create a glaze on the crust, brush with egg wash (egg whisked with a tablespoon of water or milk). You can also sprinkle sugar on top of the wash. If the pie has to cook more than 50 minutes, the sugar or egg wash may brown the crust too much, omit them if there is a long baking time.

The time it takes to bake a pie varies according to the filling.

One-Crust Pie

½	cup vegetable shortening or 1 stick of unsalted butter, or half shortening and half butter	1⅓	cups all-purpose flour, plus extra for rolling surface
		½	teaspoon salt
		3-4	tablespoons ice water

Two-Crust Pie

¾	cup vegetable shortening or 1½ sticks of unsalted butter, or half shortening and half butter	2	cups all-purpose flour, plus extra for rolling
		1	teaspoon salt
		4-5	tablespoons ice water

Divide dough in half. Roll the bottom as described above. You can either roll out the second crust and leave it whole or cut it into strips about ½ to ¾ inch wide and weave them directly on the pie filling (difficult if the filling is hot, the dough melts). It is easier to weave (over under) on a piece of waxed paper, then invert on top of the filling. Finish as described above by trimming ends, pressing the top and bottom pieces together and crimping or create a scalloped edge by pushing the edge of the crust every 1½ inches with the dull side of the knife to create scallops.

Pre-baked Pie Shell
Bake at 475 degrees

Some pies like a lemon meringue or a mousse pie may call for a crust that is pre-baked. Follow the recipe for a one-crust pie. Roll out the dough and dot with 1 tablespoon of butter cut into small bits and scattered over the center ⅔ of the dough. Butter cannot be too hard or too soft or it will break through the crust. Fold the bottom quarter of the dough up to the middle, then the top down to meet it. Seal by pressing the sides of the dough together. Fold in each of the two sides to meet in the center of the dough. Press together to seal. You now have a rectangle. Reroll to fit the pan. The biggest problem you will have prebaking a crust is that without a filling the sides of the pie tend to sag to the bottom of the pie plate. To avoid this, warm the pan and moisten the rim with water. Place the dough in the pie plate, trim and crimp the dough, as above. Prick the dough all over the bottom and sides with the tines of a fork. Take a piece of aluminum foil and lay it inside the pan on the bottom and up the sides. Fill the bottom with metal pie weights, dried beans or dry rice. Bake the crust for 4-6 minutes. If it looks "set", take the crust out of the oven and remove the weights and aluminum foil. If the dough is puffing up, prick it with the tines of a fork. Return it to the oven and continue to brown the crust. When it has reached a golden color, remove from the oven and cool on a rack.

Pie Extras

If you feel creative, add some ground nuts or a complementary spice to the crust. If you are baking a savory pie like chicken potpie or left over turkey pie, see below, add ½ cup of cheddar cheese to the dough before rolling, for example.

Bake Cookies: It's best to follow the recipes carefully. However, if you are baking large batches of cookies and want to keep costs down by using margarine, see the note above. Use the correct measuring cups, filled to the top and leveled. Don't pack in the flour or you will have more than the recipe requires. If your measuring cup has a spout and is glass or is plastic, you will get about 1 tablespoon more flour than you need. Avoid this type of cup for dry measuring, they are meant for liquids.

Chill the dough, if required, at least 4 hours. If it gets too hard, let it stand until it is malleable. Roll only a portion of the dough at a time, keeping the rest covered and in the refrigerator, if necessary. Chilled dough absorbs less flour and the cookie will be tender. Try not to over handle the dough for the same reason. Drop cookies can spread. If the first batch spread too much, try chilling the dough a bit before continuing. Leave at least an inch between cookies that are prone to spread.

Don't put too much flour on the work surface, use just enough to prevent sticking. Too much flour, tough cookies.

Do not use warm cookie sheets. Let them cool between batches.

Some cookies need to set a minute or two before removing to cooling racks or they will crumble when lifted.

Grease cookie sheets, if needed, with butter, vegetable shortening or non-stick cooking spray.

Meringues and rich dough cookies often benefit from being baked on silpat (laid on cookie sheet), or parchment paper. Cutting open a brown grocery bag and laying in on top of the cookie sheet also works well.

15

Avoid dark colored cookie sheets and thick puffy air sheets. You won't get the result you are looking for.

Berries: When purchasing, check bottom of container for mashed berries, if it is wet, select another box; check top for mold or bruises. Store berries in refrigerator in a single layer on paper-towel lined pan and cover lightly with plastic wrap. Wash just before using. Hull strawberries after you wash them to prevent absorption of water. To freeze, arrange washed and dried berries in a single layer on a flat pan and freeze. When frozen, transfer to a freezer bag and note date on it. Store up to 9 months. Blueberries freeze especially well.

Bread Crumbs: Tear up bread and whir in blender or food processor; store bread heels or crusts you don't eat in a freezer bag and make a batch when enough have accumulated. Or, whir as you go and freeze them in airtight freezer bags. Date bag with pen and use within 2-3 months; they will smell stale and flavor the food if too old.

Brew Coffee: A lot depends on how strong you like your coffee and how the coffee bean was roasted. A French roast or espresso bean is roasted longer and has an oilier consistency and therefore, will be stronger than a mocha bean. A Colombian or Arabica bean tastes different from Kona or Sumatran. Experiment. For a full-bodied cup of coffee, use 1 tablespoon of coffee per cup of water and one for the pot. If that proves too strong, increase the ratio of water to your bean selection. Automatic drip pots with a filter are easy to set up before needed and work well when serving a larger group. The coffee will continue to cook after it has dripped through; if left on the heat too long, it will become bitter. It's always good to remove the coffee to a thermos type jug to keep it warm. French glass pots which press the water down onto the grounds after steeping create a good flavor of coffee but some object to the murkiness created by the grounds floating in the water before it is pressed down. In any event, experiment with the type of pot, bean and ratio that suits you. Serve with sugar and cream, half and half or milk.

Brew Tea: Boil water in a kettle. When the water is almost at a boil, pour a small amount into the teapot and swirl the water to heat the pot; discard. Add the tea leaves of your choice, 1 teaspoon per cup and one for the pot. Pour hot water over the tea leaves; boiling water may make the tea a murky color. Steep tea for 5-6 minutes, even if you want weaker tea. You can add hot water to your tea to weaken it and yet you will have the full-bodied flavor you want. Stir tea before serving and pour through a strainer. A small pot of hot water can be served with the sugar, milk and lemon.

Butter: Most recipes call for unsalted butter, not salted. If you use salted butter, cut down the amount of salt you add. Do not substitute whipped butter as it has more water and will affect the recipe.

Compound Butters

These can be made to accentuate any meal. Have the butter at room temperature and then integrate into the butter, herbs, spices, lemon or orange juice, garlic, or anything else that would complement the meal. When thoroughly mixed, shape the butter into a pleasing shape or roll it to about ¼ inch thick on a piece of waxed or parchment paper. Keep flat and chill. Use cookie cutter, hors d'oeuvre cutters to create shapes when butter is cold.

Carving:

Chicken, Turkey, Duck and Goose

Remove from the roasting pan and tip the bird so the internal juices run back into the pan for the gravy. Put the juices to the side. Always allow the bird to sit on the cutting board for at least 10 minutes for a roasting chicken and up to 20-30 for a turkey. You can tent the bird with aluminum foil to keep it warm. You want the juices to stabilize inside and the bird to cool so it doesn't fall into bits and pieces when carving. You will need to plan your serving time accordingly. Your gravy will warm up the turkey.

You must have your knife sharpened well and have a heavy cooking fork to help hold the bird down.

First slice between the leg and the breast and come down alongside the thigh. You will remove the whole leg joint if possible, in one piece. If it proves too difficult, remove the lower leg (the drumstick), and then the thigh. Carve one side of the bird at a time. If you do not need all of the meat, it is better left on the bone, as it stays juicier. To carve the drumstick, steady it with a carving fork and cut a thick slice of meat from one side of the drumstick, along the bone. Turn the leg over so the cut side is against the board and cut off another slice, repeat twice more. To slice the thigh, hold it steady with a fork and cut slices parallel to the bone.

Next, detach the wing from the breast at the shoulder joint and cut off the wing tip, discard. Cut the wing into 2 pieces at the joint.

To carve the breast meat, hold the back of the carving fork against the breastbone and slice diagonally through the meat, starting at the bottom end of the breast. Continue until all of the meat is sliced.

Repeat with the other side.

Reserve the carcass for soup!

Roasts

Insert your cooking fork into the meat to stabilize it and slice with the grain of the meat into the size slices you desire. If the roast has ribs, have the butcher crack the bottom of them so they are easy to cut through, or you will need a heavy cleaver!

Chocolate: Pure chocolate is a thick paste made when the seeds of the cocoa bean are heated and ground. Cocoa butter is the fat extracted in the process and returned in varying amounts according to the type of chocolate being manufactured.

There are many types of chocolate, try to use the best you can find. Cocoa powder comes in 2 varieties, natural (nonalkalized) and Dutch process cocoa which adds alkali. Alkalized cocoa is darker but has a milder flavor. Different recipes call for different types of cocoa. Unsweetened is the type usually called for in baking. Bittersweet, semisweet, sweet, milk and white chocolate are the other types available. Do not substitute "candy" chocolate in a recipe as artificial flavors and additives are in it.

Coconut: To shred or grate a fresh coconut you must first drain the liquid inside it. Take a screwdriver and hammer and knock the screwdriver though one of the "eyes" of the coconut (brown circles). Drain the liquid into a bowl and reserve if you have a recipe to use it. Heat the oven to 400 degrees and bake the drained coconut for 15 minutes. Using a hammer or back of a large cleaver, break the shell and remove the meat using the point of a strong knife or small screwdriver. Remove the brown membrane with a sharp paring knife or a vegetable/potato peeler.

If you want to shred the coconut, fit a food processor with a fine shredding blade and process in batches. You can also shred it on a 4-sided grater. To shave a coconut, use a vegetable peeler and shave the edges of the coconut meat. If you do not use it all up, coconut can be refrigerated in a plastic bag for a couple of days or can be frozen for 2-3 months.

Eggs: Use large eggs in the recipes in this book. When using multiple eggs, always crack one into a dish before dropping it into the batter or dish. You don't want to ruin a recipe with a bad egg. Eggs at room temperature work best for baking. If you need to "warm" up the egg quickly, open it (or separate the white from the yolk if called for) and place in a small bowl over hot water. When egg reaches room temperature, remove it from the water bath. Test with your finger.

Egg whites are often used in frosting or decorating. Eggs today often can carry salmonella, therefore, unless you are sure of the source of your eggs, use an egg white substitute such as meringue powder or dried egg whites, if it will not be cooked.

Do not use an egg that arrives cracked in the box, as it might be contaminated.

Flour: There are many types of flour, all-purpose bleached and unbleached, whole wheat, rye, chickpea, soy and rice. There is also cake flour. I find cake baking is better done with bleached all-purpose flour or cake flour, where indicated. Unbleached does fine in breads and cookies.

Frosting:
Cake
When frosting a cake, place waxed paper pieces just under the bottom layer to catch any drips. It makes cleanup easier. Put about a ¾ cup of frosting on the first layer and spread to the edges with an offset blade spatula. Place the second layer of cake on top and frost the top. Frost the sides by taking the frosting from the bottom to the top. Smooth out. It may help to work with a tablespoon as well, taking the frosting from the spoon to

the cake. Some frostings harden quickly so you have to work undistracted.

If you want to add surface writing or decoration, use pastry bags and decorating tips to achieve the effect you are looking for. See *Cookies, for how to use pastry bag.* Use the Royal Icing recipe below.

Cookies

If you want to decorate cookies using many colors and patterns, you will need pastry bags and decorating tips. Use the Royal Icing recipe that follows:

Separate the frosting into saucers or small bowls and tint with either paste or gel food coloring to the color desired. If the frosting is too thin, add a bit of confectioners' sugar. If the frosting is too thick, use egg white to thin. You can use disposable plastic bags or the traditional treated cloth bag. If it is new you will have to cut the pointed end with a scissors to accommodate the decorating tip holder and tip you will be using. Place a decorating tip holder inside the empty bag, place the decorating tip on the outside and screw on the circular ring holder. Place the frosting in the bag and squeeze it to the tip. Fold over the top and twist it to remove air. Squeeze to decorate. Take a practice squeeze into the bowl before trying on the cookie or cake. It takes practice, don't give up. It's fun! Toothpicks come in handy as well to help push around the icing a bit or to add a dab of color here or there.

If caught short without a pastry bag or tip, you can fashion one from a small plastic bag. Make a small cut in the corner of the bag for the frosting to flow through. Piping bags can also be made with parchment paper. Cut a triangle and fold it over on itself, making a cone. Staple or tape the side. Nip the bottom with a scissors to get the size opening you desire.

You can also "paint" on the color before cooking the cookie. Dilute the food color you desire with water and with small fine pointed paint brushes, paint the cookie. You have good control if the dough is chilled. You can also sprinkle with colored sugar before baking.

Measuring: Always use the correct type of measuring cup for dry measure or liquid measure. Glass and plastic measuring cups with a pouring lip are for liquid measuring. It will give you an incorrect measure if used for dry ingredients. When measuring dry ingredients, do not pack them into the cup, with the exception of brown sugar. Always level off the top with a knife so it is flat to the top edge. When measuring liquids, place the cup on a level surface to observe the correct amount.

Nuts:
Blanching

The nut has a skin on it. To remove the skin, drop the nuts into boiling water for 3-4 minutes. Remove one to test it. Place it in a tea towel and rub. The shell should pop off. If it doesn't, boil a bit longer. Almond skins squirt off easily between your fingers.

Grinding or Chopping

If using a food processor to grind the nuts, be careful not to over grind or they will become oily and stick together. Some recipes add a bit of sugar to the nuts to help separate them. If chopping them on a cutting board, be careful of your fingers. Use an up and down motion on the nuts, rocking the knife blade.

Keep nuts in a cool dark place, or refrigerate in airtight containers if not using immediately. Nuts can get rancid quickly. Always taste one before use. To crisp them up, put the quantity you are going to use on a baking tray and put into a 400-degree oven for 4-8 minutes. Check often and turn them with a spatula. They can burn quickly.

Oil: When cooking with oil, always be careful for spatters. Gently lower foods into the oil with a slotted spoon. Anything with moisture will make the level of the oil rise dramatically and threaten a spill over. Introduce your items slowly. When frying in batches, make sure the oil temperature has a chance to get back to that called for. The more pieces you add to the hot oil, the lower the temperature will go. Do not throw used oil down the sink drain, it will clog. If you have not fried very much, you can strain the cooled oil through a cheesecloth-lined sieve into a clean airtight container and reuse. If you have fried fish or something that had a lot of intense odors, discard the oil in old coffee tins or even in a milk or juice container that you can seal!

Select your oil according to the food you are cooking. Delicate items should be cooked in a light oil, like canola, or vegetable oil. Olive oil will lend character to a meat or potato dish.

Peanut oil does well for Oriental cooking and sesame oil is a good flavor enhancement, after a dish has been cooked. Flavored oils can be made by infusions of spices or herbs and left to stand a few days.

Pastry Bags and Decorators Tips: See frosting cakes and cookies above.

Pineapple: To peel and core a fresh pineapple will require a heavy chopping knife or cleaver. First wash off the pineapple then chop off the green stalk, cutting below it into the top part of the pineapple. Cut off the bottom. Stand the pineapple upright on your cutting board and carefully slice away the skin from top to bottom. You want to cut deep enough to remove the 'eyes'. Cut the pineapple in half and into halves again the long way. You will see there is a hard core. Stand the piece vertically and slice down to remove the core. You can now cut the quarters into the size pieces or slices you require.

Some prefer to leave the skin on the pineapple and quarter it lengthwise. Remove the length of the core from each quarter. With a slender but strong knife, slice under the pineapple fruit along the edge of the skin. Then slice across the top of the quarter for your size piece. You can serve the loosened pineapple on the skin with toothpicks or a fork.

Thermometers:
Barbecue
Forks are available that read the internal temperatures of the grilled item when pierced.

Candy
Required for cooking all sorts of sweets and custards, reads higher temperatures than many other thermometers.

Frying
Can be bought as a combination candy/frying thermometer. Buy one that clips onto the side of the pan.

Instant Read
Best buy of all. Can use it anywhere at a moment's notice. Especially good for roasting poultry's internal temperature

when inserted into the thickest part of the thigh down along the back area.

Oven
It's always good to check out the real internal temperature of your oven at any given degree, as your cooking times will be affected. Place it on the rack in the center of the oven. Observe what the thermometer says and compare it to your oven setting. If it differs, adjust your oven temperatures to compensate. It is critical in baking.

Roasting
Comes with the temperatures of different meats, rare, medium and well done. Place it in the middle of the roast without touching a bone. Doesn't work well for poultry. Use the instant read type for poultry.

Turkey:
Buying
It is preferable to purchase a fresh turkey not a frozen turkey. Do not buy a self-basting turkey, as the juices added are not always the best. If you need a very large turkey, it is difficult to get the dark and white meat cooked to their best at the same time. You might want to consider two smaller turkeys. At least you get 4 drumsticks and wings! Make sure your turkey fits into your roasting pan and into your oven. Place in the center so air can circulate. Point the legs to the back of the oven as it is warmer and the dark meat takes longer to cook.

If you purchase a frozen turkey, you should defrost it in the refrigerator. Bacteria will grow in the turkey between 40-140 degrees F. Plan one day of defrosting for every 5 pounds.

Preparing
Carefully loosen the bands holding the turkey legs in place. Remove the packages inside the turkey and in the neck cavity. You should have a neck, heart, gizzard and liver. Throw away the liver or cook it separately as it will make the stock bitter; reserve the other pieces for the base of the stock that will be used with the pan drippings for gravy. Wash the inside of the turkey. Pull out any hanging pieces of innards and fat and blot inside and outside dry with paper toweling. Add salt, pepper,

basil and thyme to the inside of the bird. Put the legs back into the bands or tie (or stuff and tie). If the bird is small you can bend the wing tips under the back. Place onto a roasting rack in the pan and tuck the neck flap under the bird (or stuff the neck cavity as well and secure with a trussing pin). Smear some butter over the surface of the bird (not a duck or goose) and place in the center of the oven.

Basting Broth and Gravy
See "Thanksgiving" Chapter

Stuffing
Do not stuff the turkey until just before cooking, as bacteria will grow quickly. Do not partially cook a day ahead for the same reason and low temperature overnight cooking below 325 degrees also gives bacteria time to grow. If you decide to stuff the turkey, it can take an additional hour to roast. Do not pack the stuffing tightly into the turkey. Remove all stuffing before storing.

Time and Temperature
Allow about 18 minutes per pound of turkey or chicken. Do not rely on the pop out thermometer that may have come with the turkey. When a meat or instant read thermometer reads 180 degrees in the dark meat by the lower hip joint and 170 in the breast, it is done. The juices should run clear when pierced by a fork in the thickest part of the lower thigh, continue roasting if they don't. If the bird is stuffed, the stuffing temperature should reach 165 degrees. If the turkey is getting too dark on the top of the breast or the legs, lightly tent with aluminum foil.
Let bird sit before carving (see "Carving" above).

Yeast: Comes in a granular form or in a cake form. ¼ ounce of dry granular yeast or 1 small package is the same as 1 cake of yeast at 0.6 ounces. There is also a fast rising yeast available today. Yeast is heat sensitive and too much heat applied while dissolving can kill the yeast and your baking product won't rise. Use a thermometer to determine the liquid temperature: 110-115 degrees F is the temperature of the liquid needed if yeast is to be dissolved directly in liquid. 120-30 degrees are required if yeast is first mixed with dry ingredients (your liquid must be warmer when added). Automatic bread machines need 80 degrees for the liquid.

Zest: Zest is the product rendered when the outside of a citrus fruit is grated from the skin. You do not want to grate into the white pith area of the fruit. Wash and dry the fruit before grating.

Martin Luther King Day
Third Monday in January
Born January 15, 1929
Assassinated April 4, 1968

History

After the end of World War II, civil rights legislation was enacted by various states as well as the U.S. Congress. The goal of the legislation was to reconcile the racial inequality existing throughout the United States, and most flagrantly, in the South. U.S. Supreme Court rulings supported the legislation dealing with the integration of schools, public transportation, and expanded voter registration, all of which often contributed to civil rights demonstrations, sit-ins, harassment of blacks, violence and sometimes outright murder of black and white activists and innocents when compliance was attempted.

It was in this atmosphere of struggle that Martin Luther King found his voice, first as a Baptist minister and then as a civil rights activist, earning him the Nobel Peace Prize in 1964.

As the force of the civil rights movement gathered momentum and then fragmented into factions, some more militant than others, King is best remembered for taking the moral high road. Although his detractors pilloried him with innuendo, and attacked his morals to discredit him and the work he was doing. King's assassination served to purify his human side and focus attention on the higher cosmic morality in which he believed. In his own words:

"Our cultural patterns are an amalgam of black and white. Our destinies are tied together. . . . Somewhere along the way the two must join together, black and white together, we shall overcome, and I still believe it.

"Violence is immoral because it thrives on hatred rather than love. It destroys community and makes brotherhood impossible. It leaves society in monologue rather than dialogue. Violence ends by defeating itself. It creates bitterness in the survivors and brutality in the destroyers.

"Hatred and bitterness can never cure the disease of fear; only love can do that. Hatred paralyzes life; love releases it. Hatred confuses life; love harmonizes it. Hatred darkens life; love illumines it.

"I have a dream that one day this nation will rise up and live out the true meaning of its creed: 'We hold these truths to be self-evident that all men are created equal'."

Decoration

The African-American heritage is rich and colorful and the use of bright colors and patterns are reflected in the dresses, robes and head wear. If you don't have, or can't locate any brightly colored table linen, you might want to go to a fabric store and select a couple of yards of cloth with which to cover your table or make place mats and napkins. As always, candles create atmosphere and can coordinate with your selected color scheme. Flowers in January are usually hot house imports of early Spring-type flowers. I believe the brightly-colored, more exotic offerings would be more appropriate, even if you only buy one or three blooms and arrange them in a startling way. Baskets of multiple shapes and designs can also be gathered together to form an interesting centerpiece for your table. Flowers, fruits and nuts and breads can be tucked into them.

Martin Luther King Day Dinner for 6

Select your menu and make up your shopping list as suggested in the introduction.

Menu

Hors d'Oeuvres
Crabmeat Canapes
Bacon-Cheese Wrap-Ups

First Course
Peanut Soup

Main Course
Fried Chicken
    OR
Fried Catfish, Remoulade Sauce

Red Rice
    OR
Black-Eyed Peas

Mixed Greens
Corn-stuffed Red Peppers

Corn Bread
    OR
Hush Puppies

Dessert
Coconut Cake with Lemon Filling
    OR
Sautéed Bananas

Beverages
Iced tea and coffee

Timetable

One Day Prior
Lemon filling for cake
Cake layers if wrapped well and air tight
Clean and soak chicken in buttermilk
Make Remoulade sauce for catfish
Make peanut soup
Make black-eyed peas
Arrange flowers

Day of Party
Early in the day
Make crabmeat for canapes and toast bread
Make filling for bacon-cheese wrap-ups
Bake cake layers if not done previous day
Prepare stuffing for Stuffed Peppers
Set table
Make cake frosting and assemble cake
Fry chicken

Four Hours Prior
Make cake frosting and assemble cake
Start red rice, do not put in oven until 1½ hours prior to
    serving
Prepare mixed greens but do not start
Clean optional crayfish
Cook bacon for wrap-ups
Stuff green peppers

Two Hours Prior to Dinner
Make corn bread
Start greens
Assemble bacon-cheese wrap-ups and have ready to broil
    when guests arrive
Measure out tea and coffee and fill kettle and coffee pot
    with water

continued . . .

1¹/₂ Hours Prior to Dinner
Put rice in oven
Start greens
Toast bread for canapes
Have ingredients for bananas ready. Do not peel bananas,
    as they will turn brown

30 Minutes Prior to Guests Arriving
Assemble canapes
Put soup on stove and have ready to heat
Check rice and greens
Cut corn bread and put on plate
Make hush puppies and keep warm
Bake green peppers according to scheduled meal time

10 Minutes Prior to Dinner
Heat soup
Fry catfish
Check on all other food
Warm up black-eyed peas
Start coffee or tea

Prior to Dessert
Peel and cook bananas

Recipes

Hors d'Oeuvres

Crabmeat Canapes

Preparation Time: 10 Minutes

Equipment

Mixing Bowl
Wooden spoon
Can opener

Measuring spoons and cups
Toaster

Ingredients

1   can (6 ounces) crabmeat, well drained, flaked and picked over to remove cartilage

¼   cup mayonnaise

⅓   cup water chestnuts, fine dice

1   scallion bulb, finely minced, white part only

1   tablespoon parsley, finely minced, no stems

1   teaspoon lemon juice
    Tabasco sauce to taste
    Black pepper, freshly ground, to taste

4   slices firm white bread, lightly toasted, crust removed and cut into 2-inch rounds (4 per slice) or quarter the bread.

Combine canape ingredients in mixing bowl and refrigerate until needed. Spread on toast just prior to serving.

Bacon-Cheese Wrap-Ups

Preparation Time: 10 Minutes
Cooking Time: 5 Minutes Plus 15 Minutes
Makes 24

Equipment

Mixing Bowl
Electric mixer
Wooden spoon
Skillet or griddle
Grater
Measuring cups

Cleaver or chopping knife or mini
   food processor fitted with
   metal blade
Baking tray
Paper toweling

Ingredients

8   ounces cream cheese, room
    temperature
½   cup sharp cheddar cheese,
    finely grated
¼   cup almonds, toasted and
    cut into small pieces

2   scallions, finely diced, using
    a bit of the green
24 slices bacon
48 small, buttery-type crackers
    Parsley sprigs for garnish

Toast the almonds on a tray in a 350 degree oven until golden brown, stirring occasionally. Finely chop them when cool or place in a nut chopper or mini food processor being careful not to over process as they stick together. Place cream cheese in an electric mixer and whip until fluffy. Mix in the grated Cheddar, almonds and scallions with a spoon. Chill until ready to use.

Cook bacon on medium heat 2-3 minutes per side and drain on paper toweling. Bacon should still be limp.

Prior to serving, preheat oven to 350 degrees. Place a tablespoon of cream cheese mixture on one cracker and cover with another, a sandwich. Wrap a piece of bacon around the cracker and cheese sandwich, overlapping the bacon on the bottom. Place on baking tray.

Bake at 350 degrees for 15 minutes or until bacon is brown and crisp, remove to paper toweling and then onto a serving plate. Serve hot. Garnish with parsley sprigs.

First Course

Peanut Soup

Preparation Time: 10 Minutes
Cooking Time: 15-20 Minutes

Equipment

3 quart heavy bottom saucepan
Wooden spoon
Ladle

Mini food processor fitted with
    metal blade, optional
Chopping knife

Ingredients

3   cups dry roasted peanuts,
     finely chopped
     OR

2   cups chunky style peanut
     butter

3   cups chicken broth

3   cups milk or cream, choice
     depends on how rich you
     want the soup

3   teaspoons minced chives for
     garnish
    Salt and Pepper to taste

Combine the nuts, broth and milk and cook over medium heat, stirring constantly. Lower heat and simmer 10 more minutes.

Season with salt and pepper. Ladle into bowls and float chopped chives in each bowl.

Main Course

Fried Chicken

Preparation Time: 10 Minutes
Soaking Time: 4-6 hours
Cooking Time: 20-30 Minutes

Equipment

Heavy skillet with lid, cast iron
 best
Tongs
Plastic storage bag
Large mixing bowl
Measuring cups

Plastic wrap
Frying, candy thermometer

Ingredients

2   broiler/frying chickens (2 to
     2½ pounds each), each cut
     into 8 pieces, back and
     wing tips removed (save
     tips, backs, necks and
     freeze for stock)
2-3 cups buttermilk

2   cups all-purpose flour
2   teaspoons salt
2   teaspoons black pepper
2   teaspoons paprika
     Vegetable oil for frying,
       about 2½-3 cups

Chicken can be purchased whole or pre-cut. In either case, remove the back and wing tips and save the neck if it is in the package. These can be frozen for use in making stock at some future time. Remove any extra fat and skin hanging from the pieces. Separate the thigh and lower leg at the joint, and the breast from the wing. Lay chicken in large mixing bowl and cover with buttermilk. Cover bowl with plastic wrap and refrigerate at least 4 hours.

When ready to cook, pour oil into large heavy frying pan and heat to 360 degrees. Combine flour, salt, pepper and paprika in a plastic storage bag and shake to mix. Place 2 pieces of chicken at a time into the bag, shake to remove excess buttermilk. Coat chicken pieces completely and gently lay, skin side down, in heated oil. Lightly brown. Use tongs to turn chicken, as they won't pierce the skin and allow juices to flow out. Turn and lightly brown 2nd side. Cover pan and cook over lower heat for 10-15 minutes, depending on size of parts. Remove the lid and raise heat. Brown on both sides, turning frequently. When chicken is crisp and a nutty brown, and the juice runs clear when pierced at thickest part of piece, remove onto paper toweling and drain. Chicken is ready to serve, hot or cold.

Pan-Fried Catfish

Preparation Time: 10 Minutes
Cooking Time: 5-7 Minutes

Equipment

Heavy bottom skillet, cast iron best
Medium-size mixing bowl
Wooden spoon

Measuring cups
Metal spatula
Frying, candy thermometer
Paper toweling

Ingredients

2-2½ pounds catfish fillets, cut into 2-inch wide cross-sections
1½ teaspoons salt
1 teaspoon black pepper
2 teaspoons garlic powder or garlic salt (optional)

1 teaspoon cayenne pepper
1 cup yellow corn meal
3 cups vegetable oil for frying
Lemon wedges for garnish
Remoulade Sauce, see below

Combine seasonings and corn meal in a bowl. Heat oil in frying pan to 400 degrees. Dip catfish into corn meal mixture and fry in oil for 2½ minutes a side, or until tender and flaky. Drain on paper toweling and serve immediately. Serve with lemon wedges or Remoulade sauce.

Remoulade Sauce

Preparation Time: 10 Minutes

Equipment

Small mixing bowl
Mixing spoon
Measuring spoons and cups

Chopping knife
Plastic wrap

Ingredients

1   teaspoon capers, finely
     chopped
1   teaspoon gherkins (sweet
     pickles), finely chopped
½   teaspoon tarragon, finely
     chopped

¾   teaspoon Dijon-style
     mustard
¾   cup mayonnaise or Miracle
     Whip

Combine all ingredients, mix well, cover with plastic wrap and chill until needed.

Red Rice

Preparation Time: 10 Minutes
Cooking Time: 25 Minutes Plus 45-60 Minutes

Equipment

Large skillet, with lid
Wooden spoon
Chopping knife
Measuring spoons and cups

Large ovenproof casserole dish
Paper toweling
Can opener

Ingredients

9   slices bacon, cut into ½ inch pieces
1   cup onion, diced into small pieces
1½ green Bell peppers, cored, seeded, cut into small pieces
2   small hot peppers, cored, seeded, diced
½   teaspoon dried thyme
3   cups tomato purée, canned
1½ tablespoons brown sugar

3   cups cold water
3   cups white rice
1   cup boiled ham, diced
    OR
1   cup uncooked crayfish or shrimp, shelled and deveined

Salt and pepper to taste
2   tablespoons parsley, minced for garnish, no stems

Sauté bacon pieces in skillet on medium heat until crisp and brown. Remove from pan and drain on paper towels. Pour off half of the grease and raise temperature to medium high. Add onions and simmer until almost translucent. Add sweet and hot peppers and wilt. Add thyme and stir well. Add tomato purée and brown sugar. Combine. Stir in water and rice. Cover, reduce heat to low and cook for 15 minutes.

Preheat oven to 350 degrees. Add ham or crayfish or shrimp, bacon and salt and pepper. Stir well to combine. Pour mixture into casserole and bake at 350 degrees for 45-60 minutes, or until rice is fluffy and tender.

Black-Eyed Peas

Preparation Time: 10 Minutes
Cooking Time: 15 Minutes Plus 1 Hour

Equipment

Dutch Oven with lid
Wooden spoon
Measuring spoons and cups

Colander or sieve
Chopping knife

Ingredients

1   pound dried black-eyed peas, rinsed and picked over
6   thick cut slices of bacon, cut into ¼ inch cubes
3   cloves garlic, peeled and minced
2   medium jalapeno peppers, cored, seeded and minced

1   cup onion, diced into small pieces
¼   cup green or red Bell pepper, diced into small pieces
1½ teaspoons salt, or to taste
½   teaspoon black pepper
4   cups chicken broth
4   cups water

Heat Dutch oven and sauté bacon until fat has been extracted and bacon is semi-brown. Add hot and sweet peppers and onion and cook until soft. Add garlic and cook an additional 20-30 seconds, stirring constantly. Don't brown. Add peas and chicken broth and water. Bring to a boil. Add salt and pepper. Lower heat and cover. Cook at a simmer for about an hour or until peas are tender. Stir occasionally so mixture doesn't stick to the bottom of the pan. Add more water, if necessary.

Mixed Greens

Preparation Time: 15 Minutes
Cooking Time: 1-1$^1/_2$ Hours

Equipment

Large, heavy pot with lid, stock
   pot variety
Wooden spoon

Colander
Measuring spoons and cups
Chopping knife or cleaver

Ingredients

$^1/_2$ pound slab bacon, cubed
$^3/_4$ cup onion, finely chopped
5-6 pounds mixed greens
      (collard, kale, turnip,
      mustard, beet) or one type
      only, washed, drained,
      fibrous stem removed,
      coarsely chopped into 2"
      pieces

1   ham hock and 2 cups water
     OR
2   cups chicken broth

2   tablespoons red wine
     vinegar
1   teaspoon salt
     Black pepper to taste

Heat saucepan or stock pot and add bacon cubes, stirring until fat is rendered. Add onion and cook until it softens a bit, about 3-5 minutes. Add greens and stir. Cover tightly and cook until wilted. Add ham hock and water or chicken broth, vinegar, salt and pepper. Cover and simmer on low heat 1 to 1½ hours, until tender. Drain, and serve hot. Remaining liquid can be eaten as a broth, called "pot likker" in the South, a good lunch or light dinner served with corn bread.

Corn-Stuffed Red Peppers

Preparation Time: 15 Minutes
Cooking Time: 35 Minutes

Equipment

Large sauce pan
Medium-size skillet pan
Low sided, ovenproof casserole
    dish
Wooden spoon

Grapefruit knife
Cutting knife, cleaver
Slotted spoon
Colander

Ingredients

4   cups fresh or frozen corn
6   green bell peppers, whole
4   tomatoes
1   small onion, peeled and
        finely chopped
1   tablespoon butter
6   green olives, chopped

Salt and black pepper to
    taste
3/4 cup white unseasoned
        bread crumbs
2   tablespoons butter
Vegetable or olive oil for
    greasing casserole dish

Bring a large pot of water to a boil. Wash peppers and cut stem off of the top. Carefully remove seeds and white ribs; a grapefruit knife works well. Place in hot water for 5-10 minutes or until tender, but still a bit firm. Remove with a slotted spoon and drain well in a colander.

Meanwhile, sauté onion in 1 tablespoon of butter in the skillet until softened. Add tomatoes and corn and cook for 5 minutes. Remove from heat and add chopped olives, salt and pepper to taste. Stuff mixture into peppers. Sprinkle with bread crumbs and dot with butter. Place in greased casserole dish; do not crowd. Can be made up to an hour ahead to this point. Preheat oven to 350 degrees. Thirty-five minutes before dinner, place in oven and heat through. If they are already warm, turn up the heat to 450 degrees to brown the bread crumbs. You don't want to over cook, as the peppers will break apart.

Corn Bread

Preparation Time: 10 Minutes
Cooking Time: 25-30 Minutes

Equipment

1 medium and 1 small mixing
   Bowl
Whisk
Measuring spoons and cups
Sifter or mesh sieve

Small saucepan
9″ × 9″ square baking pan or 8-9″
   cast iron skillet
Toothpick or cake tester

Ingredients

½   cup all-purpose flour
2¾ teaspoons baking powder
1   teaspoon sugar
¾   teaspoon salt
1½ cups stone ground or regular
     yellow corn meal

1   egg
2-3 tablespoons melted butter or
     bacon drippings
¾   cup milk
     Vegetable oil, non-stick
     cooking spray or butter

Preheat oven to 425 degrees. Grease pan with butter, non-stick cooking spray or oil.

Sift flour, baking powder, sugar and salt into a medium mixing bowl. Add the corn meal. In a small separate bowl, lightly whisk egg. Add the melted butter or bacon drippings and milk to the egg. Mix well. Pour into the dry mixture and combine. Do not over beat. Place the baking pan in the oven until hot. Pour in the corn bread batter and bake for 25-30 minutes or until tester comes out dry. Cut into squares and serve warm.

Hush Puppies

Preparation Time: 10 Minutes
Cooking Time: 20 Minutes

Equipment

Heavy skillet
Mixing bowl
Measuring spoons and cups
Chopping knife

Frying thermometer
Paper Toweling
Sifter or mesh sieve
Wooden mixing spoon

Ingredients

2   cups stone ground or
       regular, yellow corn meal
1   tablespoon flour
½   teaspoon baking soda
1   teaspoon baking powder
1   teaspoon salt

3   tablespoons finely chopped
       scallions
1   cup plus 3 tablespoons
       buttermilk
1   lightly beaten egg
     Vegetable oil for frying

Sift cornmeal, flour, baking soda, baking powder, and salt into a mixing bowl. Mix in the buttermilk and egg and then the scallions. Do not over mix. Heat oil to 375 degrees and drop batter by tablespoons full into the oil (or smaller if desired). Fry until golden, turn and cook second side. Drain on paper toweling. Keep warm in 250 degree oven or under a napkin while you cook the entire batch. Serve warm.

Dessert

Coconut Cake with Lemon Filling

Preparation Time: 20 Minutes, Plus 15 Minutes
Cooking Time: 30-35 Minutes

Lemon Filling is best when refrigerated overnight. If time does not allow, refrigerate at least 4 hours.

Equipment

Medium saucepan
Small saucepan with lid
Electric mixer
2 Mixing bowls
Measuring spoons and cups
Rubber spatula
Grater
Small sieve
Juicer or reamer
Whisk

Sifter, mesh sieve
Plastic wrap
2 9″ cake pans, loose bottoms
    preferable
Toothpick or cake tester
Cooling racks
Dish towel
Candy thermometer
Spatula for frosting

Ingredients

Lemon Filling

1	cup sugar	2	tablespoons finely grated lemon rind
¼	teaspoon salt		
¼	cup water	1	tablespoon butter
½	cup fresh lemon juice, strained	5	egg yolks, beaten

In a saucepan over medium heat, combine sugar, salt, water, lemon juice and rind. Stir until sugar is dissolved. Meanwhile whisk the eggs in a small bowl. As sugar mixture comes to a boil, immediately lower the heat. Pour a small amount into the egg yolks, whisking constantly so the eggs don't scramble. Add more of the lemon syrup and pour all of it back into the saucepan. Cook on low until mixture becomes translucent and coats the back of a spoon. Put in bowl, cover with plastic wrap and chill.

Ingredients
Cake

1	cup unsalted butter, slightly softened (2 sticks)	3	cups cake flour, sifted then measured
2	cups granulated sugar	3	teaspoons baking powder
1/4	teaspoon salt	1	cup milk
4	eggs, separated	1	teaspoon vanilla

Preheat oven to 375 degrees. Grease and dust cake pans with flour or place waxed or parchment paper on bottom of greased pans. Grease and flour paper.

Cream the butter and sugar together with an electric mixer using a medium speed, until light and fluffy. Scrape down sides of bowl frequently with rubber spatula. Add the egg yolks, one at a time, incorporating each one before adding the next. Add the vanilla. Sift the flour and baking powder together into a bowl or pie pan. Alternate adding the milk and flour mixture (divide it into thirds). After each addition, beat until smooth.

In a separate, grease-free bowl and using clean beaters, whip the egg whites until stiff, not dry. Carefully fold 1/3 of the whites into batter with rubber spatula to lighten it. Fold in the balance of the whites, taking care not to deflate whites. Pour an equal amount into each baking pan and place pans in center of oven, without pans touching each other. Bake 35-40 minutes until cake starts to pull away from the sides of the pan and a tester comes out clean.

Immediately remove cake layers from pans onto a wire rack for cooling. Place a dish towel under the racks to absorb moisture. When cake layers are cool the cake is ready to fill and frost.

Ingredients
Fluffy Frosting

1	cup sugar	1 1/2	teaspoons vanilla
1/3	cup water	1 1/2	cups sweetened coconut flakes
1/3	teaspoon cream of tartar		
2	egg whites (1/3 cup)		

Remove lemon filling from refrigerator while you make the frosting.

Stir and mix sugar, water and cream of tartar in a small saucepan over high heat. Cover with lid for 3 minutes to prevent crystals from forming on sides of pan, and bring to a slow boil. Do not stir after initial mixing. Remove cover and insert candy thermometer and boil until mixture reaches 242 degrees. Meanwhile, beat egg whites until stiff peaks form when lifted by a spoon or beater. Pour hot syrup very slowly into the egg whites, beating as you pour. Syrup will spatter around sides of bowl. Try to scrape it down right away, as it hardens quickly. Add vanilla and continue to beat until the frosting holds its shape. Frost cake immediately. If frosting becomes a bit granular and sugary, beat in a little lemon juice.

Assembly

Remove filling from refrigerator about 30 minutes prior to frosting.

Place one layer of the cake on a serving platter. Arrange strips of waxed paper just under the edge of the layer to catch drippings as you frost the cake.

Spread filling on top of this first layer and cover with the other cake layer.

Spread frosting on top and then frost the sides using upward strokes of a spatula or knife.

Sprinkle coconut on the top and pat onto the sides. Remove the waxed paper and the cake is ready to serve. Cake can be garnished with thin strips of lemon peel or a thinly sliced piece of lemon, twisted.

Sautéed Bananas

Preparation Time: 5 Minutes
Cooking Time: 6-8 Minutes

Equipment

Skillet, non-stick preferable   Measuring spoons and cups
Wooden spoon   Knife
Plastic turner

Ingredients

This recipe is easier to manage if cooked in 2 batches

6   tablespoons salted butter
9   tablespoons brown sugar
1½   teaspoons cinnamon
6   bananas, sliced in half
     lengthwise
¾   cup orange juice or rum

Vanilla ice cream, optional
Sprigs of mint for garnish

Over medium heat, melt half the butter in a frying pan and add half of the brown sugar and cinnamon. When melted, add the half of the bananas and sauté about 2 minutes on each side and they begin to soften. Remove and keep warm. Repeat with the balance of the butter, sugar and cinnamon and bananas. Pour in the juice or rum and stir to combine. If pan is large enough, put bananas back into the pan. Using a match, light the liquid, the alcohol will flame and burn off. If the syrup doesn't look thick enough, remove the bananas and increase the heat to reduce the liquid until the desired consistency. Place bananas on individual serving plates and pour a bit of syrup over each. Garnish with a sprig of mint, if desired, or serve with vanilla ice cream.

Beverages

Iced Tea or Coffee

Preparation Time: 2 Minutes
Cooking Time: 10 Minutes

Equipment

Kettle to boil water   Stirring spoon
Coffee maker   Ice

Ingredients

Favorite black or herbal tea, raspberry is good, at least 1 bag or
teaspoon loose tea per cup, plus one or two for the pot.
Favorite coffee, according to taste, 1 tablespoon per cup, plus one
for the pot.

Brew coffee or steep tea leaves or bags for at least 5 minutes.
You want it stronger than usual as you will be adding ice.
Pour over ice and serve in tall glasses. If everyone likes his
tea sweetened, add sugar to taste before adding ice.

Chinese New Year
First Day of the First Full Moon
Between January 21 and February 19

History

A lunar calendar was established during the Chinese Han Dynasty somewhere between 206 and 22 BCE (before the Christmas era). This calendar established sixty-year cycles, divided into five, twelve-year increments. Each of the twelve years received an 'animal' significator, for example the rat, ox, tiger, hare (rabbit) dragon, snake, horse, sheep, monkey, rooster, dog, and boar (pig). Since every month has twenty-nine or thirty days, a double month had to be added every thirty years to keep the lunar calendar on track. The ancients reckoned the New Year had to fall on the first full moon after the sun leaves the constellation of Capricorn and enters that of Aquarius. Fourteen days of celebration ensue, ending on the fifteenth day with a Festival of Lanterns. These festivities are dominated by symbols of the Taoist yin and yang, male and female, balanced opposites, life and death (uniting the living with their ancestors), heaven and earth, the rebirth of Spring from the dormancy of Winter and symbols of or pictures of children (the future). Cymbals, gongs, drums, and firecrackers are used to chase away evil spirits who may have appeared during the passing year.

Chinese New Year is a festival where respect is paid to Ancestors in the performance of religious duties. Elders of the Clan or family are greeted and debts are paid so one can go into the New Year with a "clean slate." The celebrations end with a Festival of Lanterns of all colors and shapes and materials, with red being a favorite color. The lanterns are to attract prosperity and longevity. Children dress up in costumes and act out little plays and everyone waits to greet the dragon, one of the four divine creatures (unicorn, phoenix and tortoise being the others) who

48

will dispel any remaining bad spirits. The dragon is the highest of the creatures in the Chinese zodiac and often is portrayed with the head of a camel, the horns of a deer, the neck of a snake, the claws of a hawk, the belly of a frog and the scales of a fish. San Francisco has a Dragon Parade where a 125-foot long dragon, made of silk, velvet and fur is sinuously propelled through the streets by men hidden under the body's material. Firecrackers are lit and thrown at their feet. Floats, marching bands, stilt walkers, acrobats, martial art groups and lion dancers add to the colorful display.

There is a story that the origin of the "New Year" began in the following way. In Chinese, "Nian" means year. However, a long time ago, Nian was the name of a horrible beast or monster who preyed on people the night before the beginning of the New Year. This monster had a very large mouth and could eat many people in one bite. One year, an old man came to the monster and asked it if he could eat any other beasts of prey on the earth, as people hardly seemed to be a worthy opponent for him. That year, the monster ate other beasts. Before the old man left the village, he told the people to hang up red lanterns and red paper decorations in windows and doors to scare away Nian if he came back, as he was afraid of the color red. The old man then surprised everyone and got on the back of the beast and rode away on him! He was really one of the immortal gods. *Guo Nian,* may mean "survive the Nian" in the old days, but today it means "celebrate the New Year". The red decorations and lanterns, along with firecrackers, continue to scare away the beasts or evil spirits today.

As New Year celebrations are 15 days long, each day has its own special significance and traditional foods. The New Year is also a time when families make a special effort to be together. Homes are cleaned before New Year's Day and then all cleaning equipment is put away, as you don't want to sweep away good fortune on that day. As the holiday progresses, dirt and dust must be swept inward and carried out the back door so the family's good fortune remains. On New Year's Eve, families try to be together, play cards, games or watch television, but above all, stay awake until midnight when the fire crackers and fire works can be set off to send out the old year and welcome the new through open windows. In the morning, children receive presents, or money wrapped up in red paper packages. References to the past year are avoided, as everything should be turned towards a new beginning in the New Year. When visiting family and friends, a bag of oranges or tangerines and a red envelope filled with a new dollar bill are brought to the family. Traditions provide continuity with the past and provide the family with an identity.

Decoration

Prior to New Year's Day, Chinese families decorate their living rooms with blossoms, platters of oranges and tangerines and a circular or octagonal candy tray, the "Tray of Togetherness", containing eight varieties of dried sweet fruit. Traditionally each sweet has a special meaning: candied melon for growth and good health, red melon seed for joy, happiness, and truth, lychee nut for strong family relationships, kumquat for prosperity, coconut for togetherness, peanuts for long life, longnan for many good sons, and lotus seed for many children. Small strings of lanterns can be purchased and hung, or a red lantern can be hung at your front door. Red paper cutouts saying in Chinese "wealth, longevity and happiness", or "satisfactory marriage with many children", among others can be found in Chinese stores and groceries and hung in the house.

Setting a table for a Chinese banquet can be a daunting endeavor, but some of the basic elements of the celebration can be included easily to set a mood for a riotous party. Inexpensive chopsticks can replace flat ware, small rice bowls set at every place and dishes of condiments such as soy sauce, 'duck' sauce and Chinese hot mustard can grace the table. If you can find a 'lazy Susan' to put in the center of your table, you would be imitating how many Chinese families and restaurants handle the profusion of dishes to be shared. Votive candles at each place setting can add to the festive spirit, as can noisemakers. If you can find dragons or the 'animal of the year', add them to your table or other decorations.

Firecrackers are illegal in many states, but sparklers can usually be had. Caution should be used in lighting them indoors as sparks can burn holes. Try lighting a few on a dessert as you bring it into the dining area.

Chinese New Year Dinner for 8

Select your menu and make up your shopping list as suggested in the Introduction.

Menu

Hors d'Oeuvres
Shrimp Balls
Spring Rolls
Barbecued Spareribs
Hot Mustard, Duck Sauce

First Course
Steamed Dumplings with Ginger Soy Sauce
Honey Walnuts

Main Course
Roast Duck or Chicken with Pancakes, Hoisin Sauce
Steamed or Crisp Sea Bass or Red Snapper
Crispy Beef Sichuan
Buddha's Delight
Steamed Rice

Desserts
Orange and Tangerine Plate with Sweet Ginger Sauce
Tray of Togetherness

Beverages
Jasmine tea
Warm sake (not really Chinese but better than a sweet
    wine)

Timetable

One Day Prior
Sweet soy sauce (up to a week ahead) for shrimp balls
Make Spring Roll mixture (stuffing)

continued . . .

Prepare mustard sauce, refrigerate
Marinate spareribs
Make scallion flowers for spareribs
Make ginger soy sauce for dumplings
Make honey walnuts
Put together Tray of Togetherness for dessert

Early in the Day
Make pancakes for roast duck or chicken
Cut up vegetables for Buddha's Delight
Assemble sauce for Buddha's Delight
Assemble crispy beef, cut meat and other ingredients and
    sauce
Cut up and assemble orange and tangerine plate for dessert

Four Hours Prior
Prepare shrimp balls and sauce, do not cook
Prepare sauce for sea bass/snapper

Two Hours Prior
Start spareribs
Start duck or chicken

One Hour Prior
Fry Spring Rolls

When Guests Arrive
Fry Shrimp balls
Cut apart spareribs and serve
Steam dumplings

30 Minutes Prior to Dinner
Wash and start rice

During First Course
Cook sea bass/snapper and sauce
Cook Buddha's Delight vegetables
Cook crispy beef

Notes

Soy Sauce

There are several types of soy sauce available. If possible, obtain the dark thick Chinese variety which is made with molasses, however when using, decrease the amount of salt added to the dish. If using the more commercially available thinner soy sauce, use the amount of salt recommended in the recipes.

Recipes

Hors d'Oeuvres

Shrimp Balls

Preparation Time: 20 Minutes
30 Minutes Refrigeration Time
Cooking Time: 3-4 Minutes

Equipment

Sharp paring knife
Colander
Medium size mixing bowl
Food Processor fitted with metal
   blade
Rubber spatula

Wooden mixing spoon
Measuring cups and spoons
Deep fryer or medium size skillet
Paper towels
Plastic wrap

Ingredients

1   pound raw shrimp, shelled
      and deveined
2   eggs
¼   cup unsweetened coconut
6   water chestnuts, canned and
      well rinsed or fresh and peeled

1   tablespoon cornstarch
1   teaspoon ground coriander
½   teaspoon salt
1   quart vegetable or peanut oil
      for frying.

Rinse shrimp in a colander; peel if necessary and remove vein under outside curve by slicing a shallow slit and scraping out black, yellow or gray mass. Rinse under water and drain on paper towels.

Place in food processor with water chestnuts and coarsely process. Place shrimp and water chestnuts in mixing bowl and add the other ingredients. Mix together, cover with plastic wrap and refrigerate until ready to cook.

Heat oil in a fryer or deep-sided skillet to 375 degrees. Form mixture into bite size balls and fry for 3-4 minutes, do not crowd the pan. Cook until golden and cooked through. Drain on paper toweling. Continue to fry the balance of the mixture. Keep the shrimp balls in a 250 degree oven while you complete the balance of the recipe. Serve immediately with Sweet Soy Sauce, see recipe below.

Sweet Soy Sauce

Preparation Time: 5 Minutes
Cooking Time: 10 Minutes
Cool 1 Hour, Keeps Indefinitely

Equipment

Medium sauce pan
Stirring spoon
Measuring cups and spoons

Strainer
Air tight container

Ingredients

1½ cups granulated white sugar
2   cups Chinese soy sauce
¼   cup water
3-4 stalks of lemongrass cut into
        one-inch pieces

2   cloves garlic, peeled and
        crushed
2   star anise

Melt sugar in saucepan until sugar is completely melted and a light caramel color. You are using a larger pot than necessary because when you add the liquids it may try to bubble over. Slowly stir in the soy sauce and water, it will seize and slowly melt again. When all is a smooth liquid, add the garlic, lemongrass and star anise.

Cook 10 minutes. Cool for one hour, then strain into an airtight container. Close container and refrigerate. It will keep a month or more in the refrigerator.

Spring Rolls

Preparation Time: 30 Minutes
Cooking Time: 4-6 Minutes
Makes About 18-20
Can Be Frozen

Equipment

Cleaver or chopping knife
Cutting board
Measuring cups and spoons
Medium size mixing bowl
Small mixing bowl

Whisk
Pastry brush
Wooden spoon
Wok or deep-sided frying pan

Ingredients

1	package egg roll wrappers	2	teaspoons salt
½	pound ground beef	¼	teaspoon black pepper
2	teaspoons grated gingerroot (fresh)	1	teaspoon sesame oil
1	cup diced onion	½	teaspoon corn starch
2	stalks celery, small dice	1	tablespoon sake or vodka
5	shitake mushrooms, finely sliced	2	tablespoons vegetable, peanut or canola oil
1	pound bean sprouts		
½	cup bamboo shoots, thinly sliced, can be canned, rinse and dry	1	egg, beaten with 2 tablespoons cold water (for sealing)
1	tablespoon dark soy sauce	1	quart vegetable oil for deep frying
1	tablespoon brown or white sugar		

Using a wok or frying pan, heat 2 tablespoons of oil then add the meat and sauté until brown, breaking it up into crumbly pieces as it cooks. Add soy sauce and sugar and mix into the meat. Push to the side and add salt, pepper, gingerroot, onions, celery, mushrooms, bamboo shoots and cook about 3 minutes, stirring constantly. Bean sprouts will be added when mixture cools. Stir all together with the meat. Add sesame oil and stir through the mixture. Dissolve cornstarch into the sake or vodka and use this to thicken the pan juices. Make a well in the center of the wok and slowly stir in the cornstarch mixture. The Spring roll filling can be made ahead to this point. It needs to cool before adding bean sprouts and stuffing and cooking the wrappers.

When mixture is cool, and you are ready to serve the Spring rolls, mix in the bean sprouts, crushing them lightly. Whisk an egg with 2 tablespoons of cold water in a small bowl. Heat the oil to 365-70 degrees. Take an egg roll wrapper and place it in front of you with one corner pointing down towards you on the work surface. Place about ⅓ cup of mixture across the wrapper, leaving about ¾ inch border. Using a pastry brush, paint the border of the pastry dough with the egg. Fold up the bottom of the wrapper to cover the mixture, fold the sides across, enclosing the mixture and roll up tightly. Paint egg mixture under the final roll. The egg acts like glue. Fry immediately, 3 to 4 at a time. Do not crowd your wok or deep fryer. Dough cannot sit uncooked with filling as it gets soggy and will not crisp up. Drain on paper toweling. Do not stack the fried Spring rolls as they will get soggy as they cool. If you can't serve immediately, heat them in a 400 degree oven for about 10 minutes and serve immediately with Chinese mustard sauce and duck sauce.

If there are more Spring rolls than you require for your party, cook them and when cool, freeze them, wrapped individually in plastic wrap. When frozen they can be consolidated into a plastic bag and sealed tightly. Reheat frozen in a 400 degree oven for 15-18 minutes.

Chinese Mustard Sauce

Preparation Time: 5 Minutes
Let Sit at Least 1 Hour or Overnight

Equipment

Small mixing bowl
Whisk
Small serving bowl with spoon

Ingredients

Chinese mustard can be purchased in a jar
> OR

3	tablespoons Coleman's/dry mustard powder	½	teaspoon Chinese white rice vinegar or white vinegar, optional
3	tablespoons water		

Mix the mustard powder and water in a small bowl and make a paste. If you would like to add more tang to the mustard, add the white vinegar. Cover and refrigerate one hour, minimum or overnight. Before serving, stir to recombine. This sauce is thin. If you want a heavier mixture, add more mustard powder.

Duck (Sweet and Sour) Sauce

Preparation Time: 2 Minutes

Equipment

Small serving bowl with spoon

Ingredients

1   jar Duck Sauce or Sweet and
     Sour Sauce

This is commercially available in most supermarkets and usually quite good . . . and using it saves time!

Barbecued Spareribs

Preparation Time:
20 Minutes and Marinates 8-12 Hours or Overnight
Cooking Time: 1¹/₂-2 Hours
Garnish: 3-4 Hours Ahead or Day Prior

Equipment

Baking pan
Tongs
Cleaver or sharp butcher knife
Thin blade paring knife
Cutting board

Mixing bowl and whisk
Measuring spoons
Large rectangular dish
Plastic wrap
Aluminum foil

Ingredients

3   pounds pork spareribs or baby back ribs, flap and bottom fat removed
3   tablespoons brown sugar
2   tablespoons white granulated sugar
3   tablespoons white rice vinegar, or plain white vinegar

3   tablespoons soy sauce
1   tablespoon dry sherry or rice wine (sake)
2   small to medium garlic cloves
½   cup chicken broth
¼   teaspoon Five Spice powder

Garnish

1   bunch scallions

Ribs: Using a cleaver or butcher knife, slice apart the spareribs but leave ribs attached at the base. If necessary, cut rack of ribs in half to better fit into the dish and place them in a large dish, rounded side of ribs down. Blend together the remaining ingredients and pour over the ribs. Turn the ribs back and forth to cover with the sauce. Cover with plastic and refrigerate 8-12 hours or overnight. Turn ribs once or twice during the marinating process. When ready to cook, place on foil covered rack in a baking pan and bake in a preheated 325 degree oven for 1½-2 hours. Baste every 20-30 minutes with remaining marinade. Turn ribs after 45 minutes. If ribs are not tender, turn again and bake 15 minutes, if more time is needed, turn again and continue to cook. Baste each time ribs are turned. When done, cut apart at the base and arrange on a platter garnished with scallion flowers. Serve with the mustard and duck sauces above.

Garnish:

Prepare 3-4 hours ahead or day prior

Clean the scallions, cutting off the root end and peeling off outer leaves. Lay each scallion on the cutting board and with a thin bladed paring knife, slice about ⅓ to ½ inch into the white and several times, creating multiple thin slices. Place in a bowl of ice water and refrigerate 3-4 hours or overnight. The cut scallion ends will open up into flowers. Garnish serving dish with the scallion flowers.

First Course

Steamed Dumplings

Preparation Time:
Soaking Time: 30 Minutes;
Preparation Time: 20 Minutes
Cooking Time: 10-12 Minutes
Dumplings can be prepared in advance and cooked just prior to serving. Makes 24

Equipment

Mixing bowl
Measuring cups and spoons
Mixing spoon
Bamboo steamer/wok or frying pan to hold steamer

Spatula/tongs
Heat proof dishes or pans on which to steam and serve the dumplings.

Ingredients

8 Chinese dried black mushrooms, soaked in hot water for 30 minutes or substitute with fresh shitake or cremini mushrooms
¾ pound ground pork
½ pound raw shrimp, shelled, deveined and diced
7 water chestnuts, peeled, rinsed and cut into a small dice

¼ teaspoon salt
½ teaspoon minced fresh ginger
¼ teaspoon granulated sugar
1 tablespoon peanut butter
1 tablespoon peanut oil
1 tablespoon soy sauce
2 tablespoons cornstarch
1½ teaspoons sesame oil
1 package wonton skins, round or square

After the mushrooms have soaked in hot water and become soft (20-30 minutes), rinse, squeeze and dry them off. Remove the stems and any hard pieces that may not have softened and cut into a small dice. Place them in a mixing bowl and add the meat and shrimp. Mix well, then add the balance of the ingredients, except for the wonton wrappers. Can be made ahead, covered and refrigerated. Up to 4 hours prior to serving, make the dumplings. Take a wonton skin and hold it in the palm of your hand. Place about 1½-2 teaspoons full in the center of the skin.

61

Wrap tightly around the filling, leaving the top exposed. Tamp the filling down firmly into the pouch you are creating. It will resemble a small budding flower. Take the back of a knife and make fluted indentations around the top ⅔ of the dumpling, do not allow filling to overflow. Tap it lightly on the counter surface to flatten the bottom and place in a pan or dish on which they will cook inside the bamboo steamer or pan. When you have assembled all of the dumplings, cover and refrigerate until ready to cook.

Place a quantity of water in a large frying pan fitted with a cake cooling rack or wok large enough to fit your bamboo steamer. The size of your steamer will determine the number of layers you will have in it and the size of the dish that will accommodate the dumplings. A metal pan may cook the dumplings quicker. Bring the water to a boil. Place the dishes with the dumplings in the steamer or on a rack and cover the steamer with the lid. Steam for 10-12 minutes or until meat is cooked through. Make sure the water does not evaporate under the steamer. Keep a kettle with extra boiling water at the ready to refill, if necessary. Remove to a serving plate or serve directly on the dish on which you cooked them. You may want to loosen the bottom of each dumpling carefully before serving, in case it has stuck on the plate. Do not break the dough.

Serve with ginger soy sauce, below.

Ginger Soy Sauce

Preparation Time: 5 Minutes
Let stand 30 Minutes

Equipment

Small mixing bowl
Whisk
Measuring cups and spoons

Serving bowl and spoon
Sharp cutting knife

Ingredients

¾   cup soy sauce
1   garlic clove, peeled, finely
      minced
2   teaspoons fresh gingerroot,
      peeled, finely minced

2   teaspoons thinly sliced
      scallions, including some
      of the green leaves

Mix together soy sauce, garlic and ginger. Cover with plastic wrap and refrigerate until needed. Just before serving, wash, dry and cut off the root end of the scallion. Slice thinly, including some of the tender green leaf and float on soy sauce. You can also do this in advance and keep fresh by wrapping in plastic wrap.

Honey Walnuts

Preparation Time: 15 Minutes
Cooking Time: 20 Minutes plus 20-30 Minutes
Can be made up to 2 days in advance
and kept in an airtight container

Equipment

Colander
Medium size saucepan
Wooden spoon

Measuring cups and spoons
Baking tray, non-stick or coated
   with cooking spray

Ingredients

1   pound shelled walnuts
1½ cups sugar
1   cup water

2   tablespoons canola or
       vegetable oil

Rinse walnuts in a colander and place into saucepan. Cover with water and let soak for 15 minutes. Drain. Fill saucepan with water and bring to a boil. Add the nuts and cook until they lighten to a pale tan or until the cooking water turns dark. Drain into a colander and rinse with cold water until the water runs clear; drain.

Over a high heat, bring the sugar and water to a boil, stirring to dissolve the sugar. Add the nuts and reduce the heat to low, stirring nuts. Cook the nuts in the syrup for about 15 minutes, stirring frequently, until they are coated with the sticky syrup. If syrup becomes too sticky, add about ¼ cup water. Turn off the heat and let nuts sit in the syrup for 10 minutes.

Meanwhile, preheat the oven to 325 degrees. Strain off any excess syrup and toss the nuts with the oil. Spread the nuts out evenly in one layer on a non-stick baking tray or a baking tray lightly coated with cooking spray. Place in the oven and bake until they are crisp and dry. Check after 15 minutes and watch carefully so they don't burn. When crisp, remove from oven and cool. Store in an airtight container until serving.

Dinner

Roast Duck or Chicken with Pancakes

Preparation Time: 15 Minutes
Cooking Time: 1 Hour

Equipment

Roasting pan with rack
Small bowl
Whisk

Measuring spoons
Paper towels
Poultry skewer

Ingredients

6	pounds more or less duck or roasting chicken	3	pieces of star anise
	Salt	1	3-4-inch long stick of cinnamon
	Vodka, sake or rice wine	2	tablespoons minced fresh cilantro (coriander)
3	tablespoons soy sauce	1	inch thick slice of fresh gingerroot, slightly smashed
3	tablespoons brown sugar		
¼	teaspoon white or black pepper	3	scallions, washed, trimmed

Upon serving

6-8 cleaned, trimmed scallions, cut in quarters lengthwise, using
mostly the white

OR

12 cucumber slices, peeled, seeded and cut in 3-inch lengths by ¼
inch thick

Hoisin sauce, bottled and available in supermarkets

Preheat the oven to 400 degrees.

Line a shallow baking pan with heavy aluminum foil (or use two layers). Wash the duck or chicken inside and out, removing all membranes, internal organs and any hanging fatty pieces. Cut off the wing tips. Sprinkle salt all over the outside of the duck/chicken and rub in. Rinse off and pat skin dry with paper toweling. Rub the body cavity and outside skin with the wine. Sprinkle on more salt and rub in well. This will help to dry out the skin.

65

Mix together the sugar, soy sauce and pepper and rub into the body cavity. Place the balance of the ingredients inside the duck/chicken and close cavity with a poultry skewer.

Place the duck/chicken on the rack in the pan, breast side up. Place in oven and roast for 15 minutes. Turn duck/chicken over and roast for 15 minutes more. Turn yet again and pierce the skin all over with the tines of a roasting fork. This will allow the fat to run out. Continue to roast until the poultry is well cooked and glazed, 20-30 minutes more and about 185 degrees when tested with an instant read thermometer in the thigh near the back. Do not touch the thermometer to a bone or the reading will be inaccurate.

When cooked, remove from the oven and let stand for 10 minutes. Remove the skewer and pour out the juices that are in the cavity into a bowl. You can serve this with the poultry, if you wish.

To carve, slice off the thigh and legs, then the wings. Carefully remove the skin from the breast and cut into slices; keep to the side of the plate so it doesn't get soggy. Carve the breast and then the thighs and legs into strips and pieces. If you are using a duck, do not carve the drumstick, place it with the wings and meat on a platter. The meat will be served wrapped in pancakes each spread with about ½ to ¾ teaspoon hoisin sauce and either a piece of sliced cucumber or scallion. (Recipe follows).

To Serve:

Take a pancake and lay it on a plate. Spread about ½ to ¾ teaspoon of hoisin sauce over the surface of the pancake. Place a slice or two of duck/chicken and a piece of crisp skin on the sauce and place a piece of cucumber or scallion on top. Fold up the bottom of the pancake, and then fold over the first side, rolling it over to the other. Repeat with the other pancakes and poultry.

Pancakes for Duck or Chicken

Preparation Time: 10 Minutes
Resting Time: 30 Minutes
Cooking Time: 1 to 2 Minutes Each (8-10 Minutes Total)
Can be made ahead and reheated on a steamer

Equipment

Mixing bowl or food processor	Pastry brush
fitted with metal blade	Non-stick skillet or crepe pan
Sieve or sifter	Spatula
Measuring cups and spoons	Tea towel
Wooden spoon	Plastic wrap
Rolling pin	Steamer

Ingredients

1	cup boiling water	3	tablespoons sesame oil
2	cups all-purpose flour, plus		
	extra for rolling		Vegetable oil for cooking

Sift the flour into a mixing bowl. Add hot water in a steady slow stream, mixing with a wooden spoon to form the dough. Stir until it makes a smooth ball. If using a food processor, sift the flour into the processor and pour the water in a steady stream through the feeding tube as the machine processes the dough. In about 3-5 minutes a dough ball will form.

Cover the dough with a damp tea towel for about 30 minutes so the glutens relax. On a lightly floured surface, shape the dough into a log about 1-2 inches in diameter. Cut into 16 pieces.

Flatten each piece of dough into a 2-3 inch circle with the heel of your hand. Brush one side of each of the pieces of dough with sesame oil making sure the oil goes to the edge of the dough. Place two pieces of dough together with the oiled sides to the outside and roll into a 6-7 inch round. There will be 8 rounds.

Heat the skillet or crepe pan over medium heat. Lightly oil the pan with a scant teaspoon of oil. Place the round of dough in the pan and cook for one minute or until the pancake bubbles up. Carefully turn pancake over and cook until there are brown spots on the bottom. Remove from the pan and immediately separate the pancakes into the two pieces with which you started. One side will be brown and the other white. Be careful to control the heat and the oil so the pancakes do not scorch. Invert onto a plate and continue with the other pancakes in the same manner. When the pancakes are cool, if you are not using them immediately, cover with plastic wrap.

To reheat the pancakes, invert a heatproof dish in the steamer and lay the pancakes, in a pile, on top of it. Cover and steam for 5-7 minutes until warm and pliable.

Pancakes can be wrapped tightly and frozen for up to 3 months. Steam to reheat.

Steamed or Crisp Sea Bass or Red Snapper

Preparation Time: 15 Minutes
Cooking Time: 10-12 Minutes

Equipment

Butcher knife
Waxed or parchment paper
Large wok
Large wide Chinese strainer/
 spatula with long handle
Small mixing bowl

Small wok or saucepan
Whisk
Measuring cups and spoons
Serving dish long enough to hold
 fish

Ingredients

1   whole sea bass or red
     snapper, 1½-1¾ pounds,
     cleaned and gutted; head
     on fish
2   teaspoons white rice vinegar
     or white vinegar
3   tablespoons rice wine or dry
     sherry

1½ teaspoons salt
¼   teaspoon ground white
     pepper
½-¾ cup cornstarch
6   cups vegetable, canola or
     peanut oil

Sauce

3   tablespoons white
     granulated sugar
½   teaspoon salt
3   tablespoons dry sherry or
     rice wine
3   tablespoons white rice
     vinegar or white vinegar

1½ tablespoons dark soy sauce
1¾ teaspoons cornstarch
¼   cup plus 2 tablespoons
     chicken stock
     Pinch white pepper

continued . . .

Keep the following ingredients wrapped separately

½   cup diced onion
1   tablespoon grated or minced
     fresh ginger
1   small fresh chili pepper, can
     be Thai or jalapeno,
     minced
2   tablespoons diced carrot

Garnish

2   tablespoons thinly sliced
     scallions
     Cilantro (coriander)

Assemble the sauce ingredients and have ready to cook. This can be done earlier in the day.

Have your fish monger clean and gut the fish. Remove any extra fat. Wash inside and out and pat dry with paper towels. Lay fish flat and cut 5 diagonal slits into each side of the fish. Do not cut into the bone. Sprinkle vinegar, then wine, salt and pepper inside of the fish cavity, the diagonal cuts and the outside.

For steamed fish:
Place fish on a platter with a 1-2 inch lip and place in a steamer, or turkey roaster on a rack, two to three inches above the boiling water and cover with a lid. Steam for 10-15 minutes or until fish is cooked through and the eyes bulge.

Meanwhile, pour 1½ teaspoons of oil in a small skillet and over medium heat, add the onion and cook 3-4 minutes. Add the ginger, carrot and chili and stir briefly. Stir the liquid sauce and pour into the pan until the sauce thickens. If it gets too thick, it can be thinned with chicken or fish stock if the fish was steamed. When fish is cooked, drain off oil or broth accumulated on steaming plate. Rearrange the fish on the platter, sitting it on its belly like it's swimming, pour the sauce over the fish and garnish with cilantro.

For crispy fish:

Sprinkle cornstarch on a piece of waxed or parchment paper. Coat the fish completely, including the opening where the fish was cleaned.

Pour oil into wok and heat oil to 375-400 degrees. Place fish on the large strainer/ladle and carefully lower into the hot oil. If it does not get completely covered with the oil, ladle oil over the top of the fish and cook until brown and crisp, 10-12 minutes.

Place on a heated serving dish. Cover your hands with a cloth towel or pot holders and turn fish so it stands upright, with the stomach on the bottom of the plate, like it's swimming. Press gently to get it to sit.

Either remove all but 1½ teaspoons of the oil from the wok or use that amount of the oil in another pan and heat. Add the onion and stir and cook 3-4 minutes. Add the ginger, carrot, and chili and stir briefly. Stir the liquid sauce and pour into the pan until the sauce thickens. If it gets too thick it can be thinned with chicken stock. Pour over the fish, sprinkle with the scallions, garnish with cilantro and serve.

To carve the fish, make a cut along the side of the backbone and gently scrape off the fish. Ladle sauce over each portion.

Crispy Beef Sichuan

Preparation Time: 20 Minutes
Cooking Time: 5 Minutes

Equipment

Wok

Spatula

Measuring spoons and cups

Medium mixing bowl

Cleaver or sharp butcher knife

Ingredients

1   pound flank steak after membrane and fat removed, julienned across the grain of the meat

2   tablespoons sweet bean sauce

2½   teaspoons white granulated sugar

¼   teaspoon cayenne pepper

⅜   teaspoon hot chili or hot pepper oil

¼   teaspoon salt

1½   teaspoons Sichuan peppercorns, mashed with a mortar and pestle

3   tablespoons canola, vegetable or peanut oil

1½   tablespoons minced fresh ginger

1¾   teaspoons minced garlic

1½   cups julienned carrots

½   cup thinly sliced scallions

1½   tablespoons rice wine or dry sherry

In a medium size mixing bowl, combine the sweet bean sauce, sugar, cayenne, hot pepper or chili oil and salt.

Slice the beef across the grain into thin julienne. Julienne the carrots, mince the ginger and slice the scallions and prepare and measure the balance of the ingredients and keep in separate piles. Place them near your wok.

Heat the wok and add the 3 tablespoons of oil and make sure the whole surface of the wok is covered with the oil. When very hot, add 1 teaspoon of ginger and all of the garlic, stir. Add the balance of the ginger, scallions, ground peppercorns, stir and cook briefly, until you can smell it. Add the carrots and cook for a minute, stirring constantly. Add the beef and stir. Keep stirring the beef. When it begins to color, add the wine and stir until cooked through. Add the bean sauce mixture, stir in and heat through. Serve.

Buddha's Delight

Equipment

Nut cracker
Vegetable peeler
Sieve/colander
Paper towels
Plastic wrap
Small mixing bowl

Whisk
Wok
Cleaver or cutting knife
Measuring cups and spoons
Spatula/wooden spoon

Ingredients

4 tablespoons vegetable, canola or peanut oil
1½ tablespoons minced fresh gingerroot
12 shitake mushrooms, stems removed and thinly sliced
1 medium onion, peeled, thinly sliced
¾ pound bok choy, root end removed, washed, cut into ¼ inch slices
5 stalks Chinese or regular celery
2 carrots, peeled, sliced on the diagonal into ¼ inch slices
¾ pound snow peas, washed, ends trimmed and string removed; cut in ½ or whole, dry
½ cup water chestnuts, peeled, sliced, rinsed; if canned, rinse under water and drain, slice

1 small can baby corn cobs, rinsed and drained
5¼ by ⅜ inch slices firm bean curd, cut into cubes
¾ cup fresh lotus root, peeled, sliced into ¼ inch rounds, optional
¾ cup fresh or canned ginkgo nuts, optional
40 dried tiger lily buds, soaked in hot water for 30 minutes, squeezed dry, hard ends removed and cut in half, optional
4 tablespoons vegetable stock (chicken all right if no vegetarians)

continued . . .

72

Sauce

½	cup vegetable stock (or chicken if no vegetarians); extra may be required during cooking process	4	teaspoons dark soy sauce
		2	tablespoons corn starch
			Pinch of white ground pepper
2	teaspoons white granulated sugar	2½	teaspoons sesame oil

Note: I have included ingredients such as gingko nuts, fresh lotus root, and tiger lily buds because they lend authenticity to the dish. If you do not have access to an Oriental grocer, they can be omitted. Water chestnuts are wonderful, but rinsed canned ones are an acceptable alternative. Leftover water chestnuts can be kept in water in an air tight container in the refrigerator for a couple of weeks.

Fresh ginkgo nuts should be cracked open with a nutcracker, removed from their shells and boiled in 2 cups of water for 20 minutes. Strain in a colander and cool. Remove the skins and inside shoot. Put to the side. Or, use canned nuts.

Lotus root must be peeled. A vegetable peeler does a good job. Keep in water once sliced so they don't brown. Do not prepare until almost ready to use. Drain and dry in paper towels.

Fresh water chestnuts have a brown skin that must be removed either with a knife or vegetable peeler. Keep in water so they don't turn brown. Extras may be kept in water in an airtight container in the refrigerator for several weeks. Change the water periodically. Same storage applies to canned water chestnuts.

Combine the sauce ingredients, cover with plastic wrap and reserve to the side.

Heat the wok with the 4 tablespoons of oil. When you can see the heat rising, start the mushrooms, stirring constantly. Continue to add each ingredient in the order above, stirring well after each addition. If using fresh lotus root add it after the mushrooms. When all the ingredients have been added, add the 4 tablespoons of stock. Stir and cook for 5-6 minutes, until vegetables tenderize. Add a tablespoon of stock if it seems too dry. When the vegetables are cooked, make a well in the center of the wok and pour in the sauce. Mix well. When sauce bubbles, remove vegetables to a heated platter and serve immediately.

Steamed Rice

Preparation Time: 5 Minutes
Cooking Time: 20-30 Minutes

Equipment

Heavy bottom saucepan with   Measuring cup
    straight sides and a lid   Strainer
Wooden spoon

Ingredients

4   cups long grain rice, not   8   cups water
      converted

Wash rice under cold water in a strainer to release any impurities until the water runs clear. Place rice and water in the saucepan and cover. Do not wash rice until just before cooking as it will absorb water as it sits and will get mushy.

When water comes to a boil, lower the heat to a low setting and cook until all the moisture is absorbed and the rice no longer has a hard core to the grains. Stir and fluff. If it is still too wet, continue to cook, watching carefully that it doesn't burn. Turn off the heat and leave the lid on the pot until ready to serve. It will retain its heat for 20-30 minutes.

Leftover rice can be stored, covered in the refrigerator and warmed in a steamer or in the microwave, without adding water.

Serve in a colorful bowl with a rice ladle if you have one.

Desserts

Orange and Tangerine Plate with Sweet Ginger Sauce

Preparation Time: 20 Minutes
Cooking Time: 6 Minutes, plus 15 Minutes to Cool

Equipment

Slicing knife
Paring knife
Serving Plate

Small saucepan
Whisk
Sieve

Ingredients

3-4 navel oranges, depending on
     size, peeled and sliced
3-4 tangerines, peeled and sliced
     Kumquats, rinsed and dried,
     leave whole
1½   tablespoons peeled and
     chopped fresh gingerroot

3   tablespoons brown sugar
⅓   cup water
¼   cup fresh orange juice
     Fresh mint leaves for
     garnish

Arrange the sliced oranges and tangerines on a plate. Add kumquats in a decorative fashion.

Combine the fresh ginger, sugar, water and orange juice in a small saucepan. Bring to a boil and then lower heat and simmer for 5 minutes. Let cool for 15 minutes and strain out pulp and ginger. Pour over the fruit, decorate with sprigs of mint and refrigerate until beginning of the meal. Leave out on a counter during the meal so it is not icy cold; the flavor of the fruit is better.

Tray of Togetherness

Can be purchased or put together

Equipment

Circular tray or plate

Ingredients

8 dried sweet fruits; if traditional not available, substitute with dates, dried apricots, dried peaches and check out the canned goods in the Oriental section of the supermarket

Candied melon (can use candied watermelon from relish section of supermarket)

Red melon seed

Lychee nuts (available canned), if fresh, see Buddha's Delight on preparation

Fresh or candied kumquats

Coconut, shredded

Peanuts, sugared

Lotus seed

Longnan

Drain anything canned. Arrange in segments on a plate.

Optional Dessert Thoughts

Sautéed bananas and rice puddings are often served. See Martin Luther King Day for the bananas and St. Patrick's Day for the Rice Pudding.

Valentine's Day
February 14

History

Like many other celebrations whose roots can be found in pagan times, Valentine's Day may have its origin in the Roman Lupercalia Feast. Lupercus was a pastoral god similar to the Greek god, Pan, and was feted in a type of revelry which celebrated the rebirth of life in the Spring, the time when animals choose their mates, flowers blossom and seeds are sown. Another Roman tradition honored the Goddess, Juno Februato, in a feast during which the names of all eligible young women were placed in a box from which the young men drew a name, a type of match-making for the coming year.

In early Christian times, records indicate there were two men who had been martyred and shared the name, "Valentine". One was a priest from Rome who was beheaded in 269 by the Emperor Claudius II for refusing to worship the Roman gods. The other Valentine was the Bishop of Terni, renowned for his gifts of healing and who had been martyred about the same time. Legend says that "Valentine", while imprisoned, cured the jailer's daughter of blindness. Another legend says that while imprisoned, he fell in love with the jailer's daughter and sent letters to her signed, "from your Valentine". From that time, Valentine has been honored as the patron saint of engaged couples and lovers' quarrels.

Early Christians, drawing off of their 'pagan' heritage, recycled the idea of using the Roman 'name' box and substituted saints' names. A young woman would then draw a name of a saint and would have to emulate that particular saint's virtues through the coming year.

By the 14th century, the Roman tradition of placing girls' names in a "Valentine" box for selection by a young man was revived. Letters, sweets and flowers were sent to the fortunate girls. The French Charles, Duc d'Orleans, while imprisoned in the Tower of London in 1415 after his capture by the English in the Battle of Agincourt, expanded upon medieval traditions of 'courtly love', by sending his distant wife 'Valentines' of rhymed love letters. These letters became exemplary models of affection, love and devotion for the French court.

The Valentine tradition was exported to the United States and as early as 1723, Valentine "writers" offered booklets of verses for men to copy for their "Valentines." Responses to these verses for women were also available. "Be My Valentine" and the use of cupids, hearts and other emblems of love proliferated in cards with the advent of an inexpensive postal service. These traditions continue until today in the marketing of cards, candy and floral arrangements, jewelry, clothing and other items to an increasingly sophisticated market.

Decoration

Color schemes of lavender, pink, red, white, and delicate lace and satin bows are appropriate companions to the hearts, angels, cupids, and roses or tulips. Together they can combine to lend a voluptuous feeling to the table setting. Circular, heart-shaped white or gold paper doilies under hors d'oeuvres or under dinner plates, offset with a red or pink cloth or place mat makes the table loom special. Or, contrast a white cloth with colored napkins. Romantic color-coordinated candles will enhance the atmosphere, along with your favorite romantic music. A bowl of heart-shaped candies or red foil covered chocolates are good for after-dinner snacking.

Valentine's Day Dinner for 6 or a Romantic Dinner for 2

If you and your Valentine wish to be alone on this romantic evening, divide the recipes by ⅓. Select your menu and make up your shopping list according to the Introduction.

Menu

Hors d'Oeuvres
Heart-Shaped Herbed Cheese Round with crackers
Red Fish Roe Spread (Taramosalata)

First Course
Cold Asparagus Vinaigrette

Main Course
Cornish Hens with Black Cherry Sauce
Wild Rice with Pecans
Sugar Snap Pea Pods with Water Chestnuts
Thin Sesame Bread Sticks with Heart-Shaped Butter

Dessert
Heart-Shaped Meringues with Fresh Fruit Steeped in Fra
    Angelico
        OR
Heart-Shaped Chocolate Tart Garnished with Raspberries

Beverages
Champagne (Sparkling Wine)
Coffee or Espresso

Timetable

One Day Prior
Make meringues (can be made up to 5 days prior)
    OR
Bake chocolate tart, do not garnish
Blend and shape cheese
Combine fish roe spread

Day of Party
Blanch the asparagus
Clean the sugar snap peas and slice water chestnuts
Clean and ready the game hens
Clean fruit
Chill wine
Set table

continued . . .

One Hour Prior to Guests
Arrange cheese and crackers on serving tray (on top of a
　　lacy paper doily)
Prepare plate for roe spread
Cook rice

One Hour Prior to Dinner
Put birds in oven
Prepare vinaigrette
Macerate fruit for meringues
Prepare coffee
Put asparagus on plates without vinaigrette
Put bread sticks and butter on table

15 Minutes Prior to Eating
Warm rice over low heat
Put vinaigrette over asparagus and place on table
Have snap pea pods and water chestnuts next to stove, with
　　pan on stove

During First Course
Remove birds from oven to sit for a few minutes before
　　serving
As soon as you begin to clear first course, heat pan for vege-
　　tables. Sauté quickly
Dish up rice and garnish

Recipes

Hors d'Oeuvres

Heart-Shaped Herbed Cheese Round

Preparation Time: 10 Minutes

Equipment

Mixing bowl   Measuring spoons
Wooden spoon   Wax paper or plastic wrap

Ingredients

2   8 ounce packages of cream cheese, softened

2   teaspoons fresh chives, minced

1   teaspoon dried basil

1   teaspoon caraway seeds

1   teaspoon dried tarragon

1   teaspoon fresh ground black pepper

Paprika (optinal)

Assorted crackers of your choice

Combine all ingredients except for paprika in a bowl and stir with a wooden spoon until all is well distributed. Turn onto a piece of waxed paper, round up the mixture, flatten it slightly and using your own 'eye' or a large heart-shaped cookie cutter or mold, form into a heart shape. Dust with paprika for color and serve with crackers of your choice.

Red Fish Roe Spread (Taramosalata)

Preparation Time: 15 Minutes

Equipment

Blender or Food Processor fitted
  with metal blade
Mixing Bowl

Wooden spoon
Measuring spoons and cups
Plastic wrap

Ingredients

6   slices firm, day-old white
      bread, crusts removed
⅓   cup red fish roe (tarama),
      available in markets in
      small glass jars
¼   cup minced onion
6   tablespoons lemon juice
      (more or less)

2   cups vegetable oil
      Pita bread cut into narrow
      triangles and warmed just
      before serving. Or, small
      pita rounds (half dollar
      size) can be substituted,
      if available.

Soak 6 slices of day-old bread with crusts removed in a quantity of water so bread absorbs as much as is possible. Mix the tarama, onion and 3 tablespoons of lemon juice in the blender or food processor until smooth. Scrape the sides of bowl and blend again. Remove bread from the water and squeeze dry. With processor/blender running, alternate, adding bread then oil until smooth and thick. Blend in remaining lemon juice to taste. Cover and chill. Serve in small bowl surrounded by warm triangles of pita bread.

First Course

Cold Asparagus Vinaigrette

Preparation Time: 20 Minutes
Cooking Time: 5 Minutes

Equipment

Skillet with lid   Whisk
Large bowl with ice   Tongs
Small mixing bowl   Plastic wrap

Ingredients

Fresh Asparagus, allow 6   ⅔   cup olive oil
   per person (4 if very large)   2   shallots, finely minced
2   tablespoons red wine   2   plum tomatoes, seeded and
   vinegar   finely diced
2   teaspoons Dijon mustard

Break off tough fibrous ends from asparagus, they will separate where tender part begins. If stalks are thick, use a vegetable peeler to remove the skin from the lower half of the stem. If the stalks are pencil thin, don't peel.

Bring a small quantity of water to a boil in the skillet, enough to cover the bottom of the pan and come about half way up the sides of the asparagus. When water boils, put in asparagus and cover. Cook until barely tender. Do not over cook or allow asparagus to become limp. Pour off water and immediately plunge asparagus into ice-laden water to stop cooking process. When cool all the way through, drain off water. Wrap asparagus in plastic wrap and refrigerate until needed.

Just before serving, combine all the dressing ingredients except for tomato in a small bowl and whisk together well. Divide asparagus onto salad size plates and pour vinaigrette over the asparagus. Garnish with diced tomato across the center of the asparagus stalks.

Main Course

Cornish Game Hens with Black Cherry Sauce

Preparation Time: 10 Minutes
Cooking Time: Approximately 45 Minutes to 1 Hour

Equipment

Large Shallow Roasting Tray or Large Ovenproof Skillet if only serving 2
Cooking fork
Cutting board
Small saucepan
Knife
Sieve
Whisk
Grater

Ingredients

1 Cornish Game Hen per person (1¼ to 1½ pounds person)
1 large clove of garlic, halved
¾ teaspoon of salt
¾ teaspoon white pepper or freshly ground black pepper
Non-stick cooking spray or oil

Bottle of sweet black cherries (Morello type), 19 ounces, drained, reserve liquid
¼ teaspoon cinnamon
½ teaspoon grated lemon peel
Reserved cherry juice
1 teaspoon cornstarch

Preheat the oven to 375 degrees. Spray or lightly oil the roasting pan.

Wash the hens, inside as well as outside, removing any pieces of innards or fat then dry the inside cavity and skin.

Rub garlic halves on the insides of the hens, then rub in a combination of salt and pepper.

Roast the hens until juices run clear when pierced at the lower part of the thigh. If the hens are not golden brown, baste with juices from pan and turn up the heat to 450-500 degrees for a few minutes, watching carefully. Remove from oven and allow to set 10 minutes or so before serving on carving board. Reserve pan juices.

Sauce

Strain reserved pan juices into small saucepan. Drain cherries, reserving juice. Whisk cherry juice with cornstarch and add to pan juices along with cinnamon and lemon peel. Using a medium heat, whisk until juices thicken, if too thick, add a bit more juice (orange or grape will suffice). Stir in the cherries.

Place the game hen on individual dinner plates and divide cherry sauce on top or around sides of game hen.

Wild Rice with Pecans

Preparation Time: 15 Minutes
Cooking Time: 25-30 Minutes

Equipment

4 quart sauce pan with lid	Knife
Medium size skillet	Measuring spoons and cups
Wooden spoon	Grater

Ingredients

2	cups wild rice or combination of wild, brown and white	1	cup thinly sliced mushrooms (white or cremini)
3	cups chicken broth, stock	½	cup finely chopped scallions
2	cups water	1	tablespoon grated orange zest
		¾	cup pecans plus 2 tablespoons finely chopped for garnish
1	tablespoon vegetable oil		
1	tablespoon unsalted butter		

Bring chicken stock and water to a boil, add rice, stir and cook over low heat with lid on saucepan until water is absorbed. Do not stir until very end of cooking process. Taste to be sure rice is tender. If water is all gone and it needs further cooking, add some, replace lid and cook a while longer. Be careful it doesn't scorch on the bottom.

Melt oil and butter in medium size skillet over moderate heat. Add mushrooms and sauté until they begin to color. They will first release their juice, this must evaporate for them to brown. Stir frequently. Add the scallions and sauté until wilted. Add pecans.

When rice is ready to serve, reheat this mixture and then combine it into the rice.

When rice mixture is in serving dish, garnish top with finely chopped pecans.

85

Sugar Snap Pea Pods with Water Chestnuts

Preparation Time: 10 Minutes
Cooking Time: 3-4 Minutes

Equipment

Large skillet
Wooden spoon
Knife

Sieve
Paper toweling
Can opener

Ingredients

1   pound fresh sugar snap pea pods

1   8 ounce can sliced water chestnuts, drained and rinsed in a sieve; fresh is better, if available. Buy 8 ounces and peel; store in cold water

3   tablespoons peanut oil
½   teaspoon sesame seeds
½   teaspoon sesame oil available in Oriental section of market

Wash pea pods and dry on paper toweling. Remove the ends and any 'strings' that may loosen along the length of the pod.

Open can of water chestnuts, rinse under cold water. If whole, slice as thinly as possible.

Heat skillet and pour in oil. Add peas and sauté until crisp tender (3-4 minutes), stirring constantly; add water chestnuts and heat through. Add sesame seed oil, stir through and serve.

Thin Sesame Bread Sticks with Heart-Shaped Butter

Preparation Time: 15 Minutes

Equipment

Small heart-shaped cookie cutter
Small Mixing bowl
Wooden spoon

Rolling pin
Rubber spatula
Plastic Wrap

Ingredients

½   cup butter (1 stick) salted or
        unsalted at room
        temperature
1   package sesame bread sticks

Mash up warm butter in a small mixing bowl until it has reached a smooth consistency. Scrape out onto a piece of plastic wrap and cover with a second piece. Pat or roll to ¼-⅜ inch thickness. Place in refrigerator until almost hard. Remove and cut into small heart shapes. Place hearts on flat surface, cover and refrigerate until needed.

Dessert

Heart-Shaped Meringues with Fresh Fruit

Preparation Time: 30 Minutes
Cooking Time: About 45 Minutes
Meringues can be made up to 3-5 days prior when kept in airtight container.

Equipment

Baking (cookie) tray
Electric Mixer
Large Mixing Bowl
Spatula
Measuring spoons and cups
Food Processor fitted with metal blade or blender
3-4 inch size heart (or cookie cutter) for tracing
Pastry Bag

Medium Star Tip
Parchment paper (or brown bag)
Colander
Fork
Pencil
Metal spatula
Cooling Racks

Ingredients

4	egg whites at room temperature		1	cup hazelnuts (4 ounces), toasted (pecans or almonds can be substituted)
⅛	teaspoon cream of tartar			
½	cup plus 8 teaspoons white sugar		1	tablespoon cornstarch

To bring egg whites to room temperature quickly, separate eggs and place whites in a small bowl over warm water. Stir occasionally and test with finger.

Toast hazelnuts in a shallow baking pan in a 350 degree oven for 8 minutes. Place in a colander. Using a tea towel, rub the nuts against the sides until the skins come off. Cool.

When completely cool, place in food processor (or blender) with ½ cup of sugar and grind 15-30 seconds until fine, stopping to scrape down sides. Careful; do not over grind or nuts will become oily and stick together. Transfer to medium-size bowl. Add cornstarch and stir with fork to blend.

Position rack to center of oven and heat to 300 degrees. Lightly butter baking sheet and dust lightly with flour OR put

88

dabs of butter in the corners of the baking sheet and lay a piece of parchment or ½ of a brown paper bag on top. Butter parchment or bag and lightly dust with flour. Trace hearts onto paper spacing ½ inch apart.

Using electric mixer and large bowl, combine egg whites and cream of tartar at medium speed until soft peaks form. Increase speed slowly to high and gradually add 8 teaspoons of sugar. Beat until whites are stiff and shiny but not dry. Sprinkle ⅓ of the nut mixture into the whites and fold in with a spatula until barely combined. Repeat with remaining nut mixture. Do not over mix. Immediately spoon into pastry bag fitted with medium star tip and pipe outline of hearts. Pipe a second edge to the heart, as you want to create a lower center. Fill in the center of the hearts with remaining meringue. Remember to keep sides higher. If using meringues for 'ice cream sandwiches' or other layering purposes keep surface level.

Bake at 300 degrees for about 30 minutes. Check for doneness. They must not brown but must be dry and crackle. Reduce temperature of oven to 275 degrees and continue to bake until dry. They will firm as they cool. With large metal spatula release the meringues from the tray. If they are sticky on the bottom, continue to bake for 5 more minutes. Transfer to a cooling rack and let cool completely. Store in airtight container at room temperature for up to 5 days before use. May be frozen and kept for 1 month.

Fruit Filling

½	pint raspberries/ strawberries	½	pint blueberries
½	pint blackberries	¼	cup Fra Angelico

*Vanilla Ice cream optional

To Serve:
Rinse and drain berries; place in mixing bowl. If using strawberries, hull and quarter them. Taste each of the fruits. If they are sour, add a couple of tablespoons of sugar over the top and stir gently. Pour Fra Angelico over the berries and refrigerate until dinner is served. Bring closer to room temperature.

Just before serving, place a meringue on a plate and fill the center with fruit and a bit of the liquid from the macerated berries. Ice cream could also be served on the meringue and the berries spooned over the ice cream.

Heart-Shaped Chocolate Tart

Garnished with Raspberries and Whipped Cream
Preparation Time: 45 Minutes plus 20
Cooking Time: 25 Minutes
Chilling Time: 4 Hours to Overnight

Equipment

Heart-shaped tart pan (or 9 inch round)
Food Processor (optional) fitted with plastic blade
Pastry cutter
Mixing Bowl
Measuring spoons and cups
Rubber spatula
Fork

Rolling Pin
Electric Mixer
Pastry Bag
Large Star Tin
Bowl of Ice Water
Pie weights or dried beans
Aluminum foil
Cooling rack

Ingredients
Pastry Crust

1⅓   cups all-purpose flour
8   tablespoons (1 stick) unsalted butter, cut into teaspoon size pieces

2   tablespoons granulated sugar
⅛   teaspoon salt
3-4 tablespoons ice water

Filling

2   ounces bittersweet chocolate, coarsely chopped
2   ounces unsweetened chocolate, coarsely chopped
1½   sticks (6 ounces) unsalted butter

1   cup superfine sugar
2   teaspoons Fra Angelico, Grand Marnier or other liqueur
1½   teaspoons vanilla extract
3   large eggs, room temperature

Garnish Before Serving
Can be put together right before dinner

1   cup heavy cream
1   tablespoon superfine sugar
½   teaspoon vanilla extract
½   pint raspberries, rinsed and
       dried

Pastry Crust

The pastry dough can be made 'by hand' or by using a food processor. To make manually, place flour, salt, sugar and butter in a medium-size mixing bowl. Cut the butter into the dry ingredients until the mixture breaks into pea-size pieces. Use two knives or a pastry cutter. Add 3 tablespoons of ice water and mix with a fork. If dough is still too crumbly, add a bit more water. Turn out onto floured board and round up into a ball. Do not overwork the dough or it will become tough. Flatten and roll 1½ inches larger than the tart pan. Roll dough onto rolling pin and place over pan. Gently press into pan and cut off excess pastry.

To make dough in a food processor, place all dry ingredients and butter into bowl with plastic blade. Cover and pulse 10-15 seconds. Add 3 tablespoons of water though tube and pulse again. If it does not come together gradually add a bit more water. When it lumps together, turn it out on floured surface and proceed as above. Work quickly. If dough is too soft, refrigerate for 30-60 minutes.

Refrigerate the tart shell for 30 minutes.

Preheat the oven to 375 degrees. Prick the pie crust with a fork. Line the tart with aluminum foil and place pie weights or dried beans evenly over the surface. Bake for 15 minutes. If dough looks like it is still soft and will slide down the sides of the pan, cook a few more minutes. Remove the aluminum foil and weights. Return to oven for 10-12 additional minutes or until golden brown. Let cool on cooling rack.

Filling

Set a small heat proof bowl over simmering water, add chocolate and stir occasionally until smooth. Remove from stove and let cool slightly.

In a large bowl and using an electric mixer, beat the butter and superfine sugar until they are light and fluffy, about 3 minutes. Beat in the Fra Angelico and vanilla and then the chocolate. Add one egg and beat for 5 minutes. Repeat with other two eggs, beating for 5 minutes after each addition. Scrape down sides of bowl periodically.

Pour into tart shell and smooth top. Refrigerate until set, 4 hours to overnight.

Garnish Before Serving

Place all ingredients except raspberries in medium-size bowl and beat with electric mixer until cream is stiff. Spoon into pastry bag fitted with star tip and squeeze onto top of tart in a decorative way. Or, spread whipped cream evenly over the surface of the pie.

Garnish with raspberries on top of whipped cream.

Beverages

Champagne

Buy 2-3 bottles of dry champagne or 'sparkling' wine. Only that from the Champagne region of France can rightfully be called 'champagne'. If you are going to serve champagne throughout the meal, start with a dry one and change to a slightly sweeter champagne or rosé champagne for dessert. Ask your wine merchant for his suggestions to fit your budget.

Keep wine well chilled throughout the evening in a wine bucket.

Saint Patrick's Day
March 17

History

Saint Patrick is the Patron Saint of Ireland whom tradition says, brought Christianity and civilization to the Shamrock Isle.

Conflicting stories surround his birth. It has been said that he was born in Glastonbury, England, Scotland, Wales, or Tours, France, of Roman or Celtic parentage. Most agree that he was born sometime in the last three decades of the 4th century. He is reputed to have lived to the ripe old age of 120. One tradition surrounding the legend of Saint Patrick says that he was the son of a Roman official in Britain and his real name was Maewyn Succat. When he was sixteen years old, Patrick was kidnapped and taken to Ireland and sold as a slave. While in Ireland, he had a vision that he would escape his slavery on a ship, which would be waiting for him. After six years of captivity, he fled and found the ship of his vision, sailed to Britain and was reunited with his parents. While at home, he had another dream urging him to return to Ireland once more. Not yet prepared, he traveled to Tours, France where he entered a monastery, studied and became a priest. In 431, Pope Celestine I named him Patricius and sent him to Ireland to convert the pagan Druids and establish a Christian church.

The linking of the shamrock with Ireland comes from a legend of Patrick using the common clover as a symbol to explain the story of the Trinity to his converts. Each of the three leaves represents the Father, Son and Holy Spirit, all springing from the Godhead . . . the stem. This analogy was easy for the Druids to grasp as the shamrock had been used in ancient Celtic fertility rites to represent a triad of goddesses. The ancients had burned the shamrock's green leaves and sprinkled the ashes over fields to ensure a fruitful harvest.

Legends began to surround Patrick in his own lifetime. One legend holds that he drove the snakes from Ireland by preaching a sermon and beating a drum; snakes representing evil and the cause of the fall of Mankind from a state of Grace. It was said he raised his father and others from the dead, burned snow to make a fire, and overcame Druid treachery when they tried to poison him. Legend says he froze the Druid potion, poured off the still-liquid poison, melted the potion and then drank it. His God had rendered him invincible. Over the course of his long life, he founded many schools and colleges and organized the Church of Ireland. Because of his holiness and good deeds, upon his death, God rewarded Patrick with the right to judge the Irish at the Final Judgment. His body is reputed to lie under the Abbey of Downpatrick, in a shroud made by Saint Bridget, one of his early followers.

In Ireland, Saint Patrick's Day is the first of three days of religious devotion. The shamrock became a symbol of emerging Irish nationalism and pride of heritage in the seventeenth century when the English were occupying the island. The secularization of this saint's day is American in origin. In 1737 the Charitable Society of Boston first celebrated Saint Patrick's Day to raise money "for the relief of the poor and indigent Irishmen". The Sons of Saint Patrick in Philadelphia followed with a celebration in 1780 and New York's Veterans of the Revolution paraded in 1784. Celebrations on Saint Patrick's Day increased in scope and size over the years with New York's annual parade becoming the largest in the United States.

Corned beef, the food traditionally associated with Saint Patrick's Day in America, is not served in Ireland. For Irish-Americans, corned beef was the food eaten on the famine ships bringing large waves of immigrants to the United States in the nineteenth century and as such, has become one of America's heritage traditions.

Decoration

Green, green, still more green and shamrocks. Leprechauns, bowler hats and shillelaghs, green carnations and large "Kiss Me I'm Irish" buttons. Try to find small pots of shamrocks to set at each place setting! Or, buy a large plant and divide into mini pots; a good hostess gift for your guests. Rowdy, nostalgic, tuneful and tearful music played on bagpipes, tin whistles, Irish harps and flutes serves as a good accompaniment. A gingerbread Irish cottage roofed in thatch (shredded wheat) makes a stunning centerpiece and isn't difficult to construct.

St. Patrick's Day Dinner for 6

Select your menu and make up your shopping list as suggested in the Introduction.

Menu

Hors d'Oeuvres
Irish Smoked Salmon with capers, chopped onion and pumpernickel
Spinach/Parmesan Balls

First Course
Potato and Leek Soup

Main Course
Corned Beef with Cabbage (optional)
     OR
Irish Stew

Colcannon (potatoes and cabbage combined)
     OR
Red Potatoes with Parsley
Minted Peas

Irish Soda Bread

Dessert
Whiskey Cake
     OR
Kelly Cake
     OR
O'Connor Rice Pudding

continued . . .

Beverage
Harp Beer, Guinness, Stout, Ale
Irish Whiskey
Irish Coffee

Timetable

Day Prior
Make whiskey cake and wrap in plastic wrap
Make Kelly cake
Make potato and leek soup
Chill beer

Day of Party
Start Version 2 soda bread early, if using
Start corned beef or stew 5-6 hours before serving. Can be
    reheated.
Set table
Peel potatoes and vegetables for Colcannon; cover potatoes
    with water
Wrap vegetables in plastic wrap
Set up bar area
Clean peas
Make Spinach/Parmesan Balls, reheat later
Slice salmon and chop onions, cut bread and keep in plas-
    tic wrap
Wash red potatoes and chop parsley
Make rice pudding

2 Hours Prior
Prepare ingredients for version 1 soda bread; do not add
    liquid
Cut soda bread version 2 and cover with plastic wrap

30 Minutes Prior to Guests
Reheat or bake spinach balls
Slowly warm soup, stir often so it doesn't scorch on the
    bottom.
Chop chives for soup garnish

continued . . .

45 Minutes Prior to Dinner
Start red potatoes
Start Colcannon
Finish soda bread, version 1 and bake
Put soda bread #2 on table
Warm meat and cabbage
Start peas 12-15 minutes (5-8 minutes if frozen) prior to
    serving
Start coffee

Recipes

Hors d'Oeuvres

Irish Smoked Salmon with Capers, Chopped Onions and Pumpernickel

Preparation Time: 15 Minutes

Equipment
Slicing knife

Ingredients

½ pound smoked salmon (Irish preferable), sliced into bite sized pieces to match size of bread being served

½ cup chopped onion

½ cup capers (small variety)

Small loaf of pumpernickel bread cut into bite size squares or shamrock shapes, using cookie cutter

1 lemon cut into thin wedges for decoration or to use
Dill for garnish

Assemble the ingredients on a tray and let your guests make their own combinations.

*Some like the bread lightly buttered, your option

Spinach/Parmesan Balls

Preparation Time: 15 Minutes
Cooking Time: 45 Minutes

Equipment

Mixing bowl
Wooden spoon
Measuring spoons and cups
Sieve/colander

Whisk
Small bowl
Cookie sheet
Metal spatula

Ingredients

1 10-ounce package frozen
   chopped spinach, thawed
   and squeezed dry
3/4 cups dry, unseasoned
   breadcrumbs
1/2 cup grated Parmesan cheese

1/4 cup butter, room
   temperature
1 large egg, lightly whisked
2 cloves garlic, minced
   Salt and freshly ground
   black pepper to taste

Preheat oven to 325 degrees. Lightly butter cookie sheet.
Combine all the ingredients in a bowl and mix well. Form into 2 inch round balls and place on sheet. Bake for about 45 minutes or until lightly browned. Serve immediately.

First Course

Potato and Leek Soup

Preparation Time: 20 Minutes
Cooking Time: 40-50 Minutes

Equipment

3-4 quart saucepan with tight
    fitting lid
Food mill or blender or food
    processor fitted with metal
    blade

Wooden spoon
Ladle
Knife
Potato peeler
Large bowl

Ingredients

2   pounds potatoes (6-8 cups),
      peeled and diced or sliced
1   pound leeks (3 cups), thinly
      sliced including the tender
      green part (yellow onions
      can be substituted)
2   medium yellow onions,
      thinly sliced, in addition to
      the leek substitute
3   tablespoons unsalted butter
1   bay leaf

5   cups milk or 2 cups of milk
      and 3 cups of chicken
      broth for a thinner soup
1½ tablespoons salt
½   cup heavy cream, optional
½-¾ cup parsley leaves, minced
      in food processor; add
      after cooking soup
2   tablespoons chopped chives
      for garnish

Melt the 3 tablespoons of butter in saucepan over low heat and add sliced and diced potatoes, leeks and onions. Cover and simmer on low for 10 minutes, stirring occasionally. The vegetables will wilt and soften.

Add bay leaf, milk (and chicken broth) and seasonings, cover and simmer on low heat until vegetables are tender. Do not boil. Remove bay leaf. At this point, add the cream if desired and heat. The soup can be served as is, or put through a food mill, blender or food processor to purée the vegetables and create a smooth soup. Process the parsley leaves at this point. It will make the soup a nice light green color. Reheat on low before serving. Garnish with chopped chives after dishing out the soup.

Main Course

Corned Beef and Cabbage

Preparation Time: 10 Minutes
Cooking Time: 3¹/₂-4 Hours

Note: Corned Beef can be served with boiled cabbage and boiled red potatoes or served only with Colcannon, a combination of potatoes and cabbage, a sort of 'national' dish. Cabbage can be cooked separately, if desired, see below.

Equipment

Large 6-8 quart Dutch oven or heavy pot
Medium-size saucepan with lid

Chopping knife
Potato/vegetable peeler
Cutting board

Ingredients

4   pounds corned beef, tied with string to hold neat shape
1   sprig fresh thyme or ½ teaspoon dried thyme
1   small bunch parsley, tied together with string (about 2 cups)
1   medium onion, peeled and studded with 6 cloves
2   medium onions, peeled and quartered

1   whole carrot, peeled
*2   pounds cabbage (optional), washed, quartered, center thick rib removed as well as tough outer leaves
3   cups beef stock may be needed to cook cabbage if corned beef broth is too salty
    Black pepper, freshly ground upon serving cabbage

*Optional cabbage recipe below

Meat can be purchased already 'corned'. Drain meat and place in pot. Add all ingredients except cabbage. Cover with cold water and bring to a slow boil. Skim water often and maintain slow boil, without a lid for 3-4 hours, or until meat is tender. Remove thyme, parsley and onions. Taste the broth. If it is not too salty, add quartered, washed cabbage. If broth is too salty, boil cabbage in 3 cups of beef broth in a separate covered saucepan. Cook cabbage about 20 minutes or until tender. Do not add salt to this recipe.

100

Remove meat from the pot if beginning to fall apart and cabbage is not cooked. Place on cutting board. When cabbage is cooked, drain and lay it around the meat on a platter. A few turns of freshly ground black pepper enhances the cabbage.

Buttered Cabbage

Preparation Time: 15 Minutes
Cooking Time: 15-20 Minutes Plus 5 Minutes

Equipment

Medium to large saucepan with
    lid, depending on size of
    cabbage
String

Knife
Frying pan or microwave
Cooking fork
Casserole dish

Ingredients

1   medium-size head of
        cabbage
2-3   cups chicken stock
4   slices bacon, fried or micro
        waved

3   tablespoons butter, melted
¼   teaspoon mace
     Fresh ground black pepper
        to taste

Wash the cabbage, peeling off large tough outside leaves. Quarter and cut out the stem at the bottom of each quarter. Maintain the integrity of the cabbage and reshape into a head (ball). Tie tightly with string to keep the cabbage together in one piece.

Bring chicken stock to a boil and add cabbage. Cover with a lid and simmer until cabbage is tender, 15-20 minutes.

Meanwhile, fry or microwave the bacon, drain and cut into small bits. Melt the butter. Drain the cabbage and place in casserole dish. Pour melted butter over the cabbage, sprinkle on the mace and the bacon. Just before serving, put under the broiler for 5 minutes or until golden.

Colcannon

Preparation Time: 15 Minutes
Cooking Time: 30-40 Minutes

Equipment

1-3 saucepans for faster cooking,
with lids
Hand potato masher or electric
mixer if not available

Ovenproof dish
Cutting knife
Potato peeler
Colander

Ingredients
Saucepan #1

1½   pounds white/green
cabbage, remove tough
outer leaves and core;
quarter cabbage
1   teaspoon salt

Saucepan #2

2   pounds new potatoes with
skins (small red potatoes)
½   teaspoon mace
Salt and black pepper to
taste

2   cloves garlic, peeled and
minced
8   tablespoons (1 stick)
unsalted butter

Saucepan #3

2   medium-size leeks, well
washed and sliced into ½
inch rounds
1   cup milk

To Cook:
Saucepan #1
   Place quartered cabbage in a saucepan and cover with water. Add salt. Bring to a boil and cook for about 12-15 minutes, until tender. Remove from water, drain and slice thinly. Set aside.
Saucepan #2
   Place new potatoes in a saucepan and cover with water. Boil until tender, 20-40 minutes depending on size. Drain. Set aside in the saucepan.

102

Saucepan #3

Soak leeks in large bowl of water, then rinse under running water to remove all sand. Slice into ½ inch rounds. Place leeks in a pot and cover with milk. Simmer until tender.

Meanwhile, add mace, salt and pepper and garlic to the potatoes and mash potatoes until smooth. Add the milk from the leeks and integrate with the potatoes. Add the leeks. Do not puree; the leeks should retain their shape somewhat. If necessary, add more milk to enhance creaminess of potatoes. Add the butter and then the cabbage and mix well. The leeks and cabbage should be recognizable pieces.

Butter an ovenproof dish and pour in the mixture. Smooth the top and make a shamrock pattern on the top with the tines of a fork.

Place under a broiler until top is brown.

Red Potatoes with Parsley

Preparation Time: 5 Minutes
Cooking Time: 30-45 Minutes

Equipment

Large sauce pan with lid
Chopping knife
Cooking fork

Ingredients

Number of potatoes per person should be calculated on the size of the potato. If they are very small, 3-4 per person should be sufficient. If large, one per person may be enough with a couple of extras for 'seconds'. Cooking time will vary according to potato size, as they are cooked whole.

3-4 tablespoons minced parsley,
        no stems
4   tablespoons unsalted butter

Wash potatoes and place in saucepan with water to cover, cover with lid. Bring to a boil and maintain a slow boil until potatoes are tender when pierced with a fork.

Drain the water and return to a low heat. Jiggle the potatoes around to dry them off. Add the butter and melt it. Then add the parsley. Roll the potatoes around in the butter and parsley and turn into a serving dish.

Irish Stew

Preparation Time: 15 Minutes
Cooking Time: 2¹/₂-3 Hours

Equipment

Heavy 4-6 quart saucepan with
  lid
    OR
Heavy ovenproof Dutch Oven

Wooden stirring spoon
Butcher knife
Aluminum foil

Ingredients

3   pounds lamb neck
12 medium-size potatoes
4   large yellow onions, peeled
    and sliced thin
1   sprig fresh thyme or 1
    teaspoon dried thyme

2   cups water or enough to
    cover potatoes
   Salt and black pepper to
    taste
   Parsley springs for garnish

If baking, preheat oven to 350 degrees.

Remove fat from meat and cut into 8-10 sections; leave in bone.

Peel and slice 4 potatoes into thin slices; leave 4 potatoes whole.

In a large saucepan or ovenproof casserole, depending if cooking on top of stove or in oven, place a layer of all the sliced potatoes, ½ of the sliced onions and all of the lamb. Season with salt and pepper and add thyme. Cover with balance of onions and lay whole potatoes on top; season with salt and pepper. Add water and cover cooking dish with aluminum foil and finally, a tight lid.

Cook for 2½ hours or until potatoes and lamb are tender. If cooking on top of stove, simmer gently so lower layer of potatoes doesn't burn. As the stew cooks, the lower layer of potatoes will dissolve and should thicken the broth. If broth is too watery, remove whole potatoes upon completion of cooking and increase heat to reduce the broth and thicken it. Stir constantly so nothing burns. Serve in large dish, garnished with parsley.

Minted Peas

Preparation Time: 5 Minutes
Cooking Time: 5-7 Minutes Frozen Peas
12-15 Minutes Fresh Peas

Equipment

Sauce pan with lid
Wooden spoon
Knife

Ingredients

1	pound to 1.4 pound package frozen peas	3	sprigs fresh mint
	OR	1	sprig for garnish
2½	pounds fresh peas, shelled		

Bring ⅓ cup of water to a boil and add the frozen peas and mint. Cook according to package directions. Drain, remove mint and serve with a fresh sprig of mint on top for garnish.

If using fresh peas, shell them and place in pot with enough water to barely cover them. Add mint. Cover with a lid and cook over moderate heat until tender, 12-20 minutes depending on size and freshness of peas. Drain, remove mint and serve. Place a fresh sprig on top for garnish.

Irish Soda Bread (Version 1)

Preparation Time: 10 Minutes
Cooking Time: 30-40 Minutes

Traditional Irish soda bread is a biscuit type dough. The version usually seen in the United States is given below as Version 2.

Equipment

Mixing Bowl
Measuring spoons and cups
Sifter or mesh sieve
Spoon or fork for mixing dough

Rubber spatula
Baking (cookie) sheet, greased
Pastry cutter or two knives
Brush

Ingredients

4	cups white flour	1¼	cups buttermilk
¼	cup granulated sugar	¼	cup vegetable oil
1	teaspoon salt	2	tablespoons caraway seeds
1	teaspoon baking soda	1	cup golden raisins
2	teaspoons baking powder	1	tablespoon milk to brush on
2	large eggs		top

Preheat oven to 350 degrees.

Sift flour, sugar, salt, baking soda and baking powder into a mixing bowl, stir to blend. Add eggs, buttermilk, oil and mix with a spoon or fork to blend ingredients. You do not want to overwork the dough or the bread will become tough. Stir in the caraway seeds and raisins. Turn dough out onto greased baking sheet and mound into a 3-4 inch high circular shape with floured hands. Dough may be very sticky; that's all right. Do not over-work the dough as it will toughen.

With a sharp knife, make a cross in the center of the dough to prevent cracking.

Bake for 30-40 minutes until golden and hollow sounding when tapped.

Serve warm on a round platter and break or slice bread into wedges.

Irish Soda Bread (Version 2: type usually seen in U.S., yeast dough)

Preparation Time: 10 Minutes Plus Rising Time up to 4 Hours
Cooking Time: 30-45 Minutes

Equipment

2 Loaf pans
   OR
2 quart ovenproof bowl or casserole
Mixing bowl plus large bowl for rising
Measuring spoons and cups
Small bowl
Rubber spatula

Wooden spoon
Small saucepan
Whisk
Tea towel
Candy thermometer
Grater
Cooling racks
Pastry brush

Ingredients

¾   cup scalded milk
½   cup soft unsalted butter cut into tablespoon size pieces
3   large eggs
⅔   cup white sugar
1¼ ounce package (1 tablespoon) granular yeast dissolved in ¼ cup warm milk heated to 105-115 degrees F
5   cups white flour

1   teaspoon salt
1   teaspoon all spice
¾   cup currants
¾   cup golden raisins
½   cup candied orange or lemon peel
   Grated rind of orange or lemon
   Small amount of melted butter

In mixing bowl pour scalded milk over butter and stir until butter is dissolved. Cool until lukewarm.

Meanwhile, pour yeast over ¼ cup milk warmed to 105-115 degrees. Let dissolve and become frothy. When butter mixture has cooled a bit, add eggs, sugar and yeast mixture and blend thoroughly.

Measure currants, raisins and candied fruit into a small bowl and dust lightly with a teaspoon or so of flour to separate the pieces from each other. Add salt, flour, allspice, fruits and rind to the mixture. Add yeast bowl mixture. Mix with wooden spoon and then your hands, dipped in flour, to blend completely.

Turn out onto floured surface and knead until dough is smooth and satiny. Dough should become elastic; when a small piece is pulled up from the surface there should be tension in it. Round up dough and place in a buttered bowl, cover with tea towel and place in a warm, draft-free area until dough has doubled in size.

Turn out dough on board or counter, punch down. Divide dough into two pieces of equal size, if using loaf pans, and place into buttered loaf pans or into buttered 2 quart ovenproof casserole. Cover and let rise again until doubled in size.

Bake at 350 degrees for 30 minutes for smaller loaves or 45 minutes for larger loaf, or until browned. Loaf will have a hollow sound when tapped on the bottom.

Turn out onto cooling racks and brush with melted butter. May also be sprinkled with sugar, if desired.

Whiskey Cake

Preparation Time: 15 Minutes Plus 3-4 Hours
Cooking Time: $1^1/_4$-$1^1/_2$ Hours
*As fruits must steep in whiskey, preparation
takes several hours.*

Equipment

7 inch cake pan (8 inch will yield
   a thinner cake); adjust
   cooking time
Waxed paper
Electric mixer
2 mixing bowls

Measuring spoons and cups
Rubber spatula
Knife
Sifter or mesh sieve
Toothpick or cake tester
Cooling rack

Ingredients
Cake

1	lemon or 1 orange	3	eggs
2	tablespoons Irish whiskey	2½	cups sifted cake flour
1¼	cup sultana raisins		Pinch of salt
¾	cup unsalted butter	¾	teaspoon baking powder
¾	cup granulated sugar		

108

Peel the rind off of lemon or orange and soak in the whisky for 3-4 hours to draw out the flavor. Discard the peel and add the raisins to the flavored whiskey for about an hour or two.

Oil a 7 or 8 inch cake pan and line with waxed paper, grease this as well. Preheat oven to 350 degrees.

Using an electric mixer, cream butter and sugar until light and fluffy. Sift the flour, salt and baking powder. Add one egg at a time along with a teaspoon of the flour, beating well after each addition. Fold the balance of the flour into the egg mixture. Fold in sultanas and remaining whiskey.

Bake at 350 degrees for 1 hour. Reduce temperature to 300 degrees and continue to bake for an additional 15-30 minutes, or until tester comes out clean. An 8 inch cake pan will cook more quickly. Turn out onto cooling rack and gently peel off waxed paper.

Cool. Sprinkle powdered sugar onto top using a sifter; a shamrock stencil or doily may be used to create a pattern; or ice with a thin top layer lemon or orange frosting.

Lemon/Orange Frosting

Preparation Time: 10 Minutes

Equipment

Electric Mixer	Sifter or mesh sieve
Grater	Small mixing bowl
Juicer or reamer	Spatula for frosting

Ingredients

Juice of 1 large lemon plus grated rind (or 1 orange, plus grated rind)
About 1¼-1½ cups of sifted powdered sugar

Strain juice into small mixing bowl. Add sifted powdered sugar until a smooth spreading consistency has been obtained. The consistency of sugar will vary according to amount of juice the fruit yields. You may need juice from more than one lemon.

Place cake on serving plate. Spread a thin layer of icing over the top of cake.

Kelly Cake with Fudge Frosting

Preparation Time Cake: 15 Minutes
Cooking Time Cake: 25-30 minutes
Preparation Time Frosting: 10 Minutes
Cooking Time Frosting: 5-10 Minutes
Cooling Time Cake and Frosting: Up to 1 Hour
Frosting Time: 5-10 Minutes

Equipment

Electric Mixer
2 Mixing bowls
Measuring spoons and cups
Sifter or fine mesh sieve
Rubber spatula
2 Nine-inch cake pans

Cake tester or toothpick
Cooling racks
Medium-size saucepan
Candy thermometer
Wooden spoon
Offset spatula

Ingredients
Cake

⅓   cup of vegetable shortening
⅓   cup of butter, room
        temperature
1½   cups granulated sugar
3   large eggs, ½ to ⅔ cup
2¼   cups all-purpose flour
2½   teaspoons baking powder

1   teaspoon salt
1   cup whole milk
1½   teaspoons vanilla
        Vegetable shortening or non-
            stick cooking spray
        Extra flour for pans

Ingredients
Fudge Frosting

3   cups granulated sugar
3   tablespoons light corn syrup
1   cup whole milk
4   squares (ounces)
            unsweetened chocolate

⅓   cup butter
1   teaspoon vanilla
        Candy shamrock or green
            sprinkles, optional

Cake

Preheat oven to 350 degrees. Grease cake pans with vegetable shortening or non-stick cooking spray. Sprinkle flour around pan and cover bottom and sides; knock out the excess flour. You may want to cut a parchment circle to fit the bottom of the pan and grease and flour it as well to make cake removal easier. (See Introduction; How to Bake a Cake.)

110

With an electric mixer, cream together the shortening, butter, and sugar. Add the eggs one at a time, first breaking each into a separate dish before adding to the cake mixture.

Sift (sieve) together the flour, salt and baking powder. Measure out the milk.

Alternately, mix in the flour and milk and vanilla in two to three additions, keeping the mixer on low speed after you have added the ingredient, until it is incorporated. Stir up from the bottom of the bowl after each addition and scrape the sides of the bowl.

Pour into the prepared baking pans and bake for 25-30 minutes or until a tester comes out clean and cake pulls away from the sides of the pan. Remove the cakes from the baking pans onto a cooling rack. If it sticks a bit, run a sharp thin-bladed knife around the edge. Carefully peel off the parchment paper before the cake cools.

Fudge Frosting

This can be prepared while the cake cools, as the frosting has to cool down as well.

In a medium saucepan fitted with a candy thermometer, combine the sugar, corn syrup, milk and chocolate. Stir until sugar dissolves. Cook mixture until the thermometer reads 232 degrees F. Do not allow mixture to scorch, stir occasionally. Remove from the heat and add butter. Cool **without stirring** until the bottom of the saucepan feels lukewarm to the touch.

While frosting is cooling, prepare the serving plate. Put the first layer in the middle and place strips of waxed paper just under the edge of the cake, for easy cleanup after frosting. Make sure you have dusted all crumbs from both pieces of the cake.

When the frosting pan is lukewarm, and working very quickly, add the vanilla and beat the frosting with a mixer or with a wooden spoon. It will get hard suddenly and be almost useless. You have to catch the frosting when it is almost holding its shape. Place about ½ cup on top of the first layer and spread quickly. If it doesn't spread add a bit of milk to the frosting and stir. If it is too lose and runs, scrape most back into the pan and stir some more. Add the second layer and frost the top quickly, then the sides. The frosting will harden quickly. Add milk in drops, if necessary, to work the frosting. Remove the waxed paper strips and the cake is ready to serve.

Lay a candy shamrock or decoration on top, if desired.

O'Connor Rice Pudding

Preparation Time: 10 Minutes
Cooking Time: 45 Minutes Plus 5

Equipment

Large saucepan with lid
Wooden spoon
Measuring cups and spoons
Can opener

Sieve
Medium size mixing bowl
Whisk

Ingredients

½   cup long grain rice, not
       converted rice
1   quart whole milk
½   teaspoon salt
¾   cup evaporated milk
¼   cup heavy cream
½   cup raisins

2   large grade eggs
½   cup granulated sugar
1   teaspoon vanilla

1   teaspoon cinnamon, or to
       taste

Measure rice into a strainer and wash under cold water until the water runs clear. Pour the rice into a large saucepan. Stir in the milk and the salt and cook covered for 45 minutes, stirring occasionally.

Mix together the evaporated milk and heavy cream and add ¼ cup of the mixture along with the raisins to the rice. Stir well.

In medium size bowl, beat the eggs and sugar together then add the balance to the evaporated milk and cream and vanilla and mix well. Add about ¾ cup of the hot rice to the egg mixture and stir well. Return it all to the saucepan and cook an additional 5 minutes. Add cinnamon and pour into a serving dish. It tastes good warm or at room temperature. It can be refrigerated, covered.

Beverage

Irish Coffee

Preparation Time: 5 Minutes

Equipment

Medium-size narrow wine glasses
   or special Irish coffee glasses
Coffee pot
Electric mixer

Small bowl
Rubber spatula
Spoon

Ingredients

8   cups hot, strong coffee
½   pint rich heavy cream,
     whipped

For each serving:

1   teaspoon sugar
     Coffee to almost full glass/
       mug

1   jigger Irish whiskey
1   tablespoon whipped cream

Heat goblet in microwave. Add sugar and enough coffee to melt sugar, leave room for whiskey and cream. Stir. Add jigger of whiskey. **Do not stir.** Float whipped cream on top and serve.

Easter
First Sunday After the First Full Moon in March on, or After, the Vernal Equinox (March 21)

History

The coming of Spring has been commemorated in all cultures since the beginning of time. It is the time to celebrate the victory of life and the renewal of nature over the deathly grip of winter's sterile world of short, dark days. In the English language, the name of Easter is derived from the name of a pagan Anglo-Saxon goddess of Dawn and Spring, Eostre. For millennia, magical rituals have been performed at the Vernal Equinox, the date for sowing new seeds within Mother Earth, assuring the regeneration of life and sustenance for yet another year.

With the advent of Christianity, Easter became the day Jesus, Son of God, was resurrected from the dead after his torture and crucifixion. For devout Christians, the joyous Easter Sunday celebration is the culmination of forty days of fasting, self-sacrifice and penitence (the period of Lent). Easter, with the "Passion" of Jesus, extends a promise of spiritual rebirth and life everlasting to all mankind.

Several days of 'Carnival' or 'Mardi Gras' are a precursor to the forty-day Lenten season. It is a time of riotous partying, dancing, and games in some countries, with Rio de Janeiro, Venice and New Orleans holding the most sybaritic. Carnival was the time to use up the eggs, butter, fats and rich foods in the larder in preparation for the coming fast. For Roman Catholics, it was a last chance to eat meat, hence the derivation of the name "carnival" . . . Carne (meat) vale (farewell). In some ethnic groups, doughnuts or pancakes were/are eaten on Shrove Tuesday, the day prior to the commencement of Lent.

Fasting begins on Ash Wednesday when Catholics go to church to have ashes laid upon their brows in the sign of the cross, a reminder of their mortality and of the Biblical quote, "Dust thou art, and unto dust shalt thou return." Many believers renounce foods or pleasures meaningful to them as a form of sacrifice and discipline during the Lenten period.

The week prior to Easter Sunday is called Holy Week, the period leading up to the crucifixion of Jesus, or the 'Passion' of the Lord. Palm Sunday, the week prior to Easter, celebrates the entry of Jesus into the city of Jerusalem riding on an ass. People rejoiced and laid down their garments and branches of palm fronds upon his path to honor him as a miracle worker, healer, teacher and prophet. In many churches today, worshipers are given pieces of palm or palm crosses as they leave church in memory of this event.

As the historic 'Passion' of Jesus coincided with the Jewish Passover, Jesus celebrated a seder (ritual meal) with his twelve apostles during which, in humility and love for them, Jesus washed their feet and urged them to do the same for others in the future. 'Maundy' Thursday of Holy Week, with a word origin mandatum (command) is a reminder to remember the commandments of love which were given at that Passover meal, which became "The Last Supper". In the following centuries, kings and queens washed the feet of the poor and destitute to show their humility and love for even the lowliest of their fellow beings; maunds (gifts) were given. Thursday became a day to clean and purify the home and church altars in preparation for Easter.

Jesus knew he would be martyred and believed that his mission on earth was the sacrifice of his life so others might be saved in God. After the betrayal of Jesus to the Roman soldiers by Judas Iscariot, one of his disciples, the Romans handed him over to the Jewish high priest for sentencing. He was deemed to be a rabble-rouser and a heretic, as he called himself the Son of God, not the long-hoped for Messiah. The Jewish priest returned Jesus to the Roman Governor, Pontius Pilate, for sentencing. In reality, the religious 'establishment' was feeling threatened by the power inherent in Jesus' miracles and teachings of love and pacifism. Pilate, who had no quarrel with Jesus, offered to release him to the gathered crowd, in accordance with a Passover tradition whereby one prisoner might be released. When asked who should be released, they chose a robber, Barabbas, to be set free. Jesus was then flogged, and marched to the Hill of Golgotha with a crown of thorns (for the 'King of the

115

Jews') on his head and the cross upon which he would be crucified on his shoulder. This was "Good Friday".

Crucified in the company of two robbers, Jesus' body was
then taken down from the cross at sundown and buried in a
borrowed tomb. On the third day after his death, Sunday, a
follower, Mary Magdalene, came to the tomb and found it open
and empty. Falling down and weeping because the body was
missing, Jesus appeared to her and told her he was to ascend
to his Father. She was told to gather the disciples together and
he stood in their midst and showed them his bloody hands and
wounds, proving to them, he had overcome even death. With the
breath of the Holy Spirit upon them, he prepared them to go
forth and spread his teachings. After showing himself in several
other locations, he ascended into Heaven to sit at the right hand
of God, his Father.

Symbols of Easter

Since antiquity, the use of eggs in Spring celebrations have
been symbols of life and resurrection. The ancient Persians,
Greeks and Chinese exchanged them at Spring festivals as the
egg represented the divine sun bird, or the two halves from
which heaven and earth were made. In China, a red egg was the
symbol of life. In many middle-European countries, the richly
decorated red and white painted eggs symbolize the blood Christ
shed on Good Friday, and the white, his purity. In the year 1290,
there is an entry in the Household Accounts of King Edward I
of England, for 450 eggs to be colored and covered in gold leaf
for use at Easter.

The hare, or rabbit, another symbol associated with Easter,
was sacred to the goddess Eostre as a symbol of fertility, renewal
and return of Spring. Today he delivers the eggs!

Since the advent of Christianity, another symbol of spring,
the baby lamb, recalls the teachings of Jesus whereby he is often
represented as the Lamb of God, the Good Shepherd of believers.

Decoration

Easter is a celebration of rebirth and resurrection and the
white lily, associated with the purity of Mary, the mother of

Jesus, has long been associated with the holiday. A home laden with multi-colored Spring flowers (tulips, daffodils, anemones), forced flowering branches, (forsythia, plum and quince), enhance the décor of any room or dining table. Porcelain or small toy rabbits, baby chicks, lambs and colored eggs could be incorporated into a table display. You may want to consider using an oversized basket lined in plastic to create your own centerpiece. Inexpensive, almost flowering potted tulip, hyacinth and daffodil bulbs can be carefully removed from the clump of dirt in which they are planted and combined into your own creative arrangement. Spaces can be filled with miniature bunnies or eggs or even small Johnny Jump-ups, clover or moss. If the basket looks bare, tie a beautiful ribbon on the handle or set a color-coordinated bow among the flowers.

If there are children in the household, Easter baskets can be created inexpensively by purchasing them at craft stores and filling them with artificial paper "grass"; gear the size of the basket to the size of a child. Traditionally, chocolate bunnies, jelly beans and sugar-coated nuts can be placed in the baskets. But if you are not keen on filling children with candies, small, fuzzy, cuddly, stuffed animals, or other small toys and games can be used to fill up the space. Try to leave room for eggs gathered in an Easter egg hunt!

Decorated eggs lovingly placed in "grass," real or artificial, are often the "star" of an Easter table decoration or quest. Children love participating in dyeing them (tips to follow) and an indoor or outdoor egg hunt can be a lot of fun. If there are several children participating, you may want to dye up to three dozen eggs or more so there are plenty for all to find. The eggs don't have to be a waste . . . there's always egg salad (recipe to follow)!

Dyeing Eggs

There are many approaches to dyeing eggs:

- Put a pin prick in each end of the egg and gently blow out the egg and then paint and decorate it (carefully wrapped, they can be saved year to year).
- Trace designs in hot wax, dyeing the exposed sections, let dry, then scrape off the wax and dye other sections, after the first pattern is covered in wax.
- The easiest, hard boil and dip them into dye.

To Cook Boiled Eggs

When eggs reach room temperature, place them in a large non-aluminum, non-greasy saucepan. Do not crowd the eggs. Cover with cold water and place on medium heat. One school of thought feels if you prick the large end of the egg with a needle before cooking, it will prevent cracking. Bring water to a gentle boil for about 12-15 minutes. Place pan in the sink and run cold water over the eggs until all the hot water is displaced. Remove eggs from the pot and dry them off. They are now ready to be dyed. Dye them while still warm. Commercial Easter egg dyes are available one to two months prior to Easter in grocery and specialty stores. Most commercially packaged dyes require your having to add white vinegar to the dye, so be sure to have it on hand before you begin the project. Follow package directions. Before dyeing the eggs, use a clear wax crayon to create designs or wrap a rubber band or tape around the egg to create stripes. Be as creative as you want!

If you want to make your own 'natural' dyes, boil the eggs with yellow onion skins for a tan/brown color, red beet juice for a rosy red, spinach for green, red cabbage for blue. More esoteric colors from nature can be created using: gorse blossoms for yellow, log wood chips for purple, cochineal for scarlet, or anemone petals for green. Easier still, add food coloring to cold water and become a colorist. Violet can be made with one part red and 2 parts blue; purple with 3 parts red and 1 part blue; turquoise with 1 part green and 3 parts blue and orange from 2 parts yellow and 1 part red.

Pre-Lenten/Shrove Tuesday Specialties Recipes

Hot Cross Buns
Krapfen (Doughnuts)
Pancakes

Hot Cross Buns

Preparation Time: 15 Minutes and 2 Hours Waiting
Cooking Time: 10-12 Minutes
Makes 16 Buns

Equipment

Electric mixer or food processor
    fitted with plastic blade.
Small saucepan
2 large mixing bowls
Grater
Measuring spoons and cups
Wooden spoon
Small bowl
Whisk

Rubber spatula
Chopping knife
Tea towel or plastic wrap
2 Baking sheets
Parchment paper, optional
Pastry brush
Sharp knife
Cooling racks
Pastry bag or plastic storage bag

Ingredients

3   cups unbleached all-
       purpose flour
2   packages (5½ teaspoons) dry
       active yeast
¼   cup sugar
½   teaspoon salt
½   teaspoon grated lemon zest
¾   cup milk
¼   cup unsalted butter, cut
       into pieces
2   large eggs, beaten

½   cup raisins, or currants
¼   cup blanched, toasted,
       chopped almonds
2   tablespoons mixed candied
       fruits
    Butter for greasing 'rising'
       dough bowl
    Non-stick cooking spray,
       butter or vegetable
       shortening

Glaze

1   large egg, beaten with 1
       tablespoon milk

continued . . .

119

Icing

1	cup confectioners' sugar (powdered sugar)	½	teaspoon almond extract (or vanilla extract)
2-3	tablespoons cream or milk		

Buns

Measure the flour, yeast, sugar and zest into the large bowl of an electric mixer or food processor. In a small saucepan, heat the milk until it comes to a simmer and add the butter. Stir with spoon until the butter melts; remove from the heat. Whisk eggs in small bowl and add the whisked eggs slowly to milk and butter mixture, whisking all the time so eggs don't scramble. Add to the dry ingredients and mix over high speed until mixture is smooth and satiny (about 2 minutes). Using a wooden spoon, blend in the raisins, nuts and fruits. You may need to use your hands to mix it thoroughly. Place in a large buttered bowl and cover with a towel or plastic wrap. Place in a warm draft-free space until dough has doubled in bulk, about 1 hour.

Meanwhile, line the baking sheets with parchment paper or lightly butter, spray with non-stick cooking spray or grease with vegetable shortening.

Turn the dough onto an oiled surface and dust dough with flour. Knead dough to remove any air bubbles. Divide the dough into 16 pieces (cut in half and in half again and again). Shape each piece into a round ball being careful not to overwork the dough. Place dough, smooth side up on baking sheets, about 3 inches apart. Cover and let rise until almost doubled in size, about 45 minutes.

Preheat the oven to 400 degrees. Make the glaze and using a pastry brush, paint the tops of dough with it. With a sharp knife, slash a cross in the center of each ball.

Bake until golden brown, about 10-12 minutes. Remove from trays and cool on wire racks. When cool, make icing by combining sugar with cream or milk, adding just enough to get the sugar to a soft toothpaste consistency. Fit a small pastry bag with a small circular icing tip, or use a plastic bag and cut a small hole in a corner. Pipe the shape of a cross over the top of each bun. They are especially good when served warm.

Krapfen (Doughnuts)

Preparation Time: 15 Minutes and 2 Hours Waiting
Cooking Time: 15-20 Minutes Total
Makes 18

Equipment

Electric mixer fitted with dough
  blade
Mixing bow
Measuring spoons and cups
Rubber spatula
Whisk
Small saucepan
Lint-free, non-terry dish towel

Rolling pin
2½-3 inch biscuit cutter
Deep 6 quart saucepan or deep
  fat fryer
Frying thermometer
Slotted spoon
Paper toweling

Ingredients

4 cups all-purpose flour
1 package (2¾ teaspoons)
  active dry yeast
3 tablespoons sugar
1 teaspoon salt
1 cup milk
3 tablespoons unsalted butter
2 large eggs
6 tablespoons jam (apricot,
  strawberry, black or red
  raspberry)

Confectioners sugar or
  Super Fine sugar, for
  dusting doughnuts
Cinnamon, optional
1 quart vegetable or canola oil
  for frying

In small saucepan, heat the milk to a scald point. Pour into large mixing bowl and add butter; whisk until butter is melted. Whisk in the eggs. Add all the dry ingredients at once and process with the dough blade in the mixer until the dough is shiny, smooth and elastic. Place dough in a large oiled mixing bowl. Cover with a towel and let rise in a warm, draft-free place until the dough has doubled in size (about an hour).

Cover your work surface with a tea towel and flour it. Turn out dough onto towel and roll with a rolling pin until about ⅓″ thick. Using a 2½ inch biscuit cutter, mark out placement of circles on half of the dough. From the other half of the dough cut out the same number of rounds you have only marked on the first half. Place 1 teaspoon of jam in the center of the uncut rounds. Carefully lift and place the cut rounds on top of the jam and then using the same cutter cut through both halves of dough at the same time. This process should seal the jam within the two halves and bind the halves together.

Place doughnuts on floured tea towel and cover with another towel. Let rise until double in size, about 30 minutes.

Heat oil to 380 degrees. Carefully lower a doughnut into the hot oil on a slotted spoon, taking care not to splash yourself. Only cook as many as fit comfortably in the pan without crowding. Cook for 2 minutes until doughnuts are a golden brown. Carefully turn and cook an additional 2 minutes or until light brown. Remove from oil and drain on paper toweling. While warm, sprinkle the type of sugar you are using on the krafpen. If you like, add a teaspoon of cinnamon to the sugar for added flavor.

Corn Meal Pancakes with Maple Pecan Syrup

Preparation Time: 5 Minutes
Cooking Time: 10 Minutes Total
Makes 20–24 3–4" Pancakes

Equipment

2 mixing bowls
Measuring spoons and cups
Whisk
Rubber spatula
Small saucepan

Chopping knife
Large skillet or griddle
Vegetable oil to coat
Ladle
Large ovenproof dish

Ingredients

1½ cups yellow corn meal
½   cup all-purpose flour
1   teaspoon sugar
2   teaspoons baking powder

1   teaspoon salt
3   large eggs
1½   cups milk
4   tablespoons melted butter

continued . . .

Melt the butter in a small saucepan or in the microwave. Place the dry ingredients in a large mixing bowl and stir together to blend. In another bowl, whisk the eggs, then add the milk and whisk together. Pour into the dry ingredients and add the melted butter. Stir until blended. Do not over mix.

Start to re-warm the syrup in pan over low heat.

Heat skillet or griddle to 400 degrees. To test if the griddle is hot, sprinkle a drop or two of water on the surface; if it bounces around, heat is just right. When skillet (griddle) is hot, lightly oil surface, dabbing vegetable oil on a paper towel and rubbing over the top of the hot surface. You don't want too much oil; the butter in the pancakes will make them turn easier. I would lightly oil the pan, even if it were non-stick.

Ladle or pour the batter into the size pancakes you desire, cook a 'test' pancake for thickness. If it starts to swell up and becomes too thick for your taste, add milk to thin batter. Leave room between pancakes for spreading. Turn the pancakes when the surface bubbles and makes little holes, about 90 seconds. Turn and cook on the other side about a minute or until brown. If the pancakes are thick, be careful that they don't burn while cooking them through. Stack on an ovenproof dish and keep in the oven at about 250 degrees while you cook the balance of the batter.

Serve hot and offer the syrup in a pitcher along with butter or jam. These also taste wonderful with a nice country sausage, ham or bacon.

Syrup

Can be made 2-3 days ahead and refrigerated to blend flavors.

1¾   cups maple syrup
¼   cup chopped pecans

Simmer together in a small saucepan for 4-5 minutes. Pour into an airtight container and refrigerate until needed. Re-warm in small saucepan or microwave before serving.

Plain Old-Fashioned Pancakes

Preparation Time: 5 Minutes
Cooking Time: About 10 Minutes Total

Equipment

2 large mixing bowls	Whisk
Small saucepan	Sifter, mesh sieve
Measuring spoons and cups	Large skillet or griddle
Rubber spatula	Ovenproof dish

Ingredients

1½	cups all-purpose flour, sifted	1	egg, beaten
3½	teaspoons baking powder	1¼	cups milk
¾	teaspoon salt	3	tablespoons melted butter
2	tablespoons sugar		Vegetable oil to coat griddle

Melt butter in small saucepan or in microwave. Sift the flour, together with the baking powder, salt and sugar into a large mixing bowl. In another bowl, mix together the beaten egg, milk and melted butter. Add to the dry ingredients. Whisk until batter is smooth. Do not over mix. Follow instructions for cooking pancakes as in Cornmeal Pancakes recipe above. This batter will cook faster. Thin batter, if preferred.

You can change the flavor of pancakes as you wish, add rinsed blueberries, a teaspoon of sugar, and grated lemon peel; add bananas and ½ teaspoon cinnamon; add apples, lightly sautéed in butter with cinnamon and nutmeg . . . the combinations are yours to create.

Easter Dinner for 6

Select your menu and make up your shopping list as suggested in the Introduction.

Menu

Hors d'Oeuvres
Stuffed Celery, Snow Pea Pods, Olives
Cheddar Cheese Twisties

First Course
Minted Fresh Spring Pea Soup

Main Course
Honey-Glazed Ham with Pineapple-Raisin Sauce
Baked Macaroni and Cheese Casserole
Asparagus with Lemon Butter
Harvard Red Beets
    OR
Roast Baby Leg of Lamb Olivado
Oven-Browned New Potatoes
Buttered Beets
Cold Asparagus Salad with Shallots and Capers

Greek Easter Bread with molded butter

Dessert
Easter Lamb Cake
    OR
Coconut Custard Pie
    OR
Easter Basket or Bunny Carrot Cake

Beverage
Robust Coffee or Decaffeinated
Mint Tea
Pinot Noir wine

Timetable

One Day Prior
Bake dessert
Make soup
Make both hors d'oeuvres; do not stuff vegetables
Cook beets, make sauce
Bake Easter bread
Grate cheese for macaroni
Do table centerpiece
Make cold asparagus
Make molded butter

Easter Day
Set table
Decide on dinnertime and start ham or lamb accordingly
Make pineapple-raisin sauce
Wash potatoes and dry
Clean asparagus, if serving hot
Grate lemon for asparagus salad dressing

Three Hours Prior
Make macaroni and cheese
Stuff hors d'oeuvres

One Hour Prior to Dinner
Bake macaroni and cheese
Put beets in saucepan

Forty Minutes Prior to Dinner
Put potatoes in oven

Twenty Minutes Prior to Dinner
Slowly reheat soup
Reheat beets
Reheat pineapple-raisin sauce
Put asparagus in pan, start as sit down to eat
Put Easter bread on table with butter

Recipes

Hors d'Oeuvres

Stuffed Celery, Snow Pea Pods, Olives

Preparation Time: 30 Minutes
Can be prepared several hours or one day in advance and refrigerated, covered with plastic wrap.

Equipment

Mixing bowl
Measuring spoons and cups
Rubber spatula
Wooden spoon

Grater
Slicing knife
Small Plastic Bag or Pastry bag
　with rosette tip

Ingredients

4 stalks cleaned celery, remove long stringy fibers, cut into 2-inch
　lengths
12 snow pea pods, ends trimmed and string pulled
12-16 pitted extra large black olives
Mini carrots
Fresh Herbs for garnish

Any of the following fillings can be made and piped or spooned onto the vegetables. Mixture may have to be thinned a bit with milk to pipe into an olive.

Accent serving platter with sprigs of fresh herbs and mini carrots.

Ingredients
Cheddar/Olive Stuffing

3	ounces cream cheese	¼	cup scallions, chopped
1	cup grated cheddar cheese	2	tablespoons mayonnaise
⅓	cup black or green olives (without pimento), chopped finely	1	tablespoon red bell pepper, finely chopped
		1	teaspoon horseradish

Mix together all of the above ingredients and fill the vegetables.

Ingredients
Blue Cheese Stuffing

3   ounces cream cheese
2   tablespoons blue cheese
1   teaspoon paprika

Blend together and fill the vegetables.

Ingredients
Roquefort/Walnut Stuffing

3	ounces of cream cheese	2	tablespoons lightly roasted,
⅓	cup Roquefort cheese		finely chopped walnuts

Mix together and fill the vegetables.

Cheddar Cheese Twisties

Preparation Time: After Defrosting 10 Minutes
Refrigeration Time: 50 Minutes
Cooking Time: 12-20 Minutes
Can Be Baked 1 Day Prior, Kept Airtight

Equipment

Baking tray, 2-3
Parchment or waxed paper
Sharp knife
Grater
Measuring cups
Mixing bowl

Whisk
Pastry brush
Rolling pin
Metal spatula
Serrated knife or sharp thin-
    bladed knife

Ingredients

Flour for dusting
1 to 1½ pounds prepared or frozen puff pastry (2 sheets frozen variety)
1 tablespoon grainy mustard
1 egg beaten
1¾ cups grated cheddar cheese

Defrost pastry, keeping covered so it doesn't dry out. Cover the baking sheet with parchment or waxed paper and flour it lightly. Lay one sheet of pastry on floured baking sheet. Brush pastry with half of the egg glaze (reserve remaining) and then mustard. Cover with grated cheese. Lay other sheet of pastry over top and with rolling pin, roll pastry into a 12 × 16 inch rectangle. Refrigerate 20-30 minutes.

With very sharp knife, trim away ¼ inch from all four edges of pastry. Cut rectangle lengthwise into 30-32 strips, 16 inches long by ¼ to ⅜-inch wide, wiping blade clean after each cut and put flour on knife. Try not to pull dough. Refrigerate at least 30 minutes.

Preheat oven to 400 degrees. Take clean baking tray. Do not grease. Remove pastry from refrigerator. Twist 2 strips together, without stretching them and pinch the ends to seal them. Carefully place on baking sheet, 2-3 inches apart. Cover and refrigerate until ready to bake.

Brush twists lightly with remaining egg glaze and bake in upper portion of oven until brown and crisp, 12-20 minutes. Cool on baking sheets. When cool cut strips into 4-inch lengths with serrated knife. Serve or place in airtight container overnight. You can heat them through just before serving if you wish.

First Course

Minted Fresh Pea Soup

Preparation Time: 15 Minutes
Cooking Time: 45-60 Minutes

Equipment

2 Quart saucepan
Food processor fitted with metal
   blade or blender
Wooden spoon
Measuring cups

Can opener
Rubber spatula
Chopping knife
Measuring spoons and cups
Vegetable/potato peeler

Ingredients

3   cups chicken stock, fat
     skimmed off if there is any
     on surface, can be canned
¾   lb. shelled fresh peas (about
     3 lbs. unshelled)
½   cup peeled, diced carrots
½   cup diced yellow onion
1   cup peeled, diced parsnip
     Salt and white pepper to
     taste

½   cup heavy cream
1   tablespoon chopped fresh
     mint, no stems
¼   cup ham, diced fine
     (optional)
     Mint leaf to garnish each
     portion

Place stock, shelled peas, carrots, onion, and parsnip into saucepan and cook over medium heat until parsnips and peas are tender, about 45 minutes.

Carefully strain vegetables from stock, reserving stock. Place vegetables into a blender or food processor and add enough stock to moisten. Process until puréed. Return vegetables to stock and taste to season with salt and pepper, if desired. Can be cooked one day ahead to this point.

Add heavy cream, chopped mint and ham (optional) and heat, do not boil. Serve with mint leaf garnish.

Main Course

Honey-Glazed Ham

Preparation Time: 10 Minutes
Baking Time: $1^1/_4$-$1^1/_2$ Hours

Three types of hams can usually be found in the markets: a "Virginia" or "Smithfield" style smoked ham, a cooked half of ham (sometimes spiral cut) and ham in a metal tin. Each type of ham has its own characteristics. The Virginia or Smithfield type of ham needs to be soaked and rinsed and soaked again and then cooked. It takes about 24-36 hours to ready this type of ham for its final baking. It has a very salty, smoky taste unique to the curing process. The second and third types of hams have the most recognizable flavor and are the easiest to cook, as they already have undergone a pre-cooking process and merely have to be warmed through and seasoned. The overall preparation and cooking time is less than two hours.

If you opt for the Virginia style ham, you will usually start with a whole ham. This ham will give you a lot of leftovers if you are cooking for 6 people. Carefully follow the instructions on the packaging. Be sure to scrub the ham and allow plenty of soaking time or the ham will be inedible because of its saltiness.

If you select a pre-cooked ham, first decide if you want the flatter butt end of the more pointed shank end. There will be a bone running through the center around which you must cut when serving. These types of hams also come precut in spirals, if you prefer, and have their own seasoning packages, which are not bad. Because spiral-cut hams have more labor involved in preparation before you buy them, they tend to be more expensive. Remove the packaging from your choice of ham and place yours in a roasting pan, flat side down if its spiral cut, making sure to remove a plastic disk holding slices together.

If you select a canned ham, you will find there is no waste on the ham, as they have been prepared without a bone and are a composite of many pieces. The less expensive canned hams usually have more visible bits and pieces. These hams can be quite tasty, are easy to carve and maintain a certain even quality. They come in various weights. For a party of six, you will need at least 4-6 pounds of ham. When selecting the ham, be

131

sure there is a key on the bottom. You will need this key to open the can. Carefully wind back the metal sealing strip with the key, being careful not to cut yourself on the metal strip. The hams are often wrapped in a piece of plastic. You can pry the ham out of the can by seizing on the plastic. If you have trouble, try using a can opener on the bottom of the can so you can push from the other side. Remove the covering and place ham into a roasting pan. There will be gelatin on the surface that helps keep the ham moist, it will melt as the ham heats through.

Equipment

Roasting pan or large cast iron skillet
Toothpicks
Measuring cups
Can opener

Small saucepan and whisk if spiral cut
Small bowl
Wooden spoon

Ingredients

½ ham, butt, shank or 4-6 pound can (or if using whole ham, double the recipe)
20-40 cloves
⅓ cup brown sugar
2 tablespoons Dijon-style mustard

8 ounce can of whole pineapple slices, packed in natural juice not syrup
Handful candied or maraschino cherries

Preheat over to 350 degrees. Place ham in roasting pan and score the top of the ham into diamond/lozenge-shapes. Do not score a spiral cut ham. Insert a clove on the corners of the diamonds. Place in oven and cook for an hour. Remove from oven. Turn up heat to 425 degrees. Mix the brown sugar and mustard together and spread over the top of the ham. Return to the oven for 5 minutes. Remove and decorate with pineapple and cherries; anchor with toothpicks. Return to oven for 8-10 minutes or until fruit is heated through and sugar mixture caramelizes. Remove from oven and place on serving platter.

Serve with Pineapple-Raisin Sauce, see below.

Pineapple-Raisin Sauce

Preparation Time: 5 Minutes
Cooking Time: 20 Minutes

Can be prepared a day or two ahead and reheated
just before serving.

Equipment

Small Saucepan
Whisk
Medium size mixing bowl

Measuring cups
Can opener
Wooden spoon

Ingredients

8 ounce can of pineapple
chunks packed in its own
juices (unsweetened)
½ cup of raisins, plumped by
simmering in 1 cup of
water for about 10-15
minutes

1 cinnamon stick broken into 3
one inch pieces
2 cups pineapple juice
2 tablespoons cornstarch
1 tablespoon butter

Place raisins and cinnamon in a small saucepan, pour in 1
cup of water. Heat over moderate heat until water comes to a
boil. Lower heat to keep water at a simmer, stirring occasionally.
When raisins are plumped, remove from heat and pour into a
bowl, reserving raisin liquid in the saucepan. Drain the pineapple and add to the raisin mixture. Whisk cornstarch into the
pineapple juice and pour into the saucepan. Bring to a simmer,
stirring with a whisk, as liquids thicken. If mixture becomes too
thick, add more juice. Pour raisins and pineapple into liquid and
heat through. When ready to serve, add 1 tablespoon of butter,
stir until melted and mixed throughout. Serve in separate container along with ham.

Baked Macaroni and Cheese

Preparation Time: 25 Minutes
Baking Time: 45-60 Minutes

Equipment

Large pasta pot or 6-8 quart
    saucepan
Ovenproof casserole dish, cover
    optional
Colander or large strainer
Measuring spoons and cups
Large mixing spoon
Whisk
Grater
Small bowl
Aluminum foil

Ingredients

1   pound elbow macaroni or
      small shells
1   tablespoon salt
4   tablespoons butter
2   eggs beaten
2   cups whole milk
1   pound sharp cheddar cheese
      (or 14 ounce package),
      grated

1   teaspoon paprika
1   teaspoon salt
½   teaspoon black pepper, or to
      taste
      Extra butter for casserole
      dish

Bring about 6 quarts of water to a boil in a large pot over high heat (you want to allow room for the pasta to move around). Add 1 tablespoon of salt. Add the macaroni and stir a couple of times until you feel it isn't sticking together or to the bottom of the pot. Lower heat but keep at a rolling simmer. Stirring occasionally, cook until macaroni is almost tender, al dente. It will cook further in the oven and you don't want it to get mushy.

Preheat oven to 350 degrees.

Meanwhile, using about a tablespoon of butter, grease the inside of the casserole dish. Beat the eggs in a small bowl and beat in the milk. Add the paprika, salt and black pepper. Put to the side. Grate the cheese.

When the pasta is ready, drain it in a colander, shaking it to remove any water that may have accumulated in the tubes of pasta. Pour half of the macaroni into the casserole dish and pour half of the liquid measured out over the top, taking care to mix up the pepper and paprika from the bottom of the bowl.

Sprinkle about ⅓ of the cheese onto the macaroni and gently stir it through the pasta. Dot the layer with bits of 2 tablespoons of the butter. Add the remaining pasta, milk, and ⅓ of the cheese still left. Gently stir it into the second layer of pasta. Top casserole with remaining cheese and 2 tablespoons of butter dotted over the top. Cover tightly with a lid or aluminum foil and place into the preheated oven for about 45-60 minutes. If you like a crisp crust on the top, remove the cover for the last 15-20 minutes. The liquids should have been absorbed during the baking process. If the macaroni looks too wet, continue to bake without a lid until it is dry.

Oven-Browned New Potatoes

Preparation Time: 5 Minutes
Cooking Time: 40-60 Minutes

Equipment

Ovenproof 2-3 quart shallow dish	Cutting knife
Measuring spoons	Metal spatula
Paper toweling	

Ingredients

6	tablespoons butter or canola or olive oil	1	teaspoon Kosher salt
12-18	new potatoes, red, purple or brown, according to size (2-3 per person)		Freshly ground black pepper to taste

Preheat the oven to 375 degrees. Butter the baking dish.

Wash and dry the potatoes and slice in half. Lay in the dish and dot with butter, salt and pepper. Carefully turn once or twice during the cooking process with a metal spatula. They will pierce easily with a knife when done. Remove and serve with any green garnish you may have on hand, parsley, rosemary.

Asparagus with Lemon Butter

Preparation Time: 10 Minutes
Cooking Time: 3-5 Minutes

Equipment

Large saucepan, skillet, with lid,
    steamer
Small saucepan
Measuring spoon

Whisk
Paring knife
Juicer, reamer
Vegetable/potato peeler, zester

Ingredients

1½-2 pounds of asparagus (about
      5-6 stalks per person)
½   stick (4 tablespoons) butter

1   teaspoon fresh lemon juice
    Lemon rind curl

When buying asparagus, try to obtain the thinnest ones possible, as these are the most tender. If you can only find thick ones, you won't need as many per person. Store in a damp towel in the refrigerator. The bottoms of asparagus stalks are woody and fibrous. Break the lower ends off. You will be able to find a "break" point where the stalk becomes crisp and tender. If there are a lot of pointed pieces on the stalk, peel them off with a potato peeler. Removing the outside layer near the bottom of the stalk will make them more tender. Wash well, soaking in a water bath for a few minutes to remove any sand. Rinse and place in a saucepan or skillet with about ¼ inch of water. Cover with a lid. If you have a steamer, place it in the pot and add enough water to come up to the bottom of the steaming tray, not over the top of it. Cook at the last possible moment, best to start when you are readying the table for the main course and are putting out the other dishes. Thin spears should take no more than 3-5 minutes to cook after the water boils.

Drain and place in serving dish. Pour lemon butter (see below) over the top and serve immediately.

Lemon-Butter Sauce

Preparation Time: 2 Minutes
Cooking Time: 2 Minutes
Can be made ahead and reheated

Using a vegetable peeler or zester, remove a thin piece of the lemon rind by slowly moving around the circumference of the lemon. If you have a zester, you can make thinner strips. Squeeze lemon and put juice and butter in a saucepan and melt butter, stir, being careful not to burn or brown the butter. Pour over drained asparagus. Put rind garnish over the top.

Cold Asparagus Salad with Shallots and Capers

Preparation Time: 15 Minutes
Cooking Time: 3-4 Minutes
Can be prepared early in the day or day prior,
without dressing

Equipment

Large saucepan, skillet with lid
Vegetable/potato peeler
Chopping knife
Measuring spoons and cups
Large bowl with ice cubes and
  cold water

Small bowl to mix salad dressing
Whisk
Serving Platter and serving
  pieces
Plastic wrap

Ingredients

1½ pounds of asparagus (about
    5-6 per person), trimmed
2   tablespoons red wine
    vinegar
1   tablespoon Dijon style
    mustard

⅔   cup olive oil
2   shallots, minced
1   tablespoon capers, drained
1   cup cherry tomatoes, halved
    Freshly ground black pepper
    Salt to taste after mixing

When buying asparagus, try to obtain the thinnest ones possible, as these are the most tender. If you can only find thick ones, you won't need as many per person. Store in a damp towel in the refrigerator. The bottoms of older asparagus stalks are woody and fibrous. Break off the lowest ends. You will be able to find a "break" point where the stalk becomes crisp and tender. If there are a lot of pointed pieces, like a casing, peel them off with a vegetable/potato peeler. Removing the outside layer near the bottom of the stalk will make larger asparagus more tender. Wash well, soaking in a water bath for a few minutes to remove any sand. Rinse and place in saucepan/skillet with about a ¼ inch of water. Cover with a lid. If you have a steamer, place it in the pot and add enough water to come up to the bottom of the steaming tray, not over the top of it. They will cook 3-5 minutes after the water boils, especially thin spears. Remove when al dente. Do not over cook.

Drain and plunge into a bowl of ice cubes and cold water to stop the cooking process. When cool, drain and store at room temperature no more than 4-5 hours ahead of serving time. Can also be refrigerated, covered. Do not serve icy cold.

Whisk together vinegar and mustard. Slowly whisk in olive oil, then pepper. Taste and add salt if necessary. Careful, capers are salty. Just before serving mix in shallots, capers and tomatoes and pour over asparagus on a serving plate.

Harvard Beets

Preparation Time: 20 Minutes (10)
Cooking Time: 45-60 Minutes (15)
Can be prepared ahead one day

Equipment

Large saucepan with lid
Medium: size mixing bowl
Measuring spoons and cups
Knife

Cutting board
Whisk
Metal spoon
Cooking fork

Ingredients

2½-3 pounds fresh beets
OR
2   16 ounce bottles of beets, quartered or sliced, reserve liquid
⅔   cup sugar
4   tablespoons all-purpose flour

½   cup beet juice from saucepan in which beets were cooked
1   cup cider or white vinegar
1   teaspoon salt
4   tablespoons butter

If using fresh beets, cut off the tops right down to the top surface of the beet. If crisp and fresh, these can be saved and cooked another day as a vegetable. Cut off the long trailing end of the beet. Rinse well (they can be sandy) and place in a large saucepan with a lid. Cover with water and bring to a boil. As they boil, monitor the heat so they don't spill over; you may have to crack the lid open a bit as they cook over a slow moderate heat.

Cook until tender when pierced with a fork, about 45 minutes, depending on the size of the beet.

Remove pan from the stove and remove beets (reserving about 2 cups of beet juice, not residue in pot which may be sandy) and let cool a bit. The skin on the beet will have loosened during cooking and is easy to slip off, often without needing a knife except to cut the stem end. When peeled, slice, dice or cube beets into desired shape.

In the cleaned saucepan, mix together the sugar and flour. Add ½ cup of beet juice, flour, sugar and vinegar. Cook over medium heat, stirring or whisking constantly until mixture thickens. Taste and adjust flavoring: if too sour, add sugar, too sweet, add vinegar, too thick, add more beet juice. Add salt and butter and then the cooked diced beets. Heat through.

This dish can be made a day in advance and be reheated.

Left over beet juice can be used to dye Easter eggs!

Buttered Beets

Preparation Time: 5 Minutes
Cooking Time: 45-60 Minutes

Equipment

Large saucepan with lid
Medium size mixing bowl
Measuring spoons and cups

Knife
Cutting board
Metal spoon

Ingredients

2½-3 pounds fresh beets
        OR
2   16 ounce bottles of beets,
          quartered or sliced
2   tablespoons butter

If using fresh beets, cut off the tops right down to the top surface of the beet. If crisp and fresh, these can be saved and cooked another day as a vegetable. Cut off the long trailing end of the beet. Rinse well (they can be sandy) and place in a large saucepan with a lid. Cover with water and bring to a boil. As they boil, monitor the heat so they don't boil over, you may have to crack the lid open a bit. Cook over a moderate heat until tender when pierced with a fork, about 45 minutes, depending on the size of the beet. Remove the pan from the stove, remove beets and let cool a bit. The skin on the beet will have loosened during cooking and it is easy to slip off with a paring knife. Cut the remaining stem end down to the flesh of the beet. Slice, dice or cube into desired shape. Beets can be prepared ahead up to this point (even a day or two). Place beets in a bowl with about a cup of the beet juice, if not serving immediately, careful not to pour in pan residue. When ready to serve, reheat beets in their liquid until heated through. Drain well and melt 2 tablespoons of butter in the pan with the beets and serve.

Leftover beet juice can be used to dye Easter eggs!

Roast Baby Leg of Lamb Olivado

Preparation Time: 15 Minutes
Cooking Time: About 1¹/₂ Hours

Equipment

Roasting pan
Meat thermometer or instant
  read thermometer
Measuring cups

Small Mixing Bowl
Grater
Carving knife

Ingredients

6¹/₂-7¹/₂ pound leg of lamb
¹/₂-³/₄ cup olivado/tapenade (made with black olives and seasonings; available in jars in super markets, specialty, and some cheese stores)
Finely grated zest of medium-size lemon
Sprigs of rosemary for garnish, optional

Preheat oven to 350 degrees.

Place leg of lamb in roasting pan. Spread the olivado on the lamb and sprinkle on the lemon zest. Insert the meat thermometer taking care not to touch the bone. Place in oven and roast until thermometer reads 180-185 degrees. If you want more rare lamb remove it sooner. Remove thermometer and set lamb on serving platter. Garnish with sprigs of rosemary. Carve into thin slices and serve with the juice of the lamb created during carving.

Greek Easter Bread

Preparation Time: 20 Minutes
Resting Time: 2 hours or overnight
Baking Time: 20-25 Minutes

Equipment

Electric mixer with dough hook or food processor fitted with plastic blade
Large mixing bowl
Small mixing bowl
Measuring spoons and cups
Wooden spoon
Whisk
Grater

Small saucepan or glass bowl/cup if using microwave
Instant read or candy thermometer
Baking sheet
Parchment paper
Pastry brush
Cooling rack

Ingredients

5-6 cups unbleached all-purpose flour
2 packages dry active yeast (5½ teaspoons)
1 cup granulated sugar
1 teaspoon grated lemon zest
1 teaspoon grated cardamom
1 teaspoon salt
1 cup milk
¾ unsalted butter (1½ sticks), cut in pieces

3 large eggs, beaten
1 large egg beaten with 1 tablespoon milk for glaze
¼ cup sliced almonds, optional for garnish
1-6 uncooked eggs, dyed with Easter egg dye (see above)
Non-stick cooking spray or vegetable shortening

Heat milk in saucepan or in glass bowl/cup if using microwave. Bring to boil. Remove from heat and add butter. Stir until melted then cool milk and butter mixture to 130 degrees. While milk is cooling, mix 3 cups of flour in mixing bowl or food processor with yeast, sugar, lemon zest, cardamom and salt.

Whisk 3 eggs in a small bowl. Pour milk and melted butter and 3 beaten eggs over flour mixture. Stir with wooden spoon or beat with dough hook or paddle until dough is smooth and satiny. It will be soft and sticky. Add remaining flour one cup at a time until dough is smooth and elastic. Cover with plastic wrap and refrigerate 2 hours or overnight. Remove from refrigerator and shape, glaze and decorate (see below).

141

Dye uncooked eggs in Easter colors.

Preheat oven to 400 degrees. Bake on a greased or parchment covered cookie sheet in center of oven until golden color, 25-25 minutes. Remove from oven and place bread on cooling rack.

Twisted Ring

Divide dough into two pieces. Roll each piece into a 24-inch long rope. Place the two ropes on a greased or parchment covered cookie sheet. Twist together, curving them into a ring. Carefully join ends and pinch dough together. Place colored raw eggs in spaces between twisted pieces of dough "rope". Cover and let dough rise until doubled (30-60 minutes). Keep out of a draft and cover loosely with plastic wrap.

When ready to bake, whisk 1 egg with 1 tablespoon of milk and brush over dough. Place in center of oven for 20-25 minutes. Dough will sound hollow when cooked through.

Braided Ring

Divide dough into 3 equal parts and roll each section into a 30-inch "rope". Place on greased or parchment covered baking sheet and braid ropes gently together. Twist into a ring and pinch ends together. Place one dyed egg on joint. Follow balance of twisted ring instructions and sprinkle with sliced almonds before baking, if desired.

Easter Lamb Cake

Preparation Time: 20 Minutes
Baking Time: 50–55 Minutes (1-1¹/₂ Hours)
or until Tester Comes Out Clean
Decorating Time: 30 Minutes

Equipment

Electric mixer
Large bowl
Measuring spoons and cups
Rubber spatula
Sifter/mesh sieve
Lamb-shaped mold

Baking sheet
Toothpick, cake tester
Muffin tins, small or large egg-
    shaped molds
Cooling Rack

Ingredients

1	box prepared Pound Cake mix (1 pound, 1 ounce) OR	1	cup butter, softened
		1	cup granulated sugar
		5	eggs
2	cups cake flour, sift before measuring	1	teaspoon vanilla extract
¼	teaspoon salt		Non-stick cooking spray, vegetable shortening

Generously grease mold, paying special attention to the fragile ear, nose and neck areas. Preheat oven to 350 degrees.

If using packaged mix, follow instructions on box. Pour into face half of mold. Fill completely. **See below. Place other side (with steam vent hole) on top and make sure sides lock together. Place face down on baking sheet in center of preheated 350 degree oven. Bake 50-55 minutes or until top springs back and toothpick or cake tester inserted through hole comes out clean. Take out of oven and remove back. Let stand on cooling rack 5 minutes and then carefully remove other side of mold. Let cool completely before frosting.

If using above **recipe from scratch**, best results are obtained if ingredients are at room temperature. Generously grease and flour mold, as above. You will place mold in a **cold oven,** do not preheat.

Scrape bowl between additions. Place butter in mixing bowl and soften on medium speed, add salt and beat 4 minutes. Gradually beat in sugar and mix for an additional 2 minutes. Beat in

143

four of the eggs, one at a time, incorporating each before adding another. Beat in vanilla. Add all of the flour and beat 2 minutes. Blend in remaining egg for 15 seconds.

Pour into face half of greased mold and fill, as above and lay face down on baking sheet. **See below. Place cake in **cold oven;** turn on heat to 300 degrees. After 45 minutes, test cake through the vent in the mold with a cake tester or toothpick to see if cake is baked. Bake until tester comes out clean. Take out of oven and remove back carefully. Let stand on cooling rack for 5 minutes and then carefully remove the other side of mold. Let cool completely before frosting.

**If you have leftover batter, pour into greased muffin tins or egg-shaped molds and bake 15-20 minutes or until tests done. Cool on rack for 10 minutes and then remove from mold and cool.

Cake can be baked one day ahead and frosted with butter cream frosting, decorated and refrigerated until 45 minutes before serving. If you wish to make a marshmallow fluffy frosting it is best to frost cake the day you are serving the cake, as standing may make it "weep".

Frosting

Preparation Time: 10 Minutes
Cooking Time: 8 Minutes

Equipment

Electric mixer
Mixing bowl
Small saucepan with lid
Candy thermometer

Rubber spatula
Waxed or parchment paper
Metal frosting spatula
Spoon

Ingredients

For *Butter Cream* Frosting, see Halloween chapter and use finishing touches as described below.

Marshmallow Fluffy Frosting

1   cup granulated sugar
⅓   cup water
⅓   teaspoon cream of tartar
2   egg whites (⅓ cup)
1½   teaspoon vanilla
       Sweetened coconut flakes
          (optional)

2   large raisins or black jelly
          beans (for sheep's eyes)
       Small jelly beans to
          decorate plate

Before you start, place cake on serving plate and put strips of waxed or parchment paper along the sides to catch drips. Dust cake free of crumbs.

Mix first three ingredients in saucepan, cover and slowly bring to a boil. Remove lid after 3 minutes. This process will prevent crystals from forming. Do not stir until syrup reaches 242 degrees. While syrup is cooking, whip egg whites in a bowl with electric mixer until stiff but not dry. When syrup reaches its 242 degrees, slowly pour hot syrup over the whites, continuing to beat. Add vanilla. Beat until frosting holds shape. At the end of the process, be careful and work fast as the frosting will start to stiffen.

Working with a spatula and spoon quickly start to cover the cake with frosting. It doesn't have to be smooth, but should imitate the sheep's 'fleece'. When completely covered, pour coconut into a bowl and using your hands, pat coconut over the frosting to add to the feeling of 'fleece'.

To further decorate the lamb's face, cut raisin or jelly bean in half, if too largely proportioned for the face, and place where eyes should be.

You may want to color any remaining frosting and using pastry bags, make a wreath of flowers around the neck or a pink nose. Use your imagination. If you do not have enough icing or it is too thick, use the Christmas Royal Icing recipe for decorating sugar cookies.

Tint remaining coconut with green food coloring and scatter around the lamb; you have grass. Hide small jelly bean "Easter" eggs in the grass.

Decorate the cup cakes/egg-shaped cakes in any way you wish, making additional frosting, if necessary. If you want to simulate decorated Easter eggs, butter cream will work easier. Tint colors and go to town!

Coconut Custard Pie

Preparation Time: 40 Minutes
Baking Time: 35-45 Minutes

Equipment

9-inch pie pan
Rolling pin
Mixing bowl
Measuring spoons and cups
Wooden mixing spoon or fork
Pastry cutter or food processor
    fitted with plastic blade

Pie weights, dry beans or
    uncooked rice
Aluminum foil
Electric mixer
Rubber spatula
Knife

Ingredients

Single Crust, For Crust Recipes see Introduction

Ingredients
Custard Filling

4   eggs
⅔   cup sugar
½   teaspoon salt
¼   teaspoon nutmeg
1⅓   cups heavy cream
1   cup whole milk

1   teaspoon vanilla
1¼   cups moist shredded
          coconut (sweetened)
¼   cup coconut to sprinkle on
          top

Crust

Preheat oven to 425 degrees

Follow recipe in introduction for single crust pie and roll out. Roll onto rolling pin and place dough in pie plate and fold in edges. Moisten edge of plate with small amount of water, flip dough back onto edge and continue to finish edge as in pie dough recipe. The water will help keep the crust from slipping down the sides of the pan. Once crust is in plate, prick all over with tines of a fork and place unbaked shell in freezer for 15 minutes.

Crust must now be partially baked before filling it. Place a piece of aluminum foil over the dough and weigh down with pie weights, uncooked beans or rice.

Place in oven and bake 8 minutes or until crust begins to set; remove weights, beans, or rice and continue to bake an additional 5 minutes or so until crust is well set and will not slide down pan. Remove to cooling rack.

While crust is cooking make the filling.

Custard Filling

In a mixing bowl, beat eggs until homogenous and then add sugar, salt, nutmeg, cream, milk and vanilla. Mix thoroughly. Stir in coconut with rubber spatula and pour into pie shell. Sprinkle remaining coconut on top.

Place in 425 degree oven for 15 minutes. Reduce heat to 350 degree and bake an additional 20-30 minutes or until a knife inserted in the middle comes out clean. If you will not be serving the pie for 6 hours or more, refrigerate when cool. Take out of refrigerator one hour prior to serving.

Easter Basket or Easter Bunny Carrot Cake

Preparation Time: 20 Minutes
Baking Time: 30-35 Minutes
Icing Time: 30 Minutes

Equipment

Electric mixer
Mixing bowl
Measuring spoons and cups
Rubber scraper/spatula
Grater or food processor fitted
    with grating disk

Sifter, mesh sieve
2 9-inch cake pans
Parchment or waxed paper
Pencil
Toothpick or cake tester
Cooling racks

Preparation

Trace bottom of pan onto back side of waxed or parchment paper, cut 2.

Using room temperature butter, grease pans, place paper circles in bottom of cake pans and butter paper, sprinkle and roll flour over bottom and sides of pans; shake out excess.

Cake

2   cups flour
2   teaspoons baking soda
2   teaspoons cinnamon

1   teaspoon nutmeg
¼   teaspoon salt

Preheat oven to 350 degrees.
Sift above ingredients together into a bowl and set aside.

3   cups grated raw carrots,
        about 4 large carrots
1   teaspoon grated orange peel

1   teaspoon vanilla
1   cup chopped pecans

Mix together and set aside.

2   eggs
4   egg whites
½   cup brown sugar
½   cup applesauce

½   honey
½   cup vegetable oil
1   teaspoon vanilla

Beat 2 eggs in electric mixer until well mixed. Add brown sugar, applesauce, honey, oil and vanilla. Stir in carrot mixture, and then flour mixture. Dough is heavy.

148

In separate bowl, beat egg whites until soft peaks form. Fold half into mixture to lighten it, fold in remaining egg whites. Pour into cake pans, dividing batter in half.

Bake cakes until tester (toothpick) comes out clean, about 25-30 minutes. Cake will begin to pull away from pans. Remove to cooling racks and remove from pans. Carefully peel paper off cakes and cool.

When completely cool, frost.

Frosting
Equipment

Mixing bowl

Measuring spoons and cups

Grater

Rubber spatula

Metal spatula and spoon

Sifter, mesh sieve

Knife

Basket Option

3 Pastry bags, plastic or teflon coated

Round tip

Basket wave tip (ridges)

4-6 spring colored pipe cleaners

Coordinated bow

Pastel-colored almonds (to simulate eggs) or small candy eggs

Any small Easter decoration, bunny, chick or even real flowers

Bunny Option

12 × 14 board or cardboard covered with foil or green cellophane

2-3 Cups Shredded Sweetened Coconut

Green food coloring

M&M candies and/or jelly beans

2 squares melted semi-sweet chocolate

Small plastic bag

Ingredients
Cream Cheese/Orange Frosting

2   8 ounce packages of cream cheese at room temperature, not fat free

1   one pound box of sifted confectioner's sugar

1   teaspoon vanilla

1   teaspoon grated orange peel

1 to 2 teaspoons orange juice

149

Beat cream cheese with electric mixer until fluffy, add sifted sugar and balance of ingredients. If frosting is too stiff to spread, add juice until desired consistency is reached. If too thin to spread, add more sugar.

Basket Option

Place pieces of waxed paper on cake plate, covering edges. Place first layer on plate, paper should be able to be easily pulled out when finished, leaving a clean plate edge. Don't place under center of cake. Frost top of first layer. Place second on top. Using spatula, frost top and then thinly frost sides. Put small amount of remaining frosting in one bag with round tip and the bulk in another with basket weave tip.

Using a skewer or knife, lightly draw evenly spaced vertical lines at ¾ to one-inch intervals around the sides of cake. Pipe vertical lines with round tip from top to bottom. This is the base of the basket weave.

Using other tube of frosting, start at the top side of cake and pipe going around edge of cake, going over top of every other vertical line, remember, you are weaving. On the second row, you will go over top the verticals missed on the previous row, and "under" the ones piped before. You will probably have 4 rows of weaving. If you have any frosting left over, place to side to finish at the end.

Measure placing the pipe cleaners as a basket handle across the cake. Twist pipe cleaners together and insert one end into one side of top of cake and the other end into the other side. Mound up frosting decoratively around ends of cleaners.

Decorate the inside of 'basket' with candy or decorations. Tie bow on handle. If any icing is left over, pipe an edge around the bottom or the top edge of cake. Or, change to a star tip and tint frosting with coordinated pastel colors and make rosettes around top of cake.

If using real flowers such as Johnny jump ups, pansies, violets, anything small, crystallize them (see below) and place on cake.

Crystallized Flowers

2   teaspoons dried egg whites
      (or real egg whites if you
      have a safe egg source free
      of samonella contagion)
2   teaspoons warm water for
      dried egg whites only

Whisk
Small artist brush
Waxed paper
Granulated sugar

Mix powdered eggs and water with whisk until moisture is absorbed. Beat until foamy. If using egg whites, beat with whisk until foamy. Brush egg white onto flowers and sprinkle with sugar. Dry on waxed paper overnight until dry. Flowers can be made up to one week in advance and kept in airtight container.

Bunny option

Neatly cover board with aluminum foil or green colored paper and tape on rear to hold. Place first cake round in lower center of board, this will be the face. Place second layer on a cutting board. You will be cutting 2 semi-circular slices from top and bottom of the circle, which will be the ears. The remaining center section will be a bow tie for under the bunny's chin. Assemble pieces on board and frost. Using M&Ms or jelly beans decorate a polka dot bow tie. Use pink jelly beans for eyes and nose. Melt chocolate and pour into small plastic bag. Cut off corner, small hole, and squeeze out whiskers under noses and outline mouth.

In mixing bowl, pour out 2-3 cups coconut. Tint with green food coloring to desired grass color. Spread around bunny and dot with jelly beans for Easter eggs.

Let your own imagination run wild in decorating either of the 2 cakes.

Easter Egg Salad

Preparation Time: 15 Minutes
For 4 Sandwiches

Equipment

Mixing bowl
Wooden spoon
Chopping knife

Cutting board
Measuring cups and spoons

Ingredients

6	hard boiled eggs
½	teaspoon salt
	Black ground pepper to taste
1	teaspoon yellow or brown mustard
½	cup finely chopped celery
3-4	tablespoons mayonnaise or Miracle Whip
	Your choice of bread, toasted or not
	Any type of lettuce, watercress, sprouts to cover the bread slice, rinsed and dried

1   tomato, thinly sliced, optional

     Pickles of your choice, optional

3   bacon slices per sandwich, well cooked, crisp and drained, optional

Crack egg shell and roll between hands to loosen shell. Peel and rinse egg. Finely chop eggs and place in mixing bowl. Add chopped celery, salt, pepper, mustard, and mayonnaise. Stir gently to mix. Add more mayonnaise if consistency is not smooth enough.

Prepare bread slice. Cover lower slice with egg salad, add tomato, if desired and the lettuce, watercress or sprouts. Place second slice of bread on top and cut in half. Serve with pickles.

Summer Celebrations of Respect, Patriotism, Loyalty
Memorial Day, Fourth of July, Labor Day

As Memorial Day, the Fourth of July and Labor Day occur during the warmer months of the year and are often celebrated out of doors, I have chosen to combine them in terms of interchangeable menus. Select the foods which best serve your party and tastes.

Memorial Day
May 30
Federal Observance
Last Monday in May

History

Memorial Day was first observed May 5, 1866, in Waterloo, New York, shortly after the end of the Civil War. The day was marked by flags flying at half mast, black mourning draperies mixed with the evergreen branches of eternal life draped on buildings and a parade of veterans and other local groups marching to cemeteries to honor the war dead. Although Waterloo claims the first celebration, there is evidence that on April 25, 1866 a group of southern women accompanied a Confederate chaplain to Friendship Cemetery in Columbus, Mississippi, to lay flowers on the graves of both Confederate and Union soldiers buried there after the bloody battle of Shiloh.

The May 30th date was selected because it was near the day when the last of the Confederate army surrendered to the

Union on May 26, 1865. Memorial Day, though a sad and commemorative holiday also heralded at the rebirth of one nation, "indivisible", after the schism of civil war.

On May 5, 1868, an order from General Logan, Commander in Chief of The Grand Army of the Republic, was sent to local army posts to observe May 30, 1868.

". . . for the purposes of strewing flowers or otherwise decorating the graves of the Comrades who died in defense of their country during the late rebellion and whose bodies lie in almost every city, village, or hamlet churchyard in the land . . . to honor the memory of the departed." Believing that the holiday should be recognized by law, the Grand Army pressed state legislatures to have the day declared a legal holiday. Most states enacted legislation.

Since 1868, Arlington National Cemetery, Civil War battlefields and local Memorial Parks and monuments have been the focal points for memorial ceremonies for soldiers who died in all our wars, as well as those "unknown", lying in unidentified graves. The first soldiers buried in 1864 on the grounds of the old Robert E. Lee mansion in Arlington, Virginia, were Union soldiers. In 1866, 2,111 unknown soldiers' remains were gathered from the battlefields of Bull Run and the route to the Rappahannock River and these became the first "unknowns" buried at the site now called Arlington National Cemetery. Every war since and even those which preceded the Civil War, have made their own sad contribution to Arlington, including reburials from the Revolution and the War of 1812. The Arlington Tomb of the Unknown Soldier originally commemorated the war dead of the Second World War and the Korean War. As time goes by, unknown bodies from other wars in which the United States has participated have made their way there. It is the most visited gravesite in America.

In some areas of the country, the holiday is still called Decoration Day, referring to decorating the tombs of the soldiers with flowers. Local parades of Veterans, Militia, Boy and Girl Scouts are still popular and often end at a local war memorial or cemetery. There, wreathes are laid and flags fly on graves of those who gave their lives so that the rest of the nation can live in the peace and security Americans so often take for granted.

Fourth of July
Celebrated July 4

History

The American Revolution had been years in the making. Opposition to British laws was evidenced as early as 1761 when the British Parliament enacted the Writs of Assistance permitting customs officials to enter and search any premise they wished without cause, a transgression of the basic rights of Englishmen. Taxes to be collected from the Stamp Act of 1764, the Townshend Acts in 1767, and the Tea Act in 1773 drew increasing anger and hostility from the American colonies who felt exploited and without representation in Parliament. Colonial boycotts and increasingly violent demonstrations on the taxed goods ensued, the most famous demonstration being the Boston Tea Party. Angry citizens dressed as Indians boarded British moored ships carrying crates of tea and dumped the tea into Boston harbor.

Although there were skirmishes between colonials and the British Army over a period of time, the battles of Lexington and Concord on April 19, 1775 are seen as the real start of the American Revolutionary War. George Washington accepted command of the Continental Army on June 15, 1775.

The Continental Congress meeting in Philadelphia, Pennsylvania debated severing ties to England. These debates led to the appointment of a committee of five persons to draw up a Declaration of Independence. Thomas Jefferson, author of the Declaration, saw it through committee by July 1. After lengthy debates and eleventh hour majority approval on July 2, twelve of the thirteen colonies affirmed the formation of a new and free nation; the thirteenth colony, New York, was waiting approval from its citizens. July 4, 1776, the Continental Congress approved the Declaration. New York approved it July 9, making the acceptance unanimous. The Declaration was read in public for the first time on July 8 in Independence Square, Philadelphia.

The Declaration of Independence of the Thirteen Colonies states:

"When in the Course of human events, it becomes necessary for one people to dissolve the political bands which have connected them with another, and to assume among the powers of the earth, the separate and equal station to which the Laws of nature and of Nature's God entitle them, a decent respect to the opinions of mankind requires that they should declare the causes which impel them to separation.

"We hold these truths to be self-evident, that all men are created equal, that they are endowed by their Creator with certain inalienable Rights, that among these are Life, Liberty, and the pursuit of Happiness. That to secure these rights, Governments are instituted among Men, deriving their just powers from the consent of the governed. That whenever any Form of government becomes destructive of these ends, it is the Right of the People to alter or to abolish it, and to institute new Government, laying its foundation on such principles and organizing its powers in such form, as to them shall seem most likely to effect their Safety and Happiness.

"That these United Colonies are, and of Right ought to be Free and Independent States; that they are Absolved from all Allegiance to the British Crown, and that all political connection between them and the State of Great Britain is and ought to be totally dissolved; . . .

"And for the support of this Declaration, with a firm reliance on the protection of Divine Providence, we mutually pledge to each other our Lives, our Fortunes, and our sacred Honor."

A celebration on the Fourth of July was first observed July 4, 1777, in honor of the birth of a new nation. Celebrations of the most patriotic holiday of the American calendar have continued uninterrupted.

John Adams, to become America's second President, wrote to his wife Abigail on July 3, 1776, "The Second of July, 1776, will be the most memorable epoch in the history of America. I am apt to believe that it will be celebrated by succeeding generations as the great anniversary festival. It ought to be commemorated as a day of deliverance, by solemn acts of devotion to God Almighty. It ought to be solemnized with pomp and parade, with shows, games, sports, guns, bells, bonfires and illuminations, from one end of this continent to the other, from this time forward and forevermore." And so it has, except it has been held on the Fourth!

Labor Day
First Monday in September

History

The advent of the Industrial Revolution drew workers from farms to factories. Workers who had common interests formed themselves into unions to improve their working conditions and wages. In a sense, these new unions were replacing the old-world guild system of apprenticeships with new levels of job standards and common interest groups. In 1882, Peter J. McGuire, President and founder of the United Brotherhood of Carpenters and Joiners of America suggested to the Central Labor Union of New York that a day be set aside to honor the American worker. It was decided to celebrate such a holiday on September 5th of that year. Reviewed by the General Assembly of Knights of Labor, ten thousand workers marched around Union Square in New York City. Picnics, oratory, dancing, and fireworks followed. By 1884, the idea of a Labor Day celebration to be held on the first Monday in September had been agreed upon by the General Assembly of the Knights of Labor. Labor Day celebrations gained momentum, state by state, and on June 28, 1894, President Grover Cleveland signed a bill making Labor Day a legal holiday in the District of Columbia. By 1928, only Wyoming hadn't legalized the holiday. All fifty states celebrate the holiday today.

Decoration

As all three holidays celebrate America, red, white and blue themes are in order for all three parties. Think "stars and stripes". Since the choice of menus given here are all for outdoor celebrations (although they can be prepared indoors in case of rain), I suggest that red, white and blue disposable plates, flatware, glasses/cups and napkins be used. American flags of all sizes can be inserted into platters, flower arrangements, bushes and flower boxes. Daisies or red carnations hold up well in hot weather, and can be used with a small flag or three arranged in with them. Red, white and blue candles, citronella and regular types can be placed around the area where the meal will be served. Long citronella torches are also available and not only light an evening meal but may help to deter mosquitoes.

If you are having a daytime celebration, and you have a yard, badminton nets, horseshoes, or croquet and volley ball can be set up for friendly competitions. Children can also play these games or can be offered play dough and paints to occupy their time (outside, of course!). If you have enough guests and space, a friendly baseball game can be organized. If a pool is available, various water games and polo can while away the afternoon.

An evening celebration can include sparklers and fire-crackers, if it is permitted in your local area. A good old songfest is always a lot of fun, with or without musical accompaniment. Copy out lyrics and distribute them. Have the most musical guest lead the way. Anyone play an instrument? Have them bring it along to the party!

Always have a good sunscreen and mosquito repellant at hand for your guests and their children. They will not only enjoy themselves more at your party, but will appreciate how they feel the next day!

Menus

The following three menu options are offered:

Barbecue—Clambake—Picnic

Barbecue for 8

Select your menu and make up your shopping list as suggested in the Introduction.

Starters
Jalapeno Firecrackers
Stuffed Mushrooms
Cucumber Cups

Main Event
Barbecued Ribs
Surprise Hamburgers/Rolls
Grilled Frankfurters/Knockwurst/Rolls
    OR
Marinated Flank Steak

Pasta with Fresh Tomatoes and Olives
    OR
Baked Beans

Grilled or Boiled Corn on the Cob with Herb Butter
Yellow and Green Bean Salad

Pickles
Assorted Mustards
Ketchup

Dessert
American Flag Cake
Watermelon Granita/Peach and Plum garnish
Star Cookies

Beverage
Beer/non-alcoholic
Red Sangria
Soda/Diet and Regular
Lots of ICE!!!!!! In a Cooler with sodas and beer

Timetable

One Day Prior
Filling for cucumber cups
Sauce for ribs
Marinate flank steak
Prepare pasta 'sauce'
Cook beans for salad
Bake beans
Shuck corn
Bake cake
Bake star cookies
Make granita
Ice sodas and beer

Three Hours Prior to Arrival
Make jalapeno firecrackers
Stuff mushrooms
Stuff cucumber cups
Stuff hamburgers
Wash lettuce and slice tomatoes, onions for hamburgers, cover
Put hamburger and frank rolls on platter, slice if necessary, and cover
Make herb butter for corn

30 Minutes Prior to Arrival
Cook jalapeno firecrackers
Bake mushrooms
Start ribs, (1½ hours), rewarm sauce
Make sangria

45 Minutes Prior to Eating
Make fire
Take steak out of refrigerator
Have hamburgers and franks ready to go
Boil water for corn
Boil water for pasta
Reheat beans on low heat
Put out condiments

Recipes

Starters

Jalapeno Firecrackers

Preparation Time: 15 Minutes
Cooking Time: 4-5 Minutes, Depending on Size of Peppers

Equipment

Deep fryer or deep, large
   saucepan
Frying thermometer
Paring knife
Chopping knife
Mixing bowl
Measuring cups and spoons

Whisk
Paper toweling
Rubber or latex gloves, optional
Plastic wrap
Ovenproof serving dish
Slotted spoon

Ingredients

2   quarts vegetable or canola
     oil or Crisco for frying

Batter

2   cups all-purpose flour
1   teaspoon salt
¼ teaspoon black pepper
2   cups beer, not dark type

32 fresh jalapeno peppers, red, green or mixed
8-10 ounces Mexican queso blanco (white cheese) or mozzarella,
   small dice

Dip

2   cups sour cream
2   scallions, chopped

Pour oil or place Crisco into pot. These Firecrackers need to be fried just before eating. They can be prepared up to a point in advance. When ready to cook, heat oil to 400 degrees. Place paper towels in an ovenproof serving dish and place to the side for draining the firecrackers. Preheat oven to 250 degrees.

161

Put on rubber or latex gloves. If you don't have any, be very careful not to touch your face or eyes while cutting peppers. Wash your hands with hot, soapy water after preparing the peppers. The peppers contain an irritant making your hands feel hot and the oils will stay in your skin all day. Prepare the peppers by washing and drying on paper towels. Leave stem intact. Slice the peppers down one side but not all the way to the bottom. You want to create a pocket in which to place the cheese, but you want the pepper to still be a container. If you like things really hot, leave all or most of the seeds. Otherwise, for a more benign firecracker that won't burn your guests' mouths, remove the seeds and fibrous veins.

Chop the cheese into a small dice. Place an amount of cheese into the pocket of the pepper. Do not overstuff. If you are going to wait a while before cooking, stop at this point and cover the peppers with plastic wrap. Refrigerate and bring to room temperature before cooking if you do this several hours ahead. Don't stuff if it's going to be more than 3 hours as the cheese may get bitter tasting.

You can measure out the flour, salt and pepper, but don't add the beer until you're ready to cook. Mix in the beer with a whisk. Take a stuffed pepper and dip into the batter, turning the pepper to coat all sides. Carefully place in the hot 400-degree oil and cook until golden. Do not cook too many at the same time as the oil's temperature will lower too much. Depending on the surface area of your pan, you can cook at least 5-6 at a time. Drain on paper towels, place on an ovenproof serving plate in a 250 degree oven until all firecrackers are cooked, or serve in batches. Serve immediately upon completion of the cooking.

Place sour cream in a small serving bowl, scatter chopped scallions on top and serve next to firecrackers to cool the heat!

Stuffed Mushrooms

Preparation Time: 15 Minutes
Cooking Time: 30-40 Minutes
Can Be Prepared 3-4 Hours in Advance

Equipment

Baking dish or pan with at least
    a ½ inch lip
Mixing Bowl
Cutting board

Chopping knife
Measuring cup
Wooden spoon

Ingredients

1   pound white mushroooms,
    no bigger than 1½ inches
    across
½   pound Italian sweet
    sausage, no casing (can
    also be hot sausage)

¼   cup red wine, sherry or
    brandy
½   teaspoon salt

    Toothpicks for serving

Preheat oven to 375 degrees.

Gently wipe mushrooms with paper towel to remove any brown dirt. Remove stems and place on cutting board. Finely chop the stems. Place ½ of diced stems into a mixing bowl with the meat, liquid and salt. Stir together. Hands work well for this operation. If you feel the proportions are off and the mixture isn't holding together, add more diced mushroom stems.

Place half to a teaspoon of the mixture into the mushroom cap. You want to mound it a bit. Place mushrooms in a pan with a lip and place in oven. Cook for 30-35 minutes, until meat is browned and cooked through. If you have used larger mushrooms and more meat, the cooking time will be longer. Remove to a serving plate and serve with a toothpick in each mushroom.

If you want to step up the spiciness, add a few shakes of dried red pepper flakes to the uncooked mixture before stuffing but this might prove too much if serving the Firecrackers which are very hot.

Cucumber Cups

Preparation Time: 10 Minutes
Plus 3 Hours to Overnight

Equipment

Chopping knife
Cutting Board
Mixing Bowl
Garlic press

Spoon/rubber spatula
Cheesecloth/strainer/bowl
Teaspoon

Ingredients

1   English cucumber, about 15 inches long
1   cup plain yogurt, drained through cheesecloth at least 3 hours

1   large clove garlic, small diced or squeezed through garlic press
1   tablespoon flat leaf parsley, finely chopped, no stems

Place yogurt into cheesecloth and place in strainer over a bowl in the refrigerator for at least 3 hours, or overnight.

Remove cheesecloth with yogurt. The yogurt will be much firmer. Place in a small mixing bowl and add garlic. Flavors will meld if left for an hour or so. Add chopped parsley just before stuffing cucumber.

Peel cucumber if it has been waxed. Slice lengthwise into 2 long halves. Using teaspoon, carefully scoop out seeds, making a channel for the filling. Kept covered in plastic wrap, everything can be done up to a day ahead until this point.

Before serving, place yogurt into channel created in cucumber and slice crossways into bite-sized pieces. Serve on dish garnished with sprigs of parsley.

Main Event

Barbecued Spare Ribs

Preparation Time: 15 Minutes
Cooking Time: About 1¹/₂-2 Hours

Equipment

2-3 low baking/broiler trays with
  rims
Aluminum foil
Brush
Small sauce pan

Measuring spoons and cups
Whisk
Tongs
Carving board
Carving knife/clever

Ingredients

3-4 racks baby back ribs
      Salt
      Black pepper
1   cup molasses (unsulfured)
1   cup brown sugar
¹/₂   cup cider vinegar

1   cup Dijon style mustard
1   teaspoon Coleman's dry
      mustard powder
1   teaspoon thyme
      Hot pepper sauce to taste

Preheat oven to 350-degrees.

Enclose rimmed baking trays in heavy duty or 2 layers of aluminum foil for easier clean up. Cut off any excess fat or membrane from ribs. Lightly salt and pepper each side of the rack and place curved side down on baking sheets. You should be able to get 2 racks of ribs on each sheet. Place in center of oven and set timer for 30 minutes. If you have tongs, use them to handle the ribs. Turn ribs and cook an additional 30 minutes. Turn ribs again and cook 20-30 minutes depending on size of ribs. If they are looking brown and cooked, proceed with recipe.

While ribs are cooking, mix sauce ingredients in a small pan. When sauce comes to a boil, turn down heat and simmer 7-10 minutes. Remove from heat. After an hour and a half of cooking, the ribs are ready to be basted with the sauce. Turn up heat to 400 degrees. Turn ribs and baste first side and cook 10 minutes. Turn ribs, baste the other side and cook 10 minutes. Turn ribs a third time and baste. If they are turning too black, baste and cook only 2-3 minutes more. Remove from heat and place on cutting board. Slice between rib bones, and arrange on cutting board or platter. Provide a bowl or plate for bones and lots of napkins.

Surprise Hamburgers

Equipment
Turner for hamburgers
Grater
Slicing knife

Ingredients
4 pounds chopped round or sirloin steak. You should be able to get at
  least 4 burgers per pound of meat
16 Hamburger, Kaiser Rolls or sliced hard rolls

Fillings
½ cup grated cheddar or blue cheese
  OR
¼ cup chopped sweet pickles or pickle relish or olives

Condiments

1	Catsup	2	large tomatoes, thinly sliced
1	Mustard	1	Vidalia, red, or other sweet
	Iceberg lettuce, washed, dried, separated into single leaves		onion, sliced thin

Make a ball of grated cheese or determine what you want inside the burger. Form the meat into a patty around the stuffing. If the stuffing is in small pieces, take a portion of meat and make a well in the center, then enclose the filling with more meat. You don't want to make the patties too thick or they will take a long time to cook and get too black on the outside. Make sure that the patties are large enough to cover the surface of the roll.

Place on hot grill and cook at least 4-6 minutes per side, depending on thickness of patty, heat and preference of "doneness." Turn burgers only one time. When finished, place on roll, which can be lightly toasted on grill, and serve with condiments, lettuce, tomato and onion on separate platter.

Grilled Frankfurters/Knockwurst

Preparation Time: 5-10 Minutes
Cooking Time: 7-10 Minutes

Equipment

Tongs for turning franks
Saucepan

Ingredients

1 Package of frankfurters or knockwurst to suit your taste, regular,
all-beef, turkey
Package of frankfurter rolls, match the roll count to the number
of franks.

Sauerkraut, medium to large packet
Mustard
Catsup

Frankfurters or knockwurst (they are thicker) can be boiled
and just browned on the grill, or they can be cooked only on the
grill. Be careful that the fire isn't too hot or they will scorch
before they are heated through. They shouldn't take more than
6-10 minutes. Rolls can be toasted on grill as well.

Sauerkraut can be heated on the stove, or in a pan on the
grill.

Marinated Flank Steak

Preparation Time: 10 Minutes Plus At Least 4 Hours
Or Overnight
Cooking Time: 10-15 Minutes

Equipment

Gallon size plastic storage bag
   OR
Small garbage bag
Mixing bowl
Measuring spoons and cups

Whisk
Paring or boning knife
Meat thermometer or grilling fork
   with built-in temperature
   sensor

Ingredients

2   flank steaks, if you are not
     serving other meat
     options, about 3 pounds
     of meat
1   clove crushed garlic
2   teaspoon thinly peeled and
     sliced fresh ginger root

1½ teaspoons cinnamon
1½ teaspoons ground coriander
     seeds
1½ teaspoons ground cumin
1½ teaspoons ground black
     pepper
2   teaspoons salt

Cut excess fat off steak. Usually there is a thin membrane covering the surface of the steak. This needs to be removed so the spices better penetrate the meat. Use a paring or boning knife and slip it under the membrane; cut along the surface of the meat from one end to the other.

Mix the spices together in a bowl and rub into both sides of the beef. Place in plastic bag and refrigerate until grilling time, 4 hours to overnight.

Oil grill and cook 5-6 minutes per side, depending on how you like your meat cooked and the thickness of the steak. If unsure of the doneness, insert a meat thermometer or slice into the meat with a knife. Slicing will allow juices to drain out, so it's best not to slice. Meat becomes firmer the longer it cooks, and can be tested by pressing on the meat with your finger or the flat edge of your knife. Rare and medium meat will be softer to the touch.

Remove to carving board and allow to meat to sit 5 minutes. Slice meat diagonally across the grain into thin slices. Place on platter and serve.

Pasta with Fresh Tomatoes and Olives

Preparation Time: 20 Minutes
Cooking Time: 15-20 Minutes
All But Pasta Can Be Prepared in Advance

Equipment

Large Pasta or Soup Pot
Colander
Wooden spoon

Large, deep mixing bowl, mixing
  utensils
Slicing knife

Ingredients

1   pound box/bag of fussili,
      small shells, penne or
      other small pasta
2   teaspoons salt
5   medium-size vine-ripened
      tomatoes, skinned, seeds
      removed and diced
1½ red peppers, cored, seeded,
      cut into same size pieces
      as tomatoes
3   cloves garlic minced finely
1   pound fresh mozzarella or
      packaged brand if unable
      to locate fresh, small dice

1   cup Calamata olives, pitted,
      sliced in half
¼ to ⅓ cup extra virgin olive oil
2   tablespoons wine vinegar
      Ground black pepper to
      taste, salt if needed
1½ cups total, chopped fresh
      basil, mint, and parsley

You can have everything prepared in advanced and each item placed separately in plastic wrap. Just start the pasta water 30 minutes before you want to eat.
Cook pasta.
Fill large pot with water, allowing 2½ inches at least at the top so it doesn't overflow while cooking. Add salt and bring to boil. Add pasta and stir occasionally until pasta is al dente (to the tooth), soft but not mushy, still with a bit of firmness in the center. Remove from heat and drain in colander.

While pasta is cooking or earlier in the day, prepare tomatoes, peppers, garlic, cheese, olives. To skin tomatoes, bring a small saucepan filled with water to a boil. Drop in tomato for 20-30 seconds or until skin begins to loosen. Remove immediately and skin. Cool under cold water or in an ice cube bath.

169

Skin them one at a time so they don't cook! Core and gently squeeze, running finger around inside to loosen seeds. Cut in half and then into slices and dice, removing any seeds you may have missed.

Wash, core and seed peppers. Slice into strips and dice.

Smash garlic with flat side of large cleaver, chopping knife. It loosens the skin. Remove skin and any green bud springing from center of garlic, as it can be bitter. Finely chop.

Slice and cube cheese into small pieces.

Wash and dry herbs. Finely chop and place to the side, covered. This will be added just before serving.

Mix oil, vinegar and pepper. Whisk. You may need to add salt, depending on saltiness of olives. Wait until pasta is combined with all ingredients and taste before adding oil and vinegar. If you need salt, dissolve it into the oil mixture.

Place pasta in pasta or large serving bowl. Add ingredients and mix well, taste for salt. Add oil mixture and toss. Add herbs and toss. Serve immediately.

Baked Beans

Preparation Time: 10 Minutes
Cooking Time: Overnight Soak plus 3-4 hours Cooking

Equipment

3-4 quart Dutch oven, pot with lid
Colander
Small mixing bowl
Measuring spoons and cups

Whisk
2½ quart casserole dish with lid
  or aluminum foil

Ingredients

2   cups dried northern or navy
      beans
4   ounces salt pork, cut into
      large cubes
½   cup chopped onion
½   cup molasses

2   tablespoons catsup
1   teaspoon dried mustard
      powder, such as Coleman's
¼   teaspoon ground black
      pepper

Wash beans in a colander, cull for pebbles or bad beans. Place beans in Dutch oven or large pot and cover with cold water

170

2 inches above beans. Let soak 8 hours, overnight or follow package instructions for fast soak/boil method. Drain.

Cover beans again with fresh water and bring to a boil. Cover, reduce heat and simmer for 2 hours. Check occasionally to be sure liquid hasn't evaporated, stir. Add water, if necessary. Do not add salt at this point as it toughens the beans. Drain, if there is liquid left in the post.

Preheat oven to 350 degrees.

Grease casserole dish with butter or vegetable oil. Stir pork and onions into beans and place mixture into casserole, stir. Combine other ingredients in a bowl and pour over the bean mixture, gently moving it through the beans. Cover the beans with a lid, or tightly press aluminum foil around edge of dish to seal.

Bake at 350 degrees for 1 hour then stir beans. Continue baking for an additional hour. Check after 1½ hours of baking to be sure they aren't overcooking. If made ahead, stir before reheating, covered, in a 350-degree oven.

Best flavors are obtained by readying the beans the day before, but combine with liquids and bake the day of the party.

Grilled or Boiled Corn on the Cob with Herb Butter

Preparation Time: 15 Minutes, plus 1 hour
Cooking Time: 5-6 Minutes

Equipment

Twine
Large soup pot or skillet with lid
Brush

Tongs
Serving platter

Ingredients

12 ears of corn
1 stick butter, melted
Various herbs, cayenne pepper (¼ teaspoon), lemon or lime juice (1-2 teaspoons), your choice

To Grill

Carefully pull back green husks on cobs. Remove the silk attached to the corn. Soak cobs in water 1 hour. Dry corn off and brush with melted butter. Pull husks back over the cob, twisting ends to hold closed. Tie tops closed with a small piece of twine. Place on grill and cook for 15-20 minutes, turning corn often so it doesn't burn. Remove twine, husks and serve.

To Boil

Husk corn, remove all silk. Put 2-3 inches of water in pot and bring to boil. When water boils, place corn in pot and cover. Cook for 5-6 minutes, turning after 3 minutes. If corn is older, and has larger kernels, cook a couple of minutes longer. The more you cook the corn, the greater is the risk of it getting tough. If for some reason the corn doesn't have flavor, add a tablespoon of sugar to the cooking water.

Serve with melted butter poured over the corn.

Butter

Can be flavored by adding herbs or spices of your choice, such as basil, cayenne pepper and lemon or lime juice. You can also provide your guests with individual long rectangular dishes in which to "roll" their corn.

Yellow and Green Bean Salad

Preparation Time: 20 Minutes
Cooking Time: 10-12 Minutes

Equipment

Paring Knife
3-4 quart Sauce pan with lid
Mixing/Serving Bowl
Measuring spoons and cups

Chopping knife
Wooden spoon
2 Serving Spoons

Ingredients

¾ pound green string beans
¾ pound yellow (wax) string
    beans

1 yellow or red sweet pepper
    cut into thin strips
¾ cup red onion small dice

Dressing

½ cup olive oil
½ lemon, juiced
1 tablespoon white wine
    vinegar
1 teaspoon Dijon style
    mustard

2 tablespoons fresh oregano,
    chopped or 1 tablespoon
    dried
½ teaspoon salt or to taste
½ teaspoon cracked black
    pepper

Using a small paring knife, or your fingers, cut off the ends of each bean. Place beans in a saucepan and rinse with cold water. Drain. Put 2-3 inches of water in bottom of pan and place on high heat until water boils. Turn down to medium heat. Cook 8-10 minutes or until beans are crisp-tender. Drain water and run cold water over top to cool beans. You need to stop the cooking process. You can also place ice into the beans. Cool the beans. Recipe can be made up to a day ahead up to this point.

Combine dressing ingredients, whisk together, pour over beans and toss about an hour ahead of serving.

Desserts

American Flag Cake

Preparation Time: 20 Minutes
Cooking Time: 35-45 Minutes
Finishing Time: 20-30 Minutes

Equipment

Electric mixer
2 Mixing bowls
Measuring spoons and cups
Rubber spatula
Sifter or fine mesh sieve
8 × 12 inch baking dish
Tooth pick

Cooling rack
Thin blade knife
Serrated knife
Plastic wrap
Colander
Small saucepan
Brush

Ingredients
Cake

⅔ cup vegetable shortening
   (Crisco)
1½ cups sugar
3 eggs
2¼ cups all-purpose flour

3 teaspoons baking powder
1 teaspoon salt
1 cup whole milk
1½ teaspoon vanilla

Frosting

1½ pints heavy cream
   (whipping cream)
1 teaspoon superfine sugar
½ cup current jelly, melted

2 pints strawberries, halved
   lengthwise
1 cup plus 1 cup blueberries

This cake can be baked one day prior to use. Do not frost. Wrap in plastic wrap.

Preheat oven to 350 degrees. Grease and flour baking dish.
In an electric mixer, cream together until fluffy, shortening and sugar, scraping bowl a couple of times. Sift dry ingredients together in a separate bowl. Add eggs to sugar and shortening mixture and beat well. Add ⅓ flour mixture. Combine milk and

174

vanilla and beat in ⅓. Continue alternating dry and wet ingredients 2 more times.

Pour into baking dish and place in center of oven. Test with toothpick after 35 minutes. If it comes out clean, the cake is done. If it is wet and crumbs stick, continue to bake and test in 5-minute intervals.

Run a thin blade knife around the edges of the cake and invert onto cooling rack. Make sure there is enough space under the rack for the air to circulate well or the steam created will get the cake soggy.

To Frost

Place current jelly (no fruit pieces) into saucepan and melt over moderate heat. If you only have jam with fruit pieces in it, rub it through a fine mesh sieve into a bowl after it has melted.

Place pieces of waxed paper around edges of serving platter. Waxed paper will prevent frosting from getting onto plate and makes for an easy clean up. Do not place it too far under cake or it becomes difficult to remove. Invert cake onto platter, top of baked cake facing up. Carefully slice cake in half horizontally to make 2 layers. Use a serrated knife. If the cake layer cracks, the frosting will hold it together.

Brush jam glaze over top surface of bottom layer to prevent cake from getting soggy from cream and berries.

Place whipping cream in mixing bowl and beat with electric mixer until cream begins to solidify. Sprinkle sugar over the top and continue to beat until it is of a spreading consistency. Don't over beat or you will have butter!

Using half of the berries, place a layer of halved strawberries and blueberries over cake. Cover with a layer of whipped cream.

Place top layer of cake and spread whipped cream over top and sides of cake. Smooth surface. Using remaining berries, make a flag: a square of 50 blueberries in the upper left corner for the 50 states and 6-7 stripes of strawberries, depends on size of berries as to how many will fit, for the original 13 colonies.

Keep cake refrigerated until ready to serve. Cut cake into squares to serve.

Watermelon Ice with Peach/Plum Garnish

Preparation Time: 30 Minutes
Freezing Time: 4-8 Hours
The Ice Can Be Made 1-2 Days Prior

Equipment

13 × 9 × 2 metal pan
Blender, food processor fitted with
  metal blade
Large bowl
Fork

Rubber spatula
Measuring spoons and cups
Butcher knife
Whisk

Ingredients

4½-5 pounds watermelon (7 cups
    seeded, no rind)
½   cup granulated sugar
1   tablespoon lime juice
    Pinch of salt

10-12 peaches or plums, or a
    mixture of both.
¼   cup sugar
½   lemon juiced

Place watermelon into blender or food processor in batches and purée until smooth. Pour into large bowl as batches are puréed. When all melon has been pureed, place 4 cups back into blender, add sugar, lemon juice and salt. Mix back into the balance of the juice. Pour into metal pans.

The timing on freezing the watermelon ice will vary with the temperature of your freezer. Place in freezer for about 45 minutes or until the edges of the purée begin to get icy. Whisk the purée to distribute the frozen parts throughout. Return to freezer for approximately 45 minutes or until the purée is slushy. Whisk again to distribute frozen parts evenly. Return to freezer and freeze until solid. Remove from freezer and using a fork, scrape the ice into flakes. Freeze until ready to serve.

Peel and slice peaches or plums (or a combination of both) into a bowl. Toss with ¼ cup of sugar and juice of half a lemon.

Serve a scoop of watermelon ice with fruit on the side and star cookies (recipe follows).

Star Cookies

Preparation Time: 30 Minutes, Overnight plus 2 hours
Cooking Time: 20 Plus 5-8 Minutes per Tray

Equipment

Electric mixer
Small mixing bowl
Measuring spoons and cups
Rubber spatula
Grinder, food processor for nuts
2 Baking sheets

Star shaped cookie cutter (2-3 inches)
Rolling pin, stockinette, cotton-knit, covering (optional)
Cooling racks

Use Sugar Cookie recipe in Christmas section and decorate with red, white and blue sprinkles, multi-colored sugared bits or silver and/or gold draguees available in party and grocery stores. Apply before baking. Or, you can frost the cookies.

OR

Use the Cinnamon Star Cookie recipe in the Hanukka section of Festivals of Light.

This dough needs to sit in refrigerator overnight.

Beverages

Red Sangria

Preparation Time: 10 Minutes
Maceration Time: 1 Hour

Equipment

Large pitcher, clear glass
   preferred
Stirring spoon
Knife

Small saucepan
Cork screw
Zester

Ingredients

½   cup granulated sugar, to
       taste according to wine
       served
½   cup water
2   liters Riojo, Bardolino,
       Valpolicello or other light
       red jug wine

1   orange
1   lemon
1   peach
12 ounces chilled club soda
    Ice

As you are mixing other ingredients into the wine, you needn't spend money on the best wine available!

Make a simple sugar syrup by combining sugar and water in a small saucepan and over moderate heat, melt the sugar and bring to a boil. Remove from heat and cool. You will use this syrup to sweeten the sangria to your taste. You want to keep it refreshing, not cloyingly sweet.

With a zester or small paring knife try to cut a ribbon spiral of orange and lemon peels, leaving the end attached to the fruit. If it breaks off, don't be concerned. Do not place in the pitcher at this point. Wash, pit and slice peach into thin pieces. Place fruit into a large pitcher or container. Fill pitcher with wine, add sugar syrup to taste (2-4 tablespoons). Stir and add the lemon and orange, looping the end of the peels over the top of the pitcher and let stand for an hour for the flavors to blend.

Add ice and club soda to the wine, stir and serve.

Clam Bake for 8: at Home
or at the Beach

Menu

Select your menu and make up your shopping list as suggested in the Introduction.

Starters
Oysters in Red Sauce
Roquefort Dip with Veggies
Hot and Spicy Chicken Wings

Main Event
Clam Bake in a Pot/Pit
    OR
Clam Bake in the Oven

Red and Green Cabbage Slaw

Italian or French Bread/Baquettes

Dessert
Peach/Blueberry Pie
Red, White and Blue Cheesecake
Watermelon Slices

Beverage
Beer/nonalcoholic
Soda section including diet
Iced tea
Lots of ice!!!

Timetable

One Day Prior
Pick up seafood if your fish store won't be open on party day
continued . . .

Buy clams and remove grit, see below
Shuck corn
Make cabbage slaw
Bake cheesecake
Cut watermelon
Bake pie, optional, not preferred
Make oyster sauce
Make Roquefort dip, clean vegetables
Clean chicken wings

Day of Party
Bake pie
Prepare seafood
Prepare other ingredients for clambake
Cut bread and wrap in plastic wrap
Dig pit for clambake

Three Hours Prior to Party
Decorate cheesecake
Bake chicken wings

One Hour to 30 Minutes Prior to Party
Make sangria
Warm chicken wings

One Hour Prior to Eating
Start clambake
Set out cheesecake

Recipes

Starters

Oysters in Red Sauce

Preparation Time: 15 Minutes

Equipment

Small mixing bowl
Wooden spoon
Chopping knife/Board

Measuring spoons and cups
Serving plate with ice

Ingredients

36 oysters, opened by fishmonger, on ice

Sauce
Make one day prior

1½   cups red wine vinegar
1   clove garlic, minced
1   scallion, thinly sliced
2   tablespoons horseradish,
       bottled is fine
¼   cup parsley
¾   teaspoon cracked black
       pepper

¼   teaspoon salt
     Dash hot pepper sauce to
       taste

     Lemon wedges and parsley
       garnish

Buy oysters day of party, if possible, order in advance and tell the store you need them opened and cleaned. They will be set to go when you get them home.

Combine all of the sauce ingredients in a small mixing bowl and refrigerate 24 hours to combine flavors.

Place oysters on cracked ice, sauce in small bowl with spoon in center of oyster tray or next to it. Garnish with lemon wedges and parsley.

Stilton Cheese Dip with Fruit and Vegetables

Preparation Time: 30 Minutes
Can be Made One Day Prior

Equipment

Mixing bowl

Electric mixer

Rubber scraper

Measuring spoons and cups

Ingredients

4 ounces softened cream cheese

3 tablespoons whole milk

1 tablespoon dry white wine, or dry sherry

4 ounces Stilton (or blue cheese)

3 carrots, peeled and cut into sticks, or 2 hands full of mini carrots, washed

8 celery ribs, cleaned and sliced into thin sticks

1 endive, washed and broken into separate leaves

1 crisp apple or pear, cored and sliced into thin strips, sprinkle with a bit of lemon juice to inhibit browning

1 medium size head of radicchio or a lettuce you can remove inner leaves easily to make a bowl

Beat cream cheese, milk and wine until smooth. Crumble in the Stilton, keeping the lumps. Fold it together, cover and refrigerate overnight, if desired.

Prepare vegetables and keep crisp in ice water until serving. Cut up apple or pear just before serving. Core radicchio/lettuce. Slice bottom to make level. Wash, shake and drain upside down.

When ready to serve, place cheese mixture in center of radicchio/lettuce. Serve with vegetables and fruit on same or an accompanying platter.

Hot and Spicy Chicken Wings

Preparation Time: 20 Minutes, Plus 2 Hours
Cooking Time: 20 Minutes

Equipment

Butcher knife/cleaver
Cutting board
Large bowl
Measuring spoons and cups
Medium size sauce pan

Whisk
Tongs
Large Baking Tray with lip, not
more than ½ high

Ingredients

4	pounds chicken wings	4	tablespoons minced garlic
½	cup canola or vegetable oil	4	tablespoons peeled, minced fresh ginger
6	tablespoons finely chopped cilantro	½	teaspoon dried crushed red pepper
6	tablespoons dark soy sauce		

Glaze

2	cups rice vinegar	1	teaspoon dried crushed red pepper
1½	cups granulated sugar		
1	cup water	2	tablespoons Oriental chili-garlic sauce (bottled)
1	tablespoon minced garlic		

Wash and pat chicken dry. Remove tip of wing and cut the membrane ½ inch between the top and lower chicken joint. Wings will lie flatter. In very large bowl, mix oil, cilantro, soy sauce, 4 tablespoons minced garlic, 4 tablespoons minced ginger, ½ teaspoon dried crushed pepper. Stir sauce until blended. Add chicken wings and coat well. Cover and refrigerate 2 hours.

Preheat oven to 400 degrees. Using tongs, place chicken wings on greased baking tray and bake until they are cooked through and golden brown, about 20 minutes.

Meanwhile, place the glaze ingredients in a medium size saucepan and bring to a boil. Reduce the heat and simmer until mixture thickens and gets syrupy, about 20 minutes. Whisk occasionally.

If needed, rewarm wings and just before serving, place wings in a large bowl and pour glaze syrup over them. Toss to coat. It's a messy dish but very flavorful. Serve with dampened towels and napkins.

Main Event

Clambake on a Grill in a Pot, in a Pit, on a Stove Top

Preparation Time: 45 Minutes
Cooking Time: 30-45 Minutes
Prepare Clams One Day Prior

Equipment

Shovel	Rack, optional
30-40 quart stock pot with lid	Matches
Rack to fit bottom of pot (cooling rack should work)	Fire starter fluid, optional
	Newspaper
Sharp pointed knife	Small saucepan
Bag of charcoal	Tongs
Large barbecue grill, optional	Aluminum foil

Ingredients

12 ears of corn
8 1¼-1½ pound live lobsters
2 pounds small white onions, remove outer skins
3-4 pounds small red new potatoes, washed
5 pounds scrubbed, soft-shelled steamer clams, buy day prior
4-6 tablespoons of corn meal
Cleaned mussels, oysters, blue fish and mackerel can also be added depending on appetites and volume of guests.

Herbed Butters

1	pound butter	¼	cup minced basil
4	large garlic cloves, peeled, minced finely	¼	cup lemon juice
			Salt/pepper to taste

Try to pick up seafood the day of the party. Keep all on ice, especially live lobsters, and refrigerate clams. Put lobsters in a spare sink or large tub with ice.

Food Preparation

Place clams in a large bowl with the cornmeal and cover with salted water; refrigerator overnight. Clams will ingest the cornmeal and spit it out with grit and sand. Rinse clams before cooking.

Husk the corn and break into halves.

With sharp knife point, pierce the lobster's head at base of its "neck", severing vein, to kill it. This must be done immediately before cooking. Some people place the lobsters live in the pot. I think this is cruel. Another easy method is to have a medium-size pot of boiling water on the stove, dip in the lobster and then place in the large pot.

In a Pit or on a Grill Fire

For pit cooking on a beach, dig a hole deep enough to allow for an optional layer of stones, 6-8 inches of charcoal to come at least ⅓ of the way up the sides of the stock pot. If you are fortunate to have a beach with seaweed, you won't need a pot. Dig your pit, line with stones, if possible, and then put the charcoal on the bottom. Start the fire and get it white-hot. Place large sheets of wet seaweed over the coals for steam, and on the sides of the pit as you build your layers.

Add lobsters, another layer of seaweed, then the potatoes, onions and corn, a layer of seaweed, any fish or other seafood, seaweed, and finally the clams with a layer of seaweed on top. Cover the top layer with aluminum foil or a wet blanket held down with rocks. Some cover all with sand, but the food can get gritty. This method might take longer to cook, but you can eat it in layers! Depending on the size of the pot, the intensity of the heat and the number of layers of food, count on 35-65 minutes to cook. The clams take the least amount of time and can be eaten while the rest cooks. Discard any unopened clams.

A large barbecue grill can also be utilized. About an hour before serving time, start a fire with charcoal, newspaper and match, with or without starter fluid. The fire must have white hot coals, still slightly flaming. Pot can be set on a rack no more than 2 inches over the fire or may be set directly on the coals.

If you are using a pot, place an inch of water in the pot, a rack and then layer the pot with the freshly-killed lobsters, potatoes, onions, and then the corn, any additional seafood, and finally, the steamers on top. Cover and set on rack over coals (see above). Steam for 30 minutes or until the steamers are done. Potatoes should be able to be pierced easily. Check for water half way through the cooking process. If it has evaporated, add a bit more so the bottom doesn't burn.

On the Stove Top

Need two large pots with lids (or cover tightly with aluminum foil) and racks to fit. Pasta pot with basket preferable for one of the pots.

In a pasta pot with a basket, or large deep saucepan fitted with a rack, fill with water to bottom of basket/rack and bring to a boil. Place a layer of seaweed, if available, and the potatoes and 2 teaspoons of salt. Cover and cook about 15-20 minutes until potatoes are almost done. Place a new layer of seaweed, if available and then the onions and clams. Cook until the potatoes are tender and the clams have opened. Discard any unopened clams (mussels or oysters).

Take largest pot, place rack on bottom and fill with water to just under bottom of the rack. Bring water to a fast boil and place freshly-killed, or live lobster on the rack. Cover with fresh wet seaweed if you can get it. Cover pan and steam for 10 minutes, add corn and recover. Steam until the little legs on the lobster pull away easily and lobster is red.

Serve with herbed butters

Herbed Butters

For each variety of butter you wish to make, melt butter over low heat in a small saucepan, add herb or flavoring as desired and serve hot in a small bowl.

Clambake in the Oven

Preparation Time: 45 Minutes
Cooking Time: 1 hour

This recipe can be easily tailored to fit any number of guests, as each guest will be served an individual packet of food. Clams need to be started the day prior.

Equipment

Large bowl
Knife
Colander
1-2 baking trays, with lip
    preferable

Heavy duty aluminum foil
Tongs

Per Person Quantity

3-4	spinach leaves, raw	2	small red potatoes, scrubbed
6	steamer clams, see preparation below	1	ear corn, husked and cut into thirds
6	mussels, debearded and scrubbed		Sprigs of fresh basil and thyme
1¼	pound live lobster	¼	cup clam broth
		½	stick melted butter
2	whole scallions, cleaned, ends trimmed, leave an inch or two of green	3	lemon wedges

The day prior, place clams in a large bowl with 2-3 tablespoons cornmeal and salted water. Clams will ingest and spit out cornmeal along with grit and sand. Rinse clams before cooking.

Preheat oven to 350 degrees.

Remember quantities given are **per person.**

Cut 24-inch length of heavy-duty aluminum foil and lay flat on the counter, making sure your lobster will fit the length you cut. Arrange washed spinach leaves in center of the foil. Mound cleaned clams and mussels in the center on top of spinach. Add scallions, potatoes and corn around it all. With a knife sever the vein in the back of the lobster's neck and place it on top of all. Seal tightly, rolling and crimping edges. Place foil package on baking sheet and bake 1 hour.

Serve with melted butter and lemon wedges or herbed butter from above recipe.

Red and Green Cabbage Slaw

Preparation Time: 30 Minutes
Can Be Prepared Ahead; Needs to sit 8 Hours or Overnight

Equipment

Food processor fitted with 2mm
   shredding blade, mandoline or
   grater
Cutting Board
Large Mixing Bowl

Measuring cups and spoons
Heavy cutting knife
Whisk
Rubber spatula

Ingredients

1   small head red cabbage
1   medium size head of green
     cabbage
1   small sweet onion, finely
     chopped
2   cucumbers, peeled, seeded
     and thinly sliced
2   crisp apples, cored and
     thinly sliced or shredded
     on grater

2   cups sour cream
5   tablespoons cider vinegar
2   tablespoons granulated or
     brown sugar
2   tablespoons mustard
    Salt and pepper to taste

Cut cabbages in quarters and core. Cut into pieces to fit tube of food processor. Run cabbages, cucumbers, apples, through processor, including onions if you wish them to be in larger pieces. Remove ingredients to large mixing bowl as processor bowl fills.

Mix sour cream and balance of ingredients in small bowl. Taste for salt and pepper and sweet and sour and balance according to your tastes.

Pour over cabbage mixture and let stand in refrigerator, covered up to 8 hours or overnight.

Italian/French Bread

Preparation Time: 5-10 Minutes
Cooking Time: 10-15 Minutes

Equipment
Aluminum Foil
Knife
Cutting Board

Ingredients

2-3 loaves bread
½ cup butter (1 stick) per loaf
1 garlic clove, optional, per stick of butter

1½ teaspoon minced fresh basil or thyme per stick of butter

Bread can be served at room temperature, sliced into 1-1½ inch slices, or sliced almost through and placed in aluminum foil, wrapped and heated in a 350 degree oven for fifteen minutes. Plain or herbed butter can be spread on the slices before heating, see above recipes, but don't melt butter. Merely mash room temperature butter with either smashed garlic clove or an herb mixture of minced basil and thyme.

Desserts

Peach and Blueberry Pie

Preparation Time: 30 Minutes
Cooking Time: 35-40 Minutes

Equipment

Mixing bowl
Measuring spoons and cups
Rubber spatula
Pastry cutter or two knives
Small table fork
Rolling pin

Pastry scraper or spatula
Knife
Colander
9 inch pie pan
Small mixing bowl
Whisk

Pie Crust

1⅔   cup all-purpose flour
½   teaspoon salt
½   plus 2 tablespoons Crisco
        (vegetable shortening)
4-4½ tablespoons cold ice water

Filling

6-7   medium size peaches,
        peeled, pitted, sliced
1   pint blueberries, washed
        and dried
½   cup granulated sugar
3   tablespoons flour

1   teaspoon cinnamon, optional
        OR
1   teaspoon finely minced
        lemon peel, no white

Finishing

1   egg yolk
3   tablespoons whole milk

Preheat oven to 400 degrees.

Crust

Mix together flour, salt and shortening in large mixing bowl. Cut the mixture with a pastry cutter until you have oatmeal size pieces. Test dough with fingers. It should have a smooth consistency when rubbed between the fingers. If it feels dry add a teaspoon more shortening and cut it in, test again. Add water all at once and mix with a fork until it comes away from the sides of the bowl. If dough is too dry, add ½ teaspoon more water. Do not over mix as dough will get tough. Sprinkle about an ⅛ cup of flour on rolling surface. Pat dough into a disk and flatten with hand. Scatter a bit of flour on top of dough, lift dough and make sure there is enough underneath the dough since it will have absorbed some of the flour as you flattened it. Roll in all directions until you have a circle. You may need to add more flour as you go. Measure the size of your dough to the pan you will bake it in. It should be at least 5-6 inches larger than the circumference of the pan.

Using a dough scraper or flat spatula, gently lift upper edges of dough. Place rolling pin on top part of dough and roll dough over the rolling pin, gently scraping up the dough as you roll the pin toward you. Gently unroll dough over the top of the pie pan and pat down flat into the bottom and sides. You should have a 2-3 inch overhang. Leave it. If dough is tender, it may break. Just pinch and pat together where there is a hole.

Sprinkle 1 tablespoon of flour on bottom of crust.

Peel, pit and slice peaches about ¾ inch thick. Place in mixing bowl with blueberries. Add sugar, 2 tablespoons of flour and optional cinnamon or lemon peel. Gently stir with a spoon or your hands, careful not to break fruit. Place in pie crust and pack in the fruit evenly. Gently pull up the hanging sides of dough over the top of the pie, folding dough where necessary on itself. You should have an open section showing the fruit in the middle anywhere from 3-5 inches across.

Finishing

Whisk together egg yolk and milk and brush evenly on dough. This will aid in nicely browning the dough. You can sprinkle with granulated sugar if you wish.

Place in center of preheated oven. Pie will be done when crust is golden brown and peaches test fork tender. Remove to cooling rack. If crust is browning too quickly, lower oven temperature to 350 degrees.

Red, White and Blue Cheesecake

Preparation Time: 30 Minutes
Cooking Time: 80 Minutes
Must Refrigerate Overnight

Equipment

Electric mixer
Mixing bowl
Measuring spoons and cups
Food processor/steel blade
Small saucepan
Rubber spatula
Grater

Wooden spoon
Spring form pan (9½ inches)
Shallow baking pan (no more
   than 1 inch high)
Aluminum foil
Instant read thermometer

Crust

1½ cups chocolate wafer crumbs
      (about 28) or graham
      cracker crumbs or ginger
      snap crumbs
1   stick (½ cup) melted butter

Filling

4   eight ounce packages of
      cream cheese at room
      temperature
1½ cups granulated sugar
2   tablespoons all purpose flour
5   large eggs

½   cup sour cream
1½ teaspoons grated fresh
      lemon zest
½   teaspoon salt
1½ teaspoons vanilla

Topping

1½ cups more or less
      raspberries or
      strawberries
1½ cups more or less blueberries

Crust

Place cookies in food processor fitted with metal blade. Process until crumbs are finely ground. Melt butter, pour over crumbs and mix together with scraper or spoon. When cool enough to handle, pat buttered crumbs into bottom and lower sides of spring form pan. Tamp down crumbs with bottom of a small glass or teaspoon. Set into the refrigerator for 30 minutes while you make the filling.

Preheat the oven to 300 degrees.

Filling

Place the cream cheese in the mixing bowl of the electric mixer and beat until light and fluffy, scrape down sides. Gradually add sugar, scraping as you go. Add flour and beat in the eggs one at a time until each is blended. Add sour cream, zest, salt and vanilla. Beat until well combined. Make sure to scrape way under the bottom of the mixture to be sure it is all incorporated.

Pour into the chilled crust. Line baking pan with foil (cake may leak a bit) and place in center of 300 degree oven for 80 minutes. Check cheesecake, it will not be completely set, but if it jiggles too much cook another 10 minutes. Internal temperature should be 150 degrees on an instant read thermometer. Cake should still be a bit soft. It will set as it cools. **Do not remove from oven. Turn off heat and leave oven door ajar.** When cake is cool, remove from oven and baking tray. Cover with plastic wrap and refrigerate in the pan overnight.

To Finish

2 hours before serving, remove from refrigerator. Run a thin-bladed knife around the edges of the cake and open the spring. Remove outer band. It will be difficult to remove the bottom of the pan while so cold without cracking the cake. Leave it and try later, if you wish, when it warms or put hot towel underneath and try to loosen.

Using washed and dried raspberries, form and fill in a large star across surface of cake, covering cracks. Surround with blueberries. If you aren't going to serve immediately, put cake back in refrigerator. You don't want cake to spoil in summer heat! Remove it half an hour before serving.

Watermelon Slices

Preparation Time: 10 Minutes

Equipment
Large butcher knife
Cutting board

Ingredients
½   medium size watermelon
     Mint for garnish

Slice watermelon in half the long way and then vertically into 1 inch slices. Place on serving platter and garnish with fresh mint.

Beverage

Iced Tea

Preparation Time: 15 Minutes

Equipment
Kettle   Large heavy pitcher
Wooden spoon   Knife

Ingredients
Black or herbal tea bags or leaves
Strainer if using leaves or brewing container
Ice
Sugar, optional
Lemon, thinly sliced, optional

Bring 8 cups of water to a boil. Meanwhile, place 8 tea bags or 7 teaspoons of black tea leaves (English or Irish Breakfast tea, Earl Grey, Raspberry), favorite herbal or fresh mint leaves with stems into a large glass bowl with a lip for pouring.

Pour water over tea and let steep 10 minutes. You want it strong, as the ice will dilute it. Remove bags or leaves. Add sugar while hot, if everyone likes it sweet, it dissolves better. Garnish glasses with thin lemon slices. Pour over ice.

Picnic for 8

Select your menu and make up your shopping list as suggested in the Introduction.

When taking food away on a picnic, whether to a beach, park or boat it is extremely important to keep the perishables cold at all times. Use a cooler and ice or the blue cooling bags that can be frozen, and pack well around the food. Keep cold drinks separate so they don't crush the food.

Menu

Snacks
Jicama Cubes in Lime
Corn Chips/Tortilla Chips
Avocado Dip

Main Event
Fried Chicken (see Martin Luther King Day Chapter)
    OR
Smoked Turkey, Brie, Watercress on Baguettes/Rolls
Roast Beef, Tomato, Lettuce on Baguettes/Rolls

Savory Ham and Cheese Quiche
    OR
Devilled Eggs

Black Bean and Corn Salad
Tabbouleh

Desserts
Pecan Pie
Summer Pudding
Chocolate Chip Cookies

Beverage
White Sangria
Assorted types of Beer and Soda

Timetable

One Day Prior
Make chicken
Make quiche
Bake cookies
Make summer pudding
Make bean salad
Bake pecan pie, optional, prefer same day
Prepare baskets to carry food, utensils, napkins, cutting/
    serving knives and spoons, plates, plastic or glass wine
    glasses, salt and pepper shakers, blanket, cloth for lay-
    ing out food, freeze ice and blue freezer cubes

Day of Picnic
Start preparations as early as necessary in order to leave,
    if going somewhere else for the day

Recipes

Starters

Jicama Cubes in Lime

Preparation Time: 15 Minutes

Equipment

Medium size mixing bowl   Chopping Knife/Board
Juicer   Toothpicks
Potato/vegetable peeler

Ingredients

2   large jicamas, firm to the   Pinch of dried hot pepper
        touch   flakes
4   limes, juiced, depending on
        size

Peel jicamas with a vegetable/potato peeler. Slice into ½ inch pieces and then dice into ½ inch cubes. Jicama is a refreshing vegetable with the consistency of a cold, raw potato.

Juice limes.

Place jicamas and lime juice in a bowl, stir. Let macerate 30-60 minutes.

Sprinkle with dried hot pepper flakes, if desired, to taste. Pour off all but a bit of the lime juice and serve with toothpicks.

Avocado Dip

Preparation Time: 15 Minutes

Equipment

Knife
Juice/reamer
Wooden spoon

Medium size mixing bowl
Table fork

Ingredients

3   avocados, very ripe, peeled and mashed
1   small clove garlic, minced finely
1   medium size tomato, seeded and chopped finely

2   limes, juiced
½ to 1 teaspoon salt, to taste
    Hot sauce, optional to your taste (Tabasco, Louisiana Hot sauce)

If the avocados are very small, you may want to increase the amount of them in the recipe. Get the ripest and softest you can find, without being mushy and black.

Peel and seed avocados. Mash with a table fork, until puréed. Put into mixing bowl with other ingredients and combine well. Chill. The amounts of lime juice, salt and hot sauce will depend on the size of the avocados and your taste buds.

Serve with corn or tortilla chips in a basket.

Main Event

Fried Chicken

See Martin Luther King Day or Halloween for Recipes

Smoked Turkey, Brie, Watercress on Roll/Baguette

Preparation Time: 10 Minutes
Quantity: 6-8 Rolls

Equipment

Knife
Colander

Paper toweling
Plastic wrap

Ingredients

1½ pounds smoked turkey
1 medium-size round of Brie cheese
1 bunch watercress, washed and dried, long stems cut off
8 Hard rolls or 2 Italian/French baguettes
Butter, mayonnaise, mustard, salt to your preference, or take along to
the picnic and have each person select their preference while eating.

Precision on quantities is difficult as size of rolls and bread loaves vary and amount of meat and cheese desired on a sandwich varies from person to person. I have tried to use moderate amounts of medium-size breads.
Wash and dry watercress.
Slice rolls across middle. If using a baguette, slice lengthwise and do not slice into individual "sandwiches" until you get to the picnic.
Spread with butter, mayonnaise or mustard, or have each guest do their own at the picnic. Lay in slices of turkey and Brie and watercress. Top with other half of bread, slice rolls in half and wrap tightly in plastic wrap; refrigerate. Slice baguette into individual "sandwiches" at picnic. Wrap in plastic wrap and refrigerate.

Roast Beef, Tomato, Lettuce on Roll/Baguette

Preparation Time: 10 Minutes

Equipment

Knife
Colander

Paper toweling
Plastic wrap

Ingredients

2   pounds roast beef
     Lettuce, Iceberg or Boston
2   medium size tomatoes,
        sliced thin
     Butter, Dijon or horseradish
        mustard, mayonnaise

Salt and Pepper to taste
8   hard rolls or 2 Italian/
        French baguettes

See note in above recipes on quantities.

Slice rolls or baguettes in half and lengthwise.

Butter or spread on Dijon style or horseradish mustard, mayonnaise or let each guest add their own at picnic.

Combine ingredients onto the rolls of baguettes. Slice the rolls in half and wrap in plastic wrap. Slice baguettes into slices at the picnic. Wrap in plastic wrap. Refrigerate.

Ham and Cheese Quiche

Preparation Time: 30 Minutes
Cooking Time: 25-30 Minutes

Equipment

Pie pan
Mixing bowl
Measuring cups and spoons
Pastry cutter

Rolling pin
Baking tray
Whisk
Rubber spatula

Ingredients

1 partially cooked pie shell, see Introduction for pre-baked pie shell
but only bake about 7 minutes or until dough firms a bit
8 slices of boiled ham, cut into bite size pieces
1 cup Swiss cheese, grated
3 large eggs
1½ cups of heavy cream or whipping cream
½ teaspoon salt
⅛ teaspoon ground nutmeg
Pinch of white ground pepper
2 tablespoons butter

Preheat oven to 375 degrees.

Make and partially bake the pie shell according to instructions in the Introduction. Crack the eggs into a medium size mixing bowl and whisk until blended. Add the cream and seasonings and whisk together. Add the cheese. Lay and gently press the ham on bottom of the pie crust and pour the egg and cheese mixture over it. Dot with pieces of butter. Bake until the quiche puffs and is brown and until a knife inserted into the outside ⅓ of the quiche comes out clean. The center will settle as it cools.

When it is almost cold, cut into serving size pieces or take a knife and serving spatula with you. Cover with plastic wrap if cool or wrap in a large napkin or tea towel.

Devilled Eggs

Cooking Time: 20 Minutes
Preparation Time: 20 Minutes

Equipment

Large saucepan, non-reactive,
   heavy bottom, not aluminum
Knife

Small mixing bowl
Measuring spoons
Table fork

Ingredients

1   dozen eggs
1-2 tablespoons mayonnaise,
      Miracle Whip
1-2 tablespoons mustard,
      yellow preferred

Paprika, sweet not hot
Sliced olives, capers or dill
   sprigs, optional

Place eggs in a large saucepan and barely cover with water. Bring to a gentle boil and cook 10 minutes.

Drain and rinse with cold water. Peel eggs. Slice eggs lengthwise and pop out yolks into mixing bowl. If the white tears or is too thin in places, don't worry, the yolks will hold it all together when the eggs are stuffed.

Mash yolks with the tines of a fork until all mashed. Add mayonnaise and mustard and mix well. Taste. If dry and sweet, add more mustard. Divide yolk mixture into the whites and swirl surface with a fork. Garnish with paprika or slices of olives, capers or dill. Cover with plastic wrap, using toothpicks to keep plastic off of eggs; chill well.

Black Bean and Corn Salad

Preparation Time: 20 Minutes
Cooking Time: 3-4 Minutes

Equipment

Large mixing bowl
Cutting knife
Colander
Small saucepan

Small mixing bowl
Measuring spoons and cups
Wooden spoon
Can opener

Ingredients

2 15-19 ounce cans of black beans, drained and rinsed
3-4 ears of fresh corn, depending on size, shucked and cut off cob
½ medium red onion, peeled and diced
½ green Bell pepper, seeds and ribs removed, diced
½ red Bell pepper, seeds and ribs removed, diced
¾ cup chopped coriander or parsley

4 tablespoons red wine vinegar
9 tablespoons olive oil
1 clove garlic, smashed and finely diced
Salt and pepper to taste
Few drops of Tabasco optional

Rinse beans in a colander under cold water and drain well. Shuck corn and cut from cob by holding vertical and watching your fingers, carefully slicing down the length of the cob. Put corn in a small saucepan with a ¼ inch of water and cook 3-4 minutes. Drain immediately.

Combine beans and corn, onion and peppers into a medium size bowl. Thirty minutes before serving, whisk other ingredients together and pour over salad. Mix well. You can take the salad dressing along in a closed jar, shake and pour before serving. Chill.

Tabbouleh Salad

Preparation Time: 30 Minutes

Equipment

Large Mixing bowl
Food Processor fitted with metal
  blade
Cutting knife
Sieve

Juicer, reamer
Measuring cups
Strainer
Colander or salad spinner
Paper toweling

Ingredients

1	cup cracked bulgar wheat, very fine variety	2	large tomatoes
2	bunches parsley, curly or flat leaf variety, remove stems	6	large scallions
1	large bunch fresh mint, leaves only	1-2	lemons, depends on juiciness
		½	cup olive oil
			Salt to taste

Measure wheat into a sieve and briefly rinse under hot water, wetting through. Put aside to drain.

Wash parsley and mint leaves and spin in salad spinner or dry in paper toweling.

Place mint and parsley into food processor and pulse until it is in bits but hasn't lost its shape and become wet.

Wash scallions, removing outer hull. Cut off root end. Slice scallions into very thin slices, going into the yellow section of the stalk.

Wash tomatoes and cut in half. Scoop out seeds and squeeze gently to remove juice. Slice and dice into small pieces.

In a large bowl, combine the parsley, mint, scallions and wheat. Add the juice of one lemon, olive oil and salt to taste, at least 1 teaspoon. Combine well. Taste. If too dry start to add additional juice and a bit of olive oil. It may need more salt or juice as it stands. Add tomatoes and gently mix. Taste before serving and adjust for lemon and salt as the wheat will absorb liquids and if you are using larger wheat than preferred, you will need more liquid. Chill. Should sit at least 1 hour prior to serving.

Dessert

Pecan Pie

Preparation Time: 30 Minutes
Cooking Time: 50-55 Minutes

Equipment

Mixing bowl   Chopping knife
Medium mixing bowl   Whisk
Pastry cutter   Wooden Spoon
Measuring spoons and cups   9 inch pan
Medium saucepan   Cooling rack

Ingredients

See One-Crust Pie Recipe in Introduction

3/4   cup of granulated sugar   3   eggs, whisked in small bowl
1   cup dark Karo syrup   1   teaspoon vanilla
1/4   teaspoon salt   1   cup pecans, chopped
3   tablespoons butter   coarsely

Preheat oven to 375 degrees.

Make pie crust for single crust pie according to Introduction and put to the side.

In a saucepan, combine sugar, molasses and salt and bring to a rolling boil. Boil for 3 minutes and remove from heat.

Meanwhile, chop pecans into medium size pieces. Whisk eggs in a medium bowl.

Carefully pour a bit of the hot mixture into the egg yolk, whisking all the time. Pour yolks into the rest of the hot mixture, whisking so eggs don't scramble. Quickly add butter and stir to melt. Add vanilla.

Stir in pecans and pour into pie shell. Bake in center of the oven for 50-55 minutes and it is puffed, firm and crust golden. Remove from oven to cooling rack.

Pie can be served with ice cream or whipped cream or plain.

Summer Pudding

Preparation Time: 30 Minutes
Chilling Time: Overnight
Can Be Made Up to 2 Days in Advance

Equipment

Large 2 quart non-metallic bowl,   Wooden spoon
   6 × 6 inches   Mixing bowl
Plate   Measuring cups
Weights, cans   Large saucepan
Colander   Plastic wrap

Ingredients

2   quarts currants
2   pints (1 quart) raspberries
     OR
1   quart blueberries
1   quart black berries
2   pints (1 quart) raspberries
1½ cups granulated sugar

12   dried out 3/8-1/4 inch thick
     solid bread slices, egg
     bread not "Kiddie" or soft
     bread type
4-6 tablespoons unsalted butter
½   pint heavy cream

Wash berries, reserving a handful, a few of each, for garnish. Drain and place in saucepan with sugar and cook 12-15 minutes. Mash a bit with spoon.

Meanwhile, line bowl with plastic wrap and trail it over all sides. Butter the bread and line bottom and sides of the bowl with bread, butter side against plastic wrap. Alternate berry mixture and a layer of bread until all is used up. If there are extra berries, reserve for serving sauce. Cover with protruding plastic wrap and put a heavy plate on top of the mixture to press it down. If not enough plastic wrap, cover it with more. Weight it with several heavy cans of food from the pantry or a very heavy pot. Refrigerate 1-2 days.

A few hours before serving, whip cream in medium size bowl, adding a tablespoon of granulated sugar near the end.

Remove molded pudding by removing weights, plate and plastic from the top. Invert onto a serving plate with a rim. Remove plastic wrap carefully, garnish with reserved berries and serve with whipped cream.

Chocolate Chip Cookies

Preparation Time: 20 Minutes
Cooking Time: 9-11 Minutes
The Reliable Toll-House® Cookie Recipe

Equipment

Mixing bowl

Measuring spoons and cups

Wooden spoon

Electric mixer

2-3 baking sheets

Cooling racks

Ingredients

2¼ cups unsifted all-purpose flour

1 teaspoon baking soda

1 teaspoon soda

2 sticks (1 cup) unsalted butter, softened

1 teaspoon vanilla extract

¾ cup granulated white sugar

¾ cup packed brown sugar

2 large eggs

12 ounces chocolate chips (1 package, semi-sweet)

1 cup chopped nuts, walnuts or pecans

Preheat oven to 375 degrees.

Combine flour, baking soda and salt in a bowl. Beat butter and white and brown sugar and vanilla extract in larger mixing bowl. Add eggs, one at a time and beat after each has been added. Gradually beat in flour mixture. Stir in the chips and nuts.

Drop by rounded teaspoons full onto ungreased baking sheets and bake 9-11 minutes or until they appear firm and not too soft to the touch. Let stand for a couple of minutes before removing to a cooling rack.

Makes about 4 dozen, depending on size. Store in an air tight container or large plastic zipper bag.

Beverages

White Sangria

Preparation Time: 10 Minutes
Needs 1 Hour to Marinate

Equipment

Large glass pitcher, clear
  preferable
Long handled spoon
Small sauce pan

Knife
Cork screw
Zester

Ingredients

½ cup water
½ cup sugar
2 liters dry white wine
1 whole orange
4 slices lemon
4 slices lime

2 sticks of cinnamon
12 large strawberries, hulled
    and halved
12 ounces cold club soda
    Ice

Mix water and sugar in small saucepan and bring to a boil, melting the sugar. Remove from the heat. You will use this to sweeten the sangria to your taste, needing 2-4 tablespoons of sugar syrup.

If your pitcher is large enough to accommodate the two liters of wine and the fruit all at once, proceed to place the wine and cut fruits into the pitcher (not the orange). Add the sugar syrup and stir; taste to see if more sugar syrup is needed. If your pitcher is small, make in two batches or in another container and transfer to the pitcher for serving.

Using a zester or knife, cut the orange peel into a spiral, starting at the top and leaving attached to the orange, carefully hang over the top of the pitcher. Let marinate for one hour. Add the club soda and ice at this point, stir and serve.

Columbus Day
October 12

History

Christopher Columbus, an Italian mariner from Genoa, Italy, owed his reputation, his fortune, and imprint on history to sailing west across the Atlantic Ocean in search for a shorter route to the fabled, rich "Spice Islands" of the East Indies. After several years of petitioning the Spanish throne, he finally received financial backing from the monarchs, Ferdinand and Isabella, allowing him to set sail in three small ships, the Niña, Pinta, and Santa Maria. Although Columbus never reached the East Indies, he discovered a whole 'New World', the West Indies and the Americans, which would soon bring unrivaled wealth to Spain and other countries as well. Criticized in recent years for his poor and brutal treatment of the native Caribbean Indians, bad and self-serving colonial government and personal rapaciousness, Columbus' voyage of discovery in 1492 was, nonetheless, courageous and full of impact for the whole of the Western world. This small beginning not only imprinted the newly discovered islands and continents with Spanish culture and language, but also cross-pollinated Europe with new foods and great riches of gold and silver.

Traditionally, Columbus Day has paid homage to this great Italian and is celebrated by parades led by members of the Italian-American community. In terms of food, we can enjoy the many delicacies and foods the Italians have contributed to the "American" culture.

Decoration

The meal, whether it be an intimate family dinner or a party should celebrate the Italian culture as well as the "discovery" of

America. The Italian flag is red, green and white and these colors might be used in the color scheme of your table settings, napkins, flowers or candles. Replicas of one or all of Columbus' ships could serve as a centerpiece or be incorporated with red and white flowers and greenery. Italian music, popular or operatic, would also help to set an overall tone to the evening.

Columbus Day Dinner for 6

Select your menu and make up your shopping list as suggested in the Introduction.

Menu

Hors d'Oeuvres
Antipasto Tray*
    (Could double as a first course)
Grissini (thin bread sticks)

First Course
Minestrone Soup

Main Course
Shrimp Scampi
    Or
Veal Piccata

Fettuccine Alfredo
Spinach Sautéed with Garlic and Oil
Mixed Green Salad, Vinaigrette
Garlic bread
    OR
A Do-Ahead Meal of:
Lasagna

Desserts
West Indies Cheese Cake
    Or
Fresh Figs with Biscotti

continued . . .

Beverages
Wine: For shrimp or veal, serve a white Gavi or Pinot
   Grigio. For lasagna, a red Gattinara or Chianti
Cappuccino or Espresso
After Dinner Drink: Sambuca or Amaretto

Timetable

Two Days Prior
Roast red peppers and marinate for antipasto platter
Marinate mushrooms for antipasto platter
Chill wine

One Day Prior
Bake cheesecake
Clean Spinach
Make Soup
Make vinaigrette if antipasto is first course

Same Day
Clean shrimp according to recipe instructions; refrigerate
   packed in ice
Remove cheesecake from pan
Assemble lasagna and refrigerate; remove 1 hour before
   baking
Wash salad greens; refrigerate in plastic bag and prepare
   vinaigrette, cover with plastic wrap and put aside
Wash cherry tomatoes for antipasto
Assemble bottled or canned antipasto ingredients and serv-
   ing platter
Prepare garlic bread
Grate cheese for fettuccine; cover with plastic wrap
Sauté optional mushrooms, for fettuccini
Pound and flour veal cutlets and place in refrigerator
Squeeze lemon juice into a container and place by stove
Prepare coffee equipment
Set and decorate table

continued . . .

Thirty Minutes Before Guests Arrive
Assemble antipasto platter
Turn on oven to 350 degrees
Start fettucine water on low heat
Get ready to start lasagna . . . it will take 1½ hours to cook;
   plan dinner hour accordingly
Uncork wine; keep white chilled

Twenty Minutes Before Dinner
Check lasagna and remove foil
Place garlic bread in oven
Start shrimp or veal
Start spinach
Cook fettucine
Assemble salad and toss with vinaigrette
Remove cheesecake from refrigerator and place onto serv-
   ing platter
*Start coffee as serving dinner, if making in an automatic
   maker

Recipes

Hors d'Oeuvres

Antipasto Tray with Grissini

Cooking Time: 30 Minutes
Preparation Time: 10 Minutes

This hors d'oeuvre or first course should be served with small plates and forks. Don't forget cocktail napkins! An attractive arrangement of the components enhances the appeal of the variety of flavors offered. If serving as a first course, offer olive oil and balsamic or wine vinegar in carafes or use dressing recipe at end of antipasto segment.

Ingredients

Hard salami
Prosciutto with Endive
Asiago or Provolone cheese, cubed
Anchovies with capers
Roasted red peppers*
Marinated Mushrooms*
Artichoke hearts in a bottle
Peperonici (semi-hot pickled
    peppers in a jar)

Cherry tomatoes
Variety of green and black olives
Grissini (very thin bread sticks
    placed in a tall glass or
    container and served on the
    side)

*Should be prepared up to 2 days prior or can be purchased in glass bottles.

Roasted Red Peppers

Preparation Time: 10-15 Minutes
Cooking Time: 15-20 Minutes

Equipment

Tray with low sides, such as
    pizza pan
Sharp cutting knife

Dish to store peppers
Measuring spoons and cups
Whisk

Ingredients

2   Red Bell peppers
1   clove crushed or thinly
      sliced garlic

¼   cup olive oil
½   teaspoon oregano

Turn on oven to broil and place rack in highest position. Lightly grease or oil a small tray with low sides. Wash and dry peppers.

Place peppers on pan and place under the broiler watching carefully so they don't burn. Turn frequently as they begin to color. Skin will become blackened. Make sure that all sides of the pepper are evenly cooked, including the top and bottom. Remove from oven and cover with kitchen towel or place in brown paper bag. The steam generated by covering them will cause the skin of the peppers to loosen.

After 10 minutes, or when cool enough to handle, remove peppers, one at a time, and with sharp knife, gently remove skin. You may be able to do this procedure with your fingers.

Place pepper on cutting board and slice in half. Gently remove the core and seeds and any hanging pale ribs of the pepper. Cut into one half inch strips and place in a dish. Repeat procedure with other pepper.

Place sliced or crushed garlic over peppers, along with oregano and olive oil. Gently turn several times to mix flavors, try to keep peppers flat. Cover with plastic wrap and refrigerate. Turn peppers every 8-10 hours. Remove from refrigerator about 45 minutes before serving, as olive oil will have hardened.

Marinated Mushrooms

Preparation Time: 10 Minutes

Equipment

Piece of paper toweling
Medium size sauce pan (2 quart)
Slotted spoon
Measuring spoons and cups
Whisk
Strainer

Medium size mixing bowl
Lid or flat plate
Tall plastic or glass container to
  store mushrooms

Ingredients

1 pound small white button
     mushrooms
1½ cups water
½ cup white vinegar
1 teaspoon salt

⅓ cup olive oil
4 tablespoons white wine
     vinegar
1 clove garlic, peeled and cut
     in half

½ teaspoon salt
¼ teaspoon freshly ground
     black pepper
1 tablespoon minced Italian
     parsley, leaves only, for
     garnish

Wipe mushrooms with a damp paper towel, removing any brown dust. Remove stems and reserve for another purpose (for minestrone soup).

In a medium size saucepan, bring water and white wine vinegar to a boil, then add salt. Drop in half of the mushrooms. When the water returns to a boil, wait 45 seconds, and then remove mushrooms from the water with a slotted spoon and place in a strainer over a bowl. Repeat process with balance of the mushrooms. Place lid or flat plate on top of the mushrooms in the strainer and drain 30-40 minutes. Mushrooms excrete a lot of liquid when cooked.

Combine the other ingredients in the non-metallic container in which you will store the mushrooms. Add the mushrooms and stir gently. Cover tightly and refrigerate until 45 minutes prior to serving. Stir occasionally. Drain and place on platter. Sprinkle with minced parsley.

Assembling the Antipasto Platter

You will need a large platter whose sides are not too steep. Conceptually, you want to place the larger items on the outside of the platter and the smaller ones, like the mushrooms in the center. Serve with toothpicks placed in small items and a serving spoon, as you will provide small plates and forks for guests to use.

Prosciutto with Endive

Preparation Time: 5 Minutes

Equipment
Paper toweling or dish towel
Knife

Ingredients
2 heads of endive
8 slices of prosciutto, fat
   removed

Wash the endive and carefully separate the leaves one by one. Pat the leaves dry.

Gently take a piece of prosciutto, fold in half and roll into a tubular shape. Cut in half and place ½ on an endive leaf.

Arrange around outside edge of platter.

Hard Salami

Preparation Time: 2 Minutes

Ingredients
18 thin slices of hard or Genoa salami

Fold salami in half and half again, giving it a tricorn appearance. Alternate between endive and prosciutto.

Asiago or Provolone Cheese

Preparation Time: 2-3 Minutes

Ingredients
½ pound of sharp Asiago or Provolone cheese, cubed

Place cheese cubes on inside edge of salami and endive/prosciutto.

Anchovies with Capers

Preparation Time: 3 Minutes

Ingredients
1 small can anchovies, opened and drained of oil
enough capers as number of anchovies

Drain oil from anchovies, roll them into a circular round. Place a caper in the middle of each one.
Arrange on platter.

Antichoke Hearts

Preparation Time: 2 Minutes

Ingredients
1 jar artichoke hearts, drained of oil, arrange on platter

Peperonici (Hot Tuscan Peppers)

Preparation Time: 2 Minute

Ingredients
One jar Tuscan peppers (one-two per guest)

Drain and arrange on platter.

Cherry Tomatoes

Preparation Time: 2 Minutes

Ingredients
½ pint cherry tomatoes (½ of small basket)

Wash, dry and arrange onto platter, adding color where appropriate.

Olives

Preparation Time: 2 Minutes

Ingredients
½ cup each black, green, Calamata, or spiced olives. Whatever appeals to you.

Arrange on platter in and around cheese.

Roasted Peppers and Mushrooms

Preparation Time: 2 Minutes

Arrange prepared peppers and mushrooms toward center of platter, mushrooms in middle. Sprinkle mushrooms with minced parsley.

Offer grissini in dish or tall glasses on the side. Serve platter with small dishes, toothpicks, serving spoon and cocktail napkins.

Antipasto as First Course

Preparation Time: Same as Above

Can be served on serving platter or made up onto individual plates, one per guest.

Vinaigrette

Preparation Time: 5 Minutes

Equipment
Measuring spoons and cups
Whisk
Storage container with lid

Ingredients for Vinaigrette If Served Separately

¾	cup olive oil	⅛	teaspoon dried thyme
¼	cup white, red wine, or balsamic vinegar	⅛	teaspoon black pepper
1½	teaspoons dried oregano	½	teaspoon salt
½	teaspoon dried basil	1	crushed garlic clove

Place all ingredients in a container and whisk or shake well. Let "brew" at least 3-4 hours, or up to a day prior. Shake or whisk before use.

First Course

Antipasto
OR
Minestrone Soup

See above for antipasto recipe

Minestrone Soup

Preparation Time: 20 Minutes
Cooking Time: 1-1¹/₂ Hours

Equipment

8-10 quart soup pot
Spoon to stir
Cutting knife
Measure cups and spoons

Pasta Pot
Colander
Ladle

Ingredients

½   cup olive oil
4   carrots, peeled and thinly
      sliced
3   zucchini, diced
1   medium size yellow onion,
      small dice
4   stalks celery, sliced and
      diced
1   red pepper, seeds removed
      and diced
1   green pepper, seeds removed
      and diced
2   cups green string beans,
      remove ends and cut into
      fourths
1   cup yellow wax beans,
      remove ends, cut into
      fourths

8   cups beef broth
2½ cups peeled, seeded, chopped
      plum tomatoes
1   19-ounce can kidney beans,
      drained and rinsed
1   19-ounce can cannelloni
      beans drained and rinsed
Salt and pepper to taste
*Optional ½ pound tubular
      pasta, cooked separately,
      added last minutes
*Mushroom stems from
      marinated mushroom
      recipe, added at beginning

continued . . .

219

Clean, dice, chop all vegetables. To remove tomato skins, dip tomatoes into boiling water for 30 seconds or so. You will see skins start to loosen. Immediately remove and peel. Slice in half and remove seeds. Chop into small pieces. Hold to the side.

Heat olive oil in kettle and when hot, put in all fresh vegetables, including mushrooms, **not** tomatoes. Turn down heat and slowly cook the vegetables until translucent and soft. Season with salt and pepper to taste. Add broth and bring to a simmer, not a boil. Add tomatoes. Simmer without lid 1 hour or until all flavors have meshed.

If you are adding pasta to the soup, cook separately in salted (about a teaspoon) boiling waiter until "*al dente*," "to the tooth". Do not over cook as it has to sit in the soup pot. Drain and add to soup.

Add the canned beans and heat through. Adjust the seasonings, it may require more salt with the last additions. Soup is ready to serve.

Main Course

Shrimp Scampi

Preparation Time: 20 Minutes
Cooking Time: 5-8 Minutes

Equipment

Broiling Tray, lined with
  aluminum foil for easier
  cleaning or large skillet with
  heat-proof handle
Tongs
Sharp knife
Measuring cups and spoons
Garlic press

Colander
Cutting board, preferably plastic
Small saucepan
Whisk
Juicer or reamer
Large bowl (for storage)
Plastic wrap

Ingredients

36	large shrimp (6 per person), shelled, tail on is all right	½	teaspoon dried oregano or 1 teaspoon fresh
1	tablespoon lemon juice	¼	cup chopped parsley, remove from stems to chop as garnish
4	cloves garlic, minced or put through garlic press		
½	cup butter (1 stick)	1	lemon sliced into wedges for garnish
1	teaspoon salt		
⅛	teaspoon black pepper		

Rinse shrimp in colander with cold water. Peel shell from body of shrimp, starting by pulling the legs off the inside curve. Lay shrimp on cutting board and using sharp knife, make an incision along the back curve of the shrimp to almost the tail. Remove any black or threadlike vein and discard. On larger shrimp there may be a jelly-like substance, which should be removed. Rinse the shrimp again and place in bowl, cover with ice and plastic wrap and place in refrigerator.

Preheat the broiler about 15 minutes before serving time.

In a small saucepan, melt the butter, squeeze in garlic, add lemon juice, salt, pepper and oregano. Keep heat on low until butter is completely melted, stirring well. **This can be prepared earlier.**

Blot shrimp with paper toweling. Lay shrimp in bottom of broiler pan or skillet that has a heat proof handle. Pour butter/garlic mixture over shrimp, turning them so both sides of shrimp are well coated. Broil 5-7 minutes, until shrimp are pink. Timing depends on size of shrimp. Do not overcook or they will dry out. Place shrimp and liquid remaining in pan onto a serving platter, arrange nicely and garnish with chopped parsley and lemon wedges.

Veal Piccata

Preparation Time: 7 Minutes
Cooking Time: 5-7 minutes

Equipment

Pounding mallet
Waxed or parchment paper, or
  plastic wrap
Measuring cups and spoons

Large skillet
Cooking fork
Aluminum foil
Wooden Spoon

Ingredients

1½ pounds veal scaloppini,
  sliced into ¼" pieces; one
  to two person, depending
  on size of scallops
  All-purpose flour for
  dredging about 1 cup
½ teaspoon salt
¼ teaspoon ground black
  pepper

3 tablespoons butter
2 tablespoons olive oil
¼ cup dry white wine
4 tablespoons lemon juice
  Thin lemon slices, for
  garnish
  Finely chopped Italian
  parsley leaves, for garnish

Remove any fat or membrane from scalloppini slices. Place, one or two at a time, between 2 pieces of waxed or parchment paper or plastic wrap, and pound with mallet or small flat-bottom pan until thinner (⅛ inch). Smooth meat out to edges as you pound.

Place flour, salt and pepper on a plate or paper towel, mix well. Dredge veal in flour mixture, covering both sides well. This can be done up to one hour prior to cooking. Place veal on plate in refrigerator.

222

Melt butter and oil in heavy skillet, taking care not to brown butter. When hot and a pinch of flour sizzles in the pan, add veal in one layer and cook on medium high heat until brown on one side. Turn veal and cook on other side. Flour will stick to the pan if heat isn't high enough. If all the veal doesn't fit in the pan, cook in batches, adding more butter and oil as needed. Place cooked veal in serving dish and tent with aluminum foil to keep warm while making sauce.

When all veal is cooked drain off excess oil and add wine to the pan to deglaze caramelized bits remaining on the surface of pan. Scrape pan with wooden spoon. Add lemon juice and stir until hot and bubbling. Pour over scallops and garnish each with a slice of lemon and minced parsley.

Fettucine Alfredo with Sautéed Mushrooms

Preparation Time: 5 Minutes
Cooking Time: 25 Minutes

Equipment

Large pasta or soup pot, 8-10
   quarts
Measuring cups and spoons
Large whisk
Wooden spoon

Colander
Small bowl
Small skillet
Pasta bowl or large serving bowl

Ingredients

1	pound fettuccine noodles
1	tablespoon salt
2	egg yolks
1½	cups, small container heavy cream
¾	stick butter
2	plus 1 cup freshly grated Reggiano Parmigiano, (Parmesan cheese) Place the 1 cup of the cheese in serving dish with spoon for the table

½	tablespoon freshly ground black pepper
*1	cup mushrooms, optional (cremini or small white)
1	tablespoon olive oil
1	tablespoon butter
	Salt and pepper to taste

continued . . .

223

Wipe mushrooms with damp paper towel. Remove stems and reserve for future use. Slice thinly. Heat olive oil and butter in small skillet and add mushrooms. Sauté until golden. Remove from heat and hold in reserve. This can be done several hours ahead. Remove from skillet and place in plastic wrap by stove.

Fill pasta pot with water, add salt and bring to a boil. Add fettuccine and stir occasionally so pasta doesn't stick to bottom of pot or to itself. Cook until al dente, about 10-15 minutes. Do not overcook, as pasta will continue to cook while you make the sauce.

While pasta cooks, separate egg yolks from white and place in small bowl. Cover and save whites for other recipes. Place cheese, egg yolks, cream and pepper by the stove.

Drain the pasta in a colander and return the pot to the stove. Lower the heat and add butter, cut into tablespoon size slices. Whisk in heavy cream. Watch carefully that butter does not brown and cream does not boil. When butter is almost melted, add 2 cups of the grated cheese and stir until incorporated. Return the pasta to the pot and cover with the sauce. It will want to stick to the bottom of the pot. Keep the ingredients moving. Add the egg yolks and stir into the noodles, it thickens the sauce. If sauce is too thick, add a bit more cream (or milk if there is no more cream). Be careful not to scramble eggs on bottom of pan. Add black pepper. Pasta is ready to serve. Fold in optional mushrooms at this point. Pass extra cup of cheese on the table as pasta is served.

Spinach Sautéed with Garlic and Olive Oil

Preparation Time: 10 Minutes
Cooking Time: 8-10 Minutes

Equipment

Large skillet
Large pot or mixing bowl
Measuring spoons
Sharp slicing knife

Colander
Paper toweling
Wooden Spoon

Ingredients

2   pounds fresh spinach
3   tablespoons olive oil
3   cloves garlic, peeled and
       sliced thin
1   teaspoon salt

    Clean spinach by first rinsing/soaking in a large pot or mixing bowl full of water, to remove any sand. Drain and rinse again, and yet again if there is a lot of sand. Cut off stems and any large vein attached to the stem. Remove any soft leaves. Pat dry.

    Peel and cut garlic into thin slices.

    When ready to cook, heat olive oil in skillet, stir in garlic and cook over a moderate heat for one minute, try not to brown. Place spinach in pan and continue to stir until spinach is wilted. If spinach is not dry, you will get a lot of water in the skillet. Raise heat to evaporate. Do not overcook the spinach. Serve with the oil and garlic on spinach.

Mixed Green Salad, Vinaigrette

Preparation Time: 10 Minutes

Equipment

Colander or salad spinner
Paper towels
Knife
Measuring cups and spoons

Small mixing bowl
Whisk
Salad Bowl with serving piece

Ingredients

3   cups Romaine lettuce,
        remove root end
3   cups red leaf lettuce
3   cups Boston or Iceberg
        lettuce
1   cup arugula, optional

⅓   cup extra virgin olive oil or
        regular olive oil if not
        available

5   tablespoons red wine
        vinegar
1   clove garlic squeezed
        through garlic press or
        smashed and minced
½   teaspoon salt
        Freshly ground pepper to
        taste

Tear, do not cut, salad greens into bite-size pieces. Wash greens in cold water. If lettuce is limp, soak in iced water for about 10–15 minutes. Drain and spin in salad spinner or dry in paper toweling. Place into large plastic bag and refrigerate until needed.

Place salad dressing ingredients in small mixing bowl and whisk for a cohesive blend. Set aside; cover; whisk before use and pour over greens.

Garlic Bread

Preparation Time: 10 Minutes
Cooking Time: 15 Minutes

Equipment

Serrated knife
Garlic press/motar and pestle
Small bowl

Aluminum foil
Bread basket or large plate/
   napkin

Ingredients

1   long loaf Italian bread
1   stick softened butter
4-5 garlic cloves, depending on
      size of cloves and length of
      bread loaf
    Pinch of salt

Preheat oven to 350 degrees.

Peel garlic, put through garlic press and into a small bowl or cut into small pieces and place in a mortar with a pinch of salt. Grind garlic with pestle until a paste is formed. Slowly add butter by tablespoons and incorporate into garlic.

Slice bread into inch wide slices, taking care not to slice all the way through; leave attached on the bottom as butter would seep out when heated. Spread garlic butter between each slice. Wrap the bread tightly in aluminum foil, using two pieces together if the width is not great enough to wrap around bread.

Place in preheated oven for about 15 minutes or until heated through and butter has melted. Remove foil and place in a breadbasket or on a large plate. Cover with a color coordinated napkin and serve.

Lasagna

Preparation Time: 30 Minutes
Cooking Time: 1¹/₂ hours

Equipment

Pasta pot or large soup pot	Measuring spoons
8 × 12 inch baking dish, metal or pyrex, at least 3 inches deep	Colander
	Chopping knife
Large skillet	Aluminum foil
Wooden stirring spoon	Spatula

Ingredients

22** lasagna noodles, see below, about 1 pound
1 tablespoon salt
1 tablespoon olive oil

1½ pound chopped round or sirloin beef (hamburger style meat, but extra lean)
1 medium size yellow onion
2 cloves garlic, squeezed through garlic press or finely minced
1½ teaspoons dried oregano
1 teaspoon salt
½ teaspoon ground black pepper
1 26 ounce jar favorite tomato/spaghetti sauce
1 pound riccota cheese
1 pound mozzarella cheese, small dice

**Take uncooked lasagna noodles and place them in the pan in which you are going to bake the lasagna. Measure to see if you will need 3 or 4 noodles per layer. If noodle is too short for pan, you will have to cook additional noodles per layer, and cut them to cover the bottom of each layer. Multiply for 3 layers of noodles and add two or 3 extra for breakage. You will cook that amount of noodles.

Fill pot with water to within 3 inches of the top and bring to a boil. Add 1 tablespoon of salt and oil to help prevent noodles from sticking together. When at a full boil, add noodles and gently stir them frequently to keep from sticking together. Cook to al dente. Burner should maintain a slow boil. Drain noodles in colander and immediately rinse in cold water to prevent sticking together.

While noodles are cooking, finely chop onion with knife or in small food processor. Heat a medium size skillet with enough olive oil to film pan. You won't need too much oil as chopped meat often exudes its own fats and often water. When skillet is hot, add onions and sauté until translucent. Add chopped meat, stir and separate. If meat exudes water, raise heat to evaporate. Meat should not "brown" and get crusty, but should be cooked through. While meat is almost cooked, add garlic, salt, pepper and oregano. Combine well. When meat is cooked, remove from heat.

Preheat over to 350 degrees. Place extra piece of aluminum foil on bottom of oven to catch any juices that my run over.

Coat the bottom of the baking dish with ¼ of the tomato sauce. Add a layer of noodles, overlapping edges slightly, or leaving no space between them, cover bottom of pan. If the pan is a bit longer than your noodle, cut a noodle to fit the space. Pour half of the meat mixture evenly over the noodle. Pour ¼ of the tomato sauce over meat. Place ½ of the ricotta by tablespoons full over meat and sprinkle with ⅓ of the mozzarella. Repeat with another layer of noodles, meat, sauce, ricotta and mozzarella. Top with final layer of noodles and smooth last of sauce over top of noodles; add the remaining mozzarella across the top. Cover tightly with aluminum foil.

Either refrigerate or bake at 350 degrees for one hour. Remove foil and bake 15-30 minutes or until bubbly and cheese begins to brown ever so slightly. This will vary as to the density of the layers and size of the baking dish.

Remove from oven and let sit about 5 minutes before serving. Cut across short width of pan, across the noodles making 2-3 inch slices, then divide the long slice into 2-3 inch segments. Remove with spatula onto plates. The first piece is always hard to get out, reserve it for yourself.

Experiment with your brands of ricotta and mozzarella. Some exude more water than others and dilute the flavor of the lasagna. Don't use them the next time.

Desserts

West Indies Cheesecake

Preparation Time: 20 Minutes
Cooking Time: 1 Hour, 10 Minutes
**Make one day prior to serving

Columbus never found the "Spice Islands" which sparked his quest across the Atlantic Ocean. However, many of the West Indian islands he did locate, provide some of the spices and exotic fruits in this cake.

Equipment

Food processor or rolling pin
9½ inch spring form pan
Small saucepan
Electric mixer/bowl or hand held
  mixer
Medium size mixing bowl

Measuring spoons and cups
Scraper/rubber spatula
Foil lines shallow baking pan
Knife
Instant read thermometer

Ingredients
Crust

30 gingersnap cookies
1 stick (½ cup) plus 2 tablespoons unsalted butter, melted

Cake

4	eight ounce packages of cream cheese, softened	2	teaspoons cinnamon
1½	cups granulated sugar	½	teaspoon ground clove
2	tablespoons all-purpose flour	1	teaspoon powdered ginger
5	large eggs	1	teaspoon salt
½	cup sour cream	1	teaspoon vanilla extract

Decoration

Carambola/Star fruit, substitute with orange and a lime
  OR
1 cup heavy cream, whipped
1 teaspoon rum or orange flavored liqueur such as Grand Marnier

Crust

Place the gingersnaps in food processor and using metal blade, grind into a fine powder. OR, if you don't have a food processor, break cookies into pieces, 8-10 at a time and place them in a plastic bag, secure with baggie tie. Use a rolling pin over them several times until fine crumbs are formed. Pour into mixing bowl and repeat until all gingersnaps are crumbed.

Place crumbs in a mixing bowl and add melted butter. Stir until all crumbs are covered with butter. Pour into the bottom of spring form pan and press crumbs ½ inch up onto sides of pan and bottom, pressing hard and making sure the depth of the crumbs is even all around sides and bottom of pan. You can tamp them into place with the bottom of a small glass or small measuring cup. Put pan into refrigerator while you make the filling.

Cake

Preheat the oven to 325 degrees.

Place cream cheese in a bowl of electric mixer (or hand held mixer) and beat until fluffy and light. Scrape down sides of bowl a couple of times as you beat. Gradually add sugar and beat until it is incorporated. Beat in the flour, then the eggs, one at a time until each is mixed in. Add sour cream, then the spices and mix well. Pour filling into chilled crumb shell.

Place spring form pan onto a foil-lined, shallow baking pan and place in the middle of the oven. Cook for one hour and ten minutes. Internal temperature should be 150 degrees on an instant read thermometer. Turn off the oven and leave the door ajar with cake in the oven until the cake is cool and set. Remove from oven and when absolutely cold, cover and refrigerate overnight.

Decorating

On the day of use, remove the cheesecake from the refrigerator and place on a serving plate. Unlock the spring form and gently remove outer band. Let the cake stand a few minutes. You may be able to carefully slide a metal spatula in between the cake and bottom of pan and edge the cake onto the serving plate. If it doesn't go, don't worry. Try placing bottom of pan on hot towel. This may soften bottom enough to release it. If not, serve it as it is. Be careful it doesn't slide off plate when carrying it.

Wash and dry star fruit/carambola. The fruit has a citrus quality. Since thinly across the circumference; it slices into star shapes. If this fruit is unavailable, substitute with half of a seeded orange and lime. Slice thinly. Put to the side. Remove cake from the refrigerator when serving dinner. You can place fruit on surface of cake at this time, or right before serving, no sooner. You can twist the orange into half circles and build interesting designs on top. Or, artistically use fruit to cover cracks in cake, if there are any.

Cake can also be served with rum-flavored whipped cream on the side or piped onto top of cake in a decorative fashion.

To Whip Cream

Place cream in small bowl and beat with electric mixer until soft peaks form. Add teaspoon of rum or orange flavored liqueur such as Grand Marnier. Whip until stiff. Place in serving dish and spoon as you serve each portion or place in pastry bag with a medium size star tip and pipe around edge of cake and in center. Garnish with carambola or orange/lime.

Fresh Figs with Biscotti

Preparation Time: 10 Minutes

Equipment
Cutting board
Knife

Ingredients
2 figs per person
Store bought package of biscotti, 1-3 per person

Wash gently, dry and slice in half. Place on dessert plate with biscotti.

Beverages

Cappuccino or Espresso

Preparation Time: 5 Minutes
Cooking Time: 3-5 Minutes

Equipment
Espresso maker
Saucepan
Whisk
    OR
Coffee Pot

Ingredients
Espresso, dark roast coffee
Milk
Cinnamon, optional
Thin slice of a lemon peel, one for each cup of espresso
Sugar

Follow directions for your espresso maker for both espresso and cappuccino, if you have one. If not, prepare coffee in your regular coffee pot, one tablespoon coffee per cup. It will be strong.

Brew coffee. Just before serving cappuccino, scald milk in saucepan. Whisk until stiff and put on top of poured coffee. Garnish with cinnamon.

Halloween
October 31

History

Halloween, falling on October 31, marks the beginning of the Festival of the Dead, which includes All Saints Day on November 1 and ends in All Souls' Day on November 2. The "Christian" holiday, introduced by Pope Boniface IV in the seventh century, was to be a day of remembrance for the unknown saints and martyrs of the Catholic Church. Utilizing ages-old pagan celebrations of the Fall solstice and incorporating and transferring them into the "new" religion was a common way of gaining adherents to a new faith. Halloween, "Hallowed Evening", represented a time to pray for the souls of the dead who were believed to walk the earth on that holy evening when the veil between the seen and unseen worlds was thin. The ancient Celtic Druids honored the Sun God, Samhain, Lord of Death, who assembled the souls of those who had died during the year. If they had been sinful they were confined in the bodies of the lesser type of animals.

In America, the celebration of Halloween came with the large scale Irish immigration of the 1840's. The Irish brought traditions recalling the ancient Celtic festivals of Samhain when the spirits of the dead roamed the earth. To scare those spirits away they made large bonfires, carved large turnips and squashes and lit them with a candle, hence our Jack O'Lantern. The Trick or Treat tradition sprang, in part, from a Gaelic one whereby cakes were given away at summer's end. The receiver of the cake, in turn, would have to pray for the good of the coming harvest. It is also believed that a person born on Halloween has the ability to see and read the future in dreams or cards, hence the linking of fortune telling and witchery to the day.

In Mexico, November 2, All Souls' Day is celebrated as the Day of the Dead. Altars are prepared in the home with an ofrenda, which includes a favorite food or drink of the person who has died. Personal mementos, skull-shaped sugar candies and a special cake is also offered. Families visit cemeteries scattering marigolds on the graves and hold a graveside picnic. On November 1, toys and balloons are placed on the graves of children, who are now known as "angelitos" or little angels.

Except in religious circles and in Europe, the religious aspect of the holiday has mostly been lost to its more festive aspects.

Getting Started: The Theme

Whether a child's or an adult party is in the offing, invitations should be mailed out at least three to four weeks in advance. This is especially important if a costume party is planned. You may want to devise your own "theme" for the party and make a game out of your guests guessing the personalities they have donned. For example:

Come as you were in a past life
Come as the person you admire the most in history
Come as your favorite Disney or cartoon character
Come as your favorite Roman or movie star or animal

The permutations are endless, but nudging your guests in a direction will help them devise an original costume, using their own creativity. Play games, charades with witchy themes; be a child again! In Roman times, Ramona, the Goddess of fruits and gardens was honored for bringing the gifts of winter to man; this evening was called "Nutcrack Night". Two nuts were thrown into a fire (use your fireplace) to determine faithfulness between lovers. If the nuts were quiet and burned brightly, the couple was faithful to each other; if it cracked and jumped, they were unfaithful. If the nuts burned together, they would marry! If you peel an apple and throw a long piece of its skin into the fire, you can see the initial of the person you loved. Try it, but beware of the consequences!

Decoration

Once you have decided upon a theme, you should start thinking of how you are going to decorate the entertainment and food serving areas, as well as your doors! If you are going with a traditional Halloween theme, orange and black items are widely available, from cocktail to dinner napkins. Don't forget hand towels in the "powder room". Whether ghosts and skeletons or pumpkins, witches and black cats and bats, decide if you are after scary or cute. Don't mix too many patterns together. Use candles, black and orange. Use pumpkins, corn stalks, spider webs, witches cauldrons, broomsticks, bats, skeletons suspended over stair wells, dim lights, things that go bump in the night, things that glow in the dark, and spooky music in the background. Whether sounds available on CDs, or the classic "Night on Bald Mountain", it all adds to the mood.

Carve a scary pumpkin for outside the front door. If you live in your own house, line the sidewalks with luminerias (patterned cut paper bags filled with sand, and a lit votive candle) to light the way to your door.

Carve a pumpkin on two sides for a centerpiece using available patterns and special carving tools available in craft stores, some florists, large "sundry" stores or mail order. If photo copied or handled carefully, they can be used for many years. Always place a dish or aluminum foil under the pumpkin to protect your furniture and prevent fire if the pumpkin tips.

As pumpkins shrivel easily, coat the cut surface, inside and out, with vaseline (petroleum jelly) after carving. It will also make the entire skin of the pumpkin shine! Of course, add a candle in the middle. Allow time for this and pick out your pumpkin early on to get a good choice of shape. Keep the pumpkins cool . . . in a garage, outside (but not in sunlight), or in the refrigerator until needed.

If you're not into carving, use magic markers and paint faces on pumpkins. The pumpkins last longer, but you lose the wavering effect of the candlelight.

Make a gingerbread or graham cracker base haunted house . . . or have your guests make them!

Skeletons and wiggley, hairy rubber spiders and bats can be hung from fixtures, as can artificial spider webs. A witch's hat and small broomstick can sit in a corner or on a serving or side table with a cauldron full of punch. Or, make a life-size witch with old panty hose, stuffed with cotton batting for the face, arms and legs. Black, inexpensive witch costumes are easy to find to clothe your witch. Facial features cut from felt can be glued on. White sheets, suspended by heavy black or clear thread can double as ghosts in a dark corner. Gourds and Indian corn can be used to add color here and there.

As your guests leave at the end of the evening, give them treat bags filled with Halloween candy which you have stored in a decorated basket or witches' cauldron.

Setting the Table

It's probably best to serve your food as a buffet, as some costumes may not fit well at a sit down dinner!

When you set up a buffet table, start with your centerpiece and candles, as this will determine the space left for the food. Put the plates at the end of the table closest to where guests will enter the area. Be careful with the flow of guests so you don't get 'traffic jams' as people serve themselves and try to exit the area as others are entering the dining area. If you don't have enough plates and silverware for the number of invited guests, use heavy plastic utensils and plastic coated paper plates and napkins. Even if you have enough tableware, throwaway makes for an easy cleanup and looks festive! Place the utensils and napkins as guests leave the buffet table, so their hands have been free while selecting their food. As the suggested menu does not require a knife, fold or roll the fork in the napkin for easy pickup. Dessert utensils will be provided with dessert, as well as fresh napkins. Place a salt and pepper shaker or pepper mill adjacent to the food. Rolls and butter should be the last item picked up as it can sit on top of the food if the plate is crowded.

If your table is large enough, beverages and glasses can be placed at the end with the napkins. It is almost always better to have beverages on a separate table in another area, however, to relieve congestion. A card table or small kitchen table covered with an appropriate cloth or piece of inexpensive material can be tucked into the corner of the entertainment area making an ideal beverage table for glassware and assorted drinks. This will be your cocktail bar as well.

237

As one of the dishes you are serving will be quite hot, have a trivet available on which to place it. Put all serving dishes out in the kitchen before the party and have the serving utensils in position on the serving table. Decide on where you will place which foods. Usually meat first, then carbohydrates, then vegetables, and bread.

Halloween Buffet for 10-12

Determine your menu and make up your shopping list as suggested in the Introduction. If you decide to use only one or two of the dishes, increase their quantities accordingly. Most of the menu can be prepared ahead to free you from the kitchen and not to mess your costume!

Menu

Hors d'Oeuvres
Green Slime Punch
Jack O'Lantern Brie En Croute
Black Bean Dip with Tortilla Chips
Glazed Sweet and Sour Meatballs
Mini Halloween Pizzas

Main Course
Crispy Chicken Legs and Wings
Vampire Chili
Corn with Orange and Green Peppers
Tossed Salad with Edible Eyeballs
Cheesy Corn Bread

Dessert
Devil's Food Cup Cakes
Apple Crumb Pie
Candied Apples
Candy Corn on a Stick for treat bags

Beverages
Mulled Hot Cider

continued . . .

Cold Cider
Range of Sodas, some Diet
Rioja red wine
Chardonnay or Frascati white wine
Café Diablo

Timetable

Four to Three Days Prior
Prepare costume
Decorate house
Decorate outside, not pumpkins
Shop

Two Days Prior
Carve pumpkins
Make eyeballs
Make gummy worm ice cubes

One Day Prior
Glazed meatballs
Marinate chicken pieces
Chili
Prepare salad greens
Devil's food cup cakes
Candied apples
Candy corn on stick
Make up "treat" bags

Same Day
Bake apple pie
Form Brie
Make pizzas, do not bake
Make salad dressing
Bake corn bread, cut when cool and place on serving plate
Prepare peppers for corn
Chop coriander/parsley for corn
Prepare mulled cider
Unmold eyeballs, refrigerate

continued . . .

Three Hours Prior to Guests Arriving
Prepare and cook chicken; arrange on platter and garnish

One Hour Prior to Guests Arriving
Remove meatballs from refrigerator, place in pot
Remove chili from refrigerator, place in pot
Get corn ready to cook
Remove black bean dip from refrigerator, put in serving
    bowl with chips
Start to bake Brie, ready trap with crackers.
Place candied apples on serving plate
Make slime punch

Thirty Minutes Prior
Heat meatballs
Reheat cider
Check Brie
Heat chili, stir a lot, then turn off heat until 10 minutes
    before serving

As Guests Arrive
Bake pizzas
Serve Brie, easier to serve when sets a few minutes
Put meatballs on serving table
Set out dip

10 Minutes Before Dinner
Reheat chili
Cook corn
Toss salad, add eyeballs

Recipes

Hors d'Oeuvres

Green Slime Punch

Preparation Time: 10 Minutes

Equipment
Punch bowl   Dry Ice, optional
Ladle   Cheese cloth
Ice

Ingredients
2   quarts lime sherbet (sorbet),
          must be green
4-6   liters ginger ale
20   or so gummy worms frozen
          in ice cubes, or just in bowl
      Dry ice wrapped in cheese
          cloth, optional

Just before guests arrive, put sherbert, ice cubes and ginger ale into the punch bowl; add dry ice, it will make the punch steam. Mix carefully. If you have not frozen gummy worms into the ice cubes, add them to the punch and try to pour one into every glass served. You may want to place additional worms in the bottom of the punch bowl any way, especially if you are not using dry ice.

Jack O'Lantern Brie En Croute

Preparation Time: 12-15 Minutes
Cooking Time: 30 Minutes or until Golden

Equipment

Baking Tray with rim all around
   or small pizza pan with rim, or
   ovenproof non-stick skillet
Tea Towel
Rolling pin
Small bowl-cup

Measuring spoons
Whisk or small fork
Pastry brush, optional
Metal spatula
Sharp Knife

Ingredients

1   eight ounce round of Brie
      cheese
1   can jellied cranberry sauce
1   box frozen puff pastry
      Flour
1   egg yolk

1   teaspoon water
      Non-stick cooking spray
      Assortment of firm crackers,
        English water biscuits,
        Melba toast rounds or
        other type of cracker

Remove the pastry from the outside box and defrost one piece. Keep pastry covered with tea towel so it doesn't dry out while defrosting. Sprinkle a few drops of water on the top of the towel. There are usually 2 in a box. Place the extra sheet in plastic wrap or bag, place in box and keep frozen for another occasion.

Preheat oven to 375 degrees.

When pastry has defrosted, place on lightly floured counter top or rolling board. Roll to remove the creases in the dough and make it a bit thinner, no holes allowed.

Open the cranberry sauce and spread a few tablespoons over the center part of the pastry where the cheese will lie. Unwrap the Brie and center on top of the cranberry sauce.

Separate the egg yolk and mix with water in a small bowl or cup. Using pastry brush or your clean finger, paint the edges of the dough with the egg yolk mixture. The egg yolk acts as a "glue" to hold the pastry dough closed. Tightly fold the dough around the Brie, making sure there are no holes, as cheese will leak through them as it bakes. There will be excess dough as you fold it over; trim off so bottom is not so thick. Paint again with egg yolk, making sure the seal is tight.

Lightly spray the baking sheet with non-stick cooking spray. Place the Brie in the center of the sheet, wrapped side down. Paint the top of the Brie with egg yolk, for a nice golden color.

Take the excess scraps of the puff pastry and with a sharp knife, fashion a Jack O'Lantern face, eyes, nose, mouth. You can roll the dough into three-dimensional forms for the nose, for example, so it sticks up from the surface. Attach to the surface of the Brie with egg yolk mixture and brush the face pieces with the egg yolk.

Place in refrigerator until 30 minutes before baking.

Bake in a preheated 375 degree oven for 30 minutes or bake until it is golden.

Remove from oven and place on platter with crackers and a serving knife. Let it sit for 15-20 minutes before slicing or it will pour all over the plate.

Black Bean Dip with Tortilla Chips

Preparation Time: 15 Minutes

Equipment

Food Processor fitted with metal blade or blender

Measuring spoons
Grater or zester

Ingredients

2   19-ounce cans of black beans, reserve a ¼ cup of liquid, drain and rinse beans in cold water

2   medium size cloves of garlic, finely minced

5   tablespoons fresh lime juice
Finely grated zest from ½ lime

1   tablespoon olive oil

1   teaspoon salt

½   teaspoon black pepper
Drop of hot sauce, or to taste, optional

1   large bag tortilla chips

Place drained beans, garlic, lime juice, zest, olive oil, salt and pepper into a food processor or blender fitted with metal blade and purée until smooth. If too stiff, add reserved bean juice slowly to get pasty consistency. If not tangy enough, add more lime juice. Check for salt and add hot sauce, if desired. Place in serving dish, cover with plastic wrap and refrigerate until 30 minutes prior to serving. Remove from refrigerator and fluff up the surface of the dip with a fork. Place chips in bowl or napkin-lined bowl next to dip when serving.

Glazed Sweet and Sour Meatballs

Preparation Time: 20 Minutes
Cooking Time: 25-30 Minutes
Can Be Made One Day Prior

Equipment

6-8 quart sauce pan
Medium size mixing bowl
Measuring spoons and cups

Large skillet
Slotted spoon or spatula

Ingredients

2   pounds chopped round or sirloin steak (extra lean hamburger)
1   large egg
½   teaspoon salt
¼   teaspoon black pepper
½-¾ cup flour for dredging

Vegetable oil, such as canola for frying

1   16-ounce jar grape jelly
1½   12-ounce bottles chili sauce, looks like catsup

Pour grape jelly and chili sauce into saucepan and slowly heat, stirring occasionally until ingredients melt into each other.

Meanwhile, mix chopped meat, egg, salt and pepper in medium size bowl.

Place four on paper towel or in pie pan. Form into bite-size balls, about 1 teaspoon of meat per ball. Try to keep them uniform and compact. Drop them into the flour. Roll and cover in flour. Heat oil, about ¼ inch in bottom of pan. When hot, place a quantity of meatballs into oil; don't splash yourself, use a slotted spoon to lower them into oil. Do not crowd frying pan as you need to turn them often and gently with spatula or shake the pan to turn them. Brown evenly and remove them to the grape-chili mixture. They will finish cooking in the jam/chili sauce. Continue browning the balance of the meatballs, adding oil to the pan, if necessary. Watch the heat in the skillet as the bits of flour on bottom of the skillet may start to burn. Remove with slotted spoon. Keep sauce on moderate to low heat and stir from the bottom, taking care not to break meatballs. The meatballs will achieve a glazed effect after 20-30 minutes of cooking. Remove from heat and cool. Place in storage container in refrigerator or serve immediately with toothpicks. Reheat carefully so bottom of pan doesn't scorch.

Make sure there are small dishes or ashtrays for toothpicks available in several locations.

245

Mini Halloween Pizzas

Preparation Time: 20 Minutes
Cooking Time: 8-10 Minutes

Equipment

2 Cooking sheets
Rolling Pin
Spatula

Halloween cookie cutters or
  biscuit cutter or small glass

Ingredients

2 cylindrical containers or commercially prepared pizza dough (found in dairy area of super market) or 2 'bags' of dough if available. It's easier to work the dough in containers.
Flour
1 10-ounce jar of favorite tomato, spaghetti or pizza sauce
1 16-ounce package grated mozzarella cheese or 1 pound block, grated
Assorted toppings, your choice of small amounts of: olives, onion, peppers, garlic, Italian sweet or hot sausage, pepperoni, mushrooms, ricotta for white pizza
Oregano
Olive Oil
Non-stick cooking spray

Preheat oven to 400 degrees.

Lightly spray or oil cookie sheets with non-stick spray or a light coating of olive oil.

Sprinkle flour on work surface. Remove dough, one at a time from packaging and place on floured surface. Roll to desired thickness. Use cookie cutters (pumpkins, cats, bats, ghosts), or plain circular biscuit cutter, or small glass, to cut out shapes; place on cookie sheets, using a spatula to get them off work surface. Try not to stretch the dough.

Cover surface of each pizza with sauce and a small amount of oregano, if desired. Finish with toppings of your choice and mozzarella cheese. If you are using sausage, you will need to remove it from its casing and sauté it until brown and cooked through before using on pizzas. The pizzas can be made ahead to this point and covered and refrigerated.

Place in oven just before you want to serve them and cook for 8-10 minutes. You may want to cook them in batches, as the cocktail hour progresses so there will always be hot pizzas. The quantity made will depend on the size of your cookie cutters. If you want more, increase the amount of dough accordingly.

Main Course

Crispy Chicken Legs and Wings

Preparation Time: 10 Minutes
Standing Time: 4 Hours to Overnight, plus 30 Minutes
Cooking Time: 35 Minutes, Can Be Served at Room Temperature

Equipment

1-2 Large mixing bowls	2 Jellyroll type pans
Measuring spoons and cups	Rack
Whisk	Tongs for turning
Small bowl or cup	Paper Toweling
Small sauce pan	Plastic Wrap

Ingredients

12-15	chicken legs	3	teaspoons salt, divided in half
12-15	chicken wings with tips removed	1½	teaspoons cayenne
3	cups buttermilk	1½	cups yellow cornmeal
2½	teaspoons grated lemon zest	1	cup unflavored dry bread crumbs
⅔	cup fresh lemon juice	¾	cup grated Parmesan cheese
½	cup olive oil	1	tablespoon paprika
1	teaspoons grated lemon zest	1	stick of butter (¼ pound), melted
⅔	cup fresh lemon juice		
½	cup olive oil		
1	teaspoon dried rosemary		

Egg Wash

3 large eggs with 3 tablespoons of water and 2 tablespoons lemon juice

Wash chicken, removing any hanging skin and the wing tips. Pat dry.

In large mixing bowl, whisk together buttermilk, lemon zest, lemon juice, 1½ teaspoons of salt, oil, rosemary, and cayenne. Add the chicken to the bowl. If there is not enough room, divide between 2 bowls. Turn chicken in the mixture, cover with plastic wrap and refrigerate 4 hours to overnight.

Preheat oven to 425 degrees.

Lightly oil jellyroll pans and arrange a baking rack on the pan.

In a large bowl, combine cornmeal, breadcrumbs, Parmesan cheese, and paprika. In another bowl, whisk together the egg wash. Using tongs, remove a piece of chicken from the marinade, let excess drip off. Dip into egg wash and then coat with dry meal and crumb mixture. Place on rack to dry for 30 minutes. Repeat with remainder of chicken.

Chicken can be held up to 6 hours if covered and in refrigerator.

When ready to cook, remove the chicken from the rack and place directly on the lightly oiled pan, drizzle melted butter over the pieces and bake in middle of oven for 30-40 minutes or until crisp. Remove and drain on paper toweling. Can be served warm or at room temperature.

Vampire Chili

Preparation Time: 5 Minutes
Cooking Time: One Hour
Can Be Made One Day Prior

Equipment

Measuring spoons and cups
Large sauce pan with lid or skillet
    with cover
Wooden cooking spoon

Ingredients

3	pounds ground round or sirloin steak (extra lean hamburger)		Dried red pepper flakes to taste to increase heat, if desired. Add later when flavors have meshed
2	medium size yellow onions		
3	medium size cloves of garlic	½	cup dry red wine
3	19 ounce cans of red kidney beans	2	seeded and diced tomatoes
			Olive oil
1	2½-ounce bottle of chili powder	1	pint sour cream to serve alongside chili
1	tablespoon salt	1	pound of grated sharp cheddar or Monterey jack cheese to serve alongside chili
1	teaspoon ground black pepper		

Finely chop the onions and place into the heated pan with enough olive oil to film the bottom. Adjust the heat so the onions simmer but don't brown. When translucent, add garlic and the meat. Stir vigorously to break up the meat. You want the meat to cook through, but not brown too much. If the meat exudes water, turn up the heat until it evaporates, then lower the heat again, about 5-7 minutes.

Add salt, pepper, and chili powder and mix thoroughly.

Add kidney beans, their liquid, wine and tomatoes. Mix well and cover, turn heat to low. Stir occasionally so mixture doesn't stick on the bottom. The flavors will blend as chili cooks. After about 20 minutes, taste for salt and hotness. If you want to increase the spiciness, add more chili powder or dried hot red pepper flakes. **Warning:** The longer chili sits, the hotter it gets.

If you are making it a day before use, you may not want to increase the spiciness until reheating, then taste it. Upon reheating, if chili looks too dry, add more wine; if too runny before use, turn up heat and reduce liquid, stirring frequently to prevent scorching on bottom.

Place sour cream and grated cheese adjacent to serving bowl with spoons for service.

Corn with Green and Orange Peppers

Preparation Time: 10 Minutes
Cooking Time: 12 Minutes

Equipment

Measuring spoons	Medium size skillet
4 quart sauce pan with lid	Wooden spoon or cooking spoon

Ingredients

2	1-pound packages frozen Niblet yellow corn	½	tablespoon olive oil, canola or vegetable oil to prevent butter from burning
½	green Bell pepper, diced	4	tablespoons finely chopped coriander or flat leaf parsley, no stems, for garnish
½	orange or yellow Bell pepper, diced		
½	teaspoon salt		
1	teaspoon cumin		
5	tablespoons butter		

Dice peppers, removing membranes. Melt butter and oil in skillet, add peppers and cook until softened, but still maintain a slight crunch. Remove butter and peppers from skillet, cover and put to the side until ready for use. Can be prepared ahead.

Chop coriander/parsley, and place in plastic wrap.

Place quantity of water in saucepan, according to package instructions. When at a boil, add corn, stir and cover with lid. Stir occasionally. When corn is cooked, see package instructions, about 5-8 minutes, drain and add pepper and butter mixture. Stir and put into serving dish. Garnish with coriander/parsley.

Tossed Salad with Edible Eyeballs

Preparation Time: 20 Minutes
Refrigeration Time: 4-6 Hours
All can be made ahead

Equipment

2 rounded bottom ice cube trays or small mini muffin pans, need at least 12 'eyes'
Colander
Salad Spinner
Small mixing bowl
Measuring spoons and cups
Whisk
Salad Box and servers

Ingredients

1	box lemon gelatin (yellow)	4	tablespoons balsamic vinegar
½	pint blueberries	12	tablespoons virgin or plain olive oil
¾	head iceberg lettuce	½	teaspoon Dijon style mustard
¾	bunch Romaine lettuce	¾	teaspoon salt
½	head red leaf or Boston lettuce		Freshly ground black pepper to taste
	OR	1	medium-size clove of garlic, smashed, or finely diced
	Whatever your pleasure; quantities may vary depending on size of lettuce heads.		
	Adjust amount of greens accordingly		

Follow gelatin recipe on box.

When made, pour into ice cube trays or muffin tins and refrigerate for 20 minutes.

Wash blueberries and drain.

Gelatin will have become thicker, but not solid. Press a blueberry into the center of each "eye". And refrigerate until gelatin solidifies. To remove from molds, wrap a hot tea towel around bottom or set in hot water for a few seconds to "melt" a bit. Turn onto plate and keep cool until serving.

Wash and spin dry salad greens. Place in plastic bag and refrigerate until needed. If greens do not feel crisp, place in bowl with ice cubes for 20 minutes; drain and refrigerate.

Whisk together balance of ingredients for vinaigrette dressing. Immediately before serving, toss dressing over salad and then place eyeballs on top. If it is a sit down dinner, it is effective to put the salad greens on individual plates and center an eyeball on each one.

Cheesy Corn Bread

Preparation Time: 10 Minutes
Cooking Time: 25-30 Minutes

Equipment

8-inch square glass or metal baking dish
Mixing bowl
Measuring spoons and cups

Whisk
Small saucepan
Toothpick or cake tester

Ingredients

1 cup yellow cornmeal
½ cup white flour
¾ teaspoon baking soda
1¾ teaspoons baking powder
¾ teaspoon salt
1 cup grated sharp cheddar cheese

2 large eggs
1 cup buttermilk
¼ cup unsalted butter, melted and cooled (½ stick)
Non-stick cooking spray

Preheat over to 350 degrees.

Grease baking pan with butter. Crisco or non-stick cooking spray, getting into corners. Melt butter slowly in small saucepan or microwave.

Whisk together eggs and buttermilk in bowl. Add dry ingredients, then stir in the melted, cooled butter. Do not over-mix. Pour into prepared pan and bake. Test center of corn bread with a toothpick. It is done when toothpick comes out clean, about 25-30 minutes. Cool slightly and cut into small equal-size squares. Remove from pan and serve in dish lined with a napkin. Serve butter on side.

Desserts

Devil's Food Cup Cakes

Preparation Time: 20 Minutes
Cooking Time: 20-30 Minutes
Can be Prepared One Day Ahead

Equipment

2-5 muffin pans
Electric mixer and bowl
Measuring spoons and cups
Rubber spatula
Extra bowl
Cutting knife
Sifter or fine mesh strainer
Double boiler or small saucepan
   set within a larger pan
   containing 1-2 inches of water

Two cooling racks
Halloween paper muffin cups or
   any other
   OR
Grease muffin pans and flour
Toothpick or cake tester

Ingredients

2   cups sugar
½   cup shortening
2   large eggs
2   cups all-purpose flour
1   teaspoon baking powder
2   scant teaspoons baking soda
1   cup boiling hot coffee,
      instant can be used but
      not as good

1   cup whole milk
1   teaspoon vanilla
3   one ounce squares
      unsweetened baking
      chocolate, melted

Preheat oven to 350 degrees.

Line muffin tins with paper muffin cups or grease and flour well.

Chop chocolate into smaller pieces as it melts faster and place in double boiler over medium heat until chocolate melts. Scrape periodically. Lower heat if water boils too fast as any water splashing on chocolate will cause it to seize and be rendered useless.

Meanwhile, place sugar and shortening in electric mixing bowl and cream together until fluffy. Mix in the eggs, one at a time until incorporated. Frequently scrape sides of bowl with rubber spatula.

Measure and sift dry ingredients into extra bowl. Mix into sugar and egg mixture at a low speed, scraping often so flour doesn't fly all over.

Measure out the milk and coffee and keep vanilla bottle and melted chocolate next to mixing bowl. Do not add all liquids at once. Keeping mixer on low speed, slowly pour in liquids, alternating them and pouring in only ⅓ of each at a time. Vanilla can be added all at once after the first bit of milk and chocolate have been added. Scrape bowl after each addition. Mixture will be thin.

Pour into muffin cups, filling ⅔ full. If there is any left over, bake a second batch. Place in preheated oven for 20-25 minutes. They are done when toothpick or cake tester comes out clean. Do not let the pans touch each other, as hot air needs to circulate.

Remove cupcakes from tins and cool on racks.

Frost cake with either of the following two recipes, or both. Dip cupcakes in chocolate, black or orange jimmies, or top frosting with any other Halloween type sugar decoration that might catch your eye.

Basic Butter Cream Frosting

Preparation and Frosting Time: 15-20 Minutes

Equipment

Electric mixer, bowl
Measuring spoons and cups

Spatula, rubber and metal
Sifter/fine mesh strainer

Ingredients

3   cups confectioner's sugar (XXXX) sifted
⅓   cup softened butter
2½-3 tablespoons heavy cream

1½   teaspoons vanilla
Orange paste or gel food coloring

Combine sugar and butter in bowl with an electric mixer until fluffy. Stir in 2½ tablespoons of heavy cream and the vanilla. If consistency is too stiff to spread easily, add more cream.

Add a dab of food coloring, mixing in enough to achieve desired shade.

Spread on top of cupcakes and decorate before they harden. Cover with plastic wrap held above cupcakes with toothpicks.

Rich Chocolate Frosting

Preparation and Frosting Time: 15-20 Minutes

Equipment

Electric Mixer, bowl
Medium size sauce pan
Measuring spoons and cups

Spatula, rubber and metal
Chopping knife
Cutting board

Ingredients

8 ounces semisweet or bittersweet chocolate chips or bars broken into pieces, and finely chopped
3/4 cup heavy cream
1/2 cup unsalted butter (1 stick), room temperature

Bring cream, to a boil in a heavy saucepan. Add chocolate and immediately remove from the heat. Stir until chocolate is melted and absolutely smooth. Heat a bit more if chocolate won't all melt, taking care not to scorch. Cool to room temperature.

Cream butter in a bowl with the electric mixer, until soft. Add chocolate mixture slowly, incorporating a bit at a time. Spread immediately onto cupcakes and decorate.

Refrigerate cupcakes to maintain butter cream frosting up until 1-2 hours before serving. Keep covered with plastic wrap held above cup cakes with toothpicks.

Apple Crumb Pie

Preparation Time: 30 Minutes
Cooking Time: 45-60 Minutes

Equipment

9 inch pie pan
Mixing Bowl
Measuring spoons and
  cups

Pastry Cutter/Food Processor
  with plastic blade
Rolling Pin
Scraper

Ingredients for Crust

½   cup shortening or softened
      unsalted butter, or ¼ cup
      of each

1⅓ cups all-purpose flour
1   teaspoon salt
3-4 teaspoons ice water

Ingredients for Filling

6-8 Mackintosh, Red Delicious
      or Granny Smith apples,
      depending on apple size
4   tablespoons flour (5 if using
      Delicious)

½   cup sugar, ⅛ cup more if
      using Granny Smith
1   teaspoon cinnamon
½   teaspoon nutmeg

Ingredients for Topping

8   tablespoons (1 stick)
      unsalted butter, room
      temperature

2   cups all-purpose flour
1   cup packed brown sugar
1   teaspoon cinnamon

For the Crust: Method One, Food Processor

Place butter, salt and flour into food processor fitted with plastic blade and whirl until broken into fine pieces. Add three tablespoons ice water and blend until it pulls away from sides of container. If too dry, slowly add a few drops more of water. It doesn't last long. If over-processed, dough becomes tough.

Remove from container and place on floured work surface. Lightly flour surface of dough and rolling pin, pick up dough and make sure not sticking on bottom, add more flour, if necessary. Roll evenly, in both directions, until a circle is formed about ⅛-¼ inch thick. If dough is too wet to work, add more flour, knead it through dough and try again. Measure size of dough circle with inverted pie pan to make sure it is large enough. Carefully, with a scraper, peel dough away from work surface and roll onto rolling pin. Drape over pie pan and unroll, leaving about a ½ drape over the sides; you will roll this under for the edge of the pastry crust. Cut off any excess. Crimp pastry edge, placing index finger on edge and squeezing dough on each side, repeat around entire circumference.

For the Crust: Method Two, Pastry Cutter, The Old-Fashioned Way

Place butter, shortening, salt and flour into mixing bowl. Using a pastry cutter or two knives, cut into pea sized pieces. Add three tablespoons iced water and stir with fork. Feel dough with fingers. It should stick together, without being too dry or wet. Adjust flour or water if needed. Dough should pull away from bowl. Proceed as above. I believe this method gives a flakier, more tender pastry crust.

For Filling

Preheat over to 375 degrees.

Peel and core apples, slice in half and then into ¼ to ⅜ inch wedges. Try to maintain equal size pieces so pie cooks evenly. Place apples in bowl with all the other ingredients for the filling. Mix together and pour into the crust. Press down gently to close up gaps between apples.

For Topping

Mix all ingredients together in a bowl. Use your hands to break up the butter and mix it ito the sugar, flour and cinnamon. By pressing bits together, you will get crumbs. Sprinkle crumbs evenly over top of pie, covering all spaces and cracks; get them right up to the edge of the crust.

Place pie in a pre-heated 375 degree oven for 45-60 minutes or until crust is brown and a sharp knife slips easily into an apple slice. Remove from oven and cool on rack. I always feel it is best to bake pie the day it will be eaten as the crust is flakier and bottom won't be too soggy.

Candied Apples

Preparation Time: 10 Minutes
Cooking Time: 20 Minutes

Equipment

Measuring spoons and cups
Waxed or parchment paper, or greased paper
12-14 lollipop, ice stick pops or heavy bamboo skewers
Candy thermometer
Pastry brush/damp cloth around a fork
1 quart saucepan with lid
Sturdy box or Styrofoam piece (from craft store where pop sticks can also be purchased). Cut small slits in box with knife into which apples will be inserted to harden.

Ingredients

12 small red apples or Lady Apples, washed and dried
Options of: melted semi-sweet chocolate, shredded coconut, chopped nuts, multi color sprinkles. OR funny faces can be applied using left over syrup as glue for marshmallow pieces, licorice strips, life savers, raisins, gum drops, candy corn etc.

**The candy coating will be made in 2 batches to allow enough time for the apples to be coated before the candy hardens. Have a larger saucepan with a couple of inches of boiling water standing ready, if needed, before you begin.

Have any extra coatings you may want to apply standing at the ready as well, next to stove. The apples dry quickly.

Coating: Each of Two Times

2 cups sugar
$\frac{2}{3}$ cup light corn syrup
1 cup water
1 to 2 inches of stick cinnamon
Red food coloring

Insert sticks into the stem end of the washed and dried apples. Remove stem, if necessary. Place next to saucepan at stove.

Combine the first 4 ingredients in saucepan; stir so sugar doesn't sit on the bottom of the pan. Cover with lid until it boils

258

for about 30 seconds, stops crystallization on side of pan. Remove lid and insert candy thermometer. Do not stir. When temperature reaches 300 degrees (brittle), lower heat and maintain at 280 degrees and wipe away any sugar crystals from side of pan, if there are any, with a dampened pastry brush or damp cloth around a fork. Remove from heat and throw out cinnamon sticks.

Add red food coloring and stir in, do not over stir. **Be careful; hot sugar syrup causes nasty burns. You may want to work with an oven mitt on your hand.**

Working quickly, hold each apple by the stick and dip into the syrup, covering apple completely. You may have to tip the pan to do it. Twirl apple to spread sugar syrup evenly and place apple upright into box or Styrofoam, making sure apples do not touch. If you want to coat with chocolate of nuts, etc, dip them in a bowl of the ingredient before placing out to dry. Or, use left over syrup to apply candy faces, see above. This batch should cover 6 small size apples.

**If syrup thickens too quickly, place over pan of boiling water (creating a double boiler) to keep it liquid. When first batch is completed, wash pan and begin again. Soaking in hot water melts residue easily.

Candy Corn on a Stick

Preparation Time: 20 Minutes
Cooking Time: 10 Minutes
For "Treat" Bags
Makes 20, leftovers for Trick or Treat

Equipment

Large heavy bottom saucepan or
  Dutch oven
Large mixing bowl, or work in 2
  batches
Measuring cups
Wax or parchment paper

Clear cellophane wrap
Orange or black ribbon
  (inexpensive variety that curls
  with a scissors)
Treat bag to fit

Ingredients

50   large marshmallows
⅓   cup butter, cut into pieces
     Wooden stirring spoon
20   cups **popped** corn,
       unsalted*
2   cups "Teddy Bear" chocolate
       graham crackers, or
       similar

2½   cups candy corn
     Non-stick vegetable spray or
       vegetable oil
20   lollipop or ice cream pop
       sticks

*See Thanksgiving for how to pop corn

In heavy saucepan or Dutch oven, combine marshmallows
and butter and melt over medium-low heat. Remove from heat.
Combine popcorn and crackers in large mixing bowl, or work it
in two batches. Pour all or half of marshmallow/butter combination over popcorn and crackers and toss to coat. Add all or half
of candy corn. Stir. Lay out waxed or parchment paper. Coat
hands with non-stick spray or vegetable oil and shape mixture
into 3-inch balls. Immediately insert stick. Cool on waxed or
parchment paper. When cool, wrap decoratively in cellophane;
tie with orange or black ribbon; curl with a scissors.

Beverages

Hot Mulled Cider

Preparation Time: 5 Minutes
Cooking Time: 30 Minutes

Equipment

Coffee urn or large fondue pot or
   chafing dish (Sterno or alcohol
   fuel)
Ladle

Measuring cups
Large 6-8 quart sauce pan
Cheese cloth

Ingredients

1	gallon apple cider	½	cup raisins, optional
12	whole all spice		OR
4	cinnamon sticks		Commercially prepared
6	whole cloves		cider/spice mix

If you have a coffee urn, you can use it to prepare the cider as well as keep it hot. Place it in a central area where guests can help themselves. Plug it in 30 minutes prior to arrival of guests and forget it!

Cider can be made in a saucepan on the stove and transferred to a large fondue pot or chafing dish, in batches. Maintain heat with Sterno or alcohol burners, depending on type.

Place spices in cheesecloth and tie. Put raisins and cider in the pot with cheese-cloth filled spices and slowly heat for 30 minutes. The longer it stands the stronger the spices become. Decide how strong you like it as you go along. Remove the cheesecloth at that point.

If using commercially prepared spice mix, follow directions for quantity.

Serve in small cups.

Café Diablo

Preparation Time: 5 Minutes
Cooking Time: 10 Minutes

Equipment

Coffee pot
Chafing Dish or Fondue Pot:
   Sterno or alcohol fuel
Paring knife
Stripper (for citrus)
Measuring cups
Ladle

Strainer to fit into demitasse cups
Matches
Demitasse cups: recipe will serve
   12 for this size cup. If cups are
   larger, increase quantities in
   recipe accordingly.

Ingredients

    Favorite coffee
5   cups of freshly brewed coffee
16   demitasse sugar cubes
    (small)
3   broken sticks of cinnamon
12   whole all spice
    Peel of 2 medium-size
    oranges, removed in thin
    strips

    Peel of 1 lemon, removed in
    thin strips
1   cup brandy or Calvados
    (apple based brandy)

Do this process in front of your guests at the dessert table; it is very impressive! Have all ingredients assembled on a tray before you begin.

Turn flame on high under chafing dish or fondue pot. Mix spices, peels and sugar in chafing dish. Pour in the brandy, reserving 1 tablespoon. Pour 1 tablespoon in ladle and ignite with a match. Ladle the flaming alcohol over the sugar to melt it. It should catch on fire. Let it burn a while, then add the hot coffee and stir well. Ladle into demitasse cups through a small strainer. Garnish with a piece of peel.

Thanksgiving
Fourth Thursday in November

History

Tradition holds that Thanksgiving was first celebrated in October 1621, by the fifty-five remaining Pilgrims who had arrived on the Mayflower. Having landed the year before as a company of 102 persons, these grateful celebrants invited ninety Wampanoag Indians to join them in a feast to thank God for a bountiful harvest. The Pilgrims wanted to thank the Indians for showing them how to cultivate new world foods, such as squash, pumpkin and corn, and to hunt and fish for the wide variety of animals, fish and shellfish found in America. Without their benevolent assistance it is doubtful if the remaining Pilgrims would have survived that first winter. The celebration lasted for three days and it is said that four women and two teen girls cooked all the meals, serving partridge, duck, goose, venison, pumpkin and corn. It has not been determined if wild turkey was eaten that first Thanksgiving.

The concept of a Day of Thanksgiving derives from the old English tradition, "Harvest Home," a religious day of giving thanks for a bountiful harvest when the last of the year's crops were brought in from the fields. In America, Thursday was selected early as a day of thanksgiving, because Saturdays were days to prepare for a holy day of worship on Sunday, Monday was often a day with religious carry overs and Friday was deemed too "Roman" (Catholic) for the American Puritan ethic. Thursdays were also lecture days in old Boston where afternoon sermons were delivered in the churches. So, it was an easy adaptation to have Thanksgiving on a Thursday. Initiated on a regular basis in the 1660's in New England, the idea spread throughout the colonies during the American Revolution. In 1777, the First Continental Congress held the first National Day of Thanksgiving after the Continental Army defeated British

General Burgoyne in Saratoga, New York, on October 17. In America, as the years passed, a 'Day of Thanksgiving' was proclaimed sporadically by various State Governors at various times during the calendar year to honor victory in war, give thanks for a bountiful harvest, or just to pray for the general well being. The secularization of an autumnal harvest holiday gained momentum during the second half of the nineteeth century with the industrialization of the American economy and the resulting shift of population to cities from the farms and the seasonal rhythms of an agricultural economy. In the cities and its factories, there was little time left for recreation, much less for an appreciation of bountiful harvests. It was from this mid-nineteenth century period of urbanization that games, sports competitions and parades made their presence felt during the time traditionally set aside for prayers of Thanksgiving. In 1863, President Abraham Lincoln issued a proclamation that the last Thursday in November be set aside as a "national day of giving thanks for fruitful fields and healthful skies." The holiday bounced around in date from the last Thursday in November to the fourth Thursday until November 26, 1941, when President Franklin Roosevelt issued a proclamation that Thanksgiving would always be celebrated on the fourth Thursday in November. And so it has remained as a day of reverence and prayer for some, a day of football games and parades for others, and a feasting on autumnal produce for all.

As the Pilgrim families extended hospitality to the Indians, so today Thanksgiving is a time when a home is opened to good friends and acquaintances often isolated and far from their 'home base' in today's mobile society. Thanksgiving is a time to share.

Decoration

Thanksgiving is a meaningful occasion which warrants setting up a formal table and bringing out the "good china and silver," if you have it. White damask or autumnal colored linen, coordinating flowers, a cornucopia of fruit or harvest gourds, miniature pumpkins, colored leaves, ivy and classic candles lend a formality and solemnity to the giving of thanks. Napkins can be folded in an intricate pattern, and place cards can be used if there is a large gathering. If there are a lot of small children in the aggregate family, a separate table can be set up especially for them with appropriate paper, wooden or corn husk turkey or other colorful decorations reflecting the holiday. Having a children's table not only relieves conversational pressure for the adults, as well as the children, but it's been my experience, that over the years, bonds are formed within the peer group that go beyond the holidays. Graduating to the 'grown-up' table can become a cherished rite of passage.

Menu

Thanksgiving is a holiday where family traditions imprinted in childhood are remembered with comforting ritual over a lifetime. If there are family or childhood traditions meaningful to you, they should be remembered in the selection of the menu and exhibited in the presentation of the meal. If three are none, it is time to establish your own by always serving at least one item that everyone loves and looks forward to eating every year.

Select your dinner hour according to your family traditions, attending an early morning parade, a high school football game or Dad's need to see 'the big one' on TV that afternoon.

If everyone ends up in the family room watching a game later in the day, consider having popcorn, cheese, chips and salsa or small sandwiches on hand for post-dinner snacks.

Because a Thanksgiving meal is grandiose and filling, do not serve too many hors d'oeuvres and snacks beforehand. Keep the folks hungry. They will enjoy the meal more. Don't wait too long between the arrival of your family and guests and the serving of the meal, no more than an hour.

Thanksgiving Dinner for 10

Select your menu, there are options offered, and make up your shopping list as suggested in the introduction.

Menu

Hors d'Oeuvres
Select Two:
Cheesies
    OR
Endive Boats
    OR
Shrimp Cocktail
    OR
Popcorn, Salted, Herbed

Bowl with Mixed Nuts in Shell, Nutcracker and Small Dish
    for Shells

First Course
Corn Bisque
    OR
Oyster Stew

Main Course
Roast Turkey Garnished with Sugared Fruit
Gravy
Nana's Pennsylvania Dutch Stuffing (Bread, Vegetable,
    Potato)
    OR
Dad's Stuffing (Roast Chestnut, Sweet Potato)
Cauliflower, Brussels Sprouts Platter
Peas with Pearl Onions
Indian Succotash
Cranberry Compote with Apricots and Ginger
Canned Cranberry Sauce
Relish Tray
Pumpkin/Raisin Muffins
Herbed Baking Powder Sticks

Options
Scalloped Potatoes (if not using Potato Stuffing)
    OR
Candied Sweet Potatoes (if not using Sweet Potato Stuffing)
continued . . .

Desserts
Select 2-3 for 10 people
Pumpkin Pie
Cranberry-Apple Tart
Spice Cake with Caramel Frosting
Indian Pudding
Chocolate Dipped Apricots

Beverages
Coffee
Tea
Wine: Rose or Beaujolais Nouveau
After-Dinner Drinks: Fra Angelico, Grand Marnier, Cognac, Creme de Menthe

Timetable

One-Week Prior
Order fresh turkey: if turkey is frozen, allow 1 day for every five pounds defrosting time in the refrigerator; buy accordingly.

Two Days Prior
Shop for groceries and pick up fresh turkey
Make cheesies and refrigerate
Dip apricots and refrigerate
Put out nut bowl
Make cranberry compote

One Day Prior
Make soup
Buy oysters
Bake spice cake and frost
Bake pumpkin/raisin muffins
Bake herbed baking powder sticks
Clean endive
Make cheese filling for endive boats
Clean all vegetables
Clean vegetables for relish tray and refrigerate

continued . . .

Clean and cook shrimp, if fresh
Make Dad's chestnut dressing
Determine time you will start turkey in the morning
Make Indian pudding
*Bake pumpkin pie and refrigerate
*Bake cranberry-apple tart

*I believe pies taste better if served on the day they are baked, but if you have an early dinner hour, you should do them the day prior.

Arrange flowers and put candles in holders, arrange place cards or decide who is sitting where
Fold napkins and set table(s)

Same Day:
Start turkey when appropriate
*Bake pumpkin pie
*Bake cranberry-apple tart
*See above
Make potato stuffing, put to side, reheat one hour prior
    to serving
Pop corn
Pipe cheese blend into endive leaves
Prepare sugared fruit garnish
Make optional potato selection and prepare to bake ac-
    cording to serving time
Cook the oysters as soon as turkey is out of oven
Defrost shrimp, if frozen and cooked
Make topping for cauliflower
Whip cream for corn bisque

Thirty Minutes Before Guests Arrive:
Place cheesies in oven
Arrange shrimp on serving plate with toothpicks and cock-
    tail sauce
Place vegetables in saucepans with water, ready to cook
Put relish tray on dinner table
Take chocolate covered apricots and pumpkin pie out of re-
    frigerator

continued . . .

Arrange desserts on dining room side board or out of the
way in the kitchen
Remove soup from refrigerator
Check that stuffing and potatoes are ready to cook or are
already in the oven if appropriate to dinner hour.
Prepare coffee pot, but do not start

Twenty Minutes Before Dinner
Check on stuffing and potatoes
Reheat soup
Put muffins and bread sticks in aluminum foil and place in
350 degree oven to heat
Put butter on table
Garnish turkey and place on table if carving at table or
carve turkey and garnish platter
Open the wine

Five Minutes Prior to Dinner
Start vegetables on low heat during first course service; do
not over cook
Put corn bread and muffins on table
Ladle soup into bowls and garnish with whipped cream be-
fore guests come to the table
Start the coffee (and/or tea)

Recipes

Hors d'Oeuvres

Cheesies

Preparation Time: 15 Minutes, Plus 10
1-2 Hours Chilling Time
Cooking Time: 30-35 Minutes

The dough of this cheese-filled pastry must be chilled before it can be rolled and stuffed. It will make 4, six and one half inch 'logs.' They can be prepared 2 days ahead and even sooner, if frozen. If frozen, defrost before baking.

Equipment

Cheese grater
Mixing bowl
Measuring cups and spoons
Spatula
Electric mixer

Plastic wrap or waxed paper
Rolling pin
Jelly roll pan or pan with low lip
Non-stick cooking spray

Ingredients

1 cup unsalted butter (2 sticks or ½ pound); if using salted butter omit salt in recipe
2½ cups all-purpose flour, plus enough for dusting rolling pin and rolling surface

1 cup sour cream
¼ teaspoon salt
1 pound coarsely grated sharp cheddar cheese
Sweet paprika (optional)

Bring butter to room temperature. Place in mixing bowl and beat with electric mixer until smooth. Beat in the sour cream, then the flour and salt until all is incorporated into a dough. Take four sheets of waxed paper or plastic wrap about 12-14 inches in length.

Divide dough equally into 4 pieces and place one on each piece of paper. Dough is sticky. Cover with part of the paper/wrap and flatten a bit with palm of hand. It will make rolling easier later on. Wrap tightly and place in refrigerator for at least one hour.

When dough is firm, dust rolling surface with flour and roll one of the pieces of dough until it is rectangular in shape and about 6½ inches long by 4½ inches high. Take ¼ of the grated cheese and scatter on top of the dough, leaving the dough free from cheese about ½ inch around the edge. Starting from the long side of the dough, start to wrap the cheese-filled dough over on itself, turning in the ends after the first turn. You want to tightly wrap the dough; no cheese should protrude and there can be no holes. Pinch seam well so cheese doesn't spill out during cooking (some will anyway). Sprinkle with paprika. Wrap Cheesie in plastic wrap and place in refrigerator (or freezer if using at a later date). Repeat process with the other pieces of dough.

When ready to bake, preheat oven to 350 degrees. Use nonstick cooking spray or lightly grease a jelly roll tray or other tray with lip. Place 1-4 Cheesies on tray and place in oven for about 35-40 minutes, or until golden brown. If Cheesie is frozen, defrost and proceed as above. They should be served warm. You may want to stagger the baking time on the Cheesies so there will always be a warm batch coming. After they have set a couple of minutes, cut into 1 inch slices and place on a serving plate. They can be crumbly but taste delicious. Serve with cocktail napkins.

Endive Boats

Preparation Time: 15 Minutes
Can be prepared one day prior

Equipment

Mixing bowl
Measuring spoons and cups
Spatula
*4B piping tube

*Pastry bag
Paper toweling
Plastic bag

Ingredients

2   small heads Belgian endive
¾   cup whipped cream cheese, softened
¼   cup crumbled blue cheese
½   teaspoon dried dill

Few drops of milk, as needed
Roast pepper strips for garnish, can be purchased in a jar, or see recipe in Columbus Day

Cut bottom stem off of endive, the end at which all the leaves are joined. Carefully separate the leaves and wash in cold water. Dry on toweling and refrigerate in a sealed plastic bag. This can be done 1-2 days before serving.

Blend the whipped cream cheese, blue cheese and dill in a small bowl. Add milk, drop by drop, until a piping consistency is attained. Place into a pastry bag fitted with the 4B tip and pipe into the endive leaf. Garnish with a thin strip of roasted pepper. If you don't have the roasted pepper, sweet paprika or even a small sprig of fresh dill will add color.

If you don't have a pastry bag, spoon the mixture into the leaf and striate with the tines of a fork for a decorative effect.

If preparing a day ahead of use, place cheese mixture into plastic wrap and refrigerate until 20-30 minutes before filling the endive. It needs to soften. If it has stiffened too much overnight, add a drop or two of milk to attain the consistency needed to pipe and proceed as above.

Shrimp Cocktail

Preparation Time: 15 Minutes
Cooking Time: 3-5 Minutes

Equipment

Colander   Ice
Paring knife   Large bowl

Ingredients

1½ pounds medium-size shrimp, fresh
    OR
1-2 pounds frozen, cooked and shelled
Two stalks of fresh basil
1-2 lemons
1 bottle prepared seafood cocktail sauce/relish

Place shrimp in a colander and wash with cold water. It gets rid of the fishy smell. Drain.

To clean the fresh shrimp, peel off the shell by placing your fingers under the legs and peeling back across the fleshy back of the shrimp. You may want to leave the tail in tact for serving and holding.

Place a shelled shrimp on a cutting board and use a small knife to make an incision about ¼" deep, starting at the head end of the shrimp. Continue to cut about halfway down the back. There should be a thin black vein or a soft grey or orange-colored mass that needs to be removed. Wash under cold water again to remove any traces. Repeat with the remaining shrimp.

Place shrimp in a saucepan with enough cold water to cover the shrimp. Add the basil leaves. If none are available, a teaspoon of dry basil can be substituted. Cut lemon in quarters and place in saucepan.

Bring to a boil and turn heat down so it continues in a slow boil. The water runs over the top of the pot easily! When shrimp turn pink, they are done, about 3-5 minutes depending on the size of your shrimp. Do not over cook.

Drain immediately into a colander and rinse with cold water to stop the cooking process.

Cool shrimp, place and seal in a plastic bag until serving time. Place in the coldest part of the refrigerator. If possible, place the bag of shrimp in a large bowl and cover with ice.

273

If you have purchased frozen shrimp, defrost in bag in which they came, place in colander and rinse with cold water.

Serve on toothpicks and place on a bed of greens with the dipping sauce in the center of the tray. Have a small dish or coaster available for toothpicks. Garnish with lemon slices or wedges, if desired.

Popcorn

Preparation Time: 2 Minutes
Cooking Time: 5-7 Minutes

Equipment

Corn popper
    OR
8-10 quart pot with lid

Measuring cups and spoons
Large serving bowl

Ingredients

Vegetable oil to film bottom of pot
1½ cups popping corn
Salt to taste
1 tablespoon dried basil
1½ teaspoons dried thyme

Film bottom of pan with vegetable oil and heat until you see smoke rising. Pour in popping corn and immediately cover with lid. Shake pot until all kernels have stopped popping. Quickly pour into bowl, salt to taste and toss with herbs.

When cold, cover with plastic wrap until serving, keep out of humidity. Or, you can keep it warm in a metal bowl in a 200 degree oven. In any event, heating is a good idea.

First Course

Corn Bisque

Preparation Time: 10 Minutes
Cooking Time: One Hour

Equipment

2 Quart Double boiler . . . or one
   large pot inside another
Food Processor or Blender
Ladle
Measuring spoons and cups

Can opener
Whisk
2 Small sauce pans
Sieve, fine mesh

Ingredients

3 cans (17 ounces each) cream
   style corn
1 medium size onion, peeled
   and cut in eights
1 stalk celery, cleaned and cut
   into large pieces
3 cups chicken stock or broth
   (fresh or canned)
4½ cups milk, divided
¼ cup butter

½ cup flour
1 tablespoon Worcestershire
   sauce
1 teaspoon celery salt
   Salt and White pepper to
   taste
1 cup heavy cream for
   whipping
¼ teaspoon chili powder

Start water in bottom pan of double boiler and bring to boil.

Place corn, onion and celery into a food processor fitted with a metal blade (or use a blender) Cover and purée. Pour into the double boiler.

Add the chicken stock, your own or canned, and 3½ cups of the milk. Cover and cook 45 minutes.

Melt the butter in a separate saucepan. Stir in the flour and cook over a medium heat for about 2 minutes. Do not brown. Whisk constantly. Meanwhile, heat the other cup of milk in a separate pan and bring to a simmer. Pour into the flour and butter mixture, regulating the heat so it doesn't scorch and whisk until thick and creamy. Add the Worcestershire sauce, and celery salt. Remove from the heat.

Place the corn mixture through a fine mesh sieve. Wipe out the top pot of the double boiler. Return the corn mixture to the double boiler and whisk in the cream sauce. Add salt and white pepper to taste. Can be prepared ahead to this point.

Before serving, heat soup in a double boiler until very hot.

Whip the heavy cream until almost stiff; sprinkle in chili pepper and whip until stiff. After soup is ladled into the bowls, top with a dollop of whipped cream.

Oyster Stew

Preparation Time: 10 Minutes
Cooking Time: 20 Minutes

Equipment

3 quart sauce pan
Ladle
Wooden stirring spoon
Measuring cups and spoons

Potato peeler
Chopping knife
Whisk
2 small sauce pans

Ingredients

4	medium potatoes, peeled and diced into cubes	¼	teaspoon freshly ground black pepper
2	carrots, peeled and finely chopped	4	tablespoons flour
4	stalks celery, chopped	12	tablespoons butter (1½ sticks)
2	quarts milk	1	quart shucked oysters and their liquid
2	tablespoons chopped onion	4	tablespoons chopped parsley
1	teaspoon salt		

Have your seafood store open the oysters for you as they are difficult to pry open and the process will take a lot of time if you are not used to shucking oysters. The shells can also cut your fingers. Be sure to tell your seafood store to reserve the liquid that comes out of the shells. You need it to cook the oysters. Keep the oysters on ice until day of use. Buy oysters no more than one day prior to serving.

Combine the potatoes, carrots, celery in a 3 quart saucepan. Add enough cold water to cover vegetables, add salt and pepper. Boil until vegetables and potatoes are tender. Drain the water. Add one quart of milk to the potatoes and vegetables and bring to a simmer.

Place one quart of milk in a separate saucepan and bring to the boiling point.

Place 4 tablespoons of the butter into still another saucepan, and as it melts, add the flour and whisk together to form a roux. Do not brown, but cook for two minutes or so, stirring constantly.

Add the quart of hot milk to the roux, stirring until it has thickened. Add this mixture to the other milk, potato and vegetable mixture and whisk together until it is completely blended and thickened.

May be made ahead to this point. Reheat the soup before proceeding, being careful not to scorch the bottom of the pan.

No more than 20 minutes before serving, place the balance of the butter (8 tablespoons) into a saucepan and melt. Add the oysters and their liquid and cook until the edges curl. Add to the heated soup mixture and serve immediately. Ladle into soup bowls and garnish with the chopped parsley.

Main Course

Roast Turkey with Sugared Fruit Garnish

Preparation Time: 30 Minutes
Cooking Time: 4 to 4¹/₂ Hours Unstuffed;
4¹/₂ to 5¹/₂ Hours Stuffed
Allow 30 Minutes Rest Before Carving

Equipment

Roasting pan with rack to hold turkey slightly off bottom of pan
Paring knife
Meat thermometer, to place in thigh while cooking or instant reading thermometer

Poultry pin
Basting tube
Aluminum foil

Ingredients

22-24 pound freshly killed turkey
2 teaspoons dried thyme or 3 branches of fresh thyme
2 teaspoons dried basil or 3 branches fresh basil

Salt
Black pepper
4 tablespoons butter, softened
Non-stick cooking spray

Before you start, make sure your turkey fits into the roasting pan and the pan fits into your oven!

Preheat oven to 350 degrees.

If you are going to use a frozen turkey allow the appropriate time to defrost safely. Leave in refrigerator, wrapped, and allow 1 day of thawing for every 5 pounds of turkey.

I advise ordering a freshly killed turkey from your butcher at least one week prior to need. Even supermarket chains take orders and provide high quality turkeys, when requested.

I do not recommend using self-basting turkeys, as the basting liquid injected into the turkey flesh is usually full of chemicals. A correctly roasted turkey will be juicy and will have no need for 'additives,' especially artificial ones.

When ready to use, cook, unwrap the turkey over the sink as there will be blood in the packaging. Most turkeys are packaged with the neck and gizzard, heart and liver packed into the neck and inside cavities. You will have to carefully undo the legs from the way they have been packed, either from under a flap of skin or from being inserted into a metal or plastic brace. Do not tear or break because you want to reinsert the legs once the inside has been cleaned out and the turkey stuffed. Look inside the turkey and remove any remaining pieces, or paper bag of innards. Check the neck opening. Put the neck, heart and gizzard to the side for basting broth and gravy. Toss out the liver, unless you sauté it separately, mince it and add to the gravy at finishing time; it will give a bitter taste to the gravy if cooked with the other innards.

Wash out the inside of the turkey and remove all fatty deposits on the flaps of the turkey sides and bottom. Remove any inside pieces of innards or red spongy looking material that grows alongside the backbone. Rinse again until water runs clear. Pull any fat deposits from inside of neck flap. Check turkey for pin feathers, usually along wings, neck flap or crevices. Remove them by pulling against them with a small knife, one at a time.

Remove turkey from sink and pat inside and outside dry with paper toweling.

If stuffing the turkey, place stuffing inside the neck and abdominal cavities. Do not overstuff. Proceed as below. **Do not stuff in advance** as bacteria will grow. Once stuffed, the turkey must go immediately into the oven.

If not stuffing the turkey, mix 2 teaspoons of salt, 1 teaspoon of black pepper, thyme and basil together and rub into the cavity of the turkey. If using fresh herbs, salt and pepper the inside and place the stalks of herbs inside the turkey.

Carefully replace the legs into the band of skin or into the brace. Tie together with string if nothing is there to hold them. Pull the neck skin underneath the turkey towards the back and fasten with a poultry pin, or tuck under the bird.

Tuck the wing tips under the back of the turkey, tucking the neck skin flap underneath the wing tips. If this is too difficult, leave them as they are. The larger the turkey, the more difficult this becomes.

Spray the roasting pan with non-stick spray to prevent turkey from sticking to the sides and bottom. Place a flat rack or special turkey rack inside the pan and spray with non-stick spray. Place turkey into pan, breast side up. Smear with softened butter and place into the oven.

Prepare the basting broth; see below. Baste the turkey every 30 minutes. Make sure the liquid which forms in body cavity drains out; use baster to remove it as the turkey cooks; place juice in roasting pan. Do not baste for the last hour so skin crisps. If turkey is getting too brown on the breast or legs, cover lightly with aluminum foil.

Many turkeys come with a pop out thermometer stuck into one of the breast sides. When it pops up, the turkey should be done. Double check internal temperature with an instant read thermometer or meat thermometer placed into the thickest part of the thigh, towards the back, in several locations, a large bird isn't always done at the joint. Meat is done when thermometer registers 180-185 degrees. Legs should move easily and meat should feel soft.

When removing turkey from pan, drain any juices from the inside of the turkey into the pan.

Turkey should sit at least 20-30 minutes before cutting, and can sit more if you don't mind cooler turkey.

Basting Broth

Preparation Time: 5 Minutes
Cooking Time: 1¹/₂ hours

Equipment

2 quart saucepan
Measuring cups
Wooden spoon

Ingredients

	Turkey neck	1	sprig fresh thyme or 1
	heart, gizzard		teaspoon dried herb
1	stalk celery, cut up into 3	1	sprig fresh basil or 1
	pieces, with leaves on		teaspoon dried herb
1	cleaned, peeled carrot, sliced	1	teaspoon salt
	into 4 pieces	¼	teaspoon black pepper
1	medium size onion	4	cups water

Wash turkey neck, remove skin and throw away. Clean gizzard of fat and wash heart. Do not use the liver as it will impart a bitter taste to the broth. Reserve to cook separately, if you wish, by sautéing in a little butter and dicing into the finished gravy before serving.

Place turkey parts, and balance of ingredients into saucepan and bring to a simmer, not a rolling boil. Skim off any residue as it rises. Cook until meat on neck is tender. Use to baste turkey.

Strain broth and cool. This broth will be used for part of the gravy. Put to the side until the turkey is cooked.

Gravy with White Wine

Preparation and Cooking Time: 10 Minutes

Equipment

Wooden spoon
Whisk
Small bowl or cup

Measuring spoons and cups
Medium size saucepan

Ingredients

1 cup of dry white wine, optional
turkey broth, above
heart and gizzards, chopped fine, optional
3 tablespoons cornstarch
½ cup cold water

If there is any fat on top of the basting broth, remove it by skimming with a spoon.

After turkey has been removed from the pan, set the pan on the stove (it may require 2 burners to cover the bottom of the pan). Pour 1 cup of basting broth into the pan, to deglaze rack and pan. Scrape any brown bits off the rack and remove from the pan. Scrape the sides and bottom of the roasting pan and stir. If there is skin stuck on the bottom of the pan, try to remove as much as possible. You will strain the broth before adding the final touches. Bring to a boil. You will need 3-4 cups of gravy. The amount of liquid remaining in the pan after the turkey has been removed will determine how much extra basting broth you need to add to get your 3-4 cups. Add the balance of the broth and bring to a boil skimming off any fat that rises.

Remove from the heat and strain gravy into a saucepan. Use either a fine mesh sieve or cheesecloth.

If you have a couple of hours, let stand. Fat will rise to surface. Remove it. If you must proceed quickly to bring the meal to the table, turn up the heat under the saucepan. As the gravy begins to boil the fat will rise to the top in a froth. Remove with a spoon until clear of fatty residue. A piece of paper toweling ripped into 3-4 inch strips and pulled across the top of the gravy will also help remove the fat.

Add the white wine and continue to reduce the gravy. If you want it thicker, take an additional ½ cup of white wine or cold water and dissolve 3 tablespoons of cornstarch into the wine. Add to the gravy slowly, stirring all the while. Only add enough cornstarch slurry to obtain the consistency you want.

Add the chopped gizzards and heart and liver, if desired. Gravy is ready to serve.

Sugared Fruit Garnish for Turkey

Preparation Time: 10 Minutes
Can Be Done Several Hours Before Serving

Equipment
2 Cookie/cake cooling racks
Small mixing bowl
Whisk

Ingredients
Large bunch black grapes (about ½ pound)
Large bunch green seedless grapes (about ½ pound)
Large bunch red grapes (about ½ pound)
8 Lady Apples
6 Seckle or small red pears
1 Head curly endive or chicory or red leaf lettuce
2 egg whites or meringue powder, salmonella in uncooked egg whites can pose a problem.
2 cups granulated sugar

Rinse and drain fruit until dry. Rinse greens. Cut the grapes into attractive size bunches. The size of your turkey's circumference will dictate the amount of fruit you will need.

Whisk egg whites until they hold together and are frothy or mix meringue powder according to directions. Put sugar into a shallow mixing bowl. Dip the fruit into the egg white/meringue and immediately roll in the sugar, coating the fruit completely. Let the fruit dry on cooling racks. Keep away from moisture and steam.

When ready to assemble the serving platter, place the turkey in the center of the platter. Insert the greens into the open chest cavity and encircle the turkey with the greens. You are making a bed on which to place the fruit. Make sure the greens

283

are dry or the sugar on the fruits will dissolve. Arrange the fruits around the turkey and serve.

If the fruits are uneaten, they may be washed to remove the sugar and be served in their 'natural state' once more.

Stuffing versus Dressing

There is no difference between the two, except that often 'stuffing' refers to when it is cooked inside the turkey and 'dressing' is served on the side! If stuffing the turkey, only do it immediately before cooking, as bacteria will grow quickly and you risk becoming ill. When storing turkey after dinner, remove any stuffing, for the same reason.

Nana's Pennsylvania Dutch Stuffing Bread, Vegetable and Potato

Preparation Time: 45 Minutes
Cooking Time: 45 Minutes-1 Hour to Reheat in Casserole
Inside Turkey, Must Reach 165 degrees with
Instant Read Thermometer

Equipment

1-2 Ovenproof Casserole Dishes, with or without lid
Large skillet
6 quart saucepan with lid
Food processor
Wooden spoon/spatula
Measuring spoons and cups

Mixing bowl
Large saucepan with lid
Hand-held electric mixer or potato masher
Small bowl
Paring knife and chopping knife

Ingredients

5   pounds Idaho or Russet potatoes
1   teaspoon salt
2   medium-size yellow onions
4   celery stalks
2   green bell peppers (or 1 green and 1 red)
1   cup chopped parsley leaves, not stems
2   additional teaspoons salt
½   teaspoon black pepper

¾   loaf of 'stuffing' bread or other firm bread; doesn't have to be white, but don't use rye
1½   cups of milk
2   eggs, slightly beaten
4   tablespoons butter, plus 3 tablespoons
  Vegetable or canola oil to cover bottom of pan

Preheat oven to 350 degrees.

Butter casserole dish if not stuffing turkey.

Peel potatoes, cut into quarters and place in saucepan with enough water to cover. Add 1 teaspoon of salt, cover and cook until tender. Pour off the water and return pot to the stove. Let the potatoes 'dry' over a low heat, shaking pot constantly. Once moisture has evaporated, mash coarsely with potato masher, ricer or electric beater. If dry, add some milk to thin out a bit. They will acquire moisture from the bread and eggs to be added later. Moisture content can be increased later when assembling if dressing seems too heavy.

Take a large mixing bowl and break up the bread into small pieces in it. Pour milk over the bread and stir around. Let soak while cooking the vegetables.

Finely chop the onion, celery and peppers either by hand, or in the food processor, one at a time. If using food processor, be careful not to over-process; you want small pieces, not a purée. The longer you process, the more watery the vegetables become. Heat the skillet and add enough vegetable or canola oil to cover the bottom. Make sure there is enough oil, because the vegetables will be cooked slowly, without browning, until they are translucent and tender. Add the onions and the celery first. Once they are cooking for about 5 minutes, add the peppers. Stir frequently and regulate the heat to slow simmer. Do not let vegetables stick to the pan. If they have absorbed all the oil, add a bit more to prevent browning. Vegetables should be tender after 10-15 minutes of slow cooking. Add 1 teaspoon of salt and the ½ teaspoon black pepper and mix well. Add the chopped parsley.

Put the mashed potatoes into the skillet and stir the vegetables into the potatoes. Keep the heat very low or the potatoes will stick to the pan. The bread should have absorbed all the milk, if not, leave extra milk in bowl and mix bread into potato and vegetable mixture. Slowly add the 2 eggs and continue to mix until all is assimilated and heated through. Do not let eggs get to the bottom of the skillet or they may scramble. If mixture looks too wet, do not add all of the egg; if it is dry, add a bit of the leftover milk from the bread. The heat may be raised to dry out the stuffing if it is too wet.

Place into buttered casserole dishes or into the cavity of the turkey. Put a tablespoon of butter, cut into pieces over the top of the stuffing. Cover with a lid or aluminum foil. It may be prepared ahead and later cooked in a 350 degree oven for 45 minutes to 1 hour, immediately before serving. Remove the lid or aluminum foil during the last 15 minutes of cooking. Serve with the gravy.

Dad's Stuffing

Preparation Time: 45 Minutes
Cooking Time: 45 Minutes
May Be Prepared 1 Day Ahead

Equipment

Ovenproof casserole with lid, or
   use aluminum foil
2 large saucepans with lids
Paring knife
Mixing spoon

Measuring spoons
Large mixing bowl
Fork/masher
Poultry pin, if stuffing turkey

Ingredients

2	pounds of chestnuts** (see note below)	1	teaspoon salt
4	pounds sweet potatoes	¼	teaspoon pepper
¼	pound of unsalted butter, softened, plus 3 tablespoons	¼	teaspoon ground nutmeg
		1	teaspoon chopped chives
		2	tablespoons dry rosemary or 3 tablespoons fresh

**When buying chestnuts, check that the shell is firm against the nut. If there is an air pocket, it means the chestnut has started to dry out. Buy more than you need for the recipe as some may be spoiled inside. Those left over taste good in salads or added to a vegetable after it has cooked. If you can't buy fresh chestnuts try to find them in a jar, cooked and peeled. Some are called "marrons entiers" (French for whole chestnuts). You do not want "marrons glacés" (sugared).

Preheat oven to 350 degrees. Butter a casserole dish if not stuffing turkey.

Scrub the sweet potatoes and place in a saucepan with enough water to cover. Place lid on saucepan and cook over moderate heat until tender, 20-30 minutes. When done, remove from water and peel. Mash coarsely with a fork.

While the sweet potatoes are cooking, use a sharp knife to cut an "X" into the flat side of the chestnut, or cut around the circumference. Place the chestnuts in a large pot with a lid. Put enough water in the bottom of the pot to cover the chestnuts. Cook over moderate heat for about 30 minutes or until tender.

Remove from heat. Place a hot chestnut into a dishtowel to hold it more easily and with a sharp knife, peel away outer shell and brown inside covering. They break easily. Repeat until all are peeled. It's easier to peel them warm. You can reheat them if necessary. Reserve ¼ cup whole for garnish if serving in casserole dish. Mash the rest of the chestnuts coarsely.

Combine the sweet potatoes and chestnuts and mash together while still warm. Add ¼ pound of butter by tablespoons and incorporate. Add the salt, pepper and nutmeg. If too dry, add more butter. Mix in the chives and rosemary. Put inside the cavity of the turkey or into a buttered ovenproof casserole. If using a casserole, scatter reserved chestnuts on top and bake, covered with a lid or aluminum foil, in a 350 degree oven for 45 minutes. Stuff the turkey at the neck flap end and secure with a poultry pin; stuff cavity. Internal temperature must reach at least 165 degrees before serving.

Cauliflower and Brussels Sprout Platter

Preparation Time: 15 Minutes
Cooking Time: 12-15 Minutes

Equipment

Steamer for large saucepan with lid
Medium-size saucepan with lid
Measuring spoons and cups
Cooking fork
Small skillet
Wooden spoon

Ingredients

1	large head of cauliflower	¼	teaspoon basil
2	pints Brussels sprouts	½	teaspoon salt
¼	cup olive oil	⅛	teaspoon black pepper
1½	pieces of white bread toasted and crumbed	1	small clove garlic, finely minced
¼	teaspoon thyme	2	tablespoons minced parsley

Wash cauliflower, keeping in one piece. Remove outer leaves and remove the stalk. Make an "X" in the center of the core to facilitate faster cooking. Cut core down so cauliflower rests solidly on counter. Place in steamer and cook for 12-15 minutes until tender but not overcooked.

Crumble the toast into a small skillet. Pour olive oil, thyme, basil, salt, pepper, garlic and parsley over the bread and mix well. Heat to cook garlic without browning. Remove from the heat and put to the side for garnish. This can be done ahead of time, reserved on a saucer.

Wash and clean the Brussels sprouts, cutting the end of the stem and removing any yellow or browned leaves. Place in steamer or saucepan and cook until just tender. Do not over cook. Remove from water.

To serve, place cauliflower in the center of the platter. Scatter the Brussels sprouts in a circle around the cauliflower. Scatter the breadcrumb mixture over the top of the cauliflower.

Peas with Pearl Onions

Preparation Time: 10 Minutes
Cooking Time: 8-10 Minutes

Equipment

Medium-size saucepan with lid	Paring knife
Cooking fork or wooden spoon	Whisk
2 small saucepans	Measuring spoons and cups

Ingredients

2	one-pound bags or 1 two-pound bag of frozen peas or 4 pounds fresh peas	1	pound small pearl onions
		½	teaspoon oregano
		½	cup chicken broth

Optional Cream Sauce

2	teaspoons butter	1	cup heavy cream
3	teaspoons flour		Dash of nutmeg

Remove skin from onions* and place into saucepan with ½ cup chicken broth and oregano. Cook until tender, over moderate to low heat without a lid until all the broth is absorbed into the onions, about 10 minutes. May be cooked ahead to this point. *Or, place onions in boiling water for a minute and remove. Skins will pop off.*

Shell and wash peas, add water to cover and cook about 15 minutes, or until tender. Or, if using frozen, bring indicated amount of water to a boil and add frozen peas. Cook 5-8 minutes.

Drain peas and onions and mix together in a serving dish.

Cream Sauce

Heat butter and flour in small sauce pan and whisk for two minutes until butter has melted, but roux has not browned. Meanwhile in separate sauce pan, heat cream until just beginning to simmer. Remove from heat. Pour into the roux, stirring constantly until blended. Add dash of nutmeg and pour over the peas and onion. If sauce is too thick, add more cream.

Indian Succotash

Preparation Time: 10 Minutes
Cooking Time: 12-18 Minutes

Equipment

Large saucepan with lid
Wooden mixing spoon
Measuring cups and spoons

Ingredients

2	10-ounce boxes frozen yellow corn	¾	cup thinly sliced scallions
2	10-ounce boxes frozen green lima beans	½	cup diced green peppers or half red peppers
¼	cup butter	½	teaspoon salt
			Ground pepper to taste

Place ¾ to 1 cup of water in saucepan and bring to boil. Add lima beans and cook 10 minutes. Add corn, butter, scallions, and peppers, salt and pepper, bring to boil, cover and cook on moderate heat until all vegetables are tender. If there is too much liquid, turn up heat and reduce so sauce thickens. Serve with sauce so you don't lose the butter.

Cranberry Relish with Apricots and Ginger

Preparation Time: 10 Minutes
Cooking Time: 6-10 Minutes

Equipment

Chopping knife
Colander
Measuring cups and spoons

Medium size saucepan
Wooden spoon

Ingredients

4   cups cranberries (1 pound or 1 bag)
1½ cups sugar
1½ cups orange juice

1   cup apricots, small dice
¼ cup crystallized ginger, small dice

Wash and drain cranberries in colander. Pick over to remove any bad berries and stems.

Place in saucepan along with sugar, orange juice and apricots. Cook until berries "pop". Remove from heat and stir in ginger. Remove to serving dish.

Jellied Cranberry Sauce (Canned)

Preparation Time: 3-5 Minutes

Equipment

Can opener
Knife
Serving dish

Ingredients

2 16-ounce cans jellied cranberry sauce, chilled
1 orange, optional

Open cans at top and bottom and slide cranberry sauce onto serving plate. Cut into ⅜ to ½ inch slides; fan out. Refrigerate until needed. You can garnish with thinly sliced oranges around edge of plate.

Relish Tray

Preparation Time: 15 Minutes

1	7-ounce jar green olives with pimentos	3	carrots sliced into matchsticks
1	6-ounce can large pitted black olives	3	stalks celery sliced into matchsticks
2	bunches scallions	1	bunch radishes

Clean and peel carrots. Remove top and bottom of stem. Slice in half. Place the flat side against the cutting board and slice in half again and again. Cut into equal lengths.

Repeat with the celery, trying to make the celery stalks the same length as the carrots.

Remove the outer shell of the scallions by cutting the bottom (root) end off. Cut the top of the scallions off, but leave at least 3-4 inches of green. Use a sharp fine knife blade and cut the bulb of the scallion into sixths.

Wash the radishes and cut the top and bottom off. With a sharp knife cut petals down the sides of the radish.

Place all vegetables in cold water with ice cubes to crisp. Drain and serve on attractive tray with olives.

Scalloped Potatoes

Preparation Time: 10 Minutes
Cooking Time: $1^1/_2$ Hours

Equipment

4 quart ovenproof casserole
Food processor with 3-millimeter
    slicing blade or Mandoline
Potato peeler

Measuring spoons and cups
Cutting knife
Cutting Board

Ingredients

4   pounds all purpose potatoes,
     peeled and sliced into ⅛
     inch slices or thinner, if
     possible
1½   cups grated Gruyere or
     Swiss cheese

4   tablespoons all-purpose flour
     Salt and freshly ground
     pepper
3   tablespoons unsalted butter
5   cups chicken stock, low in
     salt

Preheat oven to 375 degrees. Butter the casserole dish generously.

Peel potatoes and rinse. Cut in half and using the food processor's 3 millimeter slicing blade, put through the feed tube. Or, thinly slice the potatoes manually. If not baking immediately, place in bowl and cover with cold water or potatoes will turn brown. When ready to use, drain well and pat dry. Place in a mixing bowl and toss with the flour and ½ cup of the cheese.

Mentally divide the potatoes into 3 portions and place the first third of the potatoes in the casserole, sprinkle with ⅓ of the remaining cheese and dot with bits of butter. Repeat two more times; top with cheese and butter. Pour the chicken broth over the potatoes and place into the oven at 375 degrees. **Do not let stand before cooking or the potatoes will quickly turn brown.** Cook for 1½ hours or until potatoes are tender.

Honey-Candied Sweet Potatoes

Preparation Time: 10 Minutes
Total Cooking Time: 45 Minutes

Equipment

Large ovenproof casserole dish
  with low sides, lightly buttered
Large saucepan
Paring knife

Small bowl or cup
Small saucepan
Stirring spoon
Measuring spoons and cups

Ingredients

6	large sweet potatoes	$\frac{1}{8}$	teaspoon nutmeg
$\frac{1}{2}$	teaspoon salt	$1\frac{1}{2}$	teaspoons grated lemon rind
$1\frac{1}{2}$	tablespoons cornstarch	2	teaspoons lemon juice
2	tablespoons cold water	$\frac{1}{4}$	cup orange juice
$1\frac{1}{2}$	cups honey	1	teaspoon salt
$\frac{1}{2}$	teaspoon cinnamon	6	tablespoons butter

Preheat oven to 375 degrees.

Butter a large ovenproof casserole.

Scrub the sweet potatoes and cook in boiling salted water, $\frac{1}{2}$ teaspoon, until tender, about 20-25 minutes. Drain and rinse with cold water.

Peel the sweet potatoes and cut in half, lengthwise. Place into prepared dish.

Dissolve the cornstarch in cold water. Put to the side.

Combine the honey, cinnamon, nutmeg, lemon rind, lemon juice, orange juice and 1 teaspoon salt in a saucepan. Bring to a boil.

Add the cornstarch mixture, stirring constantly. Keep on a medium heat. When mixture is thick and clear, remove from the heat and add the butter.

Pour mixture over the sweet potatoes and bake at 375 degrees for 15 minutes.

Pumpkin/Raisin Muffins

Preparation Time: 10 Minutes
Cooking Time: 20-25 Minutes

Equipment

Muffin tins (2½ inches in diameter) for 24 muffins or bake in batches; smaller tins may be used. Adjust cooking time accordingly.
Small sauce pan

Can opener
Measuring spoons and cups
2 Mixing bowls
Rubber scraper
Electric mixer

Ingredients

½ cup unsalted butter
1 cup sugar
2 eggs
1 cup mashed plain pumpkin (canned)
1 cup raisins
3 cups plus ½ cup all-purpose flour, divided

4 teaspoons baking powder
½ teaspoon cinnamon
½ teaspoon nutmeg
1 teaspoon salt
1¼ cup milk
   Non-stick cooking spray

Preheat oven to 400 degrees.

Grease muffin tins with non-stick cooking spray or hydrogenated vegetable shortening such as Crisco, or butter

Place the raisins in a small saucepan with enough water to cover the raisins. Plump raisins over moderate to low heat, until soft. This will be about 15 minutes. Check that water does not evaporate. Pour off any excess water.

Cream the butter and sugar until light and fluffy in a mixing bowl. Beat in the eggs, one at a time and then the pumpkin.

Sprinkle ½ cup of the flour over the raisins and fold over raisins with rubber spatula or spoon.

Sift 3 cups of flour, baking powder, cinnamon, nutmeg and salt together in a separate bowl or pie pan.

Dry ingredients and milk will be added in ⅓'s, alternating wet and dry until all are incorporated. Do not over-mix.

Fold in the raisins. Fill muffin tins ¾ full.

Bake at 400 degrees for 20-25 minutes. Tester should come out dry when done.

Smaller muffin tins will take much less time to bake. Don't over-bake or muffins will be tough.

295

Herbed Baking Powder Sticks

Preparation Time: 15 Minutes
Cooking Time: 20 Minutes

Equipment

Cookie Sheet
Pastry bag with large writing
   tube
Pastry brush (or paint brush kept
   for cooking)
Mixing bowl

Measuring spoons, cups
Rubber scraper
Pastry cutter
Fork
Cup

Ingredients

2	cups all-purpose flour	¼	cup hydrogenated vegetable
1	tablespoon baking powder		shortening (Crisco)
1	teaspoon dried thyme	1	cup milk
1	teaspoon ground sage	1	large egg
1	teaspoon salt		*Optional: Kosher salt

This recipe may be made the day ahead or 30 minutes before serving.

Preheat oven to 375 degrees.

In a medium size mixing bowl, combine the flour, baking powder, thyme, sage, salt and shortening. With pastry blender or two knives, cut in the shortening until the mixture resembles coarse pea-size crumbs.

Add the milk and stir quickly with a fork until the mixture forms a soft dough and pulls away from the side of the bowl.

Spoon dough into a pastry tube filled with a large mouth writing tube. Pipe dough into 24, 3½-inch strips onto an ungreased cookie sheet. Keep strips about ¾ inch apart.

Put the egg into a cup and beat with a fork. With a pastry brush, paint the dough with the beaten egg. If desired, some of the sticks can have Kosher salt scattered on top of them for a salt stick effect.

Bake 20 minutes, until golden. Serve warm. If serving the following day, cool the bread sticks and then place them in aluminum foil. Reheat them in a 375-degree oven for 10 minutes or until warm; serve.

Pumpkin Custard Pie

Preparation Time: 20 Minutes
Cooking Time: 45-55 Minutes

Equipment

9-inch pie pan
Pastry blender
Fork
Mixing bowl

Measuring spoons and cups
Electric Mixer
Rubber scraper

Ingredients

1 Pastry crust, see Introduction: Pie Crust.

If you have extra dough left over, make a pumpkin "cookie" by cutting it out with a knife or cookie cutter or do autumnal leaves. Bake on a piece of tin foil until golden; remove and cool. Place in center of cool pie.

1¾	cups mashed cooked pumpkin (canned)	2	tablespoons sugar
½	teaspoon salt	1¼	teaspoons cinnamon
1¾	cups whole milk	½	teaspoon ginger
2	large eggs, (½ cup)	½	teaspoon nutmeg
⅔	cup brown sugar	¼	teaspoon cloves

Place all the ingredients in a mixing bowl and beat together with an electric beater. Don't mix at too high of a speed or it will splatter all over.

Pour into a pastry-lined pie pan and bake in the center of a 425-degree oven and bake 45 to 55 minutes or until a knife inserted in the side of the filling comes out clean. The center may still look soft, but it will firm as pie cools on a cooling rack.

*This is a rich brown, spicy pie. For a lighter color and milder flavor use all white sugar and omit the cloves.

Cranberry/Apple Tart

Preparation Time: 30 Minutes
Baking Time: 20-25 Minutes

Equipment

9-10 inch pie plate
Colander
Measuring spoons and cups

Large saucepan
Wooden stirring spoon

Ingredients

Pie dough for 2 crusts, see
   Introduction: Bake a pie
   crust
2   cups fresh cranberries,
   washed
2   cups chopped, peeled apples

1   cup sugar
½   cup coarsely chopped
   walnuts
¼   cup water
1   teaspoon ground ginger

Wash cranberries in a colander. Peel and core apples and chop apples into ½ inch cubes. Chop nuts.

In a large saucepan, combine cranberries, apples, sugar, walnuts, ginger and water. Place on heat and bring to a boil, stirring constantly. Reduce heat and simmer for 10 minutes. Let cool while making pastry.

Make pastry dough and divide into two equal pieces. Roll the first and line pie pan. Reserve the second for top.

Fill pastry shell with cranberry/apple mixture.

Roll out the second piece of dough and cut into ½ inch strips; weave a lattice on a piece of waxed paper (see Introduction). Place on top of pie, trim as indicated in Master recipe and press the top and bottom crusts together and flute decoratively.

Bake at 400 degrees for 20-25 minutes, until crust is golden.

Spice Cake with Caramel Frosting

Preparation Time: 20 Minutes
Cooking Time: 35-40 Minutes

Equipment

2 9″ layer cake pans or 9″×13″ oblong pan
Electric Mixer
Mixing bowl
Rubber scraper/spatula

Measuring spoons, cups
Small saucepan
Sifter or fine mesh strainer
Small skillet

Ingredients
Cake

¾ cup soft vegetable shortening
1¼ cups brown sugar
1 cup white sugar
3 eggs (½ to ⅔ cups)
2¾ cups sifted white all-purpose flour
1½ teaspoons baking soda

1½ teaspoons cinnamon
¾ teaspoon nutmeg
¾ teaspoon cloves
1 teaspoon salt
1½ cups buttermilk
Non-stick cooking spray or vegetable shortening or butter to grease pans

Ingredients
Frosting

½ cup heavy cream
9 tablespoons butter
6 tablespoons granulated sugar

4½ cups sifted confectioners' sugar

Cake

Preheat oven to 350 degrees. Grease and flour cake pans, knocking out any excess flour.

Using an electric mixer, cream together shortening and sugar until fluffy. Thoroughly beat in the eggs. Sift together all the dry ingredients into a separate bowl or plate. Stir into the batter alternately with the buttermilk.

Divide batter between the two pans and bake 30-35 minutes; 45 minutes for larger cake, or until tester comes out clean.

Immediately remove cakes carefully from pans onto a cooling rack. Frost when cool.

This cake tastes best when made one day prior to serving.

Frosting

In a small saucepan, heat together the heavy cream and butter.

While butter is melting, caramelize granulated sugar in a small skillet by pouring the sugar into the pan and heating until sugar melts and colors to a light brown. Remove from the heat and pour three tablespoons of the caramelized sugar into the cream and butter mixture. Be careful as mixture will bubble up and could cause a severe burn. Mix with a wooden spoon until lumps dissolve. Gradually stir in the sifted confectioners' sugar and beat with an electric mixer until icing is smooth and creamy and is of a spreading consistency. Add more cream if mixture becomes too thick.

Place cake on plate and tear strips of waxed paper about 4 inches long to lay around the cake and slightly under it. This will make for a clean cake plate edge.

Spread about ¼-⅓ cup of frosting on bottom layer of cake. Place the top layer on top of it. Put about ½ cup of frosting on the top of the cake and spread around to edge. Using a spoon and knife or spatula, ice the sides of the cake working with strokes from the bottom of the cake to the top. Clean up any glitches. Swirl for patterned effect, if desired.

Remove waxed paper and clean up any icing that may have dripped onto the side of the plate. When frosting is set, cover and put in a cool place. Do not refrigerate.

Indian Pudding

Preparation Time: 20 Minutes
Cooking Time: 2¹/₂ Hours
Serve Warm

Equipment

Large saucepan
Wooden Mixing spoon
Rubber spatula
Whisk

Mixing spoons, cups
Mixing bowl
2 quart casserole

Ingredients

4   cups whole milk
1   cup maple syrup
¼   cup butter (½ stick)
⅔   cup yellow cornmeal

½   teaspoon ground dry ginger
¼   teaspoon ground nutmeg
1½   cups currants

Preheat oven to 300 degrees. Butter a 2-quart casserole.

In a large saucepan, combine 3 cups whole milk and maple syrup over medium heat until it just comes to a boil. Stir and add butter. In a mixing bowl, combine cornmeal, ginger, and nutmeg and then gradually add it to the milk mixture. Cook on low heat until thick, about 10 minutes. Fold in the currants and then place in the casserole. Pour the last cup of milk over the top of the mixture. Do not stir it. Bake for 2½ hours or until all the milk is absorbed and the top is golden. Serve warm and with ice cream if you wish.

Chocolate-Dipped Apricots

Preparation Time: 15 Minutes

Equipment

Double boiler or mixing bowl set over water in a saucepan
Baking tray lined with waxed or parchment paper
Whisk
Measuring cups

Ingredients

2 cups (12 ounces) semisweet chocolate chips
2 cups dried apricot halves

Line a baking tray with waxed paper.

Place chocolate in a bowl over simmering hot water or in a double boiler. Stir occasionally with a whisk until melted. Remove from heat.

Dip apricots, one at a time, half way into the chocolate. Shake off excess and place on waxed paper to harden. Or, place tray into refrigerator to harden more quickly. Once chocolate is hard, they may be placed into an air tight storage container and refrigerated until about an hour before use. Bring to room temperature to serve.

These will keep up to a week or longer in the refrigerator.

December
Month-Long Festivals of Light
Diwali
Hanukkah
Christmas Eve/Christmas Day

Many cultures and religions share similar symbols and concepts in the celebration of festivals commemorating their time-honored traditions and histories. Faith, goodness, innocence and holiness overcome the dark powers seeking to destroy man and his inherent goodness. The forces of 'light' overcoming those of 'darkness' has been mirrored in the astronomical progression of the seasons and celebrated in one form or another far back into mankind's prehistory. The marking of the winter solstice and the joy felt as the lengthening hours of darkness finally give way to the rebirth of the sun and its light still brings a rebirth of hope for the new year with its gradual lengthening of days bringing warmth, fecundity, and new life.

I have focused of three significant Festivals of Light mirroring the ethnic diversity now in America, all different, yet similar in feeling.

Diwali
India's Festival of Lights
Celebrated on a Lunar Calendar
Often Occurring Late October to Early November

History

Although Diwali is held during the Indian month of Kartik (late October to early November), I have included it in December as the background of the holiday is one of the forces of goodness and light overcoming those of the dark. The festival is held in honor of Lakshmi: the goddess of wealth and prosperity. Legend tells that Lord Rama, an incarnation of the powerful God, Lord Vishnu, freed his beautiful wife Sita, an incarnation of the Goddess Lakshmi, from the demon king who had abducted and imprisoned her on the island of Sri Lanka (Ceylon). Rama, absent from India for fourteen years while he fought to rescue his wife, finally overcame the dark evil demons and returned to India with her. As the couple made their way home to northern India, tradition holds that people lit small oil lamps to illuminate their path and guide the Goddess of Prosperity to their house.

The God's victory and return of the Goddess is celebrated with pageants, feasting, partying and fire works to chase away evil spirits. Deeply religious services of thanksgiving for deliverance from the bad forces of the past year are given in gaily lit and beautifully decorated temples. Indulgence in an abundance of good food helps to bring good luck for the coming year.

India offers diverse types of food, depending of the region of this large country, including vegetarian, which mirrors a deep religious respect for not taking a life for sustenance. Following is an eclectic, vegetarian dinner/buffet, with an optional chicken recipe, combining the tastes of several regions.

Decoration

As this is a festival of light, many small votive candles in clear glass containers mimic the look of the small ancient oil lamps; use many sizes and shapes for interest. Massed as well as spread across the buffet table, these small flames will reflect a myriad of light if mirrored place mats or trivets are used. Brass objects and trays also lend an Indian flavor to the setting as do multi-colored silks, exotic flowers of red and gold and carved woods. Perhaps you have a large brass tray that might double as a small table. This top could be used as a large serving platter with the rice pilaf in the center and the other dishes encircling it in small bowls. Wear a sari!

Diwali Buffet for 8 Guests

Select your menu and make up your shopping list as suggested in the Introduction.

Menu

Hors d'Oeuvres
Spiced Mixed Nuts
Savory Pakoras (Vegetable Fritters)
Paneer Pakote (Fried Fresh Cheese)

Dinner
Dal (Lentils)
Bhindi (Sauteéd Okra)
Spiced String Beans
Basmati Pullao (Rice Pilaf)
Keera Raita (Yogurt and Cucumbers)
Laccha (Salad)

Mint Chutney
Mango Chutney
Cauliflower Pickle

Tandoori Chicken

continued . . .

Chappati (Bread)
    OR
Pooris

Dessert
Firni (Almond Rice Pudding)
Malpoa (Fritters in Syrup)
Santre kie Chakle (Orange Wheels)

Beverages
Lassi (Yogurt Drink)
Spiced Tea

Preparation Note:
   Indian cooking requires the frequent use of a variety of spices, many which are available in a local supermarket. In larger cities, multi-ethnic stores will certainly carry the harder to obtain. In fact, most are used in other types of cooking and desserts, so they won't go to waste.

Ground Cumin	Mustard seed
Whole Cumin seeds	Dried Mustard powder
Ground Coriander	Black Peppercorns
Ground Cardamom	Cayenne powder (ground red
Whole Cardamom	pepper)
Ground Turmeric	Garam Masala (a spiced
Cloves	combination which can be
Cinnamon	made from the above)
Cinnamon sticks	Rose water

   Indian spices are often dry toasted in a small saucepan on top of the stove and then finely ground into a powder. Use a mortar and pestle, mini blender or even an electric coffee grinder, but if you use a coffee grinder, reserve it for spices, as the flavors linger and would flavor future coffee beans.
   Ghee is another staple that Westerners refer to as clarified butter. I will describe it below, and it is simple to produce.
   Fresh yogurt can also be easily made at home, as large quantities may be required, as can the ricotta type cheese in the recipes. They can be made ahead and stored for a couple of days. Every Indian meal also includes chutneys and pickles. These need to be made up to a week or more ahead so they can 'pickle'.

They are good with other non-Indian food as well, so the effort making them needn't be for a one time only meal.

Check your recipes ahead and make sure you have what you need. Plan your timetable accordingly.

Timetable

Three to Four Weeks Prior
Cauliflower Pickle

One Week Prior
Mango Chutney
Garam Masala

Three Days Prior
Spiced Mixed Nuts
Paneer Pakote (ricotta-type cheese)
Mint Chutney

Two Days Prior
Shop for chicken and fresh ingredients
Ghee
Garam Masala
Yogurt
Firni (Almond Rice Pudding)

One Day Prior
Sliced Oranges
Cook Beets for Laccha, peel and slice
Clean all vegetables and cut into the size pieces needed for salad and Pakoras (fritters); put in plastic bags and refrigerate
Prepare and marinate chicken
Make sure you have everything you need for the table
Arrange any flowers and candles

Day of Party
In the morning:
Make Malpoa (fritters), don't soak in syrup
Chappati or Pooris (bread)

continued . . .

Keera Raita (yogurt and cucumbers)
Set the table
Arrange a bar, if you are having one
Prepare tea spices

Four Hours Prior:
Make salad, do not put dressing on until just before serving
Cut paneer into cubes. Set in refrigerator
Arrange oranges for dessert
Remove mango chutney and cauliflower pickle from refrigerator and place in serving dishes.

Three Hours Prior:
Cook chicken
Start Dal
Soak rice, 30 minutes, drain for 30 minutes

One Hour Prior to Company:
Make batter for Pakoras and take vegetables out of refrigerator.
Have pan ready to fry Paneer Pakote and put mint chutney into serving dish
Make lassi, can be served prior to meal or with it, froth before serving

Thirty Minutes Prior to Company:
Make Pakoras and Paneer, keep warm
Set out nuts and accompaniments

Thirty Minutes Prior to Eating:
Rewarm dal
Make okra
Make spiced beans
Put keera raita on table
Put salad on table and pour over dressing
Warm chicken

Fifteen Minutes Prior:
Warm bread

continued . . .

Before Serving Desserts:
Pour syrup over fritters
Garnish puddings
Heat water for tea

To Be Made Ahead for Use in Cooking

Ghee

Preparation Time and Cooking Time: 10 Minutes

Equipment
Small saucepan
Airtight container

Ingredients
1   pound unsalted butter

Place butter in saucepan over low heat and melt. Remove from heat. When white has settled to bottom, pour off the clear yellow top part. This is the ghee (clarified butter). Place in an airtight container and use as needed for cooking and frying. You have removed most of what makes butter smoke and burn so easily. Discard the white residue. You can use ghee for any recipe where butter is needed for cooking, not baking.

Garam Masala

Preparation Time: 20 Minutes

Equipment

Mortar and pestle, mini food
   processor or coffee grinder
Airtight storage container

Measuring spoons
Small skillet
Wooden stirring spoon

Ingredients

3   tablespoons cardamom seeds
3   1 inch lengths of cinnamon
     sticks, broken into small
     pieces

1   tablespoon cumin seeds
1   teaspoon black peppercorns
½   teaspoon whole cloves
¼   grated fresh nutmeg

Place ingredients in small skillet over medium high heat (no oil) for about 5 minutes, until spices toast. Remove to a plate and cool. When cool, grind in a mortar with a pestle or mini-food processor or coffee grinder. Store in small airtight jar until needed.

Homemade Yogurt

Preparation Time: 20 Minutes
Overnight Rest

Equipment

2 quart saucepan
Large mixing bowl

Whisk
Plastic wrap

Ingredients

5 cups milk
2½ tablespoons purchased plain whole milk yogurt, unless you have
   a culture from making it before.

Boil milk. Remove from heat and cool down. Place yogurt culture in large bowl and whisk until smooth; slowly pour in warm milk. Yogurt will become watery if milk is too hot or too cold. Cover. Leave in a warm place overnight. Do not disturb it.

It should be thickened by the next morning. Refrigerate until needed. Always reserve at least 2½ tablespoons for the next culture.

Recipes

Hors d'oeuvres

Spiced Mixed Nuts

Preparation Time: 5 Minutes
Cooking Time: 15 Minutes

Equipment

Medium size frying pan
Bowl to mix spices and then nuts
Wooden stirring spoon
Measuring spoons and cups
Airtight container

Ingredients

2 cups blanched almonds (skins removed, see Introduction)
2 cups raw, unsalted cashew nuts
4 teaspoons vegetable oil
1 teaspoon coriander
1 teaspoon ground cumin
½-¾ teaspoon cayenne (ground hot red pepper), according to taste
1 teaspoon coarse salt (Kosher)

Mix spices and salt together in a small bowl. Let set 10 minutes while toasting nuts.

Place 1 teaspoon of oil in frying pan and warm over low heat. When warm, add nuts and toss for 3-4 minutes, until heated through. Add 1 more teaspoon of oil and toast until nuts are brown, about 10 minutes. Turn frequently for even coloring.

Remove to a bowl and toss with spices to eat. When cool, store in airtight container.

Savory Pakoras (Vegetable Fritters)

Preparation Time: 10 Minutes
30 Minutes to Rest
Cooking Time: 5 Minutes per Batch

Equipment

Wok or deep skillet
Slotted spoon/skimmer
Paper towel for draining
Measuring spoons
Mixing bowl

Whisk
Sifter or fine mesh sieve
Chopping knife
Ovenproof dish

Ingredients

**Note: If you are making Fried Paneer as well (recipe follows), double this batter recipe.

Batter

1½ cups chickpea flour
     (available in health food
     and specialty stores)
2   teaspoons vegetable or
     peanut oil
2   teaspoons coriander seeds,
     crushed in mortar with
     pestle

¼   teaspoon cayenne pepper
     (optional), may not want it
     in cheese fritters
2   teaspoons Kosher salt
1¼ cups cold water
     Enough vegetable oil for 2
     inches in cooking pot.

Sift chickpea flour into mixing bowl and stir/rub in the 2 teaspoons of vegetable oil. Stir in the coriander seeds, salt and the optional cayenne. Gradually whisk in the cold water. Cover and let batter rest about 30 minutes at 80 degree temperature (near warm stove or in gas oven, pilot light provides warmth).

Vegetables

**You can use one or several of the following
Cauliflower cut into flowers
Thin slices of eggplant
Thinly sliced sweet onions
Potatoes, small dice
Green or Red Bell peppers, sliced in squares
Slices of squash or pumpkin

Heat about 2 inches of vegetable oil in wok or large skillet set over medium high heat. After batter has rested, take the cut and sliced vegetables, and one at a time, dip them in the batter to fully cover. Shake off excess. Carefully put into oil using a slotted spoon. Watch the spatters. Don't crowd the pan. Adjust heat if browning too quickly. Turn fritters as they brown. Remove and drain on paper toweling when brown and cooked through. Repeat with balance of vegetables. Keep warm in ovenproof dish in low temperature oven, 200-250 degrees.

Paneer Pakote (Fried Cheese)

Preparation Time: 10 Minutes
To Finish: 1^1/$_2$ Hours

Equipment

Sieve or Colander	Rolling pin
4 layers of cheesecloth to fit sieve or colander, with extra on sides for closing and tying up	Rimmed pan
	Saucepan filled with water
	Knife
3-4 quart saucepan	

Ingredients

8	cups of milk (2 quarts)	1/8	teaspoon cayenne pepper
4	tablespoons lemon juice, strained	1/4	teaspoon mango powder
			Salt to taste
1/4	teaspoon black pepper		

Heat milk in saucepan over medium-high heat. Stir to prevent sticking or scorching on bottom. Bring to boil. Lower the heat and add lemon juice. Stir gently for 10 seconds or until curd separates from whey. Don't break up lumps. Turn off heat.

Over the sink, pour into sieve or colander lined with 4 layers of cheesecloth. Rinse with cold, gently flowing tap water to remove lemon flavor. Tie cheesecloth together and twist. Suspend over bowl to drain, or leave in sieve over bowl. This stage of the cheese is called chenna and is used in other Indian recipes. To form paneer, set cheese, still in cheesecoth, onto a clean, flat surface with a rim to catch water, and place a weight on top (a pot filled with water will do) for 30 minutes to an hour. Remove weight. Remove cheese from cloth and gently press into a square with a rolling pin. Cut cheese into ⅛ inch by ½-inch by 1½-inch rectangles. (Cheese will keep 4 days, covered in refrigerator.)

Dip cubes in the above batter and fry until brown. Drain on paper toweling. Sprinkle with a mixture of the spices and serve. If prepared ahead, loosely cover dish and reheat in a 375 degree oven for 5 minutes.

Serve with mint chutney.

Poodina ki Chutney (Mint Chutney)

Preparation Time: 20 Minutes

Equipment

Food Processor fitted with metal blade, or blender
Grater

Mixing bowl
Measuring spoons
Airtight container

Ingredients

3	cups mint leaves (no stems)		Salt to taste
½	medium-size onion	¼	cup lemon juice
1	tablespoon freshly grated peeled ginger	3	tablespoons water
2	hot green peppers, (Jalapeno-type peppers)		

Wash mint leaves and remove from stems. Place in processor or blender. Coarsely chop onion and peppers, ginger, and salt. Add to mint leaves. Pour in lemon juice and water and pulse until puréed. If too thick for a dip, add a bit more lemon juice and water. Store in airtight container in refrigerator for up to one week.

Dal (Lentils)

Preparation Time: 15 Minutes
Cooking Time: 45-55 Minutes

Equipment

4 quart saucepan
Medium size skillet
Colander

Wooden mixing spoon
Measuring spoons and cups

Ingredients

2	cups dried lentils, rinsed and picked over	8	tablespoons ghee
	Water to cover plus 2 inches	2	teaspoons ground turmeric
		2	teaspoons whole cumin seeds
4	medium size ripe tomatoes, diced	2	dried hot red peppers, finely chopped
2	large onions, finely chopped	¾	cup fresh coriander, chopped finely, no stems
4	garlic cloves, finely minced		
2	tablespoons fresh peeled ginger, finely minced		

Bring lentils and water to a boil. Reduce heat. Meanwhile, heat a skillet over medium high heat and add the ghee. Add onions and sauté until lightly browned, about 7-10 minutes. Stir in garlic and sauté briefly. Add tomatoes. Mix together well and cook until juices reduce in half. Stir in turmeric and dried red peppers. Add to the lentils. Cover and cook until tender, about 20-30 minutes, stirring occasionally. If it gets dry looking, add water. You don't want it to stick to the bottom of the pan.

In a small skillet, dry roast the cumin seeds and put in a dish to the side for garnishing.

Dal can be made earlier in the day and reheated. Don't allow it to dry out.

When ready to serve, place dal in bowl and scatter cumin seeds and chopped coriander over the top.

Bhindi (Sautéed Okra)

Preparation Time: 15-20 Minutes
Cooking Time: 5-7 Minutes

Equipment
Large skillet
Spatula

Ingredients
1½ pounds okra
1 tablespoon vegetable oil
2 tablespoons ghee
1½ teaspoons cumin seeds
1½ large sweet onions, thinly sliced
1½ fresh hot green chilies, seeded and chopped finely
1½ large tomatoes, seeded, chopped finely
2 teaspoons Kosher (coarse) salt
¾-1 teaspoon cayenne pepper
Pinch of turmeric
½ cup fresh coriander, finely chopped for garnish, no stems

Do not wash the okra as they become sticky. Wipe with a paper towel and cut off the stem and tail end. Cut into ½ inch rounds.

Heat large skillet and add vegetable oil and ghee. When hot, add cumin seeds and toast until brown. Stir in the okra and sauté for 2 minutes. Stir in onion and chilies and cook for about 5 minutes. Add tomatoes, salt, cayenne pepper and turmeric. Cook until heated through. It is preferable to keep onions on the crisp side, as it makes a nice texture contrast in the dish. Garnish with coriander when putting into a serving dish.

Posho (Spiced String Beans)

Preparation Time: 20 Minutes
Cooking Time: 15-20 Minutes

Equipment

Small skillet
Wooden stirring spoon

Mortar and pestle or grinder
2 quart saucepan with lid

Ingredients

½   teaspoon mustard seeds
5   tablespoons vegetable oil
6   cloves of garlic, finely
        chopped
1½   pounds of fresh string beans,
        ends and string removed
¾   teaspoon salt
2-3 dried red chili peppers,
        chopped

¾   teaspoon ground turmeric
1   teaspoon ground coriander

2   tablespoons raw sesame
        seeds
1½   teaspoons fresh grated
        coconut

Heat the oil in large saucepan and add mustard seeds, stirring constantly, until light brown and they 'pop'. Add garlic and lightly brown. Add balance of ingredients, cover and cook on low heat until beans are tender, about 15-20 minutes. Stir occasionally so beans don't stick.

Meanwhile, dry toast (no oil) the sesame seeds in a small skillet. Grind into a fine powder along with coconut and reserve as a garnish for the beans upon serving.

Basmati Pullao (Rice Pilaf)

Preparation Time: 1 Hour (Soaking)
Cooking Time: 20-30 Minutes

Equipment

Heavy bottomed large saucepan
with lid
Wooden stirring spoon
Measuring cup and spoon

Chopping knife (or food processor)
Wok ring (holds a wok on tip of
burner)

Ingredients

3   cups Basmati rice
4   tablespoons vegetable oil
1½   medium size onions, finely
     chopped
2   two-inch pieces of stick
     cinnamon
4   whole cloves
2   bay leaves

2   teaspoons salt
1   cup roasted, unsalted
     cashews
½   cup golden raisins, softened
     in warm water for about
     20-30 minutes, then
     drained.

Wash rice until water runs clear and let soak in pot of cold water for 30 minutes. Strain into a large sieve and let stand for 30 minutes.

Heat oil in large saucepan (or skillet) and cook onion until soft, don't brown. Adjust heat as necessary. Stir in rice, spices and bay leaf and fry for 2 minutes. Add 3 cups water and 2 teaspoons salt; bring to a boil. Cover tightly, reduce heat to low and cook until all water is absorbed and rice is fluffy, about 20 minutes. Check water level once or twice during cooking but do not stir. If you have a wok ring, place it under the pot to get it away from the direct heat. Basmati rice can easily stick and burn.

Remove from burner and let rice rest for about 5 minutes before serving; do not stir. Before serving, remove bay leaf and cinnamon sticks and fluff with a knife or fork. Stir in cashews and raisins and serve. To avoid stickiness, do not over stir or over handle the rice.

Keera Raita (Yogurt with Cucumber)

Preparation Time: 10 Minutes

Ingredients

2 cups plain yogurt (try home made)
1½ medium size cucumbers, peeled, seeded, thinly sliced
¾ teaspoon salt
¾ teaspoon ground cumin
Sprig of fresh mint, chopped for garnish

Whisk yogurt until smooth. Add the cucumbers and seasonings. Chill until serving time.

Laccha (Salad)

Preparation Time: 15 Minutes
Plus 45 Minutes to Cook Beets

Equipment

Large saucepan with lid
Cooking fork
Chopping knife
Mixing bowl
Small mixing bowl

Measuring spoons
Whisk
Paper towels
Salad bowl, servers

Ingredients

2 large sweet onions, very thinly sliced to create rings
3 large beets, washed, cooked, peeled and sliced thinly
1½ cucumbers, peeled, seeded and sliced thinly
2 large tomatoes, sliced
1½ limes, sliced
3 hot green peppers, seeds, membranes removed, sliced
6 scallions, cut in half lengthwise, root end and top removed to leave
   5 inch length
4 tablespoons fresh lemon juice
¾ teaspoon salt
Freshly ground black pepper

319

Soak onions in ice water for 30 minutes, drain, pat dry with paper towels and separate into rings.

Wash, cook, peel beets and slice thin.

Prepare the other vegetables and chill well.

Assemble close to serving time so beets don't bleed on all the other vegetables.

In salad bowl, first layer the onions and then fan the beets on top of the onions. Add a layer of cucumbers and then the tomatoes, peppers and limes. In a small bowl, mix the salt and pepper with the lemon juice and pour over the top just before serving. Place the scallions decoratively on the top.

Aamer (Mango) Chutney

Preparation Time: 15 Minutes
Cooking Time: 20-25 Minutes
Can sometimes be found ready-made in jar

Equipment
Medium size skillet with lid
Wooden stirring spoon
Air tight container

Ingredients

4	green mangoes	2	cups water
2	teaspoons vegetable oil	½	teaspoon salt
½	teaspoon cumin	4	tablespoons sugar
2	cardamom pods	1	teaspoon cornstarch
1	inch stick cinnamon	2	tablespoons milk

Wash and dry the mangoes and slice lengthwise into 6 pieces, remove seed.

Heat the oil in skillet over medium high heat and when hot, add cumin, cardamom and cinnamon. Stir for a few seconds and add the mangoes and stir for 2-3 minutes. Add water and salt stirring and scraping pan until it comes to a boil, add the sugar and stir.

Cover and lower heat. Cook for 15-20 minutes or until mangoes are soft. Taste. You may want to add more sugar, depending on the tartness of the mangoes.

In a small cup, mix cornstarch and milk into a paste. Stir into the mango mixture. You do not want it to get lumpy but thickened. You may need to raise heat for a minute to aid thickening. Remove from heat when sauce is holding together, chill in airtight container until needed.

Phool Gobi ka Aachar (Cauliflower Pickle)

Preparation Time: 10 Minutes
Pickling Time One Week

Equipment

3-5 glass jars with non-metal lids
Large mixing bowl
Wooden mixing spoon

Ingredients

1	medium cauliflower, cut into florettes	2	teaspoons coarse salt
		1	teaspoon turmeric
1	fresh, hot green chili, chopped into small pieces; removing seeds is optional (less hot)	1	teaspoon caraway seeds
		2	inch piece of fresh ginger root, peeled and coarsely grated
8	garlic cloves, peeled and coarsely chopped	1	tablespoon vegetable oil
1¼	cups white wine vinegar	1¼	cup water

Combine all ingredients in a large mixing bowl. Divide into glass jars and cover. Place in refrigerator and shake occasionally. Needs to cure for at least a week.

Tandoori Chicken

Preparation Time: 15 Minutes Plus Overnight
Cooking Time: 30-50 Minutes

Equipment

Large glass or metal rectangular dish with at least 3 inch high sides.
Mixing bowl
Whisk
Measuring spoons and cups
Roasting pan with low sides
Cooking fork/tongs

Ingredients

3 2½ pound chickens; backs and wing tips removed and quartered
⅓ cup lemon juice
½ inch fresh ginger root, peeled and coarsely chopped
¾ cup thick, plain yogurt
2 teaspoons ground coriander
1 teaspoon ground cumin
3 tablespoons garam masala (2 for marinade)
1½ teaspoons cayenne pepper
1 tablespoon sweet paprika
6 tablespoons ghee
Non-stick cooking spray

On the day prior to serving, cut up the chicken; remove back and neck, separate leg portion from breast and separate thigh and leg, cut breast into 2 pieces, remove wing tip. (Removed pieces can be frozen and used later to make stock.)

Remove the skin from the chicken and slash each piece almost bone deep in at least two to three places for a length of 2 inches.

Combine all the spices and yogurt, not the ghee. Put lemon juice in all the slashed areas and then rub the yogurt-spiced mix on the chicken pieces, and especially into the slashed areas. Cover and place in refrigerator to marinate overnight, turning a couple of times.

One half hour before cooking, remove the chicken from the refrigerator. When ready to cook, preheat oven to 500 degrees. Place chicken in low-sided roasting pan, spray with non-stick cooking spray. Sprinkle remaining tablespoon garam masala over chicken. Put chicken in oven for 10 minutes and then lower temperature to 400 degrees. Divide ghee over chicken pieces and cook 30-50 minutes or until done and juices run clear. Remove from oven and serve. If prepared in advance of use, cover lightly with aluminum foil and heat in 350 degree oven for about 20 minutes, if at room temperature.

Garnish serving platter with fresh coriander leaves.

Chappati (Flat Bread)

Preparation Time: 10 Minutes
Resting Time: 30 Minutes
Cooking Time: $1^1/_2$ Minutes each

Equipment

Hot griddle, heavy frying pan or cooking grate which fits over burner
Rolling pin
Mixing bowls (2)

Wooden spoon
Measuring cup
Damp tea towel or plastic wrap
Spatula

Ingredients

Recipe makes 15 chappati
$1^3/_4$ cup whole wheat flour plus extra for rolling
$^3/_4$ cup hot water

Put flour in medium bowl and gradually add water. Mix in with a wooden spoon or your hands. Gather dough with fingers and start to knead, if too wet, add a bit more flour. When you can get the dough out of the bowl, it will begin to hold together, place it on a whole wheat-floured surface and knead until it is smooth, about 6-8 minutes. Place in clean bowl and cover with a damp tea towel or plastic wrap. Let dough rest 30 minutes.

Heat griddle over medium low heat for 10 minutes, reduce heat to low. Knead dough briefly and divide into 15 portions. The dough may be sticky. Flour your hands. Take a portion of dough and roll into a ball. Flatten on floured surface and roll flat with rolling pin to make a $5^1/_2$ inch circle. Pick up and pat dough to rid it of excess flour. Slap down onto hot griddle. Cook over low heat for 1 minute. Brown spots will appear on the underside of dough. Turn over with spatula and cook another 30 seconds. Remove to a napkin-lined dish and cover to keep warm, or stack in foil to reheat later at 350 degrees. Repeat with remaining portions of dough.

Pooris (Puffed Bread)

Preparation Time: 15 Minutes
Resting Time: 15-20 Minutes
Cooking Time: 1-1^{1}/$_{2}$ Minutes

Equipment

Wok or deep skillet
Rolling pin
Mixing bowl

Wooden spoon
Measuring spoons and cups
Plastic wrap or damp tea towel

Ingredients

3½ cups whole wheat flour, plus
     extra for rolling surface
½   teaspoon salt

1   cup hot water
1   tablespoon vegetable oil plus
     oil for frying

Combine flour, salt and 1 tablespoon of oil in mixing bowl. Gradually add 1 cup of cold water and stir with spoon to make a soft dough. Gather dough together and knead on oiled surface for 10 minutes, until smooth. Cover with plastic wrap or damp cloth and let rest for 15-20 minutes.

Heat 2 inches of oil in a wok or heavy skillet to 375 degrees.

On oiled surface, divide dough into 20 walnut size balls. Roll each ball into a 5 inch circle. Keep remaining dough covered with plastic wrap or tea towel until ready to roll.

Carefully lay dough in hot oil and pat with a slotted spoon until it floats. Dough will puff up. Turn and cook on other side for 10-15 seconds. Do not turn again or oil will get inside dough. They should be golden in color, you may have to adjust heat as you cook the others. Drain on paper towels. Repeat with other balls of dough. Serve warm or at room temperature.

Dessert

Firni (Almond Rice Pudding)

Preparation Time: 20 Minutes
Cooking Time: 15 Minutes Plus Cooling

Equipment

Blender, food processor fitted with metal blade
2 layers of cheesecloth
Sieve
Medium size saucepan
Whisk
Measuring spoons and cups
Wooden spoon for stirring
Plastic wrap

Ingredients

⅓	cup blanched almonds	2	teaspoons rose water
⅔	cup water	2	tablespoons chopped unsalted pistachios
5	tablespoons rice flour, available at health food and specialty stores	2	tablespoons finely chopped blanched almonds
1½	cup milk	8	tablespoons pomegranate seeds or sliced strawberries
2	cups light cream		
10	tablespoons sugar		

Combine ⅓ cup almonds and ⅔ cup of water in a bowl and cover. Soak 15 minutes. Place in blender and purée. Strain in a sieve through 2 layers of cheesecloth. Squeeze out water and empty into a small bowl with rice flour. Stir and put aside.

Combine milk, cream, sugar in medium saucepan and bring to a boil, stirring constantly. Decrease heat and whisk in almond flour mixture, continue whisking to prevent lumps. Cook until mixture thickens and coats the back of a wooden spoon. Cook an additional 5 minutes on low heat. Custard is thin and will thicken as it cools. Put in bowl, don't scrape pan as bottom may have scorched. Cover surface with plastic wrap so skin doesn't form. If one does form, stir it back into custard. Cool.

When cool, stir in rose water, cover surface again and refrigerate until needed. This will keep for 3 days, refrigerated.

To serve, place in small goblets and garnish with pistachios, almonds and pomegranate berries or strawberry.

Malpoa (Fritters in Syrup)

Preparation Time: 15 Minutes
Cooking Time: 3-5 Minutes

Equipment

Small saucepan
Deep skillet or wok
Medium size mixing bowl
Whisk

Wooden stirring spoon
Measuring spoons and cups
Thermometer, candy/deep frying
Paper Toweling

Ingredients

1¾ cups flour
1½ teaspoons baking powder
¾ cup yogurt
¾ cup milk

1 cup sugar
2 cups water

Vegetable oil for frying

Combine sugar and water in small saucepan. Roll pan to dissolve sugar and boil for 10 minutes over medium heat, until golden color. Remove from heat and set aside.

In a medium size bowl, sift together flour and baking powder. Stir in the yogurt then gradually stir in the milk, stopping when batter is still thick.

Heat oil to 375 degrees. Drop batter by teaspoons into hot oil. Be careful not to spatter yourself. Fry until golden and crisp, turning balls as necessary. Drain on paper towels. About an hour before serving, place balls in a dish and soak them with the sugar syrup for 5 minutes. Drain and place on serving platter. Just before you serve, drizzle hot or cold sugar syrup over tops of balls. Garnish with mint leaves.

Santre kie Chakle (Orange Wheels)

Preparation Time: 10 Minutes
Chill at Least 2 Hours

Equipment

Large shallow serving bowl
Cutting knife

Small mixing bowl
Whisk

Ingredients

8 large oranges
1/3 cup sugar
4 tablespoons black raisins
1½ teaspoon ground fresh
  nutmeg or cinnamon

1/4 cup rose water
  Juice ½ lemon
2 tablespoons Grand Marnier
  liqueur, optional

Peel oranges and remove white pith. Slice each orange into 5-6 wheels and place in large shallow bowl. Remove any seeds.

Combine all other ingredients in a small bowl, whisk and pour over the oranges. Serve chilled with sauce spooned over oranges.

Beverages

Lassi (Yogurt Drink)

Preparation Time: 5 Minutes
Makes 4 small drinks
You may want to double the recipe

There are two types of lassi, savory/plain or sweet

Equipment

Blender or whisk
Measuring spoons and cups
Rubber scraper

Ingredients

1	cup plain yogurt	¾	teaspoon salt
5	cups cold water	¼	teaspoon black pepper

Whisk or blend until frothy and serve with the meal.

	OR	2	tablespoons rose water
3	cups plain yogurt	12	tablespoons sugar
6	tablespoons heavy cream	20	ice cubes

Blend until frothy and serve immediately; or stir before serving as it will settle in the bottom. Better after a meal or as a snack treat.

Try substituting pineapple, mango, papaya, banana for the rose water and lessen the amount of sugar. Be creative.

Spiced Tea

Preparation Time: 5 Minutes
Cooking Time: 15 Minutes
4 cups of tea; double recipe for 8 cups

Equipment

Teapot
Saucepan
Wooden stirring spoon

Ingredients

4 cups water
12 whole cloves
12 green Cardamom seeds, crushed
2 cinnamon sticks, each 2 inches long, broken
6 teaspoons black tea leaves or 4 tea bags
Sugar and milk to taste

Bring water to boil in saucepan, add spices and simmer for 10 minutes over low heat. Add tea and brew for 5 minutes. Strain into teapot and serve hot with sugar and milk on the side.

Hanukkah
A Jewish Festival of Light

History

Jewish holidays tend to commemorate experiences and events in the history of the Jewish people, as well as seasonal celebrations. Following a lunar calendar, the holidays shift in date yearly. Hanukkah, the Jewish festival of light and affirmation of faith usually falls in December.

When the Greek warrior, Alexander the Great died, the rule of his empire was divided between the ruling dynasties of Egypt and Syria. Palestine fell under the rule of the Syrian Selucid dynasty, which continued the Hellenization of Palestine initiated by Alexander. Jews were encouraged to follow Greek cultural mores, including the worship of Greek gods, whose statues were set up in their temples. The practice of animal sacrifice, though not foreign to Jews, now included that of sacrificing pigs, considered by the Jews to be unclean. Worshipping 'idols' and many other Greek practices were in total opposition to the teachings of the ancient Jewish faith. In the small town of Modi'in, an elderly Jewish priest, Mattathias, challenged and killed a Hellenized Jewish convert as he sacrificed and worshipped according to the Greek rites in the Jewish temple. Forced to flee to the desert with his five sons, a guerrilla resistance army was formed and led by one of Mattathias' sons, Judah the Maccabee. Valiantly fighting the royal troops of King Antiochus, Judah eventually liberated Jerusalem and the old Jewish Temple and helped bring the wayward Jews back to their unadulterated faith. As he sought to reconsecrate the Temple to the true Jewish religion, Judah could find only one cruse of holy oil with which to perform the purification ceremony. Lighting the Temple Menorah (candelabra) with this oil, a miracle occurred. The light burned for eight days instead of the one the quantity of oil should have allowed.

Hanukkah celebrates the valor and victory of the Maccabees (Jews) over the Hellenized Syrians (outside influences) and the restoration and rededication of the Temple with the consecrated light of pure belief. Hanukkah is a symbol of lighting the flame of faith in the human soul so that it will burn brightly for eternity and overcome the darkness of evil and indifference.

Decoration

The central decorative and religious icon in a Jewish home for Hanukkah is the menorah. A menorah, which comes in many shapes, is a holder or candelabra of nine candles, eight of which represent each of the eight days of Hanukkah. The ninth candle, the "shames", is the candle from which all others are lit. Each night of Hanukkah, one additional candle is lit until all eight are glowing on the last night of the festival.

Blue and white are traditional colors used to kindle thoughts of Israel. Setting the table to incorporate these colors will add to the sense of the holiday. One or several draidles (tops) can be used decoratively and later used for children's games, betting with Hanukkah geld (money). The Hanukkah money can be gold foil-wrapped chocolate candies usually available in net bags.

Gift giving tends to be a more western innovation to Hanukkah as it collides with the Christian Christmas season. One gift a day is frequently given the children for each of the eight days of the holiday.

Hanukkah Dinner for 6

Select your menu and make up your shopping list as suggested in the Introduction.

Menu

As Hanukkah celebrates the miracle of the holy oil, it is traditional to serve some fried dishes as part of the meal. Don't
continued . . .

think cholesterol and try to use canola or olive oils in cooking, as these oils are unsaturated fats. This is not a Kosher menu as there is a mix of dairy and meat; substitutions will be necessary if cooking "Kosher."

Hors d'Oeuvres
Mini Latkes (potato pancakes) with Cranberry Applesauce
Smoked Trout Paté
Deep-fried Parsnip Chips

First Course
Mushroom Soup

Main Course
Brisket of Beef with Dried Fruit
Noodle-Cabbage Casserole
Herbed Carrots
    OR
Red Beets in Orange-Ginger Sauce
Marinated Zucchini Salad

Dessert
Hazelnut Angel Cake with Chocolate Sauce
Cinnamon Star Cookies
Poached Pears in White Wine with Glazed Lemon Peel
Glazed Nut Clusters
Bowl of Assorted Nuts in Shells

Beverages
Coffee
Tea

Timetable

Two Days Prior
Make mushroom soup and refrigerate
Parsnip Chips and store in airtight container
Cinnamon Star cookies, store in airtight container
Glazed Nut Clusters, store in airtight container

continued . . .

One Day Prior
Smoked Trout Paté and refrigerate
Brisket of Beef
Cook red beets and sauce
Hazelnut Angel Cake
Poached Pears
Make Cranberry/Applesauce

Day of Party
4-5 Hours Prior
Make zucchini salad and refrigerate without dressing
Complete brisket recipe
Make Chocolate Sauce
Make Noodle/Cabbage casserole, do not bake
Peel and cut carrots and put in saucepan but don't cook; mince herbs
Set table

2 Hours Prior
Prepare dressing for salad and put to the side
Peel potatoes and put into cold water to keep from browning

One Hour Prior to Guests Arriving
Arrange cookies on plate
Place nut clusters in a bowl
Carefully scoop pears in serving dish, drizzle sauce and lemon peels over them and bring to room temperature
Grate potatoes, make latkes, keep warm
Put Cranberry/Applesauce in serving dish
Remove Trout Pate from refrigerator, cut pumpernickel and put on serving tray with spreader
Put parsnip chips in serving dish

Forty-five Minutes Prior to Dinner
Slowly heat up mushroom soup over low heat.
Heat noodle/cabbage casserole in 350 degree oven (needs 30-40 minutes)
Red beets go into saucepan, don't heat yet
Prepare coffee and tea pots so they're ready to go at the end of dinner

continued . . .

Twenty Minutes Before Meal
Reheat brisket
Make sure soup is ready to serve
Toss dressing on zucchini salad

During First Course
Heat beets
Cook carrots; don't forget herbs
Slowly reheat chocolate sauce and start coffee and tea as
    clearing table of main course

Recipes

Hors d'Oeuvres

Mini Latkes with Cranberry Applesauce

Preparation Time: 45 Minutes
Cooking Time: 3-5 Minutes

Equipment

Food processor fitted with thin grating blade or hand-held grater or mandoline
Food mill or fine mesh strainer
Heavy skillet
Mixing bowl

Measuring spoons and cups
Spoon for stirring
Colander, sieve
2 heavy saucepan with lid
Plastic wrap
Baking tray

Ingredients

Cranberry Applesauce

6   firm, medium-size apples, like a Rome, Cortland, Granny Smith, Mackintosh
⅛   cup granulated sugar

½   pound fresh cranberries, rinsed and picked over
½   cup granulated sugar
½   cup water
½   teaspoon cinnamon

Latkes

4   large baking potatoes, grated
1   medium to large onion, finely grated (depends on how much you like onions)
1   tablespoon lemon juice
4   large eggs

3   tablespoons flour
1   teaspoon salt
¼   teaspoon ground black pepper
    Vegetable or canola oil for cooking

Cranberry Applesauce

*Can be made up to two days ahead of use.

Wash apples, core, quarter and place in saucepan with enough water to barely cover. Add ⅛ cup granulated sugar, stir and partially cover the pan. Cook over medium heat until contents boil, lower heat and cook until apples are soft, stirring occasionally so water doesn't evaporate and apples don't scorch; about 10-15 minutes.

Meanwhile, wash cranberries and place in a second saucepan; add sugar and water and stir. Place over medium heat and cook until berries pop open and liquid evaporates a bit. Remove from heat.

Place apples into a food mill. Set over a bowl and turn mill until apples are forced through, leaving behind skin. Scrape off bottom of mill and empty. Or press through a fine mesh strainer into a bowl, "rubbing" it through with a wooden spoon, removing skins.

Place cranberries into mill and add to apples.

Taste for sugar while still warm. According to your preference and the tartness of the apples and cranberries, you may want to add more. Do so now, incrementally. Add the cinnamon and mix in. Place in serving dish and when cool, cover with plastic wrap and store in the refrigerator. Can be made ahead and brought close to room temperature before serving.

Latkes

Need to be made close to serving. Can be kept warm in a 250-degree oven.

Peel and grate potatoes with grating disk of food processor or use a hand grater. Pour lemon juice over potatoes immediately and mix throughout, as it will help prevent browning of the potatoes.

Finely grate onions and add to potatoes. Slightly beat eggs and add to mixture along with the flour, salt and pepper. Mix well.

Heat frying pan and add ⅛ or ¼ inch of vegetable oil. When hot, drop rounded teaspoons full of batter into the oil. Be careful oil doesn't get too hot and burn. Make bite size cakes. When brown on bottom, about 3-5 minutes, turn and brown other side. Remove and taste one to be sure potatoes are cooked. You may have to adjust the heat to insure complete coking. Remove and drain on paper toweling. Place on baking tray and place in 250 degree oven until ready to serve. They get soggy if they 'sit' too long.

Serve on dish with cranberry applesauce on the side.

You may want to serve these with small plates so guests can dip and eat off their own plate. Forks optional but not cocktail napkins!

Smoked Trout Paté with Pumpernickel

Preparation Time: 20 Minutes
Can be prepared up to 3 days prior to serving

Equipment

Blender or food processor fitted
  with metal blade
Mixing bowl

Measuring spoons
Mixing spoon
Rubber scraper, spatula

Ingredients

1 pound smoked trout, skinned and boned
1 stick unsalted butter (8 tablespoons), room temperature cut into
  pieces
2 tablespoons half and half or non-dairy creamer
4 hard cooked egg yolks, sieved
4 teaspoons minced fresh dill, no stems
Salt and pepper to taste
Loaf of "Cocktail" size pumpernickel bread, or cut larger size slices
  into quarters

Place trout, butter and half and half into blender or food processor for about 15 seconds. Stop and scrape down any clinging to sides. Process about another 15 seconds or until smooth.

Transfer trout mixture to a small bowl and mix in the cooked egg yolks and then the dill. Season to taste. Place in airtight container and refrigerate until use. Remove from refrigerator for about 20-40 minutes before serving. Cut thinly-sliced Pumpernickel into bite-size triangles or squares and serve with paté.

Deep Fried Parsnip Chips

Preparation Time: 15 Minutes
Cooking Time: 2-3 Minutes
Can be Made Ahead and Stored in Airtight Container

Equipment

Mandoline, food processor with slicing attachment or very sharp knife

Deep saucepan or deep fat fryer
Candy/hot oil thermometer
Paper Towels

Ingredients

3 large parsnips
Kosher salt
Vegetable or canola oil for cooking

Peel parsnips and slice very thin using a mandoline, food processor slicing attachment or sharp knife.

Heat 3 inches of vegetable oil in a deep saucepan or deep fryer to 375 degrees.

Place parsnips in oil using a slotted spoon. Stand back so you don't burn yourself. Stir. Don't crowd the pot. Cook until crisp and golden, about 2-3 minutes, stirring. Remove to paper toweling and continue with rest of parsnips. Salt each batch as it comes out of the pot. Put to the side and serve as you would any chip.

Store in airtight container, up to three days.

First Course

Mushroom Soup

Preparation Time: 20-25 Minutes
Cooking Time: 40 Minutes
Can Be Made Two Days Ahead

Equipment

Food processor fitted with metal blade
Coarse sieve
Chopping knife
Measuring spoons and cups

Large saucepan
Stirring spoon
Ladle

Ingredients

3½   tablespoons butter
3-4   finely minced shallots, depending on size
2½   pounds mushrooms, white, cremini or a mixture

10   cups chicken broth
¾   teaspoon salt
1½   teaspoon lemon juice
1   lemon, thinly sliced

Finely chop the mushrooms with a sharp knife or cut in half and place in a food processor and grind finely.

Heat the butter in a large saucepan, and add the finely minced shallots. Cook until transparent, about 3-4 minutes. Add the mushrooms and stirring frequently, cook for about 5 minutes to release the juices.

Add the chicken broth and bring to a simmer; cook uncovered for about 30 minutes. Strain through a coarse sieve into a second pot, or refrigerator container, if making in advance. You want some pieces of the mushrooms to be in the soup. Press the mushrooms to extract all the liquid. Add salt to taste and lemon juice. Before serving, reheat. Garnish soup with thin slices of lemon.

Main Course

Brisket of Beef with Dried Fruit

Preparation Time: 20 Minutes
Cooking Time: 3-3¹/₂ Hours
Can Be Made A Day Ahead

Equipment

Heavy, non-reactive, flameproof
    casserole or large Dutch oven
    with lid

Cooking fork
Measuring spoons and cups
Medium saucepan

Ingredients

4 tablespoons vegetable oil
1 large onion, coarsely chopped
2 cups beef broth
1¹/₂ cups apple cider
1 bay leaf
4¹/₂-5 pounds lean brisket of beef, trimmed of fat and membrane, or
    two smaller pieces which will need less cooking time
Salt and freshly ground pepper

Sauce

¹/₂	cup dried prunes	3	tablespoons lemon juice
¹/₂	cup dried apricots	2	teaspoons grated lemon zest
¹/₂	cup dried cherries or	3	tablespoons apple cider
	peaches, if cherries are	¹/₄	teaspoon ground ginger
	unavailable	1	cinnamon stick
¹/₄	cup brown sugar		

Preheat oven to 350 degrees.

Salt and pepper beef on all sides after you have removed
any remaining fat or gristle. On top of the stove, heat vegetable
oil over medium heat in enamel, metal casserole or Dutch oven.
Heavy metal Dutch ovens hold heat and once hot, heat needs
adjusting. Brown the beef on all sides and remove to a plate.
Add chopped onions and cook about 10 minutes, until golden,
stirring frequently and adjusting heat if necessary, as you don't
want onions to burn. If necessary, add another tablespoon of oil.
Stir in the beef stock and apple cider and deglaze the pot, by

scraping up all browned bits, which give a good flavor and color to the broth. Bring broth to a simmer. Add the bay leaf and beef, pouring any juices on the plate into the pot. Ladle broth over the beef, cover and braise in the oven for 3-3½ hours, basting ever 20-30 minutes. Turn the beef over halfway through the cooking time. Meat is done when it is fork tender.

Using a fork and spatula for support, transfer the beef to a plate until cool. When cooking liquid is cool, return meat to the broth, cover and refrigerate overnight or raise heat on broth and skim off fat as it boils up.

Next Day

Remove casserole from refrigerator and skim solidified fat off the surface and discard. Cover and cook brisket over medium heat until it is heated through, about 20-30 minutes.

Transfer the meat to a cutting board, let sit about 10 minutes and then slice across the grain into ¼-inch slices. Arrange slices on heat proof platter with sides, to accommodate broth later. Cover with foil to keep warm and so meat doesn't dry out.

While brisket is sitting on cutting board and resting, pour cooking liquid into a medium saucepan. Add the prunes, apricots, cherries or peaches, brown sugar, lemon juice, zest, cider, ginger and cinnamon stick. Cook on low heat until the fruit has plumped, about 15 minutes; sauce will thicken a bit; if too thin, raise heat and reduce, being careful not to scorch fruit. Discard the cinnamon stick. Season with salt and pepper and spoon over the warm brisket and serve.

Noodle/Cabbage Casserole

Preparation Time: 10 Minutes
Waiting Time: 1 Hour
Cooking Time: 20-30 Minutes

Equipment

Food processor with shredding
  disk
Colander
Measuring spoons and cups

2 large saucepans and lids
Stirring spoon

Ingredients

½ medium head of cabbage, trimmed and shredded
2 tablespoons salt
5 tablespoons butter (or non-dairy substitute)
Freshly ground black pepper
1 pound wide egg noodles

Place shredded cabbage into a large bowl, add salt and toss. Let cabbage sit for an hour. Drain in a colander and squeeze to remove liquid.

Melt butter or non-dairy substitute in a large saucepan. Add cabbage and sprinkle with black pepper, according to your taste. Mix well and cover pan. Cook over low heat for 20 minutes, or until cabbage is tender. Be careful not to scorch cabbage. Stir occasionally.

At the same time, heat a large pot of water. When water boils, add noodles and cook for 10-14 minutes, until tender but not mushy. Drain through a colander and add to the cooked cabbage. Mix together and serve. Or, place in buttered (non-dairy substitute) ovenproof casserole dish, cover with aluminum foil and put to side to reheat in 350 degree oven for about 30 minutes just before serving.

342

Herbed Carrots

Preparation Time: 10 Minutes Plus 10
Cooking Time: 10-15 Minutes

Equipment

2 quart saucepan with lid
Stirring spoon
Measuring spoons and cups

Ingredients

6   cups carrots, peeled and cut
     into ¼-inch rounds
½   teaspoon salt
1   teaspoon sugar

3   tablespoons butter or non-
     dairy substitute
     Minced parsley and/or
     tarragon

Place sliced carrots into saucepan with enough water to cover carrots halfway. Place cover on pan and cook over moderate heat until tender. Check the water level so they don't scorch, adjust heat or add more water, if necessary.

Pour off any remaining water. Cut butter or substitute into pieces and put in pan to melt, stir to coat carrots. When butter is melted, sprinkle herb(s) over carrots and serve immediately.

Beets in Orange-Ginger Sauce

Preparation Time: 5 Minutes
Cooking Time: 40 Minutes
Finishing Time: 15 Minutes

Equipment

Large saucepan with lid   Paring and slicing knife
Cooking fork   Measuring spoons and cups

Ingredients

2-3 bunches of beets, depending on size and number of beets in each
    bunch; about 2 pounds or six cups diced beets when cooked.
2 tablespoons butter, non-dairy substitute
3/4 cup orange juice
1/4 teaspoon cornstarch or arrowroot
1½ teaspoons minced fresh ginger root, peeled

Cut tops of beets keeping about ½ inch of the stem and either reserve to prepare another day or toss out. Place in large saucepan with water to cover. Cover and cook until tender, about 30-40 minutes, depending on size of beet.

Remove beets from water. Let stand until cool enough to handle. Cut off remaining top and bottom spike. Peel with a sharp knife. The skin should be loose and will peel off easily. Caution! Beets stain terribly!

Cut into ½ inch slices, then dice. Return to a clean saucepan and add butter or non-dairy substitute to coat the beets, then dissolve cornstarch in the orange juice and pour into pan with ginger root. Heat, stirring constantly so liquid doesn't stick to pan, if it gets too sticky, stir in a bit more orange juice. When thickened and beets are heated through, serve.

344

Marinated Zucchini Salad

Preparation Time: 15 Minutes

Equipment

Saucepan
Colander
Mixing bowl
Measuring spoons and cups

Stirring spoon
Small mixing bowl
Whisk
Garlic press

Ingredients

4-5 medium size zucchini; 6 cups in a dice
1 cup green pepper, cubed
½ cup thinly slivered red peppers
1 medium size red onion, thinly sliced
2 tablespoons minced parsley

1 tablespoon minced tarragon
1 large clove garlic, through press or finely minced
4 tablespoons balsamic vinegar
¼-⅓ cup olive oil
1 teaspoon salt
Fresh ground black pepper

Wash, then dice zucchini and place in a pot of boiling water for 1 minute. Immediately remove from pot and plunge into ice water. You want to stop the cooking. When cool, remove and drain.

Place zucchini, peppers and onion into a bowl. Add the parsley and tarragon and toss. Put into refrigerator until ready to serve.

Crush garlic into a bowl. Add salt, balsamic vinegar and oil and a few grinds of black pepper. Whisk together and toss over salad. Mix well and serve immediately.

Dessert

Hazelnut Angel Food Cake with Chocolate Sauce

Preparation Time: 20 Minutes
Baking Time: 35-40 Minutes

Equipment

10 inch tube pan with removable
    bottom
Electric mixer, bowl
Rubber spatula

Measuring spoons, cups
Sifter, fine mesh sieve
Plate or second mixing bowl
Bottle to fit hole of cake pan

Ingredients

There are several packaged angel food cake mixes that could be used to save time. If using, follow package instructions and gently fold in nuts before pouring into baking pan.
Add:
3/4 cup finely ground blanched hazelnuts (filberts) folded into batter carefully

To make your own cake

1	cup sifted all-purpose flour	1½	teaspoons vanilla
7/8	cup granulated sugar	½	teaspoon almond extract or Fra Angelico liquor
12	egg whites (1½ cups) at room temperature	3/4	cup granulated sugar
1½	teaspoons cream of tartar	3/4	cup finely ground blanched hazelnuts (filberts)
¼	teaspoon salt		

Preheat oven to 350 degrees.

Set out tube pan. Do not grease.

Measure and sift flour and 7/8 cup of sugar onto a plate.

Separate eggs. Cover yolks and return to refrigerator (they can be used to make a rich "yellow" cake).

Place egg whites, cream of tartar, salt and vanilla and almost extract or Fra Angelico into a mixing bowl and beat with electric mixer until foamy. Gradually add 3/4 cup of additional sugar, two tablespoons at a time. Beat until meringue holds stiff peaks, but is not dry.

346

Carefully sift, for a third time, the flour and sugar mixture over the meringue, gently folding it into the mixture until it disappears. Do not over-deflate egg white.

Carefully put batter into tube pan, even off and gently cut through batter with a knife to remove any air pockets.

Place in center of preheated oven for 35-45 minutes until cake begins to pull away from sides of pan and is golden brown and tester comes out clean.

Remove from oven and invert pan on bottle. A sparkling water bottle usually will fit the tube. Let hang until cool, about one hour.

Run a sharp knife along the sides of the pan and invert onto a serving plate.

Chocolate Sauce

Can be prepared a couple hours in advance and reheated.

Equipment

Double boiler, preferable, or small saucepan set inside larger with small amount of boiling water	Rubber spatula Whisk Measuring spoons and cups

Ingredients

¾ cup granulated sugar	⅓ cup light corn syrup
½ cup unsweetened cocoa powder	⅓ cup butter, non-dairy substitute
1 can (5 ounces) evaporated milk	1 teaspoon vanilla

Combine sugar and cocoa in top of double boiler. Blend in the evaporated milk and corn syrup with a whisk. Cook over a medium heat, stirring frequently. When mixture comes to a boil, boil for 1 minute and remove from heat. Stir in butter and vanilla. Serve warm.

Chocolate sauce can be drizzled over the top of the cake and the balance served at the table for those who want extra.

Cinnamon Star Cookies

Preparation Time: 15 Minutes Plus Overnight plus 2 Hours
Baking Time: 25 Minutes
Can Be Baked up to 3-4 Weeks Prior. Makes about 2 dozen

Equipment

Electric mixer
Baking trays
Mixing bowl
Rubber spatula
Measuring spoons and cups
Star-shaped cookie cutter/make
  stencil out of light cardboard
  with 8-pointed star

Rolling pin with cotton-knit
  covering
Pastry cloth
Small pastry or paint brush
Cooling racks

Ingredients

⅓ cup egg whites (about 2 large eggs), room temperature
1¼ cups granulated sugar
1½ cups almonds, do not remove skins, finely ground but not powdery
½ tablespoons cinnamon
2 tablespoons flour
2 tablespoons granulated sugar
1 cup sifted powdered sugar
Non-stick cooking spray or vegetable shortening

Place egg whites in mixing bowl and beat until soft peaks are formed when beaters are raised. Gradually add 1¼ cups of granulated sugar, 2 tablespoons at a time, beating after each addition. Continue to beat, until egg whites are thick and glossy and stand in stiff peaks (about 10 minutes).

In a medium bowl, combine almonds with cinnamon and then fold in the egg white mixture and combine well. Refrigerate overnight.

To roll out, lay down a pastry cloth or roll on cold surface or pastry board and sprinkle with the 2 tablespoons of flour and 2 tablespoons granulated sugar. Mix well and cover working surface evenly with the mixture.

Grease baking sheets using non-stick cooking spray or vegetable shortening.

Divide dough in ½. Place covering over rolling pin and roll to ¼-inch thickness. Using a star cutter, cut dough and place on cooking sheets. Repeat with other portion of dough. Gather together bits of leftover dough and roll again until all is used. Let stand for 2 hours at room temperature.

Preheat oven to 300 degrees. Bake cookies for 20 minutes. Meanwhile, mix powdered sugar with 2 tablespoons of water in a small bowl and stir until smooth. Remove cookies from oven and use brush to coat cookies with the glaze. Return to the oven for an additional 5 minutes. The surface is crusty. Remove cookies with a spatula to wire racks for cooling. Store in airtight container for up to 3-4 weeks in a cool area. Place waxed paper between layers.

Poached Pears in Wine with Glazed Lemon Peel

Preparation Time: 15 Minutes
Cooking Time: 20-35 Minutes

Equipment

Potato/vegetable peeler	Wooden spoon
Large saucepan with lid	Measuring spoons and cups

Ingredients

6	Firm Bosc or Bartlett type pears (1 per person)	1	cinnamon stick
2	cups dry white wine		Thin strips of lemon zest from skin of 1 lemon
3/4	cup granulated sugar		

Using a potato peeler, peel the pears; do not remove the stem. Cut the bottom of each pear so it is flat and will stand up.

Combine the sugar, wine, cinnamon stick, and zest in a large saucepan. Add the pears. Cover and simmer over low heat, turning the pears every 5 minutes or so, until pears are tender when pierced with a sharp knife.

Remove the pears and place upright in a serving dish. Continue to boil the syrup, increasing heat if necessary, until liquid is thick, yet can be poured, and being careful that lemon peels don't stick to bottom of pan. Pour syrup over pears and garnish tops by trailing lemon peels across the top and sides.

Glazed Nut Clusters

Preparation Time: 10 Minutes

Equipment

Large oiled tray or oiled marble
   slab
Medium-size saucepan
Measuring cup

Tea towel
Baking tray
Spoon

Ingredients

1   pound hazelnuts
1   pound almonds
        OR
    Pistachio nuts (unsalted)

        OR
    Toasted Sesame seeds
2   cups granulated sugar
    Vegetable oil

Blanch almonds to remove skins, drop in boiling water for about 2 minutes until skins loosen. Immediately remove and rub with toweling to remove skin.

Toast almonds on baking tray in 350-degree oven, stirring occasionally, until golden (about 5 minutes). Remove from oven and mix in bowl with hazelnuts.

Make small bite-size piles of nuts on the oiled tray.

Melt sugar over low heat until it melts, swirl pan. Allow it to turn a light brown color. Remove from heat and pour over clusters. It will hold nuts together as it hardens. You may need to do a little shaping with an oiled spoon. Be careful! Hot sugar syrup burns terribly.

Or, pour nuts into syrup and mix and then pour onto oiled sheet or oiled marble slab and spread out with a spoon. When hard, crack into pieces and store in airtight container.

Let pan and spoon soak in hot water; residue will dissolve and no scrubbing should be necessary on the clean-up.

Christmas
December 25

History

Christmas Eve through Twelfth Night, January 6, is one of the two most holy of Christian holidays, the other being Easter. Christmas Eve, December 24, is the most religious evening of the holiday season as it commemorates the night when Jesus was born. For devout Christians, the coming of the 'Saviour' heralds new beginnings for mankind as the birth of the Christ, the only Son of God, brings light to a dark, unenlightened world, and the birth of new hope for all. The biblical story recounts how the parents of the soon to be born Jesus traveled to the city of Bethlehem, to be counted for a census. Unable to find lodging at an inn, they had to settle for accommodations in a stable of animals. It was in these surroundings that their child was born. It is written that a bright star shone over the stable acting as a guide for shepherds and Wise Men (Magi) from the East who came bearing gifts for the infant whom they honored as the Messiah whose coming had been foretold.

Today, many celebrate Christmas Eve by going to an evening or midnight mass, often held by candlelight, where the Christmas story is told and carols of joy extolling the coming of a Messiah are sung. After this service, their fast is broken and a special meal is served. Some countries hold with a tradition that Christmas Eve is the night when the animals may receive holy communion and are, at this time only, able to talk.

As the time of year also corresponds with the winter solstice (exact dates for the solstice vary with the lunar year), many practices of pagan cultures became woven into 'Christian' traditions as the Western world converted to Christianity. December 25 was a pagan Roman holiday celebrated as *Dies Natalis Invicti Solis* (Birthday of the Unconquered Sun), marking the winter solstice, and was also an important festival of the Phrygian gods,

Attis and Mithra, whose Eastern cult came with the Roman legions to Britain. Saturnalia, a festival dedicated to Saturn, the God of Plenty, was celebrated from the December solstice until the New Year was ushered in. Trees were trimmed with treats and trinkets for Saturn, and it became a time of revelry and masquerades when no class distinctions were made; the Lord of Misrule ruled! Evergreens (non-dying with the seasonal changes) and candles were exchanged as presents; bonfires were lit on high hills to strengthen the revivifying sun on his course. Kalends, the Roman New Year, began January 1 and was celebrated for three days. Roman houses were decorated with lights, laurel, and bay leaf greenery, and presents were given to friends, children, and the poor. Divination was practiced to see what fortune the New Year would bring.

The ancient Druids held solstice rites to ensure the return of vegetation with the lengthening days. Holly, ivy, and mistletoe were symbols of life for them, as they are evergreen and bear fruit in the winter. Holly represented man and ivy, woman. Both were needed for the birth of new life. They tied fruit and other offerings onto tree branches and made plum pudding as part of their celebrations. In other cultures, mistletoe was hung over the door of a house as a talisman to ward off witchcraft and was also used to encourage healing and fertility, hence the tradition of kissing under the mistletoe. Branches of the juniper tree are often used in decorations as its sap is said to ward off evil. The juniper is the tree, it is said, which helped to hide the Holy Family as they escaped the Roman persecution on their later journey to Egypt.

Depending on locale, different Christian cultures have evolved different Christmas traditions, many stemming from their ancient past. The use of an evergreen wreath, a remnant of pagan rituals, evolved into a Christian symbol of God's eternal love; the green signifying victory over death. The Yule candle, placed in a window, guides the Christ child through the darkness. The Yule log, lit from a piece of the previous year's log is a strong Norse, Celtic, English, and French tradition honoring ancient gods and perpetual light. The log should be large enough to burn until Epiphany, Twelfth Night, when the three Wise Men came to Jesus. The tradition of the Boar's Head Feast stems from medieval England, when a scholar's book was used to fend off an attack by a wild boar. Killing the boar, the scholar then cut off the head to save his book, lodged in the boar's mouth, and brought the head back as a trophy for feasting. The Norse roasted boar to honor their god Freyr. Wassailing, Old Saxon *"waes hael,"* good health, was a drink of mulled ale, eggs, curdled cream, roast apples, nuts and spices. Nuts and candied fruit symbolized the royalty of the newborn Jesus, as these were costly items, and their golden color and aroma evoked the gold, frankincense, and myrrh given to the baby by the Three Kings from the East. Animal-shaped cookies represented the ancient burnt offerings, i.e., the sacrifice of goats, lambs, and pigs, with pig shapes often hailing the start of the Advent season. Mummers parading in costume and performing boisterous pantomimes of death and resurrection mirrors the Roman Saturnalian traditions and caroling grew out of "waits" who went from house to house singing. In France and Italy the creche (Nativity) scene is an important display, both in the church and in the home.

The first evergreen 'Christmas tree' was introduced in the Upper Rhine Valley of Germany and then later, the German, Martin Luther, a fifteenth-sixteenth century Protestant reformer, placed candles on an evergreen tree to imitate the lights of the starry heavens from whence Christ came. The tradition spread slowly to the Catholics, but the Puritans decried any celebration of Christmas as a pagan invention. Contrary to popular belief, British Queen Victoria did not erect the first Christmas tree in England, but her predecessors Queen Charlotte and George IV put up the first tree; the German spouses of the English royalty, were, most likely, behind the idea. With Queen Victoria and her German husband, Albert, the use of a Christmas tree became widespread after she put one up in Windsor Castle for Christmas in 1841. However, Charles Dickens and his successful book, *A Christmas Carol*, is perhaps most responsible for popularizing what many think of as a 'Victorian' Christmas, still imitated by many today.

It is said that the first Christmas tree in the United States—remember the Purians had decried the 'pagan' aspects of Christmas—was put up by a lonely twenty-one year old Bavarian immigrant, August Imgard, on Christmas Eve, 1847. Missing his traditions, he inaugurated another, and to this day, in Wooster, Ohio, a tree is put up to remember that first tree.

Christmas cards evolved from handmade colored papers written with a holiday sentiment. When the one penny postal service was established in England in 1840, cards began to be exchanged at longer distances. Sir Henry Cole prepared the first commercial card in 1846.

Santa Claus, a late-nineteenth-century invention, stemmed from the story of the early Christian Armenian bishop, Saint Nicholas, who gave to the poor. Indeed, St. Nicholas had made his appearance in Holland and elsewhere, placing goodies in children's shoes on December 6, his commemorative day. However, the Sinta Claus of the seventeenth-century New York Dutch had to give way to the momentum gathering with a nineteenth-century visualization of Santa in the painting by American, Thomas Nast, and the popularization of the poem, *The Night Before Christmas,* by Clement Moore. This poem popularized the idea of Santa coming down the chimney and leaving presents for the good boys and girls on Christmas Eve. In many countries, presents are not exchanged until Twelfth Night, Epiphany, the night when tradition says the Wise Men came to visit the baby Jesus. Epiphany also signals the end of the holiday season.

Overall, Christmas in America has combined as many traditions as it has cultures, making it a holiday season with variety and a wide selection of foods and confections bound up in national traditions. The Christian Festival of Light is one of Spiritual renewal by the Christ light made accessible for all Mankind.

Decoration

It is time to "deck the halls with boughs of holly," ropes of long-needle pine, juniper, bay, spruce and mistletoe. Hang wreaths on doors, put lights on bushes and trees outside and indoors, set up a profusion of candles and add color with poinsettia plants and amaryllis. Every house has its own character and should be decorated with the creativity and individuality of the owner. To avoid clutter and chaos, an underlying color scheme should be planned and a theme carried through from the Christmas tree to the mantle piece decorations to the holiday table. All hues of reds and greens, pink, silver, gold and plaid items can be found in profusion. Suit yourself on your decor, from your own national traditions to country, colonial, or modern decor. Determine your table centerpiece of greens, flowers, candles, pinecones, angels, nutcrackers, Santas, or a gingerbread house and have the table linen reflect the colors.

If you've decided you have the time to go all out, start decorating outside on the long Thanksgiving weekend or in the first week in December. It all takes longer to decorate than you think it will and it still might be warm enough not to freeze your fingers if you're hanging lights on the house, bushes or trees. Make sure you have a lot of extension cords (outdoor variety), multiple sockets, light timers and spare bulbs. Test each line before stringing them up. Avoid strings of lights where one goes out and they all go out. Make sure to encase the outdoor electrical plug connections in a waterproof plastic bag, tightly closed, or the lights might short out if it rains or snows. Place the lights on a timer, available in hardware, garden centers and craft stores. A wreath or spray of green on the door is easy to purchase if you don't have time to create one of your own design.

If you are placing electric candles in the windows to light the way for the Christ child, they can be set up in early December.

An Advent wreath with three candles, plus one, should be readied in a prominent place. Light the main candle and an additional one each of the three Sundays before Christmas.

Decide if you are having a live tree or an artificial one. The live tree should probably not go up before December 15, as it will dry out in the warmth of the house. Always put water in the base of a live tree and double-check lights for frayed cords and shorts. Don't risk a fire. Never leave the lights on when you're away from home. The same time frame is recommended for live greens, as they will also dry out quickly, especially the roped greens. There are good imitation rope greens available, and for the cost of one or two year's fresh greens, the imitations may be recycled for years. With the dimmed lights of the season, it will be difficult to tell the difference from their live cousins. Intertwining lights in their branches will also be safer.

Put a small artificial tree in your kitchen and decorate with lemons and limes studded with cloves, attach cinnamon sticks, mini cookie cutters, whisks, and gingerbread cookies with red and green ribbons tied in bows. Create an heirloom tree, adding a new significant ornament from year to year as you and your children grow older. Decorating each year will bring back floods of wonderful memories. Have a small tree that the children decorate by making their own ornaments, paper chains, cranberry and popcorn ropes and candy canes. Place a small jingle bells tree on a side table and add plaid ribbons and white lights, pinecones and bells. Create a tree using one color of ornamentation, all gold, silver or white; insert baby's breath or glittered gold or silver floral pieces. Have a "family" tree in the family room with your year to year memories and a "grown up" or sophisticated tree in the living room. Be creative and enjoy.

Involve the children in making ornaments, gingerbread houses and cookies, and even in putting on your own Christmas pageant with easily put together costumes. Type up words to Christmas Carols and popular songs and bind them together with ribbon so everyone can sing along.

Don't forget the music as you decorate and have your parties!

Christmas Dinners

If you will be doing a lot of entertaining, plan your menus, desserts, and snacks and start cooking early as soon as Thanksgiving ends. It's always good to have something on hand if last minute guests drop in and you will avoid panic by having something to serve. Stollens, certain types of cookies and cakes can be prepared ahead and frozen. Fruitcake improves as it ages. Gingerbread houses make great centerpieces, and they are fun to make. However, they are time consuming! Don't leave them to the last week before Christmas.

I am offering a casual meal for a tree-trimming party or an informal Christmas Eve, a traditional, more formal Christmas Eve meal and one for Christmas Day. As the fruitcake, stollen, mince tarts and cookies can be served at any of the meals, in addition to other desserts noted, I have placed their recipes at the end of the chapter. As gingerbread houses deserve a book unto themselves, I recommend you to *The Gingerbread Book,* by Steven Stellingwerf. The dough recipes and techniques described have proven to be infallible. If you are adventurous, make your own design and measure it out on graph paper. Be creative. I've baked everything from Hansel and Gretel houses to fortified castles and cathedrals!

Casual Christmas Eve Dinner for Six

Ideal for Tree Trimming, Present Wrapping, Carol Singing Evening

Select your menu and make up your shopping list as suggested in the Introduction.

Menu

Hors d'Oeuvres
Chips, Fritos, Pretzel Sticks, Mixed Salted Nuts
Vegetable Christmas Wreath with Sour Cream and Garlic
    Dip
Mixed Sausage Board

Main Course
Cheese Fondue with French Baguette Cubes
Apple/Grape Salad

Dessert
Tray of Christmas Cookies and/or Mince Tarts, Fruit Cake

Beverages
Mulled Wine
Flavored or Spiced Coffee or Tea

You will need a fondue pot and forks and either alcohol or 'sterno' for the heat, depending on the type of pot you have, or use a portable hot plate. Make sure to place the heated pot and its warmer stand on a trivet. Heavy ceramic pots suit a cheese fondue the best, but a metal type may be used, watching that the cheese in the bottom of the pot doesn't burn.

I am assuming the cookies and fruitcake await in a cool pantry.

Timetable

Day Prior or Early Same Day
Clean and cut vegetables for wreath, refrigerate

continued . . .

Make sour cream dip
Slice sausage and put mustards and pickles in bowls

Three-Four Hours Prior to Guests
Grate cheese
Set table
Set out dessert onto serving plates and cover with plastic
    wrap
Make apple/grape salad
Assemble vegetable wreath

One Hour Prior to Guest Arrival
Make mulled wine, don't heat
Set out chips, pretzels, nuts into bowls
Cut bread into cubes and put into serving basket, cover

20 Minutes Prior to Guest Arrival
Heat wine

Twenty Minutes Prior to Eating
Make fondue
Put bread on table
Set out salad
Prepare coffee and start towards end of meal

Hors d'Oeuvres

Chips, Fritos, Mixed Salted Nuts

Preparation Time: 3 Minutes

Place in separate serving bowls. Chips can be placed near sour cream dip.

Vegetable Christmas Wreath

Preparation Time: 20 Minutes

Equipment

Colander
Salad spinner
Paring and chopping knife
Bowl

Small mixing bowl
Spoon
Garlic press
Plastic wrap

Ingredients

Cherry tomatoes, pint size box
Head of cauliflower, cut in flowers
Radishes, carved into petals
1 cucumber, thinly sliced, preferably seedless English variety
Head of curly endive, chicory
Red pepper

Sour cream and garlic dip

Pint of sour cream
4-5 garlic cloves, squeezed through garlic press or finely minced
3 Minced chives to garnish

Wash vegetables thoroughly and drain.
Core cauliflower and break flowers into bite-size pieces.
Cut tops and tails off of radishes. With sharp knife, make a petal by taking about ¼ of the circumference of side peel from the top to about one-third of the way down the radish; continue around circumference of the radish. Place in ice water to open the flower.

359

Cut red pepper in half and remove seeds and membrane. Using a sharp knife, carve into a bow shape to put on your wreath. Cut the rest into small bite-size pieces.

Mix squeezed or minced garlic with the sour cream and allow to sit at least an hour, covered with plastic wrap, in the refrigerator to mesh flavors. Garnish with finely minced chives.

Arrange the curly endive, chicory in the shape of a wreath on a plate or tray. Place the various items to resemble decorations on a wreath. Serve with the sour cream dip in a side dish.

Mixed Sausage Board

Preparation Time: 15 Minutes

Equipment

Cutting board
Sharp medium size knife

3 small dishes and spoons or
   spreaders for mustards

Ingredients

Variety of sausages, for example:
Pepperoni
Dry cured salami with herbs or pepper coating
Hungarian sausage
Kielbassa
Garlic sausage
2 types of your favorite pickles
2 Thin baguettes, cut into rounds (leftovers can be used in fondue)
Cocktail rye or pumpernickel bread (or cut larger slices in quarters and cut Christmas shapes with cookie cutters)
Deli mustard
Dijon mustard
Horseradish mustard

Sausages will be served on a large cutting board with a knife. Slice ⅓ of each sausage and leave rest of sausage on the cutting board for guests to slice themselves. If there is a skin on it, remove it in its entirety in the kitchen.

Place mustards in small dishes/bowls with spoons.

Main Course

Cheese Fondue with French Baguette

Preparation Time: 20 Minutes
Cooking Time: 10-15 Minutes

Equipment

Fondue pot and forks
Heating material, Sterno or
  alcohol
Chopping knife

Food processor fitted with metal
  blade or hand grater
Large mixing bowl
Whisk

Ingredients

Note: Select cheese carefully. American Swiss does not melt as well as imported; a mature cheese is required. An acidic white wine is required to liquefy the cheese and make it homogeneous. If not acidic enough, add about one teaspoon of lemon juice to each ½ cup of wine. It will take about ½ cup of wine for each ½ pound of cheese. Better to start with less wine and add more if needed. Always add hot wine, not cold. If cheese separates in the cooking process or becomes lumpy during dinner, replace it on the stove and add ½ teaspoon of cornstarch. Whisk it thoroughly. If fondue is heavy, add a pinch of baking soda to lighten it.

¾ pound imported Swiss cheese, shredded
¾ Gruyere cheese, shredded
4½ tablespoons flour
1 large clove garlic
1½ cups dry, acidic white wine, like a Riesling
3 teaspoons lemon juice, if needed, see above
¼ cup kirsch (optional), add more wine if necessary for consistency
⅛ teaspoon salt
¼ teaspoon white pepper
⅛ teaspoon nutmeg

2 French baguettes (long thin loaves of crisp surface bread) cut into
  bite-size pieces
Cornichon pickles and marinated onions, optional

*Apples, celery chunks, boiled potatoes, peeled and cubed, carrot slices
  of green pepper chunks can also be served with the bread and
  dunked.

361

Cut cheese into smaller chunks and place in food processor or shred by hand on grater; don't over-process. Place the shredded cheese in a bowl and sprinkle with the flour, mix.

Cut garlic in two and rub the inside of the pot. Discard the garlic.

Pour the wine in the pot and place over high heat. Do not let come to a boil. Add lemon juice at this point, if needed.

Add cheese by handfuls, stirring constantly with a wooden spoon in a figure-eight motion until cheese is melted. Add the next handful of cheese and repeat until all the cheese has been incorporated and begins to bubble. If fondue needs thinning, add warm wine at this point. Add the kirsch, if desired, and seasonings, stir until blended and bring to the table.

Serve in the center of the table so all guests can reach the pot. They each have their own color-coded fork. They take a piece of bread on their fork and dip it in the cheese.

Apple/Grape Salad

Preparation Time: 10 Minutes

Equipment

Chopping knife
Small mixing bowl

Whisk
Salad bowl with servers

Ingredients

1½	cups diced celery (about 4 large stalks)	1	cup "Miracle Whip" or Mayonnaise
2	cups chopped firm red apples (about 3), with skin left on	1	lemon, juiced
1	cup purple grapes, pitted and sliced in half (or red seedless)		Iceberg, Romaine or Boston lettuce leaves, 1 large leaf per person
¾	cups coarsely chopped walnuts or pecans		

Prepare celery, apples, grapes and nuts. Whisk lemon juice into the mayonnaise to thin it and immediately blend it through these ingredients so apples don't turn brown. Refrigerate until use.

Serve on individual salad plates. Place large lettuce leaf (any type may be used) on individual salad plate and fill center with salad mixture.

Desserts

Plates of cookies, mince tarts, and fruitcake

Beverages

Mulled Wine

Preparation Time: 10 Minutes
Cooking Time: 10-20 Minutes

Equipment

Chafing dish/punch bowl/fondue
   pot that can withstand heat
Large saucepan
Warming candle

Trivet
Serving ladle
Match

Ingredients

4	whole allspice	1	cup granulated sugar
4	whole cardamom	8	dried apricots, cut in
1	stick cinnamon		quarters
2	bottles dry red Bordeaux	¼	cup raisins
	type wine	½	pint cognac, optional

Place spices in a piece of cheese cloth and tie top with a string.

Place spices in the saucepan and pour in the wine, sugar, apricots and raisins. Heat until the sugar dissolves and the wine comes to a simmer. Do this slowly so the spices will have time to leach into the wine. Do not boil. Remove spice bag.

Pour into a heat-proof punch bowl for serving. Pour cognac over the top at the serving table and ignite with a match. When the festive fire extinguishes, serve in small demitasse size cups with some fruit on the bottom. Keep remaining wine over a warming candle so it maintains its temperature.

Flavored or Spiced Coffee or Tea

Preparation Time: 5 Minutes
Cooking Time: 5-8 Minutes, depending on type of pot

There are many types of ground coffee available today in any supermarket. Try a hazelnut, almond/vanilla, cinnamon, mocha blend, or any other favorite you may have.

Or, for 8 cups of coffee, add 4 teaspoons ground cardamom, 2½ teaspoons cinnamon, 1 teaspoon nutmeg and 1 tablespoon of sugar to the coffee while brewing. Top brewed coffee with whipped cream (1 cup chilled heavy cream whipped until stiff with 1 tablespoon each of powdered sugar and brandy beat in at the end).

Prepare coffee ahead of the meal. Get water ready and pour flavored coffee grounds into appropriate container. Beat the optional whipped cream, cover and refrigerate. Start to brew the coffee as the meal is being served.

For tea, add the spices and sugar to the tea leaves while brewing. Omit the whipped cream, but the brandy could be served in the tea.

Formal Christmas Eve Dinner for 6

Select your menu and make up your shopping list as suggested in the Introduction.

Menu

Hors d'Oeuvres
Pine Cone Cheese Spread with Crackers
Crab Cakes
Egg Nog
Mulled Cranberry Punch

First Course
Fresh Watercress Soup

Dinner
Roast Goose
Apple and Sour Dough Bread Dressing

continued . . .

Red Cabbage
Curly Endive Salad with Balsamic Vinaigrette

Dessert
Christmas Tree Cake
Christmas Cookies

Beverages
Flavored Christmas Coffee or Tea

Timetable

One Day Prior
Make cheese spread
Make watercress soup and refrigerate
Bake and ice Christmas tree cake
Make goose stock, optional

Christmas Eve
Start goose and stock 4 hours prior to serving
Make red cabbage, can be reheated later in the day
Make apple and sour dough bread dressing up to adding
    chicken broth
Clean salad greens, refrigerate
Make salad dressing
Make crab cake batter
Arrange Christmas cookies, candies, tarts on plate and
    cover
Prepare but do not start coffee and tea

30 Minutes Prior to Guests
Put cheese spread and crackers on serving tray
Fry crab cakes and keep warm in oven
Put out cocktail napkins

One Hour Prior to Dinner
Complete dressing and bake
Slowly start to reheat soup, stir occasionally

continued . . .

20 Minutes Prior to Dinner
Warm red cabbage
Check dressing casserole
Remove cake from refrigerator
Finish gravy

Hors d'Oeuvres

Pine Cone Shaped Cheese Spread with Crackers

Preparation Time: 20 Minutes

Equipment

Electric mixer
Hand grater or food processor
   fitted with metal blade
Mixing bowl

Rubber scraper
Paring knife
Waxed paper, plastic wrap
Cheese spreader

Ingredients

1   large 1¾ pound Edam
     cheese ball or cheddar
     cheese
1   cup beer or ale
¼   cup softened butter
1   teaspoon caraway seeds
1   teaspoon dry English
     mustard (powdered)

2   cups whole almonds (with
     brown skin)
     Assorted crackers
     "Real" pine branch for
     decoration

Bring cheese to room temperature. Remove waxed rind. Cut cheese ball into wedges and grate the cheese into a bowl or use food processor. Let stand until it is very soft. Add the other ingredients and beat with an electric mixer or pulse with processor until incorporated.

Divide mixture onto two sheets of waxed paper for two pinecones or make one large cone. Shape the mixture into the shape of a pinecone. Starting at "bottom" of pinecone, make overlapping layers of almonds all the way to the "top" of the pinecone. Wrap carefully in waxed paper or plastic wrap and refrigerate until half of an hour before serving.

366

Unwrap carefully and place on a platter decorated with a pine branch and serve with crackers. You'll need a cheese spreader.

Crab Cakes with Salsa

Preparation Time: 25 Minutes
Cooking Time: 4-7 Minutes, in Batches

Equipment

Cutting knife
Mixing bowl
Measuring cups and spoons
Wooden spoon
Pie pan or plate

Cookie sheet lined with
   parchment
Plastic or plastic wrap
Skillet
Turner

Ingredients
Crab Cakes

1	pound lump crabmeat (canned or fresh)		Pinch cayenne pepper
			Salt and pepper to taste
1	large egg, beaten; plus 1 yolk if needed	½	plus 1½-2 cups Panko Japanese bread crumbs or other unflavored crumbs
¼	cup minced fresh parsley leaves	¼	cup olive oil for cooking
2	tablespoons fresh lemon juice		

Salsa

2	ripe tomatoes, seeded, juiced and diced	1	small clove garlic, minced
⅓	cup minced cilantro	2-3	tablespoons fresh lemon or lime juice
⅓	cup minced red onion		Salt to taste

Crab Cakes

If using canned crab meat, drain well through a sieve and press out excess liquid; place crab into mixing bowl. Add other ingredients, including ½ cup of bread crumbs and mix together; if 'batter' is too loose and falls apart, add an egg yolk.

367

Pour 1-2 cups of breadcrumbs into a plate or pie pan and form one-inch crab patties. Place on parchment paper, covered on a baking tray, and refrigerate until ready to cook.

Preheat the oven to 300 degrees. Heat olive oil in a skillet. Gently place crab patties into oil; do not crowd the pan and cook until light brown on both sides. Drain on paper towels and place in oven on baking tray to keep warm. Continue cooking the rest of the batch the same way.

Salsa

Core tomatoes and scoop out the seeds with your finger. Gently squeeze over the sink to remove juice; slice and dice. Mince cilantro, onion and garlic and mix with lemon juice and salt to taste. This can be made a couple of hours ahead.

Serve crab cakes with toothpicks and salsa in a side dish with a spoon. If making larger crab cakes, serve salsa on the top along with a fork and a plate.

First Course

Fresh Watercress Soup

Preparation Time: 10 Minutes
Cooking Time: 30 Minutes

Equipment

3 quart saucepan with lid   Wooden stirring spoon
Blender, food processor fitted with   Ladle
    metal blade or electric "Smart
    Stick"

Ingredients

1 medium-size onion, chopped
3 tablespoons unsalted butter
5½ cups chicken broth
1 large russet potato, peeled, cut into ½-inch cubes
4 cups packed watercress (about 4 large bunches): reserve a few leaves
    for garnish when serving
½ teaspoon salt
¾ cup heavy cream
Freshly ground black pepper

Melt butter in large saucepan over medium-low heat. Add chopped onion and sauté gently until tender and translucent, about 5 minutes. Do not brown. Stir in chicken stock and potato. Cover and simmer until potato is tender, about 15 minutes.

Meanwhile wash and dry the watercress, cutting bottom ¼ inch off stem. Both the leaf and the stem will be used in cooking.

When potato is tender, add the watercress and the salt and simmer until watercress is wilted and tender, about 4-6 minutes. Remove from the heat.

Purée in batches. Hold on lid of blender or processor and do not overfill or it will spill all over and you might get burned from the hot liquid, or use a "Smart Stick" device, which can purée directly in pan.

Pour soup into a clean saucepan and add heavy cream. If serving soon, rewarm; if serving the next day or later in the day, pour into a storage container and refrigerate.

Taste to adjust seasonings. If too thick, extra cream can be added. This might especially be true if refrigerating. Bring to a simmer before serving. Ladle into bowls and garnish with a fresh watercress leaf.

Dinner

Roast Goose

Preparation Time: 10 Minutes
Cooking Time: About 3-4 Hours According to size of Goose

Equipment

Shallow roasting pan with rack
Basting bulb
Instant read thermometer
Cooking fork
2 quart saucepan
3 quart saucepan
Large cutting knife or cleaver

Cup
Fat can (empty coffee can is ideal)
Aluminum foil
Whisk
Large sieve
4-cup measuring cup/glass bowl

Ingredients

1 12-14 pound goose, giblets and neck reserved

Stock
Cook while goose is roasting or day prior

	Neck, heart, gizzard	5	sprigs fresh parsley
2	tablespoons vegetable or canola oil	2	bay leaves
2	cups chopped onions	3	cups chicken broth, more may be needed
1	cup chopped carrots	4	cups of water
5	sprigs fresh thyme or 1 teaspoon dried	1	teaspoon salt
		1/4	teaspoon pepper

Gravy

1 cup tawny port, preferred, or sherry or red wine
2½ tablespoons chopped fresh thyme or 2½ teaspoons dried
4 cups stock
3 tablespoons cornstarch

Fresh or frozen and defrosted goose may be used. As a goose is very fatty, this method seeks to rid the goose of fat by pouring hot water over the skin throughout the cooking process, so you must be available throughout the cooking process. Pull and cut

370

off as much extra fat as you can from the chest cavity and around the neck areas.

Preheat the oven to 425 degrees. Position rack in center of oven.

Cut off the first joint of the wing, the tip using a cleaver or very sharp knife. Wash and pat the goose dry. Do not truss. Prick the skin all over, especially the fatty areas, with the tines of a fork. Place on rack in roasting pan and roast for 15 minutes.

Meanwhile, bring 2 cups of water to a simmer in a saucepan. Reduce oven temperature to 350 degrees. Open the oven door and using a baster, remove any fat in the roasting pan. Baste goose with simmering water and return goose to oven. Continue to roast, baste with hot water, and remove fat and excess basting water every 20 minutes until the goose is done, about 2 hours and 45 minutes. It should register 175 degrees when an instant read thermometer is inserted into the fattest part of the thigh, without touching the bone. If goose is getting too brown, tent lightly with aluminum foil.

Drain any watery liquid from goose into the roasting pan. Place goose on carving board, sprinkle with salt and pepper, and tent with foil.

Pour off water from roasting pan and skim any fat from remaining pan juices. Place roasting pan over high heat and add ¾ cup of port or wine and chopped thyme. Boil until a glaze consistency is attained, scraping the bottom of the pan.

This will take about 5 minutes. Mix the cornstarch with ¼ cup of port or wine in a small bowl or cup and set aside. Add the 4 cups of stock made the day prior or while the goose was cooking and then the cornstarch mixture. Stir constantly while bringing to a boil. Reduce heat and simmer until gravy thickens, stirring or whisking constantly, about 5 minutes.

Carve goose and serve with gravy. Goose is carved in the same manner as a turkey or chicken; see Introduction.

Stock
Discard the liver. Chop the heart and gizzards. Cut the neck into 2-inch lengths with a cleaver or very sharp heavy knife. Heat oil in a heavy Dutch oven or saucepan over medium heat. Add the heart, gizzards and neck and sauté until brown, about 15 minutes. Add the onions, carrots, thyme, parsley and bay leaves and sauté until golden. Scrape bottom of pan often. Add

3 cups of broth and 2 cups of water. Bring to a simmer and cover partially. Continue to simmer for 1 hour and 15 minutes. Skim the surface of the broth occasionally to get rid of the foam.

Strain the stock into a large glass measuring cup or bowl. Discard solids. Skim any fat from the surface. You will need 4 cups of broth. Add additional chicken broth if amount is insufficient. Broth can be made a day ahead to this point. Cover and refrigerate. Skim off additional fat from the top before reheating.

Apple and Sour Dough Bread Dressing

Preparation Time: 20 Minutes
Cooking Time: 20 Minutes
Baking Time: 45 Minutes
Can be prepared one day ahead up to addition of chicken broth.

Equipment

Very large mixing bowl
Measuring cups and spoons
Large skillet
Wooden stirring spoon
Chopping knife
Large buttered casserole

2 baking sheets
Metal spatula
Small bowl
Whisk
Plastic wrap

Ingredients

1-1½ pounds day-old sourdough bread
7 tablespoons unsalted butter
1 medium sweet onion, thinly sliced
1 teaspoon dried thyme
3 medium baking apples, peeled, cored, and cut into ¾-inch cubes
½-¾ cup low salt chicken broth
½ cup minced fresh sage
3 large eggs, beaten to blend

Position rack in center of oven and preheat to 425 degrees.

Remove crusts from the bread (these can be reserved and ground up into breadcrumbs and frozen for another use). Cut bread into ¾-inch cubes. Arrange cubes of bread on two baking sheets and bake until golden, stirring occasionally. Do not burn! Transfer to a large mixing bowl. Melt 3½ tablespoons of the butter over medium-high heat in a heavy large skillet. Add onions and ½ teaspoon of thyme and sauté until the onions are golden and tender, stirring frequently. This should take about 8 minutes. Transfer onion mixture to the bread cubes.

Melt the remaining 3½ tablespoons of butter in the same skillet and add the apples and ½ teaspoon of the thyme. Sauté until apples are golden but firm, about 5 minutes. Stir into the bread and onion mixture. This may be prepared 1 day ahead to this point. Cover with plastic wrap when cool.

Butter a large casserole dish. Preheat oven to 350 degrees. Whisk the eggs and add ½-¾ cup of chicken broth, depending on volume of dish, and minced sage A larger volume of broth will produce a softer bread in the casserole. Pour combined liquids over the bread, onion and apple mixture and combine. Pour into the casserole and bake at 350 for 45 minutes or until crusty on top.

Red Cabbage

Preparation Time: 10 Minutes
Cooking Time: One Hour

Equipment

Four-sided grater or food processor fitted with 1 or 2 millimeter slicing/shredding disk

Large non-reactive saucepan with heavy bottom, or Dutch oven with lid
Stirring spoon

Ingredients

1	medium-size head of red cabbage, shredded	1	teaspoon caraway seeds
5	tablespoons vegetable oil	2	bay leaves
1	small onion, finely chopped or run through food processor with metal blade	1	teaspoon sugar
		1	tablespoon white vinegar
		1	teaspoon salt

Peel off tough outer leaves from the cabbage. Cut the cabbage into quarters and remove the center fibrous spine and tough bottom piece. Cut to fit pieces into the tube of the processor, and using a slicing disk, shred the cabbage. Or, grate cabbage on a grater, being careful not to shred your knuckles and nails!

Heat oil in 2½ quart round enameled cast-iron casserole or heavy bottomed pot. Sauté the chopped onion for about 6 minutes, or until softened. Add the shredded cabbage, caraway seeds, bay leaves, sugar, vinegar and salt. Stir to combine the ingredients. Cover and simmer over low heat for about an hour, or until cabbage is tender. Stir occasionally. Check the pot and add ¼ cup of water if there is any danger of cabbage sticking to the pan. Taste after about 30 minutes and adjust seasoning, sourness, if necessary. You may want to add more vinegar. When cabbage is finished, discard the bay leaves. Although I recommend serving the dish hot with the goose, this cabbage may also be served cold.

Optionally, this dish may be cooked in a 350-degree oven for one hour, or until tender. Cover and check for moisture content as cabbage bakes.

Curly Endive Salad with Balsamic Vinaigrette

Preparation Time: 10 Minutes

Equipment

Colander or salad spinner
Small bowl

Whisk
Salad bowl and tossing utensils

Ingredients

1   medium-size head of curly endive
2   ripe Anjou or Bosc pears, peeled and thinly sliced
½   cup walnut halves
¼   cup olive oil (virgin preferable)

4   tablespoons balasamic vinegar
½   teaspoon salt
¼   teaspoon black pepper or 2-3 turns of a pepper mill

Tear the endive into bite-size pieces, discarding tough stems. Rinse with cold water and dry with paper toweling or in a salad spinner. Refrigerate in a plastic bag if not serving immediately.

Combine dressing ingredients in a small bowl. This can be done ahead. Whisk to combine elements before pouring over salad.

Just before serving, peel and slice the pears and immediately combine with halves of walnuts and endive in a salad bowl. Pour prepared dressing immediately over greens and toss. Pears will brown if not covered in dressing (or lemon juice).

Desserts

Christmas Tree Cake

Preparation Time: 20-25 Minutes
Baking Time: 30-40 Minutes

Equipment

Electric mixer
Mixing bowl
2 medium size mixing bowls
Measuring spoons and cups
Rubber spatula/scraper
Sifter or fine mesh sieve
Zester or fine grater
Juice reamer, squeezer

Christmas tree-shaped baking mold, available in most large hardware or discount chain stores
Large cooking rack
Pastry bay with star and piping tips
Food coloring

Ingredients
Cake

2½	cups all-purpose flour	½	cup unsalted butter (1 stick), softened
1	teaspoon baking soda		
¾	teaspoon salt	1½	cups sugar
1	cup buttermilk	3	eggs
1	teaspoon grated lemon zest		Non-stick cooking spray
3	tablespoons fresh lemon juice		

Preheat the oven to 350 degrees. Grease and flour baking pan. I recommend using a non-stick cooking spray to get into all the crevices.

Sift and combine flour, baking soda, and salt in a small bowl. In a second bowl, combine the buttermilk, lemon zest, and lemon juice.

In large mixing bowl, beat the butter and sugar until combined. Add in the eggs, one at a time until incorporated. Mentally divide the flour and liquid mixture into thirds, and alternately beat into the butter, sugar and egg mixture.

Pour into mold and bake in center of oven until toothpick comes out clean. It will begin to pull away from the side of the pan.

Remove cake from mold onto cooling rack. Frost when cool. Start icing, as it has to chill before applying to cake.

Vanilla Butter Cream Frosting
Equipment

Small saucepan with lid	Rubber spatula, scraper
Pastry brush	Plastic wrap
Candy thermometer	Disposable pastry bags
Electric Mixer	Assortment of decorating tips,
Mixing bowl	star, dots
Measuring spoons and cups	

Ingredients

1¼	cups sugar	Leaf green, red, yellow food
⅓	cup water	coloring
5	egg whites at room	*Choice of*
	temperature	Silver dragees
	Pinch of salt	Chocolate jimmies
⅛	teaspoon cream of tartar	Red hots
3	sticks (1½ cups) unsalted	Multi-colored sprinkles
	butter, softened	Gum drops

Separate the egg whites, reserving the yolks, covered, in refrigerator for another recipe. If whites are cold, place them in a small bowl and set over a larger bowl of hot water for two minutes or so. Stir with finger to test for room temperature.

In a small heavy saucepan, combine the sugar and water and swirl in pan over moderate heat. When sugar is dissolved, cover for a minute to wash down the sides of the pan and dissolve any remaining sugar. Remove lid and place thermometer in liquid. Cook until it reaches 248 degrees F.

Meanwhile, place room temperature egg whites and the salt in a mixing bowl and mix until foamy. Add the cream of tartar and beat the whites until they are stiff, not dry. With the mixer running, pour the sugar syrup in a slow constant stream into the whites. Continue to beat until cool. Beat in the butter a little at a time. Chill, covered, until it reaches a spreadable consistency.

Place cake on serving plate and surround with strips of waxed paper tucked just under the edge of the cake. It makes for a clean plate at the end! You should have about three cups of butter cream frosting. Reserve about a cup for decoration. Tint the larger portion with leaf green food coloring. I prefer using the paste color as it is more intense in color and doesn't thin down the frosting as liquid drops tend to do. A little goes a long way. Use liquid drops if paste is not available. Tint to desired shade of green (or have a white tree) and frost the cake using a small spatula to give the effect of branches, swirling down and out.

Decide how you want to decorate your tree . . . a gold star at the top? Balls of red and gold? A garland? Divide the balance of the icing into saucers or small bowls and color as you desire. If you want to make balls or stars on the tree, insert the star-shaped tube on the end of the pastry bag. Roll the bag down to the frosting and squeeze. Garlands can be piped on using a piping tube and a clean pastry bag with another color.

Does your tree need a brown trunk? Use chocolate sprinkles and press on.

Silver dragees or red hots (cinnamon drops), small gum drops, sprinkles, holiday decorative sugars could all be used instead of colored frosting; make the tree your own. Or, put powdered sugar in a sieve or flour sifter and gently knock white "snow" over the cake just before serving. Remove waxed paper and clean up edges of plate with barely damp paper towel.

Do not refrigerate.

Christmas Day Dinner for 8

Select your menu and make up your shopping list as suggested in the Introduction.

Menu

Hors d'Oeuvres
Eggnog
    OR
Mulled Cranberry Punch
Stilton Cheese Tart
Chicken Liver Paté with Toast Points and Crackers

First Course
Puffed Christmas Tree

Main Course
Prime Ribs of Beef with Horseradish Sauce
Roast Potatoes with Rosemary
Glazed Carrots
String Bean Tree
Christmas Salad
Popovers

Dessert
Buche de Noel
Mince Meat Tarts
Assortment of Christmas Cookies
Fruit Cake

Beverages
Coffee and tea served with candy canes or sticks of rock
    candy
Cocoa with marshmallows or candy canes for children

Timetable

Day Prior
Make Buche de Noel
Prepare and bake pastry for Stilton tart, cover tightly when cool
Bake Christmas tree puffs and store in airtight container when cold
Make liver paté
Peel and slice carrots, put in plastic bag in refrigerator
Clean string beans and store in plastic bag in refrigerator
Wash salad greens

Christmas Day
Make eggnog or mulled cranberry punch . . . can be made day prior
Check meat weight and schedule cooking time for dinner
Peel and cut potatoes and hold in cold water until one hour prior to dinner
Make horseradish sauce
Make toast points for paté

Two Hours Prior to Dinner
Prepare stuffing for tree puffs
Bake Stilton tart
Bake mock plum pudding and sauce
Toast almonds for string beans
Make salad dressing

30 Minutes Prior to Guests
Arrange paté and toast points
Put Stilton tart on serving plate
Heat mulled cranberry punch
Warm eggnog, if desired warm, can also be served cold

60 Minutes Prior to Dinner
Dry potatoes and put in oven
Make popovers
Prepare coffee and tea but do not start
Prepare cocoa mixture

continued . . .

379

10 Minutes Prior to Dinner
Heat puffs and stuff
Start carrots
Start string beans
Toss salad with dressing
Set out horseradish
Start coffee and tea

Recipes

Hors D'Oeuvres

Eggnog

Preparation and Cooking Time: 6-8 Minutes

Equipment

Large saucepan
Mixing bowl
Measuring cups and spoons

Whisk
Wooden stirring spoon

Ingredients

3 cups whipping cream
1½ cups half and half
9 large egg yolks
¾ cup sugar
1½ teaspoons ground nutmeg

9 tablespoons dry Sherry
Additional ground fresh
nutmeg for garnish

Simmer cream and half and half in a saucepan. Whisk egg yolks and sugar in a bowl to blend. Gradually whisk half of cream mixture into egg mixture and return to saucepan. Whisk in balance. Stir over medium-low heat until it coats back of spoon and thickens, about 4-5 minutes. Regulate heat. Do not boil. Strain into mixing bowl and add nutmeg. Cool slightly. Cover and chill if making day prior or serving cold.

To serve, divide eggnog into serving cups and stir 1 tablespoon of sherry into each cup. Garnish with grated nutmeg and serve.

Mulled Cranberry Punch

Preparation and Cooking Time: 10–15 Minutes

Equipment

2 quart saucepan
Measuring cups
Wooden stirring spoon

Cheesecloth
String

Ingredients

1 quart cranberry juice
2 cups apple cider
¼ cup golden raisins

5 cloves
5 whole allspice

Garnish with thin orange slices threaded on cinnamon sticks, one per person.

Place cloves and allspice into center of cheesecloth and tie. Mix juices, raisins and spices in saucepan and heat slowly until warm. Serve warm in cups with raisins in bottom of each cup. Garnish with orange and cinnamon stick.

Stilton Cheese Tart

Preparation Time: 1 Hour 30 minutes, Includes
Refrigerator Time
Cooking Time: 30-35 Minutes

Equipment

14″ × 4½″ rectangular flan form
    set (or 9″ tart pan with
    removable fluted rims)
Baking (cookie) sheet
Food processor fitted with plastic
    blade
Measuring spoons and cups
Rubber spatula, scraper
Metal weights for pastry or 3 cups
    dried beans or raw rice

Aluminum foil
Medium size saucepan
Measuring spoons and cups
Whisk
Mini prep or nut chopper
Cooling rack
Plastic wrap

Ingredients

Pastry Dough

Can be made one day ahead and refrigerated.

¾   stick (6 tablespoons) cold
      unsalted butter
4   ounces cream cheese, cut
      into small pieces

1   cup all-purpose flour
½   teaspoon salt

    Combine all ingredients in a food processor and pulse the motor until the dough begins to form a ball. Gather dough into a ball and remove onto a piece of plastic wrap. Flatten slightly, wrap and chill for about an hour (or overnight).
    On a floured surface, roll dough into a ⅛-inch thick rectangle, slightly larger than flan mold. Place in mold, trim excess dough and crimp edges decoratively. Place on baking sheet.

Ingredients
Tart

⅓ cup walnuts, ground fine, plus 6 attractive halves for garnish

½ cup half and half

3 ounces Stilton cheese, crumbled

2 large eggs
Watercress or other greens for garnish

Preheat oven to 425 degrees.

Sprinkle ground walnuts over tart shell. Prick bottom and sides of shell with a fork. Refrigerate 30 minutes.

Line shells with aluminum foil and fill with weights or dried beans or raw rice and bake in 425 degree oven for 10 minutes. Carefully remove foil and weights. Bake the shell 5-6 additional minutes or until golden. Remove from oven and cool on rack.

Meanwhile, in a saucepan, bring the half and half to a simmer and add Stilton. Stir until just melted, controlling temperature so it doesn't scorch. Remove from heat and cool slightly. Whisk eggs and pour a few drops of warm cream into the eggs (if mixture is too hot, the eggs will scramble), pour in the rest, whisking as you pour. Place mixture in shell and bake at 375 degrees for 30-35 minutes, or until a knife, inserted into the custard ½ inch from the edge, comes out clean. Let tart cool at room temperature, then carefully remove the flan form. Transfer the tart to a serving platter. Garnish top with walnut halves and greens around portions of the platter. Cut cross-wise to serve.

Chicken Liver Paté with Toast Points and Crackers

Preparation Time: 3 hours Waiting Time, 10 Minutes Prep
Cooking Time: 20 Minutes
Must Be Done One Day in Advance

Equipment

Food processor fitted with metal blade
Medium-size skillet
Small terrine or mold
Mixing bowl

Measuring spoons and cups
Stirring spoon
Plastic wrap
Colander

Ingredients

12 large chicken livers
1 tablespoon finely chopped parsley
3 tablespoons finely-chopped onion
Pinch of thyme
2 tablespoons olive oil
7 oz. white fresh breadcrumbs
8 tablespoons cold milk

1 egg yolk
Salt, pepper to taste
Non-stick cooking spray or vegteable oil
6 Slices white bread, crusts removed, rolled thin and lightly toasted
Water Crackers

Two or three hours before you are going to make the paté, clean the livers, removing the little veins and membranes and cut away any green-looking matter (gall . . . which would make for a bitter taste). Place livers in a bowl with 4 tablespoons cold milk, cover and soak in refrigerator for 2-3 hours. Drain livers and pat dry with paper towels. Season with salt and pepper. (Discard milk.)

Heat olive oil in skillet, when oil smokes, add livers and sauté until brown, turning with spatula frequently. Place in colander to drain. Add onion to oil, reduce heat so they don't brown . . . they should be golden, about 10 minutes.

Meanwhile soak the breadcrumbs in 4 tablespoons of milk. Fresh breadcrumbs can be easily made by placing torn up white bread into the food processor and pulsed until desired size is obtained. Extras can be frozen in a plastic bag for further uses.

Saving heels of bread and freezing until a batch is obtained is an inexpensive way to use all your bread pieces.

Drain the breadcrumbs and squeeze to remove moisture. Place crumbs and livers in food processor and pulse briefly. Scrape into the skillet and mix in the chopped onion, parsley, thyme and egg yolk. Cook over a low heat, stirring constantly with a wooden spoon, allowing it to come to a brief boil. The moisture will cook out. If it gets too dry and sticks to pan, add 2 tablespoons additional milk. Season to taste with salt and pepper.

Place in a greased terrine or other mold, line with enough plastic wrap to hang over the sides, oil then add paté and cover with the sides of the plastic wrap. Refrigerate for 24 hours for flavors to mesh. Turn out onto a serving platter and serve with Toast Points and Crackers and a bit of greenery.

First Course

Puffed Christmas Tree

Preparation Time: 15 Minutes
Cooking Time: 10 and 10 Minutes

Equipment

Cooking (cookie) sheet
Christmas tree cookie cutter
Skillet
Measuring spoons and cups

Metal spatula
Pastry brush
Fork

Ingredients
Crust

Puffed Pastry; 1 box frozen puffed pastry, thawed (takes about 20 minutes)
1 egg, whisked with 1 tablespoon water
Flour
Rolling pin

Unfold a sheet of puffed pastry dough onto a floured surface. Roll slightly and with a Christmas Tree cookie cutter, cut out the number of trees required for the amount of guests, make up any left over as well (they can be frozen, once baked). Lift carefully with spatula, so they don't stretch. Place on ungreased cookie sheet and prick all over with a fork. Brush tops, not sides, lightly with egg mixture. Bake in preheated 350 degree oven for about 15 minutes or until golden brown.

Remove from tray with spatula and cool. Can be made ahead and stored in air-tight container.

Ingredients
Filling

3 cups thinly sliced mushrooms
18 stalks of asparagus, bottom end trimmed off and sliced in 1½ inch pieces cut on the diagonal
½ teaspoon thyme
½ teaspoon basil

¼ teaspoon salt
¼ teaspoon freshly ground pepper
3 tablespoons butter
1 tablespoon oil
¼ cup heavy cream
¼ cup dry white wine

Melt butter and oil in a skillet and add thinly sliced mushrooms. Stir and cook until the moisture has exuded. Add the asparagus, herbs and salt and pepper. Stir until tender, but not overcooked. Add wine and cook until liquid is reduced by ½; add cream and heat.

To Serve:
Divide up the amount of filling onto salad-size plates, shaping into a triangle. Drizzle wine flavored juices over them. Top each with a puff pastry Christmas tree and serve immediately. If trees are puffed a lot and they can be easily split, cut them in half and put vegetables between the two halves. They chill quickly.

Main Course

Prime Ribs of Beef with Horseradish Sauce

Preparation Time: 10 Minutes
Cooking Time: 2-3 Hours, depending on size of roast, figure 18
minutes per pound for medium

Equipment
Large roasting pan
Meat thermometer/Instant read
   thermometer

Ingredients
4 rib roast (about 10½ pounds) on the bone, trimmed with bone cracked
   for easier carving
1 teaspoon dried rosemary or two stalks of fresh
Few turns of pepper mill, cracked black pepper

Preheat oven to 350 degrees.

Place meat side up, bone on bottom, inside pan. Put cracked pepper over the top and sprigs of fresh or dry rosemary. Insert meat thermometer into fleshy larger end of roast, making sure that it does not touch a bone. If not uniform in size, the smaller end will cook faster creating some more well-done meat. Place in oven and cook until the meat is the cooked to your taste, rare, medium etc., check on thermometer. Remove when finished and place on garnished platter. Serve immediately as meat will continue to cook a bit as it stands.

Carve into ½-inch slices and serve with horseradish sauce on the side.

388

Horseradish Sauce

Preparation Time: 10 Minutes
Can be made 3 hours ahead

Equipment

Hand-held mixer
2 Mixing bowls, 1 chilled
Rubber spatula, scraper

Juicer, reamer
Measuring spoons and cups
Plastic wrap

Ingredients

1   cup heavy cream
¼   cup prepared (bottled) white
      horseradish, drained
2   teaspoons lemon juice

1   teaspoon Worcestershire
      sauce
¼   teaspoon salt

Using a chilled mixing bowl, whip cream with electric mixer until almost stiff.

Combine other ingredients in a second bowl and then fold in the whipped cream. Place in serving dish, cover and refrigerate until needed.

Roast Potatoes with Rosemary

Preparation Time: 15 Minutes
Cooking Time: 45-60 Minutes

Equipment

Potato/vegetable peeler
Measuring cups and spoons
Ovenproof dish with low sides

Cooking fork
Paper towels
Knife

Ingredients

10-12 baking potatoes, peeled, Idaho or Russet preferred
¼ cup olive or vegetable oil
2-3 cloves garlic, peeled and diced, optional
2 tablespoons dry rosemary or 3 tablespoons fresh, pulled off stems
1 tablespoon Kosher salt

Preheat oven to 375 degrees.

Wash potatoes after peeling and dry with paper towel. Cut in half lengthwise and then into quarters or into 1½ inch slices the long way. Dry off the pieces.

If there are more pieces than room in your cooking dish, use two dishes, covering the bottom of each generously with oil. They will not brown nicely and will become mushy if too crowded in the baking dish.

Rub oil over all sides of the potatoes as you are placing them into the dishes. Sprinkle with chopped garlic, salt and rosemary and place in oven. If the potatoes seem to be cooking faster than they are browning, turn up the heat to 450 to brown. Depending on the potato and size of the pieces, they will take 45-60 minutes. Turn several times with a spatula after 30 minutes.

OR

If there is adequate room in your roasting pan next to the meat, surround the roast with them. Sprinkle with rosemary and salt, omit the garlic unless you don't mind the flavor in the meat, and roast for about 45 minutes to an hour, turning several times to brown in the fat rendered from the meat. This is a good, easy option but many don't like the taste of the meat fat on the potatoes, especially, if a vegetarian is coming for dinner!

Glazed Carrots

Preparation Time: 10 Minutes
Cooking Time: 15-20 Minutes

Equipment

Large saucepan with lid   Colander
Wooden spoon for stirring   Grater
Potato/vegetable peeler

Ingredients

10-12 carrots, or 24 smaller carrots, peeled, halved and cut into two-
  inch pieces
    OR
1½ pound bag of baby carrots, pre-peeled, rinsed well
3 tablespoons butter
½ cup orange juice
2 tablespoons orange liqueur such as Grand Marnier
2 teaspoons orange rind, grated
Pinch of nutmeg
2 tablespoons chopped parsley for garnish, no stems

Place carrots in saucepan with all of the ingredients, cover
and cook on medium heat for 10 minutes, depending on size of
carrot. Do not overcook. These can be started while first course
is being served. Remove lid and allow to glaze while rest of dinner is being put out. Garnish with parsley when placed in serving bowl.

String Bean Tree

Preparation Time: 10 Minutes
Cooking Time: 8-10 Minutes

Equipment

Large saucepan with lid or
   steamer
Colander

Cooking fork
Small skillet or baking sheet
Spatula

Ingredients

2 pounds of fresh string beans, whole
½ cup toasted whole almonds or sliced almonds
3 tablespoons butter
   OR
Bits of diced red pepper or pomegranate seeds to decorate "tree" instead of nuts and butter

Trim ends off beans and pull off string. Wash and place in plastic bag and refrigerate if doing ahead or put into saucepan with one inch of water or steamer set over an inch or two of water. Cover and cook 8-10 minutes, test bean, they should be a bit crisp. They can cook during first course on moderate heat. Drain.

Nuts can be prepared early in the day, put on saucer and covered. If almonds have skin on them, place in a small pot of boiling water for one to two minutes. Remove an almond from the pot. If skin sides off easily by squeezing nut between fingers, remove all nuts and drain. Remove the other skins. Pat dry.

In a small skillet, melt 3 tablespoons butter and add almonds. Stir frequently. They will brown suddenly. Remove from heat and the pan as they will continue to brown. Set aside until serving time (this can be done ahead). Nuts can also be browned in a 350 degree oven on a cookie sheet without using butter. Watch toasting process, they turn color very quickly. Remove from oven and put to side in a smaller container.

Place beans on a low platter, forming bunches of beans into the triangular Christmas tree shape. Sprinkle nuts, diced red pepper or pomegranate seeds on the beans to resemble tree decorations and serve.

Christmas Salad

Preparation Time: 10 Minutes

Equipment

Salad spinner   Whisk
Small bowl   Juicer or reamer
Measuring cups and spoons

Ingredients

4   endives   1   lemon, juiced
1   bunch watercress   ⅓   cup olive oil
    Seeds from ½ pomegranate ½   teaspoon salt
    or ½ red pepper, small   ¾   teaspoon Dijon style
    dice   mustard

Wash endives. Cut in half lengthwise. Lay on flat side and cut into thin slivers. Place in salad bowl or plastic bag and refrigerate until ready to use. Cut off bottom of watercress stems below the leafy part. Separate, wash and spin dry in salad spinner. Remove and cut into thirds. Add to endive.

Cut a pomegranate in ½ and remove membrane and place seeds in separate cup and reserve, careful as the juice stains. Or, cut a red pepper in half and remove seeds, membrane and stem. Thinly sliver half of the pepper and dice into small pieces. Add to greens.

In a small bowl, whisk the balance of the ingredients together and pour over salad and toss right before serving.

Popovers

Preparation Time: 10 Minutes
Cooking Time: 35-45 Minutes
May be prepared ahead and reheated. Makes 24

Equipment

2 Muffin pans (12 muffins total)
 or special popover pan
Mixing bowl

Measuring cups and spoons
Whisk
Paring knife

Ingredients

4 large eggs
2 cups unsifted all-purpose
 flour
2 cups whole milk

1 teaspoon salt
2 tablespoons melted butter
 Butter for pans or non-stick
 cooking spray

Preheat oven to 450 degrees. Butter muffin pans or use with non-stick cooking spray. **You will need to bake 2 batches.**

Beat eggs slightly in a bowl with a whisk and then add other ingredients. Do not over mix.

Pour into muffin pans until each cup is half full. Bake for 15 minutes at 450 degrees and then reduce heat to 325 degrees for an additional 25-30 minutes or until golden brown. During the last 5 minutes, prick the side of the crust of the muffins with a small pointed knife tip. This will allow steam to escape and leave the popover crisp, not soggy. Remove from pans until completion. To reheat, place on a cookie sheet in a 350 degree oven for 7-10 minutes or until hot through and through.

This is an easy, non-greasy substitution to Yorkshire pudding, which is a similar batter cooked in the beef grease.

Dessert

Buche de Noel
Yule Log

Preparation Time: 45 Minutes
Cooking Time: 20-30 Minutes Plus 1 hour
Finishing Time: 25 Minutes

Although time-consuming to make, a Buche de Noel is an impressive and tasty dessert. In addition to the cake, a filling/frosting and meringue must be prepared. The filling/frosting must sit a while, therefore I make it prior to the cake. The meringue "mushrooms" take about an hour in a slow oven, but aren't needed until the final assembly just prior to serving. Therefore, they can be made ahead with the filling and stored in an airtight container until needed. The cake can be made, filled and rolled a day prior.

Equipment
Frosting/filling

Heat-proof bowl
Small saucepan
Candy thermometer
Whisk
Electric mixer

Mixing bowl
Measuring spoons and cups
Rubber spatula or scraper
Bowl for refrigeration
Plastic wrap

Ingredients
Italian Meringue

3   egg whites
¼   scant teaspoon cream of
         tartar

Pinch of salt
1⅓   cups granulated sugar
⅓   cup water

Butter Cream

12 ounces bitter sweet or semi-sweet chocolate, cut into pieces
3 tablespons strong coffee
1 tablespoon vanilla extract
2 sticks softened unsalted butter (1 cup)

Place the chocolate and coffee in a double boiler or in a bowl inside a medium-size saucepan and melt the chocolate. Careful not to get water in the chocolate or it will seize and be unusable. Put to the side when all is melted.

Separate yolks from whites and reserve for cake and other uses. Place egg whites into a mixing bowl and start to beat. When whites get frothy, add the cream of tartar and salt. Beat until stiff peaks form.

While egg whites are beating, mix sugar and water in a small saucepan over high heat. Do not stir, gently swirl pan until sugar is dissolved. Cover and boil rapidly for about 20-30 seconds. Uncover pan and place thermometer in pan. Cook until temperature reaches 238 degrees. Pour the sugar syrup into the beaten egg whites and beat on a high speed until the mixtures cool. It will have a satinlike texture and will hold stiff peaks when lifted with a spoon or spatula.

Beat the warm chocolate into the cool meringue mixture. Gradually beat in the butter until all is incorporated. Chill the butter cream until it reaches a spreading consistency.

Frosting can be covered and refrigerated until ready to use. Bring to spreading temperature before use. Leftover frosting can be frozen. You will need some to build the meringue mushrooms.

Equipment
Meringue Mushrooms

Small baking sheet	Mixing bowl
Parchment paper	Measuring spoons and cups
Pastry bag fitted with ³⁄₁₆″ tube or tip opening	Rubber spatula, scraper
	Sharp knife
Electric mixer	Air tight container or plastic bag

Ingredients

2	egg whites at room temperature		Pinch of cream of tartar
	Dash of salt	½	cup superfine sugar

Preheat oven to 200 degrees. Line a cookie sheet with parchment.

Beat egg whites until they are frothy. Add the salt and cream of tartar. Beat until soft peaks form. Add two tablespoons of the sugar at a time until all is incorporate. Beat until stiff, glossy peaks form.

Fill pastry bag with meringue mixture and pipe onto parchment covered tray. You want to pipe meringue mushroom "caps" and stems separately. The caps are mounded and then the top is smoothed over with a fingertip. The stems should be broader at the bottom and brought to a point at the top. You will need about 8-10 mushrooms tops and stems of various sizes. If you still have meringue left over, pipe Christmas wreaths, by piping the meringue into circles. Try to make them the same density as the mushrooms so they cook in the same amount of time. Sprinkle multi-colored sugars on them or red cinnamon drops for holly berries.

Place tray in center of oven and bake 45 minutes to an hour or until they are crisp and crackle. Remove from oven and cool on the baking tray. When cool, remove them carefully. You may have to loosen from paper with a sharp knife blade. Place into airtight container or sealed plastic bag until ready to use. Serve meringue wreaths on cookie platter. They will get soggy if left out.

See below for how to make meringue mushrooms under Decorating the Buche

Equipment
Cake

12×16 jelly-roll pan/cookie sheet with a lip all the way around (about ½ inch deep)	Measuring spoons and cups
	Parchment or waxed paper
	Small saucepan
Electric mixer	Pastry brush
Mixing bowl	Sifter or sieve
Rubber spatula, scraper	Damp tea towel

Ingredients

3	large eggs at room temperature, separated	1	tablespoon sugar
1	egg yolk	1	cup cake flour
½	cup sugar	3	tablespoons melted butter plus 1½ teaspoons melted for coating pan
¼	teaspoon vanilla or almond extract		Flour
	Dash of salt		Powdered sugar
¼	teaspoon cream of tartar		

Cut a piece of waxed paper or parchment paper to fit the pan allowing a couple of extra inches at each end. Using some of the 1½ teaspoons of melted butter, lightly coat the pan with a brush, then place the waxed or parchment paper over the pan, fitting it in tightly and overlapping the ends of the pan a bit. Brush melted butter over the paper and sides and lightly flour, knocking out any excess flour. Put to the side.

Preheat over 350 degrees.

Place the 4 egg yolks into the mixing bowl and set over warm water until tepid. Begin to mix with electric mixer and slowly add sugar. Mix to a light lemon yellow color and yolks form a ribbon when beater is lifted. Mix in vanilla or almond extract.

With a clean bowl and beaters, beat egg whites until frothy and add a dash of salt and cream of tartar. Beat until soft peaks are formed and add 1 tablespoon of sugar over the top and beat until stiff peaks are formed.

Add about a third of the egg whites to the egg yolk mixture and fold together gently with rubber spatula. Add half of the cake flour and fold into the mixture. Add the balance of the egg whites and flour and fold until almost blended. Add the 3 tablespoons of melted butter and fold into the batter. Do not over-mix or the egg whites will deflate.

Pour into the prepared pan and spread evenly over the surface. Bake in a 350-degree oven for 12-20 minutes. Check cake. It is done when it starts to pull away from the side of the pan, is puffed and a pale brown color, fingerprint doesn't show. You don't want to overcook or it will crack when rolled. Remove from oven and let cool in pan for about 3 minutes. Place powdered sugar in a sifter or sieve and shake over the cake until covered. Place a piece of waxed paper over the cake.

Wet a kitchen towel and ring well. Lay towel on the waxed paper and turn pan upside down onto a counter or table area. Leave the pan on the cake for about 15 minutes. Remove the pan. Slowly peel back the waxed paper if ready to fill with the frosting. If not, loosen the waxed paper and trim the side of the cake removing any over-browned edges. Replace the waxed paper and slowly roll up tightly into a roll, using the waxed paper that was on the bottom of the pan to guide you. You will keep a piece of waxed paper on each side of the cake so it doesn't stick to itself. Roll tightly and place in a plastic bag until ready to use. I recommend finishing immediately.

Finishing/Decorating the Buche
Ingredients
Powdered cocoa
Powdered sugar in sieve
Fresh currants, if available or pomegranate seeds
Greens, holly pieces

Gently unroll cake, or if still flat, remove top piece of waxed paper. Spread about a third of the frosting/filling on the cake. Using the waxed paper under the cake to help, tightly roll the cake from the narrow end. At a diagonal, slice a narrow piece from each end of the cake. These will be used to make a gnarled "knob" on our Yule "log". With the tip of a small sharp knife, cut out a small circle from the side of the cake and place the "knob" of the cake into the hole. A bit of frosting may be necessary to make it stay. Form knobs to look like a broken tree branches. You can use one or the two ends, if you wish, staggering them on the sides of the log.

Reserve about ⅛ cup of frosting. Cover and refrigerate for making the "mushrooms." With the remaining frosting, cover the cake and "knobs." You may want to leave the ends unfrosted to resemble a cut log, but if not serving soon, the cake could dry out. I usually cover the ends and swirl the frosting with the tines of a fork to resemble the rings on a log.

Using a fork, pull the tines down the length of the log to resemble bark. Carefully place cake on serving plate and refrigerate until frosting is firm. Cover with plastic wrap, using toothpicks to hold frosting away from cake. Remove about an hour or so before serving.

At this point:
Finish the meringue mushrooms. Gently make a small hole in the "cap" portion of the mushroom with a pointed knife. Take softened butter cream, and place a bit on the tip of the meringue "stem," and put into the cap. Repeat with the other meringues. Place the mushrooms around the "knob" of the log and across a part of the top of the cake, as it pleases you.

Place pieces of evergreens around cake. If you have fresh currants, use a spray on top of the cake, or place pomegranate berries to resemble holly berries. Use holly leaves and berries if you don't have the fruit berries. Make sure you don't serve berries to guests!

With your fingers, dust the mushrooms lightly with cocoa powder to make the meringues look like wild mushrooms. Lightly dust the cake and branches with powdered sugar to resemble "snow" by tapping a sieve gently with a knife or sifting gently. You don't want too much. Cake is ready to serve. Small pieces are sufficient, as it is a very rich cake.

Recipes for Use throughout the Season

All the recipes below can be made in advance and either frozen until needed, or kept in airtight containers.

Fruitcake

Preparation Time: 45 Minutes and Overnight
Cooking Time: 3 Hours and 15 Minutes
The Fruitcake should be made at least two weeks before serving.

Equipment

10-inch tube pan
Large brown paper bag
  OR
Paper or foil candy cup/muffin cups and pan into which they fit. It makes bite-size servings, which also work well on cookie platters.
Electric mixer
2 Mixing bowls
Measuring spoons and cups

Wooden mixing spoon
Chopping knife and board
Plastic wrap
Scissors
Pencil
Ruler
Sifter or mesh sieve
Toothpick or cake tester
Waxed paper or medium-size bowl
Cheesecloth
Airtight storage container

Ingredients

*Note: Raisins must macerate overnight

1 pound golden raisins
½ pound black raisins
¼ pound dried currants
½ cup dark rum or brandy*, or use orange juice
Combine the above in very large mixing bowl, cover, and let stand overnight

1 pound candied pineapple, cut in thin wedges
½ pound red-candied cherries, cut in half or ¼ pound green, ¼ pound red cherries
¼ pound candied citron, cut in thin strips
⅛ pound candied lemon peel, cut in thin strips
⅛ pound candied orange peel, cut in thin strips

401

Add to raisin mixture and stir.

Preheat oven to 275 degrees.

To line the tube pan with heavy paper, use heavy brown paper or 'grocery' bag, cut length at seam and open out the base of the bag to flatten it. Using a ruler, mark an 18-inch circle in pencil and cut out. Place tube pan in the center of the circle and trace around the base of the pan and the inside of the tube. With the pencil lines to the outside, fold the paper into eighths and cut off the tip, the inner circle of the tube. Open up the circle and cut from the outside edge down each fold line to the second pencil circle. Grease the tube pan and the paper as well, (the side with no pencil marks on it) with vegetable shortening. Fit the paper, greased side up into the tube pan. By having cut the folds, the paper fits into the pan and the side 'leaves' can be adjusted to lie flat on the sides of the pan.

OR

Grease muffin tins and line with paper or foil cups.

Batter

1½	cups flour	1	cup granulated sugar
½	cup flour	1	cup brown sugar, packed
½	teaspoon mace	5	eggs, slightly beaten
½	teaspoon cinnamon	1	tablespoon milk
½	teaspoon baking soda	1	teaspoon vanilla or almond extract
¼	shelled, blanched, coarsely chopped almonds		
¼	pound shelled, coarsely chopped pecans or walnuts		Rum or brandy, optional
		2-3	slices of apple
½	cup butter (1 stick) softened to room temperature		

Sift 1½ cups of flour with spices and baking soda onto a piece of waxed paper. Set aside.

Combine ½ remaining cup of flour with nuts and add to fruits and toss lightly. It will help to separate the fruits and reduce stickiness.

In large bowl, with electric mixer on medium speed, beat butter until light. Gradually beat in the granulated sugar and then the brown sugar. Beat until light and fluffy, scraping bowl to incorporate butter. Beat in eggs, milk, and extract, and mix until combined. Beat in the flour and spice mixture on low speed until well mixed.

Pour this batter into the fruits and nuts and mix well using a heavy wooden spoon or your hands, which will work better!

Place batter into prepared pan-pressing down to remove air and make even all around. Bake 3 hours and 15 minutes in the center of the oven, or until a tester comes out clean. Place cake on cooling rack for 30 minutes. Turn pan upside down and remove. Gently peel paper from cake. Cool completely.

OR

*Place paper or foil candy or muffin holders in muffin/mini muffin pans. At Christmas there are usually paper and foil cups available with holiday designs on them. Put batter in each cup, about ¾ full. Place in oven and bake anywhere from 45 minutes to an hour, depending on size of cup. Test with toothpicks and cook until it comes out clean. Remove to cooling rack.

To Store

If storing the tube pan cake, wrap the cooled cake in a piece of cheesecloth soaked in rum and brandy. Place cake in container with a lid and put a couple slices of apple on top of cheesecloth to help maintain moistness. Fit lid tightly. As cheesecloth dries out, rewet with brandy.

Store the small cakes in an airtight container.

To Decorate

Remove cake to a plate and remove cheesecloth. Glaze the cake with the recipe below and garnish with pieces of candied cherries, angelica cut in shapes, and nuts.

Equipment

Small saucepan	Sieve strainer
Paring knife	Small bowl
Pastry brush	

Ingredients

1	cup of apricot jam
⅓	cup rum or brandy

Combine ingredients in a small saucepan until the jam is melted. Place through a strainer into a small bowl and brush onto the cake or mini cakes. It may take more than one application. Decorate top, using bits of candied cherries (red and green) to make holly leaves.

403

Mince Tarts

Filling may be made up to five days prior and tarts can also be made ahead and frozen. Filling should sit at least overnight for flavors to blend. Individual tarts are suggested as they easily fit onto a platter with other cookies and fruit cake cups and can be served easily on other occasions. If you prefer, the filling can be placed into a two-crust pie, baked and served warm with vanilla ice cream.

Equipment
Filling

Large 2-3 quart, heavy bottom
    saucepan
Wooden mixing spoon
Measuring spoons and cups

Ingredients

5	Granny Smith or other firm apple, peeled, cored, and chopped into ¼-inch dice	2	tablespoons unsalted butter
1	cup dark raisins	1	tablespoon cider vinegar
1	cup golden raisins	½	teaspoon salt
¼	cup mixed candied citrus peels	1½	teaspoons cinnamon
1	teaspoon grated lemon zest	1	teaspoon ground allspice
1¼	cups firmly packed brown sugar	¼	teaspoon ground nutmeg
		¼	teaspoon freshly ground black pepper
		¼	cup rum or brandy, optional

In a heavy saucepan, combine all ingredients **except liquor** with 1½ cups of water. Bring mixture to a boil, stirring frequently. Cook for about 40 minutes or until liquid is very thick. Add the rum or brandy and stir until almost all the liquid is evaporated. Cool filling and store overnight in refrigerator or up to 5 days in an airtight container.

Equipment
Tarts or Pie

9″ Pie pan or individual small tin tart shells (2-3 inches)
Mixing bowl
Pastry cutter or food processor fitted with plastic blade
Rolling pin
Measuring spoons and cups
Fork or mixing spoon

Bring filling to room temperature
Christmas cookie cutter
Metal spatula
Non-stick cooking spray
Baking tray
Pastry brush
Cooling rack

Ingredients

2 crust dough recipe in Introduction
1 egg
Granulated sugar to sprinkle on top of crust

Preheat oven to 400 degrees.

Using basic 2-crust pie dough as described in Introduction, roll out first half, and place in pie pan. Place filling into pan. Roll second piece of dough and place over the top. Cut off anything that hangs down more than an inch. Roll top dough over the bottom dough and seal together. Crimp edge as with any pie. Using a Christmas cookie cutter, cut out center piece of dough. Reserve to side. If there are any scraps of dough left over, they can be cut into holly-leaf shapes or stars etc. In a small cup, mix an egg with a ¼ teaspoon of water. Brush on top of pie. Place the cut out shapes decoratively on top of the pie. Sprinkle with granulated sugar and bake at 400 degrees until crust is a golden brown, about 30-45 minutes.

OR

Roll pie as usual. Place individual tartlette tins upside down on dough and cut around each tin, allowing enough dough to extend up the sides of the tin. For easier removal from the tins, spray each with a non-stick cooking spray. Gently, using a spatula if necessary, place the pieces of dough into the tins and crimp the edges. Allow enough dough to rise over the edge so you can grab it later upon removing tarts from pan. Do NOT fold it over the edge of tin or it will break up when you try to remove the tart. Fill the tarts with mince filling. Leave at least ¼ inch at

405

the top so they don't cook over, which will cause sticking. Place on a cookie sheet in a 400 degree oven and cook until lightly browned, about 10-20 minutes, depending on size. Remove from oven and place on a cooling rack. When cool, remove tarts from tins. If they are sticking to the tins, take a sharp, thin knife and try to gently slide it down between the crust and side of the tin. They are ready to serve, refrigerate, or freeze until ready for use. To freeze, place on a cookie tray in the freezer. Wait until they are hard and then place into a firm-sided freezer container. Bring to room temperature to serve or heat in oven for a few minutes.

Mock Plum Pudding

Preparation Time: 15 Minutes
Cooking Time: 1 Hour

Fool proof, and tasty. This dessert should be served warm with hard sauce or even vanilla or cinnamon ice cream.

Equipment

6 cup fluted mold, greased
Electric mixer
Mixing bowl
Measuring spoons and cups
Knife

Can opener
Rubber spatula
Toothpick or cake tester
Small saucepan
Whisk

Ingredients
Pudding

1   pound can or jar of purple
     plums (2 cups)
1   package prepared
     gingerbread mix
½   teaspoon salt

1   cup raisins, golden preferred
½   cup chopped walnuts
     Non-stick cooking spray or
     vegetable shortening

Sauce

     Plum syrup plus water to
       make 1½ cups
¼   cup sugar

2   tablespoons cornstarch
1   tablespoon lemon juice

Using non-stick cooking spray or vegetable shortening,

406

grease a six-cup fluted mold or similar baking container . . . the height looks good.

Preheat oven to 375 degrees.

Drain plums, reserving syrup for plum sauce. Remove the pits and cut into small pieces.

Prepare the gingerbread mix according to the package instruction. Stir in the salt, plums, raisins and walnuts.

Pour into the mold and bake about an hour, or until a toothpick comes out clean. Immediately remove from the mold onto a serving plate.

While the 'pudding' is baking, prepare the sauce.

Plum Sauce

Add water to reserved plum syrup to make ½ cups of liquid. Combine sugar and cornstarch in small saucepan. Gradually whisk in the plum liquid. Stir frequently and cook until mixture boils for one minute. Remove from heat and add the lemon juice. Serve warm and spoon over each slice of the plum pudding as it is served.

Hard Sauce

This is to be served on top of the plum pudding and plum sauce, instead of ice cream and can be made ahead and refrigerated in the serving bowl.

Ingredients

6	tablespoons butter
1	cup sifted powdered sugar
1	tablespoon boiling water
⅛	teaspoon salt
1	teaspoon vanilla
½	cup heavy cream

Cream butter and sugar until fluffy. Add boiling water, salt and vanilla. Beat until creamy.

In another bowl whip the heavy cream until it holds its shape. Fold into the butter and sugar mixture and refrigerate until serving.

Stollen

Preparation Time: 45 Minutes
Rising Time: About 2 Hours
Baking Time: About 35 Minutes
Recipe makes 2 loaves, which Can Be Frozen

Equipment

2 Large mixing bowls
Small mixing bowl or glass
  measuring cup
Medium-size saucepan
Measuring spoons and cups
Rubber spatula
Mixing spoon

Grater
Candy or instant read
  thermometer
Whisk
Plastic wrap
2 baking sheets
Cooling racks

Ingredients

5   cups unsifted all-purpose
      flour
1   cup unsifted flour
1½ teaspoons ground cinnamon
¾   teaspoon ground mace
⅛   teaspoon ground cardamom
2   packages active dry yeast
½   cup warm water (112-115
      degrees F)
1   cup milk scalded
1   cup granulated sugar
½   teaspoon salt

¾   cup butter, melted
2   tablespoons butter, melted
2   large eggs, lightly beaten
1   cup golden raisins
¼   cup diced mixed candied
      fruits
¼   cup diced dried apricots
    Grated rind of 1 lemon
½   cup coarsely chopped
      blanched almonds
    Powdered sugar

Using a large bowl, mix together 5 cups of flour, cinnamon, mace and cardamom.

In a smaller bowl, pour yeast over the warm water. If the water is too hot it will kill the yeast, if not hot enough it won't 'proof' (get bubbly), check with thermometer which should read 100-110 degrees. Set to the side.

Scald milk and melt butter together in small saucepan.

In a third bowl, combine the scalded milk, granulated sugar, salt and ¾ cup of butter. When the temperature of the milk lowers to 110 degrees, pour in the yeast and water mixture and stir to combine. Beat in the eggs with a whisk.

Gradually stir in the flour and spice mixture and if necessary, about an additional cup of flour. It depends on how much the dough will incorporate. Dough should be firm, yet a bit sticky.

Turn dough onto a floured board. You may need to work in additional flour if it sticks to the board too much. Add in the fruit and nuts and keep kneading the dough, folding and turning it until it becomes elastic and shiny and smooth and if a piece is pulled up, it releases back into the dough without breaking.

Place dough into a large greased bowl. Cover loosely with buttered plastic wrap and let rise in a warm place until it doubles in bulk, about 1 hour or so.

Punch down dough and turn over. It will collapse into itself. Let rest about 10 minutes. Divide dough into two equal pieces. Roll each piece into a 6 × 10 inch rectangle and brush with some of the two tablespoons of melted butter. Fold one long side to the center and then overlap the other long side. Turn dough over and shape into a tapered loaf, a bit wider in the center than the ends. Place each in center of its own buttered cookie sheet, paint with melted butter and cover with plastic wrap.

Let rise in a warm place for an additional hour or until doubled in bulk.

Preheat oven to 375 degrees. Bake in the middle of the oven for 30-35 minutes or until golden brown. It is wise not to crowd the oven. Bake separately to allow heat to circulate evenly. Remove to wire racks to cool and then sprinkle with powdered sugar before serving.

Stollens freeze well in airtight containers. Sprinkle with powdered sugar before serving.

Cookies

Gingerbread Cookies

Preparation Time: 30 Minutes
Baking Time: 15-20 Minutes
Decorating Time: According to Your whims

Equipment

Electric mixer
Mixing bowl
Measuring spoons and
  cups
Rubber spatula
Double boiler
Candy or instant read
  thermometer
Whisk
Small bowl
Rolling pin
Baking tray

Parchment paper, non-stick
  cooking spray or vegetable
  shortening
Cooling racks
Assorted cookie cutters and/or
  traditional gingerbread boys
  and girls
Pastry bags (can be plastic) and
  piping tubes ⅛ inch maximum,
  and small star tube.
Plastic wrap, waxed paper
Airtight containers

Ingredients

Yield will depend on size of cookie cutters.
My grandchildren love oversized Santa Clauses.

Cookie Dough

1   cup dark molasses,
        usulphured
1   cup light or dark brown
        sugar
4½   teaspoons ground ginger
3½   teaspoons ground cinnamon
¾   tablespoon baking soda

1   cup (2 sticks) unsalted
        butter at room
        temperature
2   large eggs, lightly beaten
6   cups sifted all-purpose flour
      Currants

Royal Icing

1 cup sifted powdered sugar
1 large egg white, meringue powder or powdered egg white
Food coloring to achieve the designs you want

Preheat the oven to 325 degrees and line baking sheets with parchment paper or grease them with non-stick cooking spray or vegetable shortening.

Place the molasses, sugar, ginger, and cinnamon in a large double boiler over medium heat. Stir. When the sugar has melted, add the baking soda and stir. Remove from heat when mixture bubbles up.

Place butter in large mixing bowl. Add the hot molasses mixture and stir well. Let mixture cool to about 90 degrees F. While mixture is cooling, whisk eggs in small bowl, then add. Beat mixture on a low speed and gradually add the flour, about 1 cup at a time.

Shape the dough into a rectangle and place on a well-floured surface and with a rolling pin, roll until dough is ¼ inch thick. Cut into desired shapes and place cookies onto the parchment paper and baking trays. You may need a metal spatula to pick up the cookie from your floured work surface. Gather leftover dough together and repeat until you've used all the dough.

If you want to add currant eyes, buttons, etc., press into dough now. Place baking sheets in the center of oven and bake for 15-20 minutes, or until firm to the touch; do not overbake. Remove to cooling racks.

When cookies are cool, they are ready to ice.

Mix the powdered sugar and egg whites in a small bowl. You need a consistency that will squeeze through an icing tube. Thin with egg white or thicken with additional sugar. You can divide the icing into small cups and color with food paste coloring to achieve any color you may wish.

Scoop frosting into a variety of disposable plastic pastry bags fitted with tips; see Introduction for more information. These bags can be purchased in a gourmet/kitchen department of up-scale hardware stores or specialty shops. You will need piping tubes with a ⅛ inch opening, maximum, and perhaps a star/rosette shape for diversity, experiment, narrower openings will render better details on the cookies. Let your imagination go! So cookies don't break when icing, try to leave them flat on cookie sheets or pans with edges until they dry. When icing is hard, store in airtight containers. Place waxed paper or plastic wrap between layers of cookies so they don't stick to each other.

Sugar Cookies

Preparation Time: 20-30 Minutes
2 Hour Chilling Time
Baking Time: 6-10 Minutes
Makes about 4 dozen cookies, depending on size of Cookie Cutters

Equipment

Electric mixer
Mixing bowl
Additional bowl
Measuring spoons and cups
Sifter or mesh sieve
Waxed paper, plastic wrap
Rubber spatula
Rolling pin

Cookie cutters in Christmas
  shapes
Cookie trays
Metal spatula
Cooling racks
Decorating bags and tips for
  piping, fine-point paint brushes
Airtight container

Ingredients

1½ cups sifted powdered sugar
1   cup room temperature
     butter (2 sticks)
1   large egg
1½ teaspoon vanilla
2½ cups all-purpose sifted flour

1   teaspoon baking soda
1   teaspoon cream of tartar
    Non-stick cookie spray or
     vegetable shortening or
     room temperature butter

Place sifted powdered sugar and butter into a bowl and mix until fluffy. Add the egg and vanilla and mix thoroughly. Sift the dry ingredients into a small bowl and then mix into the dough, which will become stiff. Gather dough together and lay on a piece of waxed paper or plastic wrap. Flatten and refrigerate 2 hours minimum. Dough can be made ahead and baked another day.

Preheat oven to 375 degrees and lightly butter baking trays or spray with non-stick cooking spray, or vegetable shortening.

Divide dough in half and place on well-floured surface. Roll as thin as you can and cut into shapes. Make sure there is always plenty of flour under the dough as you roll it out. Sprinkle a bit on the surface, as well. You will probably require a spatula to get the cookie off the surface. Be patient. The thinner the cookie, the less it will spread when baked. If dough gets too hard to handle, return to the refrigerator for a few minutes. Allow at least 1½ inches between cookies on the tray as they spread when baked. If dough has warmed a bit, place baking tray in refrigerator for 10 minutes or so to firm it up.

Sprinkle cookies with colored sugars or bake plain, to be decorated with icing later. Or, you can "paint" the cookies with color combining 1 teaspoon of light corn syrup and ¼ teaspoon of water and then the food coloring. Use a small paint brush and create your designs, you can even add the sparkling sugar on top of the paint for added dimension.

Bake 6-10 minutes or until delicately golden. Thinner cookies bake faster and they burn quickly . . . be careful and check after 5-6 minutes! Let stand on cookie trays for a couple of minutes to harden a bit, especially if the design is intricate. Carefully remove to wire racks for cooling. They are very delicate cookies and break easily. You will never have baked enough!

Use icing recipe in Gingerbread cookie recipe after the cookies have cooled. When icing is hard, store in airtight containers. Place waxed paper or plastic wrap between layers to minimize breakage.

This dough can also be rolled into a log shape, wrapped in waxed paper or plastic wrap and chilled. Remove from paper and roll in colored sugar and cut into ⅛-inch slices. Or, put a colored food paste into the dough before refrigeration, roll into a log and proceed as above. Bake as standard recipe.

Pinwheels

Preparation Time: 20 Minutes
3 Hour Chilling Time
Baking Time: 6-10 Minutes
Makes about 5 dozen cookies

Equipment

Electric mixer
Mixing bowl
Smaller mixing bowl
Measuring spoons and cups
Rubber spatula
Sifter or mesh sieve

Small saucepan/bowl or double
  boiler
Metal spatula
Rolling pin
Waxed paper or plastic wrap
Baking rays
Cooling racks

Ingredients

¾ cup total of shortening and butter (combined half and half)
1 cup granulated sugar
2 eggs
1 teaspoon vanilla extract
1½ cups all-purpose white flour
1 teaspoon salt

2 squares unsweetened chocolate, melted and cooled

Mix shortening and butter, sugar, eggs, and vanilla in a large bowl. Sift flour, baking powder and salt into the batter. Mix well. Divide dough in half. Wrap one piece into plastic wrap or waxed paper and flatten; refrigerate. Mix melted chocolate into the other half of the dough. Wrap in plastic wrap or waxed paper, flatten and refrigerate.

After dough has chilled about 2 hours, remove from refrigerator and place plain dough on well-floured surface. Roll into a 9×12 inch rectangle.

Flatten chocolate dough and roll separately to the same size. Place it on top of the plain dough. It may break up. Don't worry. Press it together to cover as well as you can. It's not an easy process to work. When the white dough is covered, except for a small margin around the edges, start to roll the dough from the long side. Fold in the ends of the dough as you make the first

414

turn or two. Continue to roll into a tight log/cylinder. Seal seam by squeezing dough together. Turn seam to bottom and shape the log until it is uniform thickness. Roll onto a sheet of waxed paper or plastic wrap and roll up. Carefully lift and place in refrigerator until it is firm, about 1½ hours.

Preheat oven to 400 degrees.

Remove from refrigerator, unroll paper, and place on lightly floured surface. Using a thin bladed, sharp knife, cut into ⅛-inch slices and place on ungreased baking sheet. You may want to lift with a spatula so they don't distort. Bake 6-10 minutes. Remove to cooling racks and when cool place in airtight containers.

Chocolate Drops

Preparation Time: 10 Minutes
Refrigeration Time: 3 Hours, or Overnight
Baking Time: 10-12 Minutes

Equipment

Electric mixer
Mixing bowl
Small bowl
Rubber spatula
Measuring spoons and cups
Sifter or mesh sieve
Double boiler or bowl inside
　saucepan

Wooden stirring spoon
Baking sheets
Metal spatula
Cooling racks
Airtight container

Ingredients

½ cup vegetable oil
4 squares unsweetened baking chocolate, melted in double boiler
2 cups granulated sugar
4 large eggs
2 teaspoons vanilla
2 cups all-purpose sifted flour

2 teaspoons baking powder
½ teaspoon salt
Non-stick cooking spray or vegetable shortening or butter at room temperature
1 cup powdered sugar

Mix oil, chocolate, and granulated sugar in a bowl and blend

415

with an electric mixer. Beat in one egg at a time until well mixed. Add vanilla. Stir sifted flour, baking powder, and salt into mixture. Cover the bowl and refrigerate several hours or overnight.

Preheat oven to 350 degrees. Grease baking tray or use non-stick cooking spray.

Place powdered sugar into a small bowl. Drop teaspoonfuls of chocolate dough into the sugar. Roll in sugar and form into balls. Place onto baking tray about 2 inches apart, as they spread.

Bake 10-12 minutes. Do not over-bake or they will be tough. They should hold their shape and be almost firm to the touch. Let rest a minute before removing them to cooling racks. Store in an airtight container.

Traditional Thumbprint Cookies

Preparation Time: 20 Minutes
Baking Time: 10-12 Minutes
Makes about 3 dozen cookies

Equipment

Electric mixer
Mixing bowl
Measuring spoons and cups
Rubber spatula
2 small bowls
Whisk

Sifter or mesh sieve
Small food processor or spice/nut grinder
Baking trays
Cooling racks
Airtight container

Ingredients

½ cup butter (1 stick), at room temperature
¼ cup brown sugar, packed
1 large egg, separated
½ teaspoon vanilla
1 cup all-purpose sifted flour

¼ teaspoon salt
¾ cup finely chopped nuts (pecans, or walnuts)
Raspberry or other tinted jellies

Preheat oven to 350 degrees.

Mix butter and sugar in a bowl with the electric mixer until light and fluffy. Separate egg white into a small bowl and reserve; add egg yolk and vanilla to the batter, and beat thoroughly. Blend sifted flour and salt, and mix into batter.

416

Lightly whisk the reserved egg white. Place chopped nuts in another bowl. Make balls from the dough, using about a teaspoon of dough. Drop into the egg white and then into the nuts. Place on ungreased baking tray and then press the center of each cookie with your thumb to make an indentation. Bake 10-12 minutes or until set.

Remove to a rack and cool. Fill the thumbprints with a bit of jam and store in airtight container or freeze. If stacking cookies, place waxed paper between layer so they don't stick to each other.

Coconut/Apricot Macaroons

Preparation Time: 10 Minutes
Baking Time: 20 Minutes
This recipe makes about 20 Macaroons

Equipment

Electric mixer
Mixing bowl
Measuring spoons and cups
Rubber spatula

Baking tray
Metal spatula
Cooling racks

Ingredients

3   egg whites at room temperature
1¼ cup sifted powdered sugar
1   teaspoon vanilla
1¾ cups flaked sweetened coconut

¼   cup finely diced dried apricots
¼   cup sifted all-purpose flour
     Room temperature butter
     Flour for baking tray

Preheat oven to 325 degrees. Butter and flour a baking tray.

Dice apricots. Using the electric mixer, beat the room-temperature egg whites until frothy. Gradually beat in the powdered sugar and then the vanilla. Continue to beat until egg whites are very stiff and form peaks that don't collapse.

In a small bowl, combine the coconut, apricots and flour then fold gently into the egg white mixture. Try not to overmix or deflate egg whites.

417

Spoon by teaspoonfuls onto the greased baking tray about 2 inches apart. Bake in middle of oven for 20 minutes or until a light golden color and slightly firm to the touch. Immediately remove to cooling racks with spatula.

New Year's Eve
December 31

History

New Year's Eve is the culmination of a month of celebrations. Coming on the heels of the winter solstice, our pagan ancestors celebrated the turn of the New Year with rites and rituals whose intentions were to ward off the barrenness of winter and herald the coming of spring and its fertility. Therefore, in some cultures, the celebrations welcoming in the new year included the killing of a symbol of the old year, in some cases the 'old' king. This 'killing' might be symbolic using a scapegoat (animal or human) upon whom the tribe's or community's sins were heaped and who was then turned out of the society to wander and die. Or, sometimes, they literally killed the king, leader or a substitute. As new fires were built or a Yule leg kindled, sexual license and intoxication with drink and merriment was often concealed behind masks. Celebrations might continue up to three days and include ritualistic combat, mummers, dancing, and finally, a pledge of new resolve to redeem past bad or hedonistic behavior of the last few days or year. In later cultures, the New Year has been ushered in with bells tolling the death of the old year, Father Time giving way to the Baby of a New Year, whistles, noisemakers, and gun shots, parades and in recent years, football games.

With the arrival of the New Year, fortunes are told, ritual meals eaten, and superstitions attended to. For example, you could have good or bad luck for the coming year depending on who was the first person to cross the threshold after midnight of the old year. Strangers would bring luck. The Pennsylvania Dutch might eat pork loin or ham with sauerkraut to bring health and riches into the New Year. In parts of Tennessee, clothes are washed on New Year's Day to wash someone out of the family. In the Ozarks, a full salt shaker will bring prosperity in the coming year, the Louisiana Creoles might wear something new for good luck, and the Chippewa Indians called the day, Kissing Day. In Philadelphia, Pennsylvania, there is still a colorful and lively "Mummers" parade where the participants prance and dance to the rhythms of incredible banjo playing while balancing tall, feathered headpieces and wearing elaborate costumes.

Decoration

I am suggesting a formal, elegant, intimate dinner party for this New Year's Eve. An evening at home, away from the crowds and noise. You might even request that your guests "dress up" in a tuxedo, suit or dressy outfit. As the house may still be decorated for Christmas, it might be an appropriate time to change the table decoration, if there was one, and replace it with a beautiful bowl of fresh cut flowers. Bring out the best table linen, a wine cooler, and candles. If you have a fireplace, you may want to put a small table in front of it, drape it with a beautiful cloth, flowers, and eat in front of a roaring fire. Of course, the requisite noise makers, balloons and plumed hats can be added as the evening progresses towards the magic hour, or included as part of the centerpiece, to be cannibalized later. Consider more champagne at midnight.

New Year's Eve Dinner for Six

The menu offered is elegant and expensive. If it is over your budget, there are suggested alternatives. As the night is long, you might want to invite your guests for eight o'clock, but make sure you tell them they will be receiving a full dinner! Select your menu and make up your shopping list as suggested in the Introduction.

Menu

Hors d'Oeuvres
Mushroom stuffed phyllo pastries
Caviar with all the trimmings
    OR
Baby scallops, skewered

Ice Cold Vodka
Champagne (Dry) or White wine

First Course
Watercress and Endive Salad with warmed Goat Cheese
    (or Brie if using garlic toast)
Focaccia Olivada
    OR
Roasted Garlic Toast (if serving pork roast)

Main Course
Crown Roast of Lamb
    OR
Crown Roast of Pork

Aubergine (Eggplant) and Parsley Tomatoes
Broccoli with Parmesan
Mashed Potatoes

Dessert
Gateau St. Honore

Beverages
Tisane (Herb Tea)
Espresso

Bordeaux or Merlot red wine with dinner

Timetable

One Day Prior
Freeze Vodka bottle in a milk or coffee container

continued . . .

Mushroom stuffing for pastry hors d'oeuvres
Wash salad greens and store in airtight bag in refrigerator
Bake puffed pastry for cake and store airtight
Make pastry cream
Make paper frills for end of lamb or pork bones (see recipe
    for directions)

Day of Party
Make focaccia dough and bake (skip if making garlic toast)
Make 'cage' for cake
Clean broccoli and blanch, prepare casserole dish
Prepare caviar and trimmings or marinate scallops, don't
    cook
Make toast points
Roast garlic
Prepare roast and have it oven-ready, refrigerate
Make eggplant and tomatoes
Warm mushroom filling and stuff phyllo pastries, refrig-
    erate
Peel potatoes and cover with cold water
Set table
Whip cream
Make salad dressing
Assemble cake only, do not add pastry cream

Two Hours Before Guests Arrive
Slice baguette for garlic toast and brown
Take meat out of refrigerator and bring to room temper-
    ature

One Hour Before Guests Arrive
Start meat, if appropriate to scheduled dining hour
Prepare beverages but don't start

Thirty Minutes Before Guests Arrive
Bake phyllo pastries
Put out caviar and accompaniments
Thread scallops on bamboo skewers, cook after guests
    arrive
Put pastry cream into cake and finish cake

continued . . .

Thirty Minutes Before Dinner
Check internal temperature of roast and plan the rest of
    cooking accordingly
Start potatoes
Put broccoli casserole into oven
Goat cheese rounds onto baking tray
Put butter and milk in saucepan for mashing potatoes

Five minutes before dinner
Warm goat cheese, toss salad with dressing and place on
    individual salad plates; top with warm cheese
        OR
Broil garlic toast with cheese on top and put on salad
Warm eggplant and tomatoes

Before Dessert
Place 'cage' on cake
Cook beverages

Recipes

Hors d'Oeuvres

Mushroom Stuffed Phyllo Pastries

Preparation Time: 30 Minutes
Cooking Time: 15 Minutes
Can be made in advance and frozen unbaked up to 2 months.
Makes 36

Equipment

Medium-size skillet
Metal spatula
Damp cloth
Rolling pin
Mixing bowl
Measuring spoons and cups

Chopping knife
Food processor fitted with metal
  blade
Medium-size skillet
Wooden stirring spoon
Baking tray

Ingredients

12 sheets frozen phyllo dough, thawed (18 × 14-inch sheets), keep
  covered with damp cloth until ready to use, as it dries out quickly
½ cup unsalted butter, melted (1 stick)
3 leeks
4 tablespoons olive oil
1½ pounds mixed types of mushrooms
1½ tablespoons fresh thyme or ¾ tablespoon dried thyme
½ teaspoon salt
¼ teaspoon fresh ground black pepper
¼ cup beef stock
Non-stick cooking spray or vegetable shortening

    To clean leeks, split in half lengthwise. Soak in a large bowl of cold water, sand should filter to the bottom. Remove the leeks from the bowl and repeat the process. Rinse once more under a running tap.

    Remove the tops and root end and finely slice into ½ inch lengths.

    Wipe mushrooms clean, slice finely, then chop into a small dice or place in food processor and pulse to fine dice.

Warm skillet over medium heat and add 1 tablespoon of olive oil. Sauté leeks for about 5 minutes, or until soft, stirring frequently. Do not brown them. Remove to a bowl.

Add 1 tablespoon of oil to pan and sauté mushrooms until soft, about 3 minutes. Return leeks to pan.

Add thyme, salt, pepper and stock and cook over high heat, continually stirring until liquid is reduced to a thick, syrup consistency. Set aside to cool.

Unroll phyllo pastry. Keep what you're not using covered with a damp cloth. Lay out a sheet of phyllo and brush with melted butter. Lay a second sheet on top and repeat. Cut crosswise into 6 equal strips. Take 1 teaspoon of mushroom/leek filling and place about 1 inch from the end of one of the pastry strips. Starting at the end where the filling is, fold over one of the points, corners, over the filling so it lines up with the other side of the strip, forming a triangle. Continue folding like a flag all the way up the strip, using up the length of dough. Continue with the other 5 strips and repeat until you have used up the dough and filling. At this point, the hors d'oeuvres can be frozen for up to 2 months, or refrigerated until just before serving time.

When ready to bake, preheat the oven to 375 degrees. Place on baking sheet covered with non-stick cooking spray, brush pastry with melted butter and cook for 15 minutes or until golden. Serve immediately. If using frozen triangles, do not thaw before cooking. They will take a bit longer to cook.

Caviar with Iced Vodka or Champagne

Preparation Time: 20 Minutes
Freezing Time for Vodka: 1-2 days

Equipment

Tray which can hold 2 bowls: one for crushed ice and a smaller dish
   that can be set over ice for the caviar
Small demi-tasse spoons
Cardboard milk or juice container or coffee can to fit bottle of vodka
Leaves, flowers or food coloring to decorate ice
Rolling pin
Fine mesh sieve
Chopping knife or food processor fitted with metal blade

Ingredients

Black caviar, Beluga is probably the best, but very expensive. Select
   one to suit your budget. Chill well
6 hard boiled eggs, sieve yolks and whites separately
1 medium size sweet onion, finely diced
Toast points (12 slices firm white bread)
½ stick unsalted, room temperature butter, molded into an attractive
   shape or cut into curls or merely decorated with the tines of a fork
1 lemon, cut into wedges
1-2 bottles dry champagne, iced
Liter of favorite vodka

Cut top off of cardboard waterproof container or coffee can
and fill with water. Loosen cap of vodka bottle then close. Put
vodka bottle in center, spill off any excess water and freeze upright. Food coloring can be added to color the ice, or leaves, pine
branches, holly or flowers can be set into the water, adjust them
as it freezes. When it is frozen, dip in hot water; it should slip
out of container. Return to freezer until needed. Serve the bottle
in the block of ice on a tray or in a wine cooler. You will have
chilled vodka without needing ice. Serve in small attractive
glasses.
   Using a rolling pin, flatten each slice of bread and cut off
crusts. Toast and then cut into 4 triangles. You should have
48 pieces.
   Assemble serving tray with iced caviar in the center (always
serve in a dish embedded in crushed ice).

426

Surround with toast points. Eggs, butter and onions can be served either on the tray, if there is room or in separate dishes surrounding the caviar. Garnish with lemon wedges.

Each guest makes their own combination: bread, butter, caviar, onion and egg on top, lemon juice, or anyway, they enjoy it.

This may be served with iced vodka or iced champagne.

Baby Skewered Scallops

Preparation Time: 15 Minutes
Cooking Time: 3-5 Minutes

Equipment

Bamboo skewers, about 3-4 inches in length, soaked in water for 30 minutes before using. Longer ones can be broken to the correct length.
Colander

Mixing bowl
Whisk
Knife
Plastic wrap
Paper toweling

Ingredients

1 pound baby scallops
3 tablespoons lime juice
1 tablespoon olive oil
Parsley, minced, no stems, for garnish

Rinse scallops in cold water, drain and dry off with paper toweling. Marinate scallops in lime juice and oil, covered in refrigerator, for at least 3-4 hours before serving.

Place one scallop on each skewer. Broil under high flame for 1-2 minutes a side and serve on a platter with a parsley garnish. Cook longer if you prefer well-done.

427

First Course

Watercress and Endive Salad
Warmed Goat Cheese

Preparation Time: 10 Minutes
Cooking Time: 2 Minutes

Equipment

Baking tray
Salad or large bowl to mix
Small mixing bowl
Whisk

Knife
Juicer, reamer
Salad spinner
Metal spatula

Ingredients

2 bunches watercress
2 Belgian endive
1 'log' mild goat cheese, cut into 6 slices
Pinch of paprika
1 lemon juiced and strained, need 3-4 tablespoons
5 tablespoons olive oil
½ teaspoon salt
1 teaspoon Dijon style mustard

Cut stems off watercress, wash and spin dry. Wash endive. Cut off root end. Cut endive in half and then slice vertically into as many fine pieces as possible. Add to the watercress and refrigerate in a plastic bag until needed.

Whisk together the lemon juice, oil, salt and mustard and reserve until serving time.

Just prior to serving, slice the goat cheese into 6 slices and sprinkle a bit of paprika on the top of each slice. Place under the broiler for only a minute or two until warmed through. Remove from broiler.

Mix salad together with the dressing. Divide equally among the individual salad plates. Place a round of cheese in the center of each salad and serve immediately with Focaccia Olivada.

Focaccia Olivada

Preparation Time: 25 Minutes
2 Hours Rising Time
Cooking Time: 40 Minutes

Equipment

Mixing bowl
Measuring spoons and cups
Rubber spatula
Small bowl or glass measuring
  cup
Whisk
Fork

Candy or instant read
  thermometer
Small paring knife
Baking sheet
Cooling rack
Tea towel or plastic wrap

Ingredients

1 envelope dry yeast, ¼ ounce
1 cup warm water, 105-115 degrees F
3 cups (plus some for kneading) unbleached all purpose flour
1 cup oil cured, pitted olives, chopped
¼ cup olive oil
1 teaspoon salt
Olive oil
6 tablespoons olivada (a black olive paste, sometimes called tapenade
  and available in bottles in supermarkets or fresh at specialty and
  cheese stores)
Coarse (Kosher) salt

In a small bowl, dissolve the yeast in the cup of water. Let
stand 10 minutes. It will foam up.

Meanwhile, pit and chop the oil cured olives.

In a mixing bowl, mound 3 cups of flour and make a well in
the center. Add the dissolved yeast, chopped olives, ¼ cup olive
oil, and 1 teaspoon salt. Mix ingredients together. If dough is
too wet, slowly begin to work in extra flour. When holding a ball
shape, place on lightly floured work surface and knead until it
is smooth and elastic, about 10 minutes. If dough is too sticky,
work in more flour. Scrape off counter periodically.

Mound up the dough, dust top with flour and place in a bowl
in a draft free place. Cover with a damp towel and let rise until
doubled in bulk, about 1½ hours. Dough can be refrigerated for

a couple of hours at this point. Bring back to room temperature and continue.

Grease a baking tray with olive oil. Punch down the dough and knead on lightly floured surface for about 2 minutes. Divide dough in half. Roll first piece into a 7 × 11 inch rectangle, or circle, and transfer to baking sheet. Spread olivada to within an inch of the borders. Roll second piece of dough to fit over the first. Gently place on top of olivada. Press all edges with the tines of a fork to seal. Let dough rise in a draft free place, covered with a tea towel or piece of plastic wrap, for 30 minutes.

Preheat oven to 400 degrees. Brush dough with olive oil and sprinkle with coarse salt. Bake about 40 minutes. It is cooked when the loaf sounds hollow if tapped on the bottom. Remove to a cooling rack and serve warm or cold. I suggest cutting into small serving size pieces and arranging on a small plate.

Roasted Garlic Toast

Preparation Time: 5 Minutes
Cooking Time: 20 Minutes

Equipment

Small ovenproof skillet   Small bowl
Baking tray   Fork
Knife   Plastic wrap

Ingredients

1 loaf French bread (baguette) sliced into 24 pieces
1½ tablespoons butter
1 large head garlic, not peeled
Small round of Brie cheese, cut to fit onto baguette slices

Preheat oven to 350 degrees. Slice bread and bake until golden brown, no more than 10 minutes. Check as they bake. They can brown suddenly. Remove from oven and cool.

Melt butter in small oven proof skillet and add garlic. Toss to coat with butter and place in oven with pointed side up. Bake until tender in center when pierced by knife, about 20 minutes. Cool slightly and peel. Put peeled garlic in a small bowl and mash with a fork. Cover until ready to spread on bread. When ready to serve, spread garlic on bread, add round of cheese and place under preheated broiler until warm.

Main Course

Crown Roast of Lamb

Preparation Time: 5 Minutes
Cooking Time: 60-75 Minutes

Equipment

Roasting pan with rack
Paper frills (papillote), purchased
  or home made (see below)
Instant reading thermometer
Small bowl

Spoon
Aluminum foil
Garlic press, optional
Chopping knife

Ingredients

1 crown roast (ribs section of 2 loins, standing upright in a circle), almost room temperature
1 tablespoon salt
1 teaspoon freshly ground black pepper
3 tablespoons fresh rosemary; 1½ tablespoon dried
2 tablespoons lemon zest
2 cloves of garlic, squeezed through press or finely minced, optional
2 tablespoons olive oil
Fresh rosemary, mint or parsley for garnish

Have butcher prepare crown roast (2 loin ribs in a circle) by tying together with string and cracking bone at bottom. The ribs will stand upright in a circle or crown.

Preheat oven to 350 degrees.

Cover tips of bones with aluminum foil to prevent burning. Place meat on rack in roasting pan.

Mix salt, pepper, rosemary, lemon zest, garlic, and olive oil in a small bowl and rub into the roast. It should take 45 minutes to an hour for rare meat (125 degrees internal temperature) or 15 to 30 minutes more for medium rare (135 degrees). Remove from oven and replace foil bone coverings with paper frills. Place on platter and let sit about 10 minutes before serving.

Immediately prior to serving, put mashed potatoes into the center of the roast, and garnish with mint, fresh rosemary or parsley for color.

431

Paper Frills (Papillotes)

Preparation Time: 20 Minutes

Equipment

Scissors
Cellophane tape
Staples
Waxed or parchment paper,
    aluminum foil or colored tissue
    paper that has some body

Cut paper into length of about 25 inches by 5 inches. Fold lengthwise, twice and open the last fold to reveal a scored line. Using scissors, cut strips along the folded side ¼ inch apart just down to the folded line.

Open the paper and fold the other way, inside out; do not crease. The frills will have a rounded shape this way. Staple or tape along bottom edge. Roll the paper around your finger or a pencil, depending on the size of the rib to be covered, at least twice so the layers are staggered a bit to make the frill fluffy in appearance. Secure with tape.

Crown Roast of Pork

Preparation Time: 5 Minutes
Cooking Time: About 1¹/₂ to 2 hours (185 degrees
Internal Temperature)

Equipment

Roasting pan with rack   Small mixing bowl
Paper frills, papillotes (*see above*)   Aluminum foil

Ingredients

Crown roast of pork (2 rib sections of loin, tied together and standing
   upright in a circle and cracking bone at bottom)
3 tablespoons fresh sage, 1½ teaspoon dried
1 tablespoon salt
1 teaspoon fresh ground black pepper
1 tablespoon oil

Fresh sage or parsley for garnish

To form a crown roast, have butcher tie together with string,
2 rib loins to form a circle, a crown. The ribs stand upright.
   Preheat oven to 350 degrees.
   Place almost room temperature meat on roasting rack.
Cover bone tips with aluminum foil to prevent burning.
   Mix sage, salt, pepper and oil in a small bowl and rub onto
the exterior of the meat. Put into center of oven and check for
being done at 185 degrees, with instant read thermometer.
   Remove from oven to platter. Remove foil tops and replace
with paper frills. Put mashed potatoes into center of roast imme-
diately before serving and garnish with fresh sage or parsley.

Aubergine (Eggplant) and Tomatoes with Parsley

Preparation Time: 10 Minutes
20-30 Minutes to Drain
Cooking Time: 15 Minutes Plus Reheat Time of 5 Minutes

Equipment

Large skillet	Vegetable peeler
Sieve/colander	Garlic press
Large mixing bowl	Large cleaver or chopping knife
Wooden spoon	Paper Towels

Ingredients

2 pounds eggplant (about 8 cups large dice)
1½ teaspoons salt
Olive oil or vegetable oil
5 medium-size tomatoes
¾ cup coarse ground white bread crumbs, unseasoned
3 tablespoons thinly sliced scallions
1-2 large cloves garlic, mashed or finely diced
6 tablespoons finely chopped fresh parsley, no stems
¾ teaspoon dried thyme
¾ teaspoon dried basil

Using a vegetable peeler or knife, remove the skin from eggplant. Slice lengthwise into ¾-inch slices. Slice these slices lengthwise into ¾-inch wide slices. Then cut the strips into ¾-inch cubes. You need 8 cups. Toss in mixing bowl with the salt and let stand 20-30 minutes.

Core the tomatoes and gently squeeze out juice and seeds. Slice into ¾-inch slices and dice into ¾-inch cubes.

Immediately before cooking eggplant, drain in sieve or colander and pat dry with paper toweling.

Film a heavy skillet with about ⅛ inch oil and heat until hot. Add eggplant to make 1 layer; do not crowd pan. You will need to make batches. Turn and stir frequently. You want them to become tender and lightly brown. Eggplant burns easily. If they are brown before tender, lower heat and cover for 2 minutes or so. Remove from pan into a sieve over the mixing bowl to catch oil. Return oil to pan and reheat. Add another batch of eggplant and continue this process until all are cooked.

434

Make sure there is oil in pan or add a bit more and add the tomatoes. Toss until barely heated through and remove from pan.

Add more oil to the pan and add the bread crumbs until lightly brown. Add the scallions and garlic and toss gently for a couple of minutes. Remove from heat. Can be prepared ahead up to this point. Reheat bread crumb mixture, add eggplant and heat until they are hot through and sizzling. Add tomatoes in last 30 seconds to warm. Garnish and toss with the parsley and herbs and serve immediately.

Broccoli with Parmesan

Preparation Time: 10 Minutes
Cooking Time: 15-20 Minutes
Can be prepared ahead

Equipment

Ovenproof casserole dish	Knife
Large saucepan	Vegetable, potato peeler
2nd large pot or mixing bowl filled with ice	Plastic wrap or waxed paper

Ingredients

2	pounds broccoli
6	tablespoons butter
½	cup grated Parmesan cheese

Bring a large saucepan full of water to a boil. Meanwhile, clean the broccoli, discarding the bottom 2 inches of stem. Remove the tops of the broccoli, leaving approximately an inch or so below the 'flower.' With a vegetable peeler, remove the tough outer layer of skin from the stalks. Slice the stalks into ¼-inch rounds.

When water comes to a boil, toss broccoli and stems into the water for 3-4 minutes. Quickly remove and plunge into a pot or bowl of ice water to stop cooking process. When cool, drain.

Using a tablespoon of the butter, grease the inside of an ovenproof casserole dish. Dust the bottom and sides with 2 tablespoons of the grated cheese.

Melt 4 tablespoons of butter. Place half of the broccoli in the bottom of the casserole dish and pour half of the butter and ½ of the cheese over it. Place the balance of the broccoli in the dish, arranging the 'flowers' into a pleasing pattern on the top. Cover with the rest of the butter and cheese. Loosely cover with plastic wrap or waxed paper and set aside.

To heat, preheat oven to 350 degrees. Remove plastic wrap and place uncovered casserole into oven to heat through, about 15-20 minutes. When butter begins to sizzle, place under a hot broiler to brown the cheese. Serve immediately.

Mashed Potatoes

Preparation Time: 10 Minutes
Cooking Time: 12-15 Minutes

Equipment

Large saucepan with lid
Small saucepan
Potato peeler

Potato Masher or hand held
electric mixer

Ingredients

4 pounds Idaho or Russet potatoes
2 teaspoons salt
1¼-1½ cups milk, heated
6 tablespoons butter, melted into the milk

Peel potatoes and cut into quarters or eighths. Place potatoes in saucepan and cover with water. Add salt. Cover and bring to a boil over moderate heat. Adjust heat, as necessary to prevent boiling over. Cook until potatoes are tender, about 12-15 minutes. Do not overcook or potatoes will get mushy.

Drain water off potatoes and return pot to heat. Shake potatoes to remove any moisture that may be clinging. Turn off heat.

Meanwhile, heat milk and butter together in a small saucepan or in a cup in the microwave; do not boil. Using either a potato masher, ricer or electric mixer, begin to break up the potatoes. When fluffy, start to add the milk/butter mixture as you continue mixing. Incorporate as much as needed to achieve a texture pleasing to you. If potatoes are not going to the table immediately, which they should be, add a few extra drops of milk as the potatoes will stiffen up while standing. Replace lid until serving. Stir up and place in serving bowl, or inside center of crown roast.

They can be kept in a warm 200 degree oven for 10-20 minutes, but they will begin to dry out.

Dessert

Gateau St. Honore

Preparation Time: 40 Minutes
Baking Time: 50 Minutes
Assembly Time: 20 Minutes

This showy cake is built on a pie crust foundation and topped with a 'halo' of pâte à choux, or cream puffs, which may be filled with chocolate pastry cream and are affixed to the 'halo' with caramel. The center of the cake is filled with a luscious chocolate cream filling. The puffs are finished off with a chocolate coating. The entire center of the cake is enclosed in a golden caramel 'cage'.

This elegant cake has multiple steps, most which can be prepared in advance by a day or more, if you freeze the pastry. The cake can be assembled earlier in the day, but the pastry cream should not be added until just before serving, as the puffs of pastry will become soggy. Each stage, which can be made and stored prior to the day of use, will be noted.

Equipment

2 baking trays (non-stick preferable)
Medium-size sauce pan
Small sauce pan with lid
Wooden spoon
Strainer
Food processor fitted with plastic blade, or pastry cutter
Paring knife
Fork

Aluminum foil
Cooking weights or dried beans or heavily-weighted cake pan
Electric mixer, hand held
Pastry bag with ½-inch round tube opening
Plastic wrap or waxed paper
Small bowl
Whisk
Cooling rack

Cake Base: Can be made in advance
Ingredients

1½   cups all-purpose white flour
7   tablespoons unsalted butter
1   tablespoon shortening
¼   teaspoon salt
¼   cup ice water

1   tablespoon sugar
1   lightly beaten egg
      Non-stick cooking spray or butter

Place flour, butter, shortening and sugar in food processor and pulse until mixture has the consistency of coarse meal. (Or, cut ingredients with a pastry cutter.) Turn on processor and gradually add water, stopping when dough begins to hold together. Check dough and see if it holds together. If it does, gather in a ball and remove to a piece of plastic wrap. If it is still too dry, add a bit more water and pulse again. Refrigerate dough in plastic wrap or waxed paper for an hour or more. (Dough can be made up to a week ahead or frozen.)

Preheat oven to 425 degrees.

Remove dough from refrigerator and place on lightly floured surface. Flour top of dough and roll to about ¼ inch thickness. Roll dough onto rolling pin and lay out on non-stick or greased baking pan. Using an inverted 10-inch pie or cake pan, gently place it on top of dough, and cut around it with a knife. Remove excess dough.

Prick dough all over with a fork so it doesn't rise as it cooks. Place buttered aluminum foil onto which cooking weights or dried beans or a heavily weighted buttered cake pan has been placed, on top of the pastry dough.

Bake for 12 minutes or until dough is no longer soft. Remove aluminum foil and weights, or pan. Brush pastry with a lightly beaten egg and bake until golden, about 10 more minutes. Cool on a rack. When cool, put in airtight container, plastic bag, or freeze until needed.

Pâte à choux: Can be made in advance
Ingredients

1	cup water	¼	teaspoon salt
½	cup unsalted butter, cut into pieces (1 stick)	1	cup all-purpose flour
		3-5	large eggs

Place butter, water, salt in a heavy saucepan and bring water to a boil over high heat. Reduce heat to medium and add all the flour at once, stirring with wooden spoon until mixture leaves sides of pan and forms a ball. Transfer dough to a medium-size bowl and using an electric mixer, add 3 eggs, one at a time, incorporating each one before adding another. Batter should hold soft peaks, like when you're beating egg whites. If batter is still too stiff, break an additional egg in a small bowl and beat lightly. Slowly add additional egg to the mixture by drops until the correct consistency is achieved. The eggs make the puffs rise so you want to get as many as possible into the batter without getting it too soft, however, better less than too much.

Preheat oven to 425 degrees.

Butter and flour 2 baking sheets. Using the same 10″ inverted pan, lightly trace an outline into the flour.

Fit the pastry tube to a pastry bag, turn down sides of bag, and fill bag with the dough, no more than half way. Close tightly, twist. Grasping bag firmly, push dough into tip and squeeze a circle around the inside of the traced circle about the width of your thumb. This is the 'halo'. Then squeeze the balance of the dough into 1¼ inch diameter puffs around the rest of the baking sheet and onto another, if needed. Allow about ¾ inch space between the puffs for expansion during baking. Brush the circles and 'halo' with the left over beaten egg, rounding the tops of the puffs with the brush.

Bake for approximately 20 minutes. When beginning to brown, turn oven to 350 degrees for an additional 10 minutes, or until puffs have risen and are brown and crisp. Remove puffs from oven and with a thin skewer or knife tip, pierce the side of each puff to allow steam to escape. Prick the halo in a few places. Turn off oven heat and return halo and puffs to oven for about 10 minutes with door closed and an additional 10 minutes with door ajar. Cool on a rack.

These may be kept in an airtight container or frozen if making in advance. Warm until crisp at 350 degrees for 10 minutes before use if made a day or more prior.

Ingredients
Chocolate (or Vanilla) Pastry Cream:
Can be made one to two days prior.

1 cup milk
1½ teaspoons gelatin
2 tablespoons Fra Angelico or rum, orange liqueur or juice
¼ cup plus 2 teaspoons superfine sugar
3 eggs, separated, room temperature
1 tablespoon all-purpose flour
1 tablespoon cornstarch
Pinch of salt

1 ounce unsweetened baking chocolate, finely chopped
1 ounce semi or bitter sweet chocolate, finely chopped
1 teaspoon vanilla extract

**If making vanilla pastry cream, add a 2-inch-long piece of vanilla bean, cut open, to milk while cooking. Strain out after mixture has cooked, and omit chocolate and vanilla extract step.

In a small bowl, soften the gelatin in the liqueur, rum or juice. Set to the side. Separate eggs, reserving whites in a mixing bowl. Combine ¼ cup sugar and egg yolks in a medium-size bowl and with an electric mixer beat at high speed until the mixture 'forms a ribbon' when beaters are lifted, about 5-7 minutes. Gently mix in the flour, cornstarch, and salt. Put milk into heavy-bottomed saucepan and bring to a boil. Gradually whisk hot milk into the egg mixture. Strain mixture back into a clean saucepan. Whisk constantly to prevent lumping and sticking, adjusting heat. Reduce heat and boil until the consistency of mayonnaise, whisking all the time, about 2-3 minutes. Remove from heat.

Whisk gelatin mixture into the hot pastry cream. If making chocolate cream, add it to gelatin and hot pastry cream. Whisk until chocolate is melted, add vanilla. If using vanilla bean pastry cream, strain mixture into gelatin and hot pastry cream mixture.

In another bowl, beat egg whites until soft peaks form. Gradually beat in the remaining 2 tablespoons of sugar and beat until whites are stiff but not dry. Fold ½ the whites into the pastry cream with a rubber spatula, to lighten, then gently fold in the balance, blending well. Press plastic wrap to the surface of the pastry cream so a skin does not form and refrigerate until firm. Can be prepared 1 to 2 days in advance.

Prior to assembly:

Chocolate Glaze for Tops of Puffs
½ pound semi or bittersweet chocolate, finely chopped
½ cup whipping (heavy) cream

Bring cream almost to a boil. Remove from heat and whisk in the chocolate, stirring until melted.

Caramel and Cage
Cage can be made several days prior but needs to be kept in an airtight container or it will collapses. The cage can be eliminated and fresh fruit can be placed on top of the pastry cream filling.

441

Ingredients

2   cups sugar
½   cup water, heated to boiling
¼   teaspoon cream of tartar

Grease the bottom of a large mixing bowl whose diameter will fit over the center, open section of the cake. Cover with aluminum foil and grease, smoothing out any creases; leave about ½-inch lip at bottom. The rounded bottom will be used to build the 'cage'.

Combine all ingredients in a small saucepan, swirling pan to dissolve sugar. When sugar is dissolved and liquid is beginning to thicken, cover with a lid until bubbles are thick. Remove cover. Continue to swirl pan until color begins to turn to a light caramel color and falls in fairly thick strands from a fork. Remove from heat.

Using a fork, start to weave a lacy pattern over the bottom of the greased mixing bowl, crisscrossing back and forth for strength. Put a heavier rim of loops around the bottom. Be careful, as hot sugar burns terribly! You may want to wear a potholder glove or a heavy rubber glove to protect your hands.

Reheat over low heat, as necessary.

As soon as the caramel is set, about 10 minutes, gently loosen, and raise aluminum foil off surface of bowl. Beginning at side farthest away, gently gather the foil into a ball in your hand, rotating and loosening it from the 'cage'. Replace the cage onto the surface of the bowl and leave in place until needed. Can be made in advance but needs to be kept in an airtight container.

Whipped Cream

1   cup heavy cream
1   tablespoon sugar

With an electric mixer, whip the cream until it begins to thicken. Add the sugar and beat until thick. Cover and refrigerate it not using immediately.

Assembly

Place the pie crust bottom on a serving platter. Count the number of puffs you will need for covering the circumference of the 'halo,' each touching the one next to it.

You have an option: you can either fill the puffs with pastry cream, or not. If filling, they need to be done close to serving because dough will get soggy, so it can be a problem at a party. To fill puffs, put an amount of pastry cream into a bag fitted with the tube and insert the end of the tube into the hole you made to allow the steam to escape. Squeeze a small amount of cream into the puff. Repeat with the other puffs.

Dip the tops of the puffs into the chocolate mixture and set aside to dry.

Caramel can be reheated on low heat, if necessary or make a new batch if it is too dark or it is another day from when you made the cage.

Using a fork, drizzle a small quantity of caramel on edge of pie shell. Secure the 'halo' to the shell. Dip the bottom of each puff into the caramel and secure on the 'halo,' touching one to the other until the 'halo' is full.

Immediately before serving, fill the center with the pastry cream. Put whipped cream into a pastry bag and make rosettes between the puffs on the outer edge of the cake, on pipe a scroll of whipped cream around the edge of the pie crust. Carefully place the cage over the center of the cake. If there are 'bare spots,' decorate with whipped-cream swirls.

Serve!

The cage can be eliminated. Fruit is also a nice addition to the center of the cake if using vanilla pastry cream.

Recipe Index

Hors D'Oeuvres

Antipasto Tray, 212	Columbus Day
Avocado Dip, 197	Summer Picnic
Bacon Cheese Wrap-ups, 32	Martin Luther King Day
Black Bean Dip, 244	Halloween
Brie En Croute/Jack O'Lantern, 242	Halloween
Caviar, 426	New Year's Eve
Celery, stuffed, 127	Easter
Cheddar Cheese Twisties, 128	Easter
Cheese Dip Stilton, 182	Summer Clam Bake
Cheese Rounds, Herbed, 81	Valentine's Day
Cheese Spread, Pine Cone, 366	Christmas Eve
Cheese Tart, Stilton, 382	Christmas Day
Cheesies, 270	Thanksgiving
Chicken Liver Paté, 384	Christmas Day
Chicken Wings, Hot and Spicy, 183	Summer Clam Bake
Christmas Wreath/Vegetable, 359	Christmas Eve
Crab Cakes, 367	Christmas Eve
Crabmeat Canapes, 31	Martin Luther King
Cucumber Cups, 164	Summer Barbecue
Endive Boats, 272	Thanksgiving
Focaccia Olivado, 429	New Year's Eve
Garlic Toast, Roasted, 430	New Year's Eve
Jalapeno Firecrackers, 161	Summer Barbecue
Jicama Cubes/Lime, 196	Summer Picnic
Latkes (Mini Potato Pancakes), 335	Hanukkah
Meat Balls, Glazed, 245	Halloween
Mushroom in Phyllo, 424	New Year's Eve
Mushrooms, Stuffed, 163	Summer Barbecue
Oysters in Red Sauce, 181	Summer Clam Bake
Pakoras (Vegetable Fritters), 312	Diwali
Paneer Pakote (Fried Cheese), 313	Diwali

Parsnip Chips, Deep Fried, 338   Hanukkah
Pizzas, Mini Halloween, 246   Halloween
Popcorn, Salted/Herbed, 274   Thanksgiving
Red Fish Roe (Taramosalada), 82   Valentine's Day
Scallops, Skewered, 427   New Year's Eve
Shrimp Balls, 54   Chinese New Year
Shrimp Cocktail, 273   Thanksgiving
Smoked Salmon, Capers, 97   St. Patrick's Day
Smoked Trout Paté, 337   Hanukkah
Spareribs, Barbecued, 59   Chinese New Year
Spiced Mixed Nuts, 311   Diwali
Spinach/Parmesan Balls, 98   St. Patrick's Day
Spring Rolls, 56   Chinese New Year
Stilton Dip with Veggies, 182   Summer Clam Bake

First Course

Asparagus Vinaigrette, Cold, 83   Valentine's Day
Corn Bisque, 275   Thanksgiving
Dumpings, Steamed, 61   Chinese New Year
Minestrone Soup, 219   Columbus Day
Mushroom Soup, 339   Hanukkah
Oyster Stew, 276   Thanksgiving
Pea Soup, Fresh Minted, 130   Easter
Peanut Soup, 33   Martin Luther King Day
Potato and Leek Soup, 99   St. Patrick's Day
Puffed Christmas Tree, 386   Christmas Day
Watercress Soup, 368   Christmas Eve

Main Course

Meat / Poultry:
Beef, Brisket with Dried Fruit, 340 Hanukkah
Beef, Prime Ribs, 388   Christmas Day
Beef, Sichuan, Crispy, 71   Chinese New Year
Chicken, Crispy Legs and Wings, 247 Halloween
Chicken, Fried, 34   Martin Luther King Day
Chicken, Tandoori, 322   Diwali
Chicken, Roast with Pancakes, 65   Chinese New Year

Chili, Vampire, 249	Halloween
Cornish Hens, Cherry Sauce, 84	Valentine's Day
Corned Beef, 100	St. Patrick's Day
Duck Roast with Pancakes, 65	Chinese New Year
Frankfurters/Knockwurst, Grilled, 167	Summer Barbecue
Goose, Roast, 370	Christmas Eve
Ham, Honey Glazed, 131	Easter
Hamburgers, Surprise, 166	Summer Barbecue
Irish Stew, 104	St. Patrick's Day
Lamb, Crown Roast, 431	New Year's Eve
Lamb, Roast Leg Olivado, 140	Easter
Pork, Crown Roast, 433	New Year's Eve
Spareribs, Barbecued, 165	Summer Barbecue
Steak/Flank, Marinated, 168	Summer Barbecue
Turkey, Roast, 278	Thanksgiving
Veal Piccata, 222	Columbus Day

Seafood

Cat Fish, Fried, 35	Martin Luther King Day
Clam Bake, Grill, Pit, Stove Top, 184	Summer Clam Bake
Clam Bake, Oven, 187	Summer Clam Bake
Shrimp Scampi, 221	Columbus Day
Sea Bass or Red Snapper, Steamed or Crisp, 68	Chinese New Year

Fondue / Quiche / Sandwich

Baguette/Roll, Smoked Turkey, Brie, 198	Summer Picnic
Cheese Fondue, 361	Christmas Eve
Ham and Cheese Quiche, 200	Summer Picnic
Roast Beef, 199	Summer Picnic

Pasta / Noodles

Fettucine Alfredo/Sautéed Mushrooms, 223	Columbus Day
Lasagna, 228	Columbus Day
Macaroni and Cheese, 134	Easter
Noodle/Cabbage Casserole, 342	Hannukah
Pasta/Fresh Tomatoes, Olives, 169	Summer Barbecue

Potatoes
Colcannon and Cabbage, 102   St. Patrick's Day
Potatoes, Mashed, 436   New Year's Eve
Potatoes, Oven-Browned New, 135   Easter
Potatoes, Red with Parsley, 103   St. Patrick's Day
Potatoes, Roast with Rosemary, 389   Christmas Day
Potatoes, Scalloped, 293   Thanksgiving
Sweet Potatoes, Candied, 294   Thanksgiving

Rice
Basmati Pullao (Pilaf), 318   Diwali
Red Rice, 37   Martin Luther King Day
Steamed White Rice, 74   Chinese New Year
Wild Rice with Pecans, 85   Valentine's Day

Butters / Condiments / Dairy / Dips / Sauces
Balsamic Vinaigrette, 374   Christmas Eve
Cauliflower Pickle, 321   Diwali
Chutney, Mango, 320   Diwali
Chutney, Mint, 314   Diwali
Cranberry/Applesauce, 335   Hanukkah
Garam Masala, 310   Diwali
Ghee, 309   Diwali
Ginger Soy Sauce, 63   Chinese New Year
Gravy/White Wine, 282   Thanksgiving
Horseradish Sauce, 389   Christmas Day
Hot Mustard Sauce, 58   Chinese New Year
Pineapple Raisin Sauce, 133   Easter
Red Sauce, 181   Summer Clam Bake
Remoulade Sauce, 36   Martin Luther King
Salsa, 367   Christmas Eve
Sour Cream and Garlic Dip, 359   Christmas Eve
Soy Sauce, Sweet, 55   Chinese New Year
Vinaigrette, 218   Columbus Day
Yogurt, 310   Diwali

Stuffings / Dressings
Apple/Sour Dough, 372   Christmas Eve
Stuffing, Dad's (Sweet Potato/ Chestnut), 287   Thanksgiving
Stuffing, Nana's (Bread/Vegetable/ Potato), 285   Thanksgiving

Vegetables

Asparagus, Lemon/Butter Sauce, 136	Easter
Asparagus Vinaigrette, 83	Valentine's Day
Aubergine (Eggplant)/Tomato, 434	New Year's Eve
Beans/Baked, 170	Summer Barbecue
Beets, Buttered, 139	Easter
Beets, Harvard, 138	Easter
Beets/Orange-Ginger Sauce, 344	Hanukkah
Bhindi (Okra), 316	Diwali
Black-Eyed Peas, 38	Martin Luther King Day
Broccoli/Parmesan, 435	New Year's Eve
Buddha's Delight, 72	Chinese New Year
Cabbage, Buttered, 101	St. Patrick's Day
Cabbage, Red, 373	Christmas Eve
Carrots, Glazed, 391	Christmas Day
Carrots, Herbed, 343	Hannukah
Cauliflower/Brussels Sprouts, 288	Thanksgiving
Colcannon/Potato, 102	St. Patrick's Day
Corn, Grilled or Boiled, 172	Summer Barbecue
Corn with Peppers, 250	Halloween
Dal (Lentils), 315	Diwali
Greens, Mixed, 39	Martin Luther King
Peas, Minted, 105	St. Patrick's Day
Peas with Pearl Onions, 289	Thanksgiving
Peppers Stuffed with Corn, 40	Martin Luther King Day
Spinach/Garlic and Oil, 225	Columbus Day
String Beans, Spiced, 317	Diwali
String Bean Tree, 392	Christmas Day
Succotash, Indian, 290	Thanksgiving
Sugar Snap Peas, Water Chestnuts, 86	Valentine's Day

Salads

Apple/Grape, 362	Christmas Eve
Asparagus, Cold/Shallots, Caper, 137	Easter
Bean/Yellow and Green, 173	Summer Barbecue
Black Bean and Corn, 202	Summer Picnic
Cabbage Slaw, Red and Green, 188	Summer Clam Bake
Christmas, 393	Christmas Day
Cranberry Compote/Ginger, Apricots, 291	Thanksgiving
Curly Endive, 374	Christmas Eve

Devilled Eggs, 201	Summer Picnic
Easter Egg, 152	Easter
Keera Raita (Yoghurt/Cucumbers), 319	Diwali
Laccha (Indian), 319	Diwali
Peppers, Red Roasted, 213	Columbus Day
Marinated Mushrooms, 214	Columbus Day
Mixed Green/Vinaigrette, 226	Columbus Day
Relish Tray, 292	Thanksgiving
Taboulleh, 203	Summer Picnic
Tossed with Edible Eyeballs, 251	Halloween
Watercress/Endive/Goat Cheese, 428	New Year's Eve
Zucchini, Marinated, 345	Hanukkah

Bread

Bread Sticks, Sesame, 87	Valentine's Day
Chappati, 323	Diwali
Corn Bread, 41	Martin Luther King Day
Corn Bread, Cheesy, 252	Halloween
Easter Bread, Greek, 141	Easter
Focaccia Olivado, 429	New Year's Day
Garlic Bread, 227	Columbus Day
Garlic Toast, Roasted, 430	New Year's Eve
Herbed Baking Powder Sticks, 296	Thanksgiving
Hot Cross Buns, 119	Easter
Hush Puppies, 42	Martin Luther King Day
Italian/French Bread, 189	Summer Clam Bake
Irish Soda, 106, 107	St. Patrick's Day
Krapfen (Doughnuts), 121	Easter
Pancakes, Cornmeal, 122	Easter
Pancakes, Chinese, 67	Chinese New Year
Pancakes, Old-Fashioned, 124	Easter
Pooris, 324	Diwali
Popovers, 394	Christmas Day
Pumpkin/Raisin Muffins, 295	Thanksgiving
Stollen, 408	Christmas

Desserts and Cakes

American Flag Cake, 174 — Summer Barbecue
Angel Food Cake/Hazelnut, Chocolate Sauce, 346 — Hanukkah
Buche de Noel (Yule Log), 395 — Christmas Day
Carrot Easter Basket or Bunny Cake, 148 — Easter
Cheesecake, Red, White and Blue, 192 — Summer Clam Bake
Cheesecake, West Indies, 230 — Columbus Day
Chocolate Tart, Raspberries, 90 — Valentine's Day
Christmas Tree Cake, 375 — Christmas Eve
Coconut Cake/Lemon Filling, 43 — Martin Luther King Day
Devil's Food Cup Cakes, 253 — Halloween
Easter Lamb Cake, 143 — Easter
Fritters in Syrup (Malpoa), 326 — Diwali
Fruit Cake, 401 — Christmas Day
Kelly Cake (White/Chocolate Fudge), 110 — St. Patrick's Day
Meringues/Fresh Fruit, 88 — Valentine's Day
Spice Cake, 299 — Thanksgiving
St. Honore, Gateau (Cake), 438 — New Year's Eve
Whiskey Cake, 108 — St. Patrick's Day

Frostings / Sweet Sauces
Basic Butter Cream Frosting, 254 — Halloween
Caramel Frosting, 299 — Thanksgiving
Chocolate Frosting, 255 — Halloween
Chocolate Fudge Frosting, 110 — St. Patrick's Day
Chocolate Sauce, 347 — Hanukkah
Cream Cheese/Orange Frosting, 149 — Easter
Lemon/Orange Frosting, 109 — St. Patrick's Day
Marshmallow Fluffy, 145 — Easter
Vanilla Butter Cream Frosting, 376 — Christmas Eve
Whipped Cream, 442 — New Year's Eve

Candy / Nuts
Candied Apples, 258 — Halloween
Candy Corn on a Stick, 260 — Halloween
Chocolate Dipped Apricots, 302 — Thanksgiving

Honey Walnuts, 64   Chinese New Year
Nut Clusters, Glazed, 350   Hanukkah
Spiced Mixed Nuts, 311   Diwali

Cookies
Biscotti, purchased, 232   Columbus Day
Chocolate Chip, 206   Summer Picnic
Chocolate Drops, 415   Christmas
Cinnamon Star, 348   Hanukkah/Summer
    Barbecue
Coconut/Apricot Macaroons, 417   Christmas
Gingerbread, 410   Christmas
Pinwheels, 414   Christmas
Sugar, Cut Outs, 412   Christmas/Summer
    Barbecue
Thumbprint, 416   Christmas

Fruit
Bananas, Sautéed, 46   Martin Luther King Day
Figs, 232   Columbus Day
Orange and Tangerine/Sweet Ginger
    Sauce, 75   Chinese New Year
Orange Wheels, Spiced (Santre kie
    Chakle), 327   Diwali
Poached Pears in White Sauce, 349   Hanukkah
Tray of Togetherness, 76   Chinese New Year
Watermelon Ice, 176   Summer Barbecue
Watermelon Slices, 194   Summer Clam Bake

Pies
Apple Crumb Pie, 256   Halloween
Chocolate Tart with Raspberries, 90   Valentine's Day
Coconut Custard Pie, 146   Easter
Cranberry-Apple Tart, 298   Thanksgiving
Mince Tarts/Pie, 404   Christmas Day
Peach and Blueberry Pie, 190   Summer Clam Bake
Pecan Pie, 204   Summer Picnic
Pumpkin Pie, 297   Thanksgiving

Puddings
Almond Rice (Firni), 325   Diwali
Indian Pudding, 301   Thanksgiving
Pastry Cream, Chocolate & Vanilla,
    440   New Year's Eve

451

Plum, Mock (cake), 406
Rice Pudding/O'Connor, 112
Summer Pudding, 205

Christmas Day
St. Patrick's Day
Summer Picnic

Beverages

Café Diablo, 262
Cappuccino, 233
Cider, Hot Mulled, 261
Coffee, Flavored & Spiced, 364
Coffee, Iced, 47
Coffee, Irish, 113
Cranberry Punch, Mulled, 381
Egg Nog, 380
Espresso, 233

Halloween
Columbus Day
Halloween
Christmas Eve
Martin Luther King's Day
St. Patrick's Day
Christmas Eve
Christmas Day
New Year's Eve/Columbus
  Day

Lassi (Yogurt) Savory & Sweet, 328
Mulled Wine, 363
Punch, Green Slime, 241
Sangria, Red, 178
Sangria, White, 207
Tea, Flavored, 364
Tea, Iced, 47, 194

Diwali
Christmas Eve
Halloween
Summer Barbecue
Summer Picnic
Christmas Eve
Martin Luther King Day/
  Summer Clam Bake

Tea Spiced, 329
Vodka, Iced, 426

Diwali
New Year's Eve